Resisting the Dehumanization of Refugees

RESISTING THE DEHUMANIZATION OF REFUGEES

EDITED BY
YASMEEN ABU-LABAN, MICHAEL FRISHKOPF
REZA HASMATH AND
ANNA KIROVA

◊ AU PRESS

Copyright © 2024 Yasmeen Abu-Laban, Michael Frishkopf, Reza Hasmath, and Anna Kirova
Published by AU Press, Athabasca University
1 University Drive, Athabasca, AB T9S 3A3

https://doi.org/10.15215/aupress/9781771994101.01

Cover design by John van der Woude, JVDW Designs
Cover image "Brain and heart connection" by stellalevi (iStock Images)
Printed and bound in Canada

Library and Archives Canada Cataloguing in Publication

Title: Resisting the dehumanization of refugees / edited by Yasmeen Abu-Laban, Michael Frishkopf, Reza Hasmath, and Anna Kirova.
Names: Abu-Laban, Yasmeen, 1966– editor. | Frishkopf, Michael Aaron, editor. | Hasmath, Reza, editor. | Kirova, Anna, editor.
Description: Includes bibliographical references and index.
Identifiers: Canadiana (print) 20230589316 | Canadiana (ebook) 20230589324 | ISBN 9781771994101 (softcover) | ISBN 9781771994118 (PDF) | ISBN 9781771994125 (EPUB)
Subjects: LCSH: Refugees—Social conditions.
Classification: LCC HV640 .R47 2024 | DDC 305.9/06914—dc23

This book has been published with the help of a grant from the Federation for the Humanities and Social Sciences, through the Awards to Scholarly Publications Program, using funds provided by the Social Sciences and Humanities Research Council of Canada. We also acknowledge the financial support of the Government of Canada through the Canada Book Fund (CBF) for our publishing activities and the assistance provided by the Government of Alberta through the Alberta Media Fund.

This publication is licensed under a Creative Commons licence, Attribution–Noncommercial–No Derivative Works 4.0 International: see www.creativecommons.org. The text may be reproduced for non-commercial purposes, provided that credit is given to the original author. To obtain permission for uses beyond those outlined in the Creative Commons licence, please contact AU Press, Athabasca University, at aupress@athabascau.ca.

Contents

Acknowledgements ix

Introduction 3
    Yasmeen Abu-Laban, Michael Frishkopf, Reza Hasmath,
    and Anna Kirova

1. Theoretical Perspectives on Dehumanization and Resisting It 21
    Yasmeen Abu-Laban, Michael Frishkopf, Reza Hasmath,
    and Anna Kirova

Part I The Role of Immigration Policies and the Media in the Dehumanization of Refugees

2. Dehumanizing or Humanizing Refugees? A Comparative Assessment of Canada, the United States, and Australia 41
    Yasmeen Abu-Laban

3. Migrant and Refugee Precarity as a Double Movement: A Case Study of Dehumanization and Humanization in the Canada-US Borderlands 65
    Jeffrey M. Ayres

4. Resisting Dehumanization Through Resettlement Based on Full Refugee Experiences 91
    Fariborz Birjandian

5. Conflating Migration, Terrorism, and Islam: Mediations of Syrian Refugees in Canadian Print Media Following the 2015 Paris Attacks 103
    Nariya Khasanova

Part II   The Role of Educational Institutions and Programs in the (De)humanization of Refugees

6. A New School and New Life: Understanding the Experiences of Yazidi Families with Children   125
   Pallabi Bhattacharyya, Labe Songose, and Lori Wilkinson

7. "Where Are You From?": A Personal Perspective on the Struggles of Youth Living Between Two Cultures   151
   Jwamer Jalal

8. Precarious Inclusion: Refugees in Higher Education in Germany   167
   Encarnación Gutiérrez Rodríguez

9. (Not) Meeting the Needs of Refugee Students: Toward a Framework for the Humanization of Education   195
   Anna Kirova

Part III   Countering Dehumanization: State Apologies and New Approaches

10. When the State Says "Sorry": Jewish Refugees to Canada and the Politics of Apology   225
    Abigail B. Bakan

11. State Apologies and the Rehumanization of Refugee, Indigenous, and Ethnic Minority Groups   247
    Reza Hasmath, Benjamin Ho, and Solomon Kay-Reid

12. Home, Hope, and a Human Approach to Displacement   269
    Jim Gurnett

Part IV Enacting (Re)humanization: Refugee Agency and the Arts

13. A Life of Many Homes: Reflections of a Writer in Exile   287
    Jalal Barzanji

14. Locating Kurdish Cultural Identity in Canada   303
    Louise Harrington and Dana Waissi

15. How Can Music Ameliorate Displacement, Disconnection, and Dehumanization?   329
    Michael Frishkopf

16. Music, Weapon of Change, Weapon of Peace: Thomas Mapfumo, Chimurenga, and the Power of Music in Exile   349
    Thomas Mapfumo, Chiedza Chikawa, and Michael Frishkopf

17. Music Enacting (Re)humanization: Concert Introduction, Program, and Link   379
    Michael Frishkopf

Contributors   389
Index   397

Acknowledgements

This volume aims to explore both the dehumanizing discourses, policies, and structural forces that impact refugees and the ways that refugees and their allies contest these. In undertaking this aim, we utilize a transdisciplinary approach that brings together academics, practitioners, and those who have experienced being coded as "refugees." In pursuing this aim and producing this transdisciplinary volume, we have many organizations and people to thank.

From Athabasca University Press, we are exceptionally grateful to Pamela Holway for her time, her guidance, and her always thoughtful support. From the very start, Pamela was enthusiastic to potentiate the ideas that emerged in this volume, and we also thank the anonymous reviewers who provided constructive and helpful comments on our work. We are so pleased to have worked with Athabasca University Press and to have this book be open access, as opposed to guarded behind a paywall.

This volume is an outgrowth of a specialized workshop entitled "Ethics, Rights, Culture and the Humanization of Refugees" held at the University of Alberta on February 6–8, 2020, in conjunction with International Week. From the University of Alberta International–Global Education, we were delighted to have the support of and work with Nancy Hannemann and Carrie Malloy on the 2020 International Week (an annual educational event devoted to understanding and finding solutions to global issues). From the Faculty of Arts, we also thank the events manager Cindy Welsh for her expert backing during our workshop.

For direct financial support, we thank the Kule Institute for Advanced Study (and its former director Geoffrey Rockwell). We are grateful to several units at the University of Alberta for their generosity: the Faculty of Arts and the Arts Conference Fund, the Faculty of Education for providing a Conference Fund and a venue for the workshop, and the Faculty of Science (and Sandeep Agarwal in particular). A big thank you to the Department of Music and the Canadian Center for Ethnomusicology. We also acknowledge, with appreciation, the Canada Research Chairs Program and the Canadian Institute for Advanced Research.

We extend our deepest appreciation to Elder Stanley Peltier for holding a welcoming smudging ceremony at the opening of the workshop and reminding us of our responsibilities as settlers on the ancestral, traditional, and unceded territory of Treaty 6, the Métis homelands, Region 4. This is a gathering place that encompasses seventeen First Nations in central Alberta, including the Dene Suliné, Cree, Nakota Sioux, and Saulteaux peoples whose living languages, histories, and cultures impact and influence the diverse personal and professional communities in which the University of Alberta is located and where many of the workshop's participants live and work. His welcoming words of wisdom to the workshop's participants guided our two-day work.

We were very fortunate to have dedicated support for our work at different junctures. We thank University of Alberta PhD student Nariya Khasanova for her expert research assistance. We also thank Dr. Salina Abji for her expert editorial assistance.

Not least, we are very indebted to our contributors. For many of us, the February 2020 workshop and "Transpositions" concert (a recording of which can be linked to through this volume) were the last major "in-person" events we attended before the declaration of COVID-19 as a pandemic by the World Health Organization and the lockdown measures that followed. That we were able to meet was a gift. The restrictions and border closures that followed stood as reminders that openness to human mobility is not a given, and this profoundly impacts refugees.

We thank all our contributors for meeting deadlines and illuminating the challenges and resistances to the dehumanization of refugees.

Yasmeen Abu-Laban, Michael Frishkopf,
Reza Hasmath, and Anna Kirova

Resisting the Dehumanization of Refugees

Introduction

Yasmeen Abu-Laban, Michael Frishkopf,
Reza Hasmath, and Anna Kirova

How do we talk about "refugees," a term that in itself may contribute to some not seeing the people behind the label? Some contest the distinction between refugees and migrants (Hamlin 2021). The distinction has even been characterized as a false binary that obscures "the multifaceted conditions and considerations that shape refugee-migrant journeys" (Hyndman and Reynolds 2020, 68). Others contest the definitions and frameworks provided by the United Nations High Commissioner for Refugees (UNHCR) or, in the case of Palestine refugees, the United Nations Relief and Works Agency (UNRWA). Some discuss refugees in numerical terms: we know there are more international migrants and refugees on the move today than at the end of World War II. According to the United Nations Department of Economic and Social Affairs (2021), there were approximately 281 million migrants in 2020, more than double the number at the turn of the twenty-first century. As a distinct class of migrants, "refugees" account for 12 percent of this figure; this is likewise up 9.5 percent relative to 2000. Over the 2010s, forced displacement has increased at an alarming rate relative to voluntary migration. This trend is set to continue in the 2020s, witnessed, for example, in March 2022 by the almost 3.39 million refugees who fled Ukraine due to Russian military aggression—marking one of the largest refugee crises in Europe since World War II (UNHCR 2022).

Numbers, like labels, can mask individuals and the complexity of individual experiences, identities, and circumstances. Indeed, statistics can be used to construct a sense of "crisis" and/or to evoke a fear of refugees who are deemed threatening to national security or a way of life. In this book, we sometimes use statistics, but we use them with different intent—to draw attention to the reality of displaced people who have experienced persecution, violence, and uprooting. We do not homogenize refugees as "vulnerable" (and in need of "our" compassion) or "powerful" (and therefore a threat to "our" security). Rather, we approach refugees as people who, by circumstances of violence and possible dehumanization, are forced to flee and as a result can experience precarity and marginalization. Prior to or after resettling, refugees may also experience forms of dehumanization. Because of this variety, we believe that each individual, and each individual story, matters, as do the ways in which those labelled as refugees and their allies resist dehumanization. For this reason, we focus on not only the experience of dehumanization but resistance to it.

The book largely focuses on realities pertaining to urban Canada within a comparatively informed frame of reference that is attuned to the developments and research findings of other national, regional, and international contexts. This focus is appropriate, since migration is truly a global phenomenon, and all world regions both send and receive migrants today. However, migration is also a national phenomenon involving the crossing of state borders with implications for national citizenship and belonging. Nations like Canada that emerged as a result of settler colonialism have used, and continue to use, migration in their nation-building project, which also involved the expropriation of land and dispossession of Indigenous peoples (Abu-Laban 2020). Migration is also a local phenomenon, today especially involving cities. In the Canadian context, 35.6 percent of the national immigrant population is in Toronto, followed by Vancouver (13.1 percent), Montréal (12.4 percent), Calgary (5.4 percent), Edmonton (4.1 percent), and Ottawa (3.4 percent; Statistics Canada 2017). It is notable that over the past fifteen years, the share of recent immigrants to Canada's prairie provinces has more than doubled. In the province of Alberta, for example, the share of new immigrants went from 6.1 percent in 2001 to 17.1 percent in 2016. Alberta is also the province exhibiting a disproportionately high number and increasing growth rate of white supremacist groups (Mosleh 2019). Not incidentally, this observed reality concerning xenophobic backlash was one of the main motivations for convening the workshop that spurred the writing of this book.

Against this backdrop, *Resisting the Dehumanization of Refugees* provides urgent insight and policy-relevant perspectives that go beyond traditional attempts at "managing" refugees. Uniquely, the book takes a transdisciplinary perspective, understood not as a "unified theory of everything" but rather as "research that integrates not just across disciplines, but across non-academic sources of insight from stakeholders and practitioners" (Repko, Szostak, and Buchberger 2016, 74–75). As such, this book brings together scholars across disciplines, with practitioners in the fields of refugee and immigrant settlement, as well as refugees who contribute experiential knowledge and analysis. Consistent with the central theoretical, methodological, and practice-based concerns of the humanizing approaches, including *deep contextualization* (i.e., social, historical, economic, and cultural context) and *voice* (who can speak and what can be heard), one of the major goals of this book is making space for the "telling" of refugees' stories themselves.

We are pleased that over the past five years, there has been more scholarly and policy attention paid to the issue of refugees and dehumanization. In this spirit, this book stems from a workshop held at the University of Alberta in February 2020. The workshop was markedly distinctive insofar as it paid close attention to the lived experience of dehumanization, allowing for "reflecting upon our understanding of what it means to be human or inhuman" (Oliver 2011, 86). In different ways, contributors to this book have included reflections on the lived experiences of migration. Since there is no single experience of migration that can capture the complexities and diversity of lived experiences, we hope that the authors' biographies also bring to light the richness of experiences from which the authors approach the question of refugees and (de)humanization. Some contributors in this transdisciplinary collection grapple with what humanization means in relation to key disciplinary traditions; others offer insight into how dehumanization is experienced as well as how it is resisted before, during, and after resettlement.

The state of the world when it comes to the everyday realities of the global refugee cohort is concerning. The growth of xenophobic populism, racism emanating from the COVID-19 pandemic, continued war, environmental catastrophes, and ongoing dislocation are daily news items. There are uncomfortable underlying conversations about which refugee cohorts should have priority to receiving countries. For instance, in 2022, the Canadian government indicated it would accept an "unlimited number" of migrants and refugees from Ukraine (see Tasker 2022). The government's stance received widespread support from the general public—with over 80 percent of Canadians supporting this plan, according to the Angus Reid Institute (2022). This stands in extreme contrast to Canadian support for the government's commitment to settle 25,000 Syrian refugees in 2015—at that time, only 39 percent of Canadians supported the government's plan. Moreover, the Ukrainian program sharply contrasts with Canada's actions and responses to Palestinians, largely refugees already under the mandate of UNRWA, displaced again in the Gaza Strip as a result of the 2023 Israeli war on Gaza. Here, not only did Canada support Israel's military actions; it only offered to support the applications of one thousand Palestinians with relatives in Canada in a program critics charged with being potentially "meaningless" as people could not leave the area (Osman 2024). The fact that Canada is home to 1.36 million Canadians of Ukrainian descent and that less than 80,000 of some 500,000 Canadians of Arab ancestry claim Syrian descent may superficially explain variations in the level of public support for receiving refugees from both cohorts (Statistics Canada 2017). Yet the vast majority of Ukrainians migrated to Canada between 1891 and 1952 and are thus multiple generations removed from contemporary Ukraine. For example, only 4.3 percent of those who identified as being of Ukrainian descent exclusively spoke the language at home, and 7.5 percent spoke either English or Ukrainian at home (Statistics Canada 2017). Accordingly, seeming discrepancies in responses and public attitudes have been approached less in relation to numbers than ethno-racial background, or "white privilege" (see Hasmath 2021), whereby European migrant groups are privileged and humanized relative to non-European refugee groups who are often dehumanized. This, in many ways, might be seen as a return to the policy practice of Canada's first wave of post–World War II migration (1945–67), where people with European backgrounds were prioritized for entry and settlement (see Hasmath 2012; Abu-Laban and Gabriel 2002; Abu-Laban, Tungohan, and Gabriel 2023).

Such national-based perplexities in Canada find echoes globally. For instance, much of the Western media coverage given to the 2022 crisis in Ukraine presented it as a shocking state of affairs, precisely since it was happening in Europe and not in the developing world. This led the US-based Arab and Middle Eastern Journalists Association to warn against journalistic coverage that associates tragedy with peoples of the Middle East, Africa, South Asia, and Latin America and "dehumanizes and renders their experience with war as somehow normal and expected" (cited in Bayoumi 2022). More to the point, the fact that many European politicians responded with sympathy and open borders to Ukrainians, while positive from the vantage point of human rights, also presented a jarring contrast to responses to Syrian and other visible and ethno-racialized minority refugee groups fleeing for their lives (Bayoumi 2022). So too did the fact that many non-Ukrainian residents fleeing Ukraine (such as workers and students from India and Morocco) encountered obstacles both in Ukraine and at borders with neighbouring European states (Human Rights Watch 2022).

Given the saliency of issues and questions that confront us both in Canada—as a country with a continued history of settler colonialism of Indigenous peoples and racism—and globally, we believe that the time is right to systematically address the dehumanization of refugees and to consider ways to resist it. We see the pages that follow to be of relevance to academics and students in a number of disciplinary areas that cover themes relating to immigration, race, ethnicity, public policy, and social policy in Canada and beyond. We also see this edited collection as relevant to practitioners working in the field of immigrant and refugee settlement, policy-makers, educators, and recent and settled refugee communities. The authors of the chapters that follow look at specific areas of concern and are cognizant of their specialization and focus. However, as a collective, the chapters in this book present a complex picture. While there are no singular or simple solutions to the dehumanization of vulnerable groups, since "vulnerability" itself is subject to different readings (see Anderson and Soennecken 2022), the book as a whole points the way to the synergies that might be developed to potentiate multiple sites and strategies for resistance. Following chapter 1, which addresses how "dehumanization" has been understood across disciplinary boundaries, this book is divided into four subsequent sections addressing immigration policies, educational encounters, state apologies, and the arts.

The Role of Immigration Policies and the Media in the Dehumanization of Refugees

In chapter 2, Yasmeen Abu-Laban asks whether policy and policy-makers contribute to the humanization or dehumanization of refugees. Abu-Laban investigates this question by assessing policy developments and discourses with a focus on the years 2015–20 in Canada, the United States, and Australia. These three jurisdictions share considerable similarities in their formation as settler colonies and dispossession of Indigenous peoples, their historically racially exclusionary immigration policies, and their forms of continued settler privilege. Abu-Laban argues that while there has been a trend toward dehumanization—seen in criminalizing and punishing refugees and asylum seekers through policies relating to preventing entry, detention, and deportation—it is nonetheless the case that elected officials have a strong role to play in countering dehumanizing portrayals of refugees. The distinct role Prime Minister Justin Trudeau has played in humanizing refugees, both in Canada and in relation to the international community, is highlighted as providing an alternative discourse, especially in contrast to America's Donald Trump. The chapter also features a discussion of the Global Compact on Refugees, approved by the United Nations General Assembly in December 2018, which gained Canada's and Australia's support but not that of the United States.

In chapter 3, Jeffrey M. Ayres addresses the Canada-US Safe Third Country Agreement (STCA) pertaining to refugees. His analysis suggests that over the past several years, changing border processes have produced and/or shaped a duality of migrant precarity along the Canada-US border. The duality of precarity refers to the contradictory processes of globalization and contestation. On the one hand, government border policy reforms "from above" respond to globalization-influenced migration flows, often in dehumanizing ways. On the other hand, these may contrast with potential humanizing and human-rights-expanding interventions and claims-making by civil society actors on behalf of migrants "from below." Ayres's chapter illustrates how the Canada-US borderlands have become a site of contestation for challenging Canadian and US refugee and asylum policies—including the STCA. Ayres theorizes how both the humanizing (pro-refugee) forces and the dehumanizing (anti-refugee) migrant forces play out in relation to the structural conditions imposed by neoliberalism, precarity, and more recently, the COVID-19 pandemic. With a focus on the border between Québec, New York, and Vermont, especially at Roxham Road, he examines important transboundary interactions. Specifically, he shows how the civil society transboundary interaction that is pressuring for formal changes to bordering norms and regulations illustrates a stark departure from the oftentimes negative media portrayal and partisan discourse surrounding asylum seekers and refugees. This highlights the human rights commitment of migrant-serving groups on both sides of the border.

Chapter 4 addresses the critical issue of whether we trust others to be good and to do right when past experiences have been negative and harmful.

Specifically drawing from his experience as a refugee as well as work and leadership in the settlement sector, Fariborz Birjandian asks how we can collectively restore refugees' faith in humanity through individual efforts, public policy, community engagement, and other interventions. Birjandian's analysis shows the importance of what happens before, during, and after resettlement in Canada, noting that Canada is one among some twenty-five countries globally that are formally committed to resettling refugees. In breaking down what is often experienced by many resettled refugees into different stages, Birjandian draws our attention to the profound trauma associated with being forced to flee and the ways this may be amplified or mitigated in the journey, the wait to find a country for resettlement, and resettlement itself. He calls for settlement and integration policies not only to focus on immediate needs as they do in Canada but to go further to better take into account what individual refugees have experienced emotionally and even spiritually before arrival, as well as what they encounter en route. Such a holistic approach points to the value of boosting access to mental health support as well as being attuned to the additional pressures faced by many refugees, especially those who have recently arrived and who may have faced additional challenges during the COVID-19 pandemic when it comes to isolation, employment, and safe jobs.

In chapter 5, Nariya Khasanova analyzes Canadian media portrayals of Syrian refugees following the 2015 Paris attacks. Through a close analysis, she shows how media portrayals of refugees as either sympathetic or threatening depend on framing, current events, and their sociopolitical contexts. While the tragic photo of toddler Alan Kurdi's lifeless body on a beach in Turkey stirred tremendous compassion for Syrian refugees in Canada, Khasanova shows how the media mood shifted abruptly with the Paris attacks and putative connections to Syrians in France. Syrian refugees to Canada had formerly been framed by religion (Islam), but this frame was now conflated with a conflict frame, thereby linking three discourses: asylum seeking, Islam, and terrorism. Such framing, Khasanova argues, heightened by the ongoing Canadian election season, promoted Islamophobia, amplifying a dehumanizing discourse contrasting Syrian refugees with Canadian values. This was achieved by referencing narratives of Islamic terrorism and antisemitism, implying that their immigration posed a threat to Canadian life and values, representing an "Other" opposed to the "West." Indeed, most of the articles uncritically linked Syrian refugees, Islam, and violence, failing to give voice to the refugees themselves. However, distinctive newspaper discourses also revealed contrasting political alliances, supportive (the *Globe and Mail*) or critical (the *National Post*) of Liberal government policies. While the *Globe and Mail* mainly presented facts about government policies, the *National Post* tended to present opinion pieces grounded in Orientalist discourses linking Muslims with violence and antisemitism and raising the spectre of security threats. However, a few opinion pieces in both newspapers encouraged a critical response to dehumanization, portraying Syrian Muslim refugees as hapless but peaceful and poised to become good Canadian citizens. Overall, Khasanova's analysis demonstrates the tremendous potential for the media to play a constructive role in encouraging a more humane approach. Yet such voices and perspectives are all too often eclipsed by the larger political and economic factors driving media representations.

The Role of Educational Institutions and Programs in the (De)humanization of Refugees

This section focuses on the role educational institutions and educational programs offered by not-for-profit organizations play in the lives of refugee children and youth as they resettle in their host countries. Research shows non-profit organizations have historically played a crucial and significant role in the lives of immigrants (see Ramakrishnan and Bloemraad 2008). Although refugees typically no longer experience the same level of threats to their safety during resettlement, they are faced with the challenge of navigating an entirely new society with its institutions and their sometimes difficult-to-understand rules and regulations. For refugee children and youth, educational institutions are places where most of a culture's dominant discourses are exchanged, everyday conventional acts are observed, and new ways of doing things are learned. In particular, schools are considered by scholars as potential sites for social-emotional support for refugees and war-traumatized youth (Sullivan and Simonson 2016). Unfortunately, schools can also reinforce existing inequalities and thus contribute to the dehumanization of refugees when social differences, pre- and post-migration trauma, experiences of social exclusion, bullying, racism, and marginalization due to school practices of testing and labelling are ignored. Moreover, because teachers and other school personnel possess important intercultural competencies to varying degrees, students of non-European descent are not treated equally in a system perpetuating the dominant Eurocentric culture, values, and norms through its curriculum and organization.

Consistent with previous research, the study in chapter 6, reported by Pallabi Bhattacharyya, Labe Songose, and Lori Wilkinson, reveals a range of dehumanizing pre-migration experiences among Yazidi refugees in Canada. Study participants reported highly traumatic experiences of torture, prolonged captivity by ISIS, rape, sexual slavery or other forms of enslavement, witnessing murder, and the rape or torture of family members. The chapter focuses on the impact of such highly traumatic pre-migration experiences on the participants' adjustment and adaptation to life/learning/work after resettling in Canada as well as the impacts of these experiences on their young children. The study challenges resettlement practices adopted by the society at large that do not meet the specific needs of this particular population of people who suffer multiple traumas, including the trauma of adjusting to post-resettlement life in Canada. Such ineffective practices include lack of flexibility in offering English as a second language classes, lack of mental health support and care, lack of financial support, barriers to accessing services, and barriers to accessing employment. The authors' critique of such practices is based on the recognition that meeting the complex needs of highly traumatized refugees cannot work unless it is approached through a trauma lens. The major contributions of the chapter are Yazidi refugees' first-person accounts, which put a human face to traumatic experiences and their impacts during resettlement. Overall, the researchers advocate for the adoption of trauma-informed practices in resettling refugees as a practical approach to humanizing refugees after resettlement in Canada. Such strategies include providing sustainable and secure funding to settlement agencies, planning and investing in providing assistance to highly traumatized refugees prior to their arrival in Canada, and extending eligibility for services, including language learning beyond the current three-year period, as critical in meeting their needs.

Using a first-person narrative account, Jwamer Jalal begins chapter 7 with the question "Where are you from?" as a way of exploring the "purgatory of identity" that many first-generation refugees and immigrants who grew up in Canada experience. Examples of situations in which the question was asked include encounters with officials (e.g., police, teachers) as well as with peers and members of the general public in both the host country and the country of origin. Jalal's analysis of these situations demonstrates how the question acts as a vehicle of othering as well as an indicator that first-generation immigrants belong nowhere. The chapter thus contributes to our understanding of what it means to experience dehumanization. More specifically, the chapter exposes harmful discourses and policies that may contribute to the othering experienced by immigrant children as well as their desires for belonging to their non-immigrant peer group in school and to the society at large. Jalal also offers an important critique of the conception of national identity from which Brown and Muslim citizens are excluded. In his account of how obtaining legal citizenship is a "false promise" to Brown citizens, he illustrates how citizenship does not necessarily lead to a sense of belonging for those who are not considered to be "true" Canadians (i.e., white, monolingual English speakers, and Christian). The chapter concludes by considering potential solutions to the adversities experienced by first-generation youth that could foster a movement toward inclusiveness and belonging. Jalal describes specific examples of community-based youth programs grounded in cultural wealth theory (Yosso 2005) that can help first-generation immigrants regain pride in their cultural heritage and begin to develop a healthier bicultural identity. In this way, the chapter contributes to our understanding of the practical approaches taken by some not-for-profit organizations toward educational programs that aim at rehumanizing refugees during and after resettlement in Canada.

Chapter 8 brings attention to the inclusion of refugee youth, especially those who are in the process of seeking asylum, within post-secondary educational institutions in Germany. Unlike other European nations, between 2015 and 2017, German society experienced a period of partial hospitality, mobilized by different social actors welcoming refugees and enabling their arrival. Encarnación Gutiérrez Rodríguez's study of a pilot program, Branch Out, is analyzed in the context of the implementation of the New Pact of Asylum and Migration, as adopted on September 23, 2020. The goals of the pilot program were threefold: (a) to be a bridge between the university and persons seeking asylum in Giessen, (b) to offer these persons introductory access to the university, and (c) to establish a transcultural learning space for major and minor students pursuing bachelor's degrees in social sciences as well as persons seeking asylum participating in this course. Despite creating common courses, the refugee students, other ERASMUS students, and the German students did not meet on equal terms. Refugee students' access through the audit program did not provide them with regular student status. Language barriers, othering, and racism were reflected in the classroom. The chapter highlights systemic barriers to refugees' access to post-secondary education. By pointing to the potentials and limits of transcultural learning within the context of seeking asylum, the chapter offers a critique of the current post-secondary educational provisions for refugees regarding the unrealized potential of building anti-racist intersectional and transcultural learning projects in German post-secondary higher education in the future. The chapter also offers specific recommendations for reforms in post-secondary educational institutions in Germany that would lead to easier access for refugees. These include adjusting the requirement for German-language proficiency, which currently prevents refugee students who are participating in pathway programs from access to the university; taking into account potential health problems related to depression and trauma; and addressing financial barriers to refugee students' access to higher education.

While chapters 6, 7, and 8 focus on issues of othering faced by refugees as they encounter the education system in the countries in which they resettle, chapter 9 provides a brief historical overview of the origins of the practices of homogenization. It traces such practices including "schooling the body" through a space-time continuum of school life, objectification, stereotyping, racism, and othering to the mid-seventeenth century. In her analysis of educational theories and practices that have created universal benchmarks for a "civilized" modern human that in turn have positioned those who are different as less than human, Anna Kirova examines the dimensions of dehumanization that have detrimental effects on refugee and immigrant students' experiences of schooling in their host countries. The chapter also offers a critical analysis of essentialism and assumptions of normalcy that still exist in multicultural and anti-racist educational theories and practices, which have contributed to the persistence of "othering" those who do not fit the very norms these educational theories are aimed at eradicating. The chapter offers a framework for the humanization of education based on the key concept of interculturalism—"alterity" as a recognition of the Other's perspectives, as a possibility for questioning one's own. The chapter proposes that a pedagogical understanding of all children as strangers whom we can never fully know can allow educators to get "rid of the normalcy assumptions and essentialism" within themselves to attempt to transgress the deeply entrenched norms, rules, and codes meant to assimilate the Other into a homogeneous same. It calls for pedagogy that enacts alterity as a movement toward the richness and brilliance of the heterogeneous Other and also bears responsibility for who they are. The chapter concludes that only then can schools become sites where the educational experiences offered to all children, including those who come from refugee backgrounds, truly respect the alterity of the Other.

Countering Dehumanization: State Apologies and New Approaches

This section examines the idea of humanization through the prism of state apologies. In chapter 10, Abigail B. Bakan offers a case study of the over 900 German Jews seeking refuge from Nazi Germany in 1939 via the infamous ship called the MS *St. Louis*. They were repeatedly turned away—from Cuba, the United States, and finally Canada—and forced to return to Europe. Subsequently, 254 of the MS *St. Louis* passengers were killed in the Holocaust. On November 7, 2018, Prime Minister Justin Trudeau apologized for Canada's refusal to accept these Jewish refugees. Bakan argues this apology was long overdue, yet the narrative of this particular apology also asserted a certain narrow and distorted definition of antisemitism in the process. Bakan notes that antisemitism was described as centrally including criticism of the state of Israel, defense of Palestinian rights, and specifically the Boycott, Divestment and Sanctions movement. In the chapter, Trudeau's problematic apology and the condition of Jewish refugees to Canada are considered from the perspective of anti-racist and feminist theory and policy based on a close examination of documents and context. What does it mean when a nation says "sorry" for heinous crimes? In an age of apology—including the Truth and Reconciliation Commission of Canada on the Indian residential school system and its 94 Calls to Action—how can states and social movements advance solidarity while redressing oppression based on difference? This question of solidarity is especially pertinent in a settler colony like Canada where Indigenous peoples and other racialized minorities have experienced different forms of state harm and where many have benefitted from the colonial project at the expense of Indigenous peoples.

Chapter 11 argues most state apologies are qualitatively about rehumanizing the apologizer and seldom the apologized party, such as the refugee, Indigenous, or ethnic minority groups. That is, the apology seeks to redeem, atone, and/or restore trust in the apologizer. Authors Reza Hasmath, Benjamin Ho, and Solomon Kay-Reid take a relatively unique angle and look at the rare instances when state apologies are employed to rehumanize the apologized group. The authors employ a novel framework by bridging insights from the literature about apologies, which has focused on how apologies function, and the literature on truth and reconciliation, which has focused on countering dehumanization through "rehumanization." They pose three analytical queries: (1) How are apologies different toward refugee, Indigenous, and/or ethnic minority groups when the goal is to rehumanize the apologized party, not the apologizer? (2) What happens to the apologizer in such apologies? (3) What can be learned by jointly considering the apology and truth and reconciliation literature on how to make an effective apology? The chapter suggests that while the function of an apology is often to rehumanize the apologizer, paradoxically, an apology is really only effective if the intent is to rehumanize the victim, the apologized group.

In chapter 12, Jim Gurnett, a former member of the Legislative Assembly of Alberta and past executive director of the Edmonton Mennonite Centre for Newcomers, proffers a powerful argument for critical self-reflection, calling attention to the hypocrisy of refugee policy in Canada. While determined by principle in theory, the policy is characterized by political expediency in practice. The Universal Declaration of Human Rights, to which Canada is a signatory, affirms that home, citizenship, and asylum are basic human rights. Yet not only does Canada often refuse refugees, but Canadians also fail to critically examine their complicity in creating refugees through their willing participation in an oppressive global system that directly or indirectly causes people worldwide to seek refuge in Canada. Many Canadians often blithely consume goods manufactured and distributed through a global system of exploitative cheap labour, resulting in economic displacement. Canada provides weaponry to oppressive regimes to boost its military-industrial sector, resulting in political persecution. Canada thus seeks political and economic advantage at the expense of human rights, producing refugees streaming to the West. Canada admits a few thousand of these refugees—usually only the wealthiest, best educated, and best positioned to serve its economy—but excludes most of the poor. The chosen few are welcomed at the airport with gifts and fanfare, before television cameras and smiling politicians. But this is all spectacle more than principle: millions of others (indeed, the vast majority) are excluded. The loss of home is traumatic, and yet Canada provides scant resources addressing refugees' mental health, many of them suffering from PTSD, a condition exacerbated by uncertainty and life at the poverty line. If Canada seeks to become a global leader toward a more just world, one that recognizes refugees as "siblings in the human family," its citizens must critically examine Canada's refugee policies as well as the practices creating refugees in the first place. Human rights must take precedence over financial and political considerations, and home is a right.

Enacting (Re)humanization: Refugee Agency and the Arts

Chapter 13 is an autobiographical recollection of the events surrounding Jalal Barzanji's imprisonment during Saddam Hussein's regime in Iraq and Barzanji's family's journey to Canada. The theme of being at home, losing a home, and finding a new home is central to the chapter. The role of the library as an institution—as "palaces for the people," to use Eric Klinenberg's (2018) words—is explored in relation to the main theme of home as an intellectual home. The building of the Erbil Public Library, like the bodies of the prisoners, was violated when Hussein's regime converted it into a prison. The descriptions of torture, humiliation, and other violations of human dignity while in this prison are juxtaposed with Barzanji's experiences of writing poems in his prison cell. Some of the poems written while in prison are included in the chapter and exemplify the role of art and artistic expression in resisting dehumanization, particularly for those who have been subjected to imprisonment as a violent and severe form of dehumanization. The chapter ends with regaining one's humanity after resettlement. Thus, the chapter addresses how art, as an epistemological approach to humanizing (or rehumanizing), can be beneficial for refugees during resettlement in Canada.

Chapter 14, by Louise Harrington and Dana Waissi, examines the relationship between cultural production and exiled Kurdish people. As a group, exiled Kurdish people are often referred to as the world's largest stateless nation, subjected to intense dehumanization in several jurisdictions. The chapter asks how the cultural production of literature and music might operate as a site for Kurdish identity in exile. The authors' hypothesis is that addressing this question will uncover what a Kurdish cultural identity among a widely dispersed community might be founded on. The cartographic absence of a recognized, bordered Kurdistan has fostered the belief that Kurdish cultural identity cannot be unified. Therefore, the chapter examines both the literary and the musical outputs of Kurds from 1969 to 2019 to trace the patterns of "Kurdishness" at the heart of two significant forms of the culture. This approach acknowledges that Kurdish identity is likely located in multiple places, not in a singular site or form. It reveals how the literature and music of the Kurds make visible their historical plight and cultural identity even through the processes of exile and resettlement in Canada.

In chapter 15, Michael Frishkopf takes as his focus resisting dehumanization through music. This chapter develops a theory of transcultural music as a social technology for global human development. This is achieved by weaving connections: enhancing inclusive, diverse, resilient social linkages through resonant interactions across perceived social boundaries of culture or community. As Frishkopf insists, culture and community are concepts that should be treated not as countable nouns but rather as indivisible continua, albeit exhibiting regions of greater or lesser density. Transcultural music thus has the capacity to extend what can be termed the social fabric (empathetic connections among social subjects), as opposed to the social network (communicative connections among social positions). Importantly, transcultural music is shown to be a generative tool for the creation of grassroots solidarities. These are solidarities that are diverse and inclusive yet also cohesive and resilient insofar as they transcend or erase top-down boundaries of culture and community. As the chapter indicates, such solidarities can become the productive basis for a broader, more connected social fabric, both paradigmatically (as a generative model) and syntagmatically (as a connective nucleus).

Chapter 16, by Thomas Mapfumo, Chiedza Mapfumo, and Michael Frishkopf, centers on the story of Thomas Mapfumo as a musician activist in exile. In doing so, the authors explore music's power to catalyze connection and change. Through a trialogue of interviews supplemented by archival research, the chapter recounts the life story of Thomas Mapfumo, a Zimbabwean musical icon and a tireless musical critic of injustice and corruption in his country. Born in a rural town of colonial Rhodesia, where he imbibed traditional folk music, his family later moved to the city, where he absorbed popular local and American styles. After his initial career singing covers, Mapfumo and his band developed a new genre called Chimurenga ("struggle"), fusing popular southern African styles with traditional *mbira* music, closely linked to pre-colonial life, and evoking the power of the people for freedom and justice. Singing to support the liberation struggle against the white Rhodesian regime, in 1980, he celebrated Zimbabwe's independence under newly elected leader Robert Mugabe, participating in a massive concert featuring Bob Marley and the Wailers. But corruption quickly set in, and a decade later, he was criticizing Mugabe in song. "Music is a weapon," Mapfumo has said, and the potency of that weapon was revealed not only through its effectiveness but also in the severity of the regime's response to its celebrated musical critic. The repression, persecution, and brutality of Mugabe's regime produced many Zimbabwean political refugees over subsequent decades, including Thomas Mapfumo himself. Forced into exile in 2000, he moved, together with his family, to the United States. But his music sustained his connections to the homeland, where he remained a potent force even while far away. Meanwhile, his band expanded to include American musicians, connecting him to various American music scenes. His many North American concert tours and festival appearances, along with radio play, garnered wide exposure. He helped link up the Zimbabwean diaspora while developing passionate new fans among North Americans. Amplified by many media appearances on platforms as widely disseminated as NPR and the *Guardian*, as well as local newspapers and radio stations, his music contributed greatly to raising general awareness of Zimbabwe's dire political conditions and galvanized the Zimbabwean opposition in exile. Ultimately, the power of Mapfumo's music to unite against injustice helped catalyze political change. In 2017, Mugabe was forced from power, and Mapfumo returned to a triumphant concert in 2018.

Chapter 17 contains the link to an online concert program, as well as being based on Frishkopf's pre-concert talk called "Beyond Words: Transpositions: Music for Resilient Sustainable Communities." Frishkopf centers on the power of music to support refugees undergoing a process of social transpositions. By weaving resilient, humanized connections, music can enable refugees to maintain social and cultural connections to their homelands while supporting social integration in their host societies. As the concert convincingly shows, music is not only aesthetically beautiful but also physiologically and psychologically powerful. It moves, distracts, and entertains us individually. But music is also a remarkably powerful social technology like no other. Some use that power for profit or power, but as Frishkopf points out, music can also be deployed for social good. He also introduces the concert program.

In concluding this volume with a concert program, we aim as editors to signal the tremendous and as yet not fully tapped potential of the arts to be a vehicle for discussion, experience, and resisting dehumanization. This and the other findings illuminated in the chapters of this transdisciplinary collection are offered to scholars, practitioners, and those who have experienced refugeehood as a starting point for a wider public conversation about resisting the dehumanization of refugees.

References

Abu-Laban, Yasmeen. 2020. "Immigration and Settler-Colonies Post-UNDRIP: Research and Policy Implications." *International Migration* 58, no. 6 (December): 12–28.

Abu-Laban, Yasmeen, and Christina Gabriel. 2002. *Selling Diversity: Immigration, Multiculturalism, Employment Equity and Globalization*. Peterborough, Canada: Broadview.

Abu-Laban, Yasmeen, Ethel Tungohan, and Christina Gabriel. 2023. *Containing Diversity: Canada and the Politics of Immigration in the 21st Century*. Toronto: University of Toronto Press.

Anderson, Melissa Mary, and Dagmar Soennecken. 2022. "Locating the Concept of Vulnerability in Canada's Refugee Policies at Home and Abroad." *Laws* 11 (2): 1–25S.

Angus Reid Institute. 2022. "Half of Canadians Back Sending Lethal Aid to Ukraine; Most Prefer Humanitarian Assistance, Sanctions Against Russia." March 16, 2022. https://angusreid.org/ukraine-russia-canada-aid-nato/.

Bayoumi, Moustaf. 2022. "They Are 'Civilised' and 'Look like Us': The Racist Coverage of Ukraine." *Guardian*, March 2, 2022. https://www.theguardian.com/commentisfree/2022/mar/02/civilised-european-look-like-us-racist-coverage-ukraine.

Hamlin, Rebecca. 2021. *Crossing: How We Label and React to People on the Move*. Stanford, CA: Stanford University Press.

Hasmath, Reza. 2012. *The Ethnic Penalty: Immigration, Education and the Labour Market*. Burlington, VT, and Surrey, UK: Ashgate.

Hasmath, Reza. 2021. "What Salience Does White Privilege Have in Non-diverse Societies?" Paper presented at the virtual American Sociological Association Annual Meeting, August 6–10, 2021.

Human Rights Watch. 2022. "Ukraine: Unequal Treatment of Foreigners Attempting to Flee." March 4, 2022. https://www.hrw.org/news/2022/03/04/ukraine-unequal-treatment-foreigners-attempting-flee.

Hyndman, Jennifer, and Johanna Reynolds. 2020. "Beyond the Global Compacts: Re-imagining Protection." *Refuge* 36 (1): 66–74.

Mosleh, Omar. 2019. "Alberta Home to Disproportionate Number of Hate Groups, Report Says." *Star*, April 23, 2019. https://www.thestar.com/edmonton/2019/04/23/alberta-home-to-disproportionate-number-of-extremist-groups-report-says.html.

Oliver, Sophie. 2011. "Dehumanization: Perceiving the Body as (In)human." In *Humiliation, Degradation, Dehumanization: Human Dignity Violated*, edited by Paulus Kaufmann, Hannes Kuch, Christian Neuhäuser, and Elaine Webster, 85–97. New York: Springer.

Osman, Laura. 2024. "Canada to Accept 1000 Applications from Canadians' Relatives Seeking Way Out of Gaza." CTV News, January 2, 2024. https://www.ctvnews.ca/politics/canada-to-accept-1-000-applications-from-canadians-relatives-seeking-way-out-of-gaza-1.6708119.

Ramakrishnan, S. Karthick, and Irene Bloemraad, eds. 2008. *Civic Hopes and Political Realities: Immigrants, Community Organizations, and Political Engagement*. New York: Russell Sage Foundation.

Repko, Allen, Rick Szostak, and Michelle Buchberger. 2016. *Introduction to Interdisciplinary Studies*. 2nd ed. Thousand Oaks, CA: SAGE.

Statistics Canada. 2017. "Immigration and Ethnocultural Diversity: Key Results from the 2016 Census." *Daily*, October 25, 2017. https://www150.statcan.gc.ca/n1/daily-quotidien/171025/dq171025b-eng.htm.

Sullivan, Amanda L., and Gregory R. Simonson. 2016. "Systematic Review of School Based Social Emotional Interventions for Refugee and War Traumatized Youth." *Review of Educational Research* 86 (2): 503–30.

Tasker, John Paul. 2022. "Canada Prepared to Welcome an 'Unlimited Number' of Ukrainians Fleeing War." CBC News, March 3, 2022. https://www.cbc.ca/news/politics/canada-unlimited-number-ukrainians-1.6371288.

UNHCR (United Nations High Commissioner for Refugees). 2022. "Refugees Operational Data." https://data2.unhcr.org/en/situations/ukraine.

United Nations Department of Economic and Social Affairs. 2021. "International Migration 2020 Highlights." January 15, 2021. https://www.un.org/en/desa/international-migration-2020-highlights.

Yosso, Tara J. 2005. "Whose Culture Has Capital? A Critical Race Theory Discussion of Community Cultural Wealth." *Race, Ethnicity and Education* 8 (1): 69–91.

1 Theoretical Perspectives on Dehumanization and Resisting It

Yasmeen Abu-Laban, Michael Frishkopf, Reza Hasmath, and Anna Kirova

In this chapter, we grapple with the manner in which dehumanization and humanization have been approached across disciplinary boundaries. As the editors of this book, we are a multidisciplinary team spanning political science, education, and ethnomusicology and have brought together other scholars in such diverse disciplines as comparative literature and sociology. We are fully aware of how humanization as a concept has been both unevenly and variably taken up across disciplines. Whereas fields like political science and economics have not made heavy use of the concept, others such as philosophy and particularly social psychology have. Below, we trace emergent themes from disciplinary traditions that have given consideration to humanization and point to ways our knowledge can be expanded by pushing disciplinary boundaries.

A range of disciplines have clear connections to the issue of humanization. The conceptualization of humanization presupposes a shared ethical framework denoting what it means to be human. We recognize that any such framework is shaped by socio-historical forces that reflect "unequal geographies of knowledge production" (Brankamp and Weima 2021, 5). In this and other ways, the Western philosophical tradition can be instructive in establishing a conceptual ethical and moral baseline. Foremost, being human intricately involves an experiential element. It is to experience ourselves as both the subject and the active spectator of objects in the world (see, e.g., Heidegger 2008). It is our ability to think consciously and ultimately to create and distinguish valid ethical knowledge claims about the world around us (see, e.g., Wittgenstein 2001). If human beings are social creatures, as Marx and Engels ([1845] 1998) assert, then humans can only develop their true nature in society. Being human thus has a socio-cultural and moral element, whereby there are formal and informal societal norms, rules, rights, behaviours, and expectations that are imparted onto us and are in turn embodied, codified, and governed by a society's legal jurisprudence and political, economic, and social institutional structures.

Commonplace in understanding the act of being human and being afforded humanizing qualities within the psychological, sociological, and political spheres is the notion that humanization can be seen as empathizing with the common ethical humanity of the Other. This can be expressed at the individual level as well as performed in the groups, institutions, and structures of a society, whether political, legal, economic, social, or cultural. In other words, we recognize the humanity of others through connections—established through communications, live or mediated—from which we infer, affectively, that "they" are like "us," subjects rather than objects. Likewise, we ourselves are human for others to the extent that "we" are perceived as connected to "them." In fact, full humanistic recognition requires both directions to obtain and form a cycle: one must feel the other recognizing one's humanity to fully recognize that of the Other and even to recognize oneself as human. Likewise, one's humanity appears in one's recognition of the Other, as in a mirror. Full humanistic recognition requires bidirectional connections underlaid with affect or emotive elements. Emmanuel Levinas's (1991) philosophy of ethics summons a responsibility for the alterity of the "Other" as separate and different from oneself. Levinas's overarching claim is that the ethical relation with the Other is the condition of possibility for all human consciousness. Phenomenologically, alterity is concerned with "the otherness of the other" (van Manen 2014, 64), which makes the Other uniquely who they are. Michael Frishkopf and Anna Kirova explore these elements in their respective chapters.

Such bidirectional connections must pervade a community to ensure robust collective recognition. Analyzing the epistemological basis for coordinating collective action, Michael Chwe (2001, 19) has called attention to "common knowledge," which can be recursively defined as that which everyone knows and which everyone knows is common knowledge. Collective recognition of humanity, by contrast, requires a "common feeling": a felt intuition of the Other as human, together with the feeling that such intuition is shared (Frishkopf 2021, 64). One then recognizes the Other in oneself, a mutual inclusion. If our humanity depends on the humanity of others, then our humanity is a mutuality we can all share within a socio-cultural context. Mutualities consist of qualities and faculties whose existence depends on a relationship between human beings. However, as Paulo Freire (2000) demonstrates, and a key point that we stress, *Our humanity is bound among the humanity of others through processes of both humanization and dehumanization.*

Dehumanization is the act of debasing the individuality of the Other as a subject and, instead, treating the individual as an object. In this commonplace act, accepted social norms, rules, rights, behaviours, and expectations that apply to every "human" do not apply (or are perceived not to apply) to the Other. Dehumanization can occur among individuals, socio-cultural groups, or institutions of a society. For example, ethno-racial group(s) and refugees can be targeted by state actors or state-organized institutions delegitimizing their status and power in society through exclusion and/or violence. This case is demonstrable in Abu-Laban's chapter on refugee policies in the United States, Canada, and Australia as well as Harrington and Waissi's chapter on Kurdish cultural identity.

Dehumanization proceeds from disconnection, rendering subject as object. Sophie Oliver (2011, 85) posits that the "standard definitions of dehumanization define the concept in terms of a negation of such positive 'human' qualities as individuality, autonomy, personality, civility, and dignity." While some scholars reserve the word for the most extreme cases (e.g., American dehumanization of African slaves, Nazi dehumanization of Jews, Hutu dehumanization of Tutsis), others recommend a continuum of objectification, from "casual indifference" at one end to full-fledged "dehumanization" at the other (Rector 2014, 9–10). In many cases, particularly following trauma, the dehumanization of the self is also common due to both a disconnection from others who would affirm one's humanity and a loss of connection to one's world, culture, and identity.

In nearly all traditional cultures, the possibility of complete dehumanization (and the horrific atrocities that may follow) is by no means inevitable; while a certain suspicion of strangers may be common, such societies also uphold values of hospitality as a means of interacting with outsiders (Pitt-Rivers 2012). During such interactions, "the stranger" may be personally unfamiliar but occupies a familiar status as "guest." Derrida (2000) clarifies the dual meaning of the word *hôte* in French to mean both "host" and "guest." His idea is that hospitality, seen as a welcome to cross the threshold and join the host in their place, meets difficulties. The host who welcomes becomes a guest to the guest they are welcoming. They both receive from the house or place they are in. The welcome of the other who comes without invitation is exhausting whether the other is welcomed out of guilt (from the host) or out of his or her vulnerability.

Moving from philosophy to the vantage point of social psychology, dehumanization can be understood as "denying humanness to others, introducing an asymmetry between people who have human qualities and people who are perceived as lacking these qualities" (Volpato and Andrighetto 2015, 31). Notably, when we are considering the basis by which an asymmetry is introduced between an "in-group" and an "outgroup," it is relevant to observe that they can take place along a variety of axes—including gender, sexuality, ethnicity, race, socio-economic status, and citizenship, among others; these often involve legal or perceived differences in status (Haslam and Loughnan 2014, 407–10).

Social psychological studies in the field dating from the 1970s to the 1990s have addressed dehumanization in relation to mass violence. These studies have asked how the perceptions that victimizers hold of victims may lessen the normal restraints governing violence as well as how perceptions of value differences and demonizing labels can fuel inter-group conflict (Haslam and Loughnan 2014, 401). Social psychological studies have also shown that a propensity to dehumanize can stem from a variety of factors, including feeling part of an in-group, feeling part of an in-group that has historically been accused of inflicting harm on an outgroup, seeing an outgroup as a threat, and having a sense of personal power (Haslam and Loughnan 2014, 414). There is some debate within social psychology about the explanatory utility of the focus on dehumanization. Critics have charged, for example, that comparisons to non-humans are not always negative (e.g., calling a toddler a "little monkey"), that outgroup members can be (negatively) labelled in ways that only apply to humans, and that being perceived as less than human does not always lead to harm (Over 2020, 5–10). However, other social psychologists have defended the concept by arguing that work on dehumanization does not suggest all animal metaphors are dehumanizing, that dehumanization is conceptually distinct from prejudice and labels that might be "human" but derogatory, and that the consequences of dehumanization are not just about harm (Vaes, Paladino, and Haslam 2020). We submit that such a perspective of dehumanization needs to be taken seriously.

We find the social psychological work on dehumanization to be relevant precisely because the dangers associated with dehumanization are well documented and go beyond psychological harm. Indeed, at the extreme, they can and do include violence and atrocities (Volpato and Andrighetto 2015, 31), a feature relevant to the growing number of works in genocide studies that make conceptual use of dehumanization (Haslam and Loughnan 2014, 401). However, social psychologists also trace a link between dehumanization and a lessening of pro-social behaviour (relating to empathy and sharing) as well as antisocial behaviour (e.g., aggression and excluding others). Put differently, there is a cost to dehumanizing behaviour that may be incurred by both those who are on the receiving end and those who do it. The costs make it worthwhile to study dehumanization and to ask how it might be mitigated.

We find the existing social science research on refugees and dehumanization to be illuminating. For instance, Brankamp and Weima (2021, 1) interrogate the dehumanization of politics and wider dehumanizing societal sentiments toward refugees in Europe and North America by drawing connections between the "existing systems of racialized inequalities, dispossession, and differential mobility that has grown out of histories of empire and a militarized liberal world order built on racial capitalism." Refugees are typically dehumanized and are placed in a precarious position in several respects: (1) due to experiences of violence, disconnection from homeland and lack of connection to the host society; (2) exclusion of basic fundamental human rights enshrined in international jurisprudence, whether civil or political rights or economic, cultural, and social rights; and (3) exclusion from power, increasingly across generations as growing numbers of protracted refugee situations suggest (Abu-Laban 2021). Dehumanization is often exacerbated in refugee camps, where besides relative material deprivation, there is no connection to either the sending state or the receiving state, and identity loss accompanying the dehumanization of the self is also common. But the fact that dehumanization is typically driven by systemic forces means that it may be reversed once political or economic factors inhibiting rehumanization are removed. People have the capacity to humanize the Other, given a suitable context—that is, one enabling and promoting common feeling and mutuality. It is in this sense that our work is ethically grounded in critical scholarship:

challenging researchers to re-examine and re-think humanity, the meaning of being human, the conditions of dehumanization, and those who are subjected to them. In this transdisciplinary collection, the prominent place of contributions from refugees themselves speaks to our commitment to widening the circle of knowledge production, challenging dehumanizing views of refugee identity by broadening our horizons to see beyond their experiences of displacement, torture, imprisonment, and other forms of dehumanization and embrace their success in retaining their humanness as writers, poets, and musicians.

From another lens, refugees have been subject to media, partisan, and popular discourses that construct them as a "threat." For instance, media stereotyping in settler societies such as Canada and Australia has promoted negative characterizations of refugees (see, e.g., Khasanova's chapter; McKenzie and Hasmath 2013). This negativity primes the general public to view refugees in a dehumanizing light (see, e.g., Hasmath 2012). An individual's tendency to dehumanize refugees is associated with unfriendly verbal and nonverbal behaviours toward them. Moreover, some recent work posits that governments and political leaders can either feed refugee dehumanization or challenge it with alternative messaging, in keeping with their stated humanitarian and human rights obligations (see, e.g., Abu Laban's chapter; Esses, Medianu, and Sutter 2021, 284–86). This brings us to consider strategies to resist dehumanization.

Strategies for Resisting Dehumanization

Moving from the theoretical to the pragmatic, the idea of challenging dehumanization—or, put differently and as a shorthand, rehumanization—is important because it allows us to establish a framework for understanding a shared common trust or distrust with the Other. Political scientists have pointed out that acts of rehumanization can help de-escalate conflict, violence, civil strife, and/or even genocide. Practitioners of conflict resolution have repeatedly suggested that we are less likely to rationalize engaging in such acts if we see the Other as a human being while maintaining minimal levels of mutual respect and trust (see, e.g., Saguy et al. 2015). Once all parties are able to empathize through recognition of shared humanity and basic ethical norms, they are more likely to listen, build, and engage in constructive resolution (see, e.g., Halpern and Weinstein 2004). This can even lead to taking responsibility, apologizing, and reconciling with the Other, as discussed in Bakan's and Hasmath, Ho, and Kay-Reid's chapters.

Increasing Inter-group Contact

For sociologists, fostering inter-group contact has been an essential component of rehumanizing the Other—that is, increasing social trust between groups, improving between-group relations, engendering forgiveness for past transgressions (see Hasmath, Ho, and Kay-Reid's chapter), and creating a more differentiated perception of the outgroup. Pettigrew et al. (2011) found that the optimal conditions for inter-group contact—equal status, common goals, the absence of inter-group competition, and authority sanction—facilitate greater rehumanization potential. Cross-group friendships are particularly effective at promoting positive attitudes toward the outgroup (see Turner et al. 2007). These effects are usually generalized beyond the confines of an individual's relationship with members of another group, to the outgroup at large. Additionally, these positive effects can occur, although to a lesser extent, merely by having an in-group friend with outgroup friends (see Pettigrew et al. 2011).

Recent research in contact theory has suggested that in much the same way as negative portrayals of outgroup members can increase bias and dehumanize the group—see, for example, Khasanova's chapter in this volume for discussions on the media's representation of Syrian refugees—positive portrayals can reduce prejudice (see Dovidio, Eller, and Hewstone 2011). Although vicarious contact in this form has fewer positive consequences, it can still help reduce prejudice and improve sentiments toward the outgroup. Significantly, this has been found to occur even in scenarios that involve ethno-racial or religious conflicts (see, e.g., Bilali and Vollhardt 2013). An additional benefit of vicarious contact via positive mass media is that it can influence a significant number of viewers, allowing the effects to occur faster at a population-wide level (see Vezzali et al. 2014).

Multicultural Education

In the context of integrating newcomers into host societies, education is described in multiple ways. In some cases, multicultural education is approached as an outcome of the successful integration of newcomers. In other cases, it is treated as a means of integration, since achievements in these areas can exert a recursive influence (see, e.g., Ager and Strang 2008). As an answer to cultural pluralism in society, multicultural education was conceived not only as a way of managing diversity and the integration of newcomers into the larger society but also as a way of providing continuity to the ongoing dialogue about the nature of multiculturalism. In Canada, it emerged as an application of the federal multicultural policy within many provincial education systems (James 2003). Thus, it has been linked to the influence of the original federal multiculturalism in Canada, the first country to adopt such a policy, which promoted ethno-cultural retention (Abu-Laban 2014).

From its inception, the goal of multicultural education "has been to foster appreciation of the cultural heritages of others towards increasing inter-group harmony" (Lund 2003, 5). However, as Ghosh and Abdi (2004) conclude, multicultural education programs only theoretically give access to all ethno-cultural groups, and these programs have not resulted in equal participation in the educational or economic sphere (see, e.g., Hasmath 2012). Other scholars have argued that such programs have solidified the boundaries between majority and minority cultures while reproducing white dominance (e.g., Kirova 2015).

Critiques of multicultural education, therefore, reveal tensions between theory and practice. Moreover, critiques also reveal how practices based on universalist structuralist theories may limit the ability to respond to the individual needs of marginalized people who do not fit within the generalized theoretical approaches. Kirova's chapter reviews the promises and failures of multicultural and anti-racist education, particularly in regard to their essentialism and assumptions of normalcy.

In response to the widespread sense among some political and intellectual elites in pluralistic societies worldwide that multiculturalism has failed (see, e.g., Hasmath 2011)—an argument even heard in Canada, where multiculturalism policy has flourished for over half a century as a national policy—there is an ongoing "debate about the future of multiculturalism as a concept or model and whether inherited ideas of multiculturalism need to be replaced with new 'post-multicultural' approaches in an era of 'hyper-diversity'" (Kymlicka 2009, 36). As a consequence, there is an emerging new theme in multiculturalism. In seeking new "post-multicultural" approaches, the various initiatives undertaken by the very institutions, including schools, charged with the task of facilitating the integration of newcomers into the larger society need not lose sight of the multiple causes of such hyper-diversity, the most prominent among which are the ongoing armed conflicts that threaten the very humanity of those who have been forcefully displaced from their homes, including children who were taken away from their mothers' arms or have witnessed their parents and other relatives being tortured and murdered. As Hollenbach (2019, 5) aptly puts it, "When persons are displaced as refugees, they fall through the cracks of a world shattered by war or injustice." Jalal Barzanji's experience of imprisonment during Saddam Hussein's oppressive regime in Iraq (see Barzanji's chapter), and, more recently, the experiences of the Yazidi people following the American-led war, reveal unspeakable crimes against humankind. These crimes, which produce the refugee flows we see today, are also interconnected with long histories of colonialism and colonial institutions (see Nyers 2019).

The unprecedented displacement of children poses even greater challenges for the world's education systems. This is especially apparent when we recognize the fundamental rights of refugees to access education, earn a livelihood, and seek justice when wronged. However, as noted in Encarnación Gutiérrez Rodríguez's chapter addressing Germany, education is not often included in humanitarian responses to refugees. While free access to primary education is a child's right, access to post-secondary education is seldom mentioned in the inclusion of refugees in education.

Dialogical Approach

A rehumanizing approach to knowledge production has its roots in Freire's (1972) popular education in Brazil and his moral philosophy, which advocated a dialogical approach to the world and the liberation of the oppressed. Freire determined that rehumanization occurs via dialogue through which the oppressors and the oppressed can become more fully human. He argued that this dialogic inquiry "must be directed towards humanization—the people's historical vocation" (Freire 2000, 85). In order to overcome oppression, this dialogue "cannot be carried out in isolation or individualism, but only in fellowship and solidarity" because "no one can be authentically human while [preventing] others from being so" (85). He describes our humanity as bound among the humanity of others. Both the oppressed and their oppressors, all people can attempt to regain or to realize their full humanity or, in Freirean terms, their fuller humanity. Therefore, regardless of whether participants in dialogue are oppressors or oppressed, their rehumanization depends on the humanization of those in relation to them. As Alexander Sidorkin (1999, 12) puts it, "A failure to affirm the being of the other brings myself into Freirian non-being."

To factor the Freirean approach to rehumanization in educational contexts, for example, educators have to succeed in creating dialogic spaces that would allow refugee students to regain their full humanity, especially since some of them have lost a part of their sense of self and their identity. A dialogue facilitating a horizontal relationship of mutual trust among participants must be founded upon love, humility, and faith in humanity. Those who cannot fully participate in the dialogue cannot develop their full humanity or even live life to its fullest. The language barriers to participation in dialogue encountered by refugee students are noted in Kirova's, Gutiérrez Rodríguez's, and Bhattacharyya, Songose, and Wilkinson's chapters.

Expressive Culture and the Arts

Performing arts can induce "common feeling" (Frishkopf 2022, 78) through mutual participation. Music provides a good example, and similar considerations apply to all the performing arts. Treating music broadly—following Small's (1998) generalized notion of "musicking"—to include a range of musical activities, from performing to dancing to toe-tapping or simply listening, musical participation engenders emotion, emotional recognition, and deeply felt humanistic connection. The generation of "common feeling" does not presume that everyone responds to music in the same way or even that participants think that they do. Music offers multiple layers of meaning, some of them limited by culture, while others enable intercultural comprehension or, at least, the intercultural recognition of meaningfulness. Observing others' responses to musical stimuli confirms an intuitively felt recognition of their humanity, even without necessarily understanding music in the same way. Other collective activities—sharing a meal, say, or conversation (if allowed by a common language)—may induce a similar recognition. However, music and dance provide several uniquely humanizing properties resulting from their ability to communicate emotion broadly, across large collectivities, and beyond language.

Touching is perhaps the most intimate form of human connection through mutual feeling. Composer and soundscape theorist Murray Schafer (1994, 11) has described hearing as a form of "remote touching": "Touch is the most personal of the senses. Hearing and touch meet where the lower frequencies of audible sound pass over to tactile vibrations (at about 20 hertz). Hearing is a way of touching at a distance and the intimacy of the first sense is fused with sociability whenever people gather together to hear something special."

Dance, varying widely in form and meaning across cultures yet providing a layer of transcultural mutual comprehension, frequently implies a socialized touch. But even without touch, dance enhances the power of music's remote touch through visual communication of rhythm and form.

Music and dance, being both collective and relatively abstract, offer the greatest transcultural power to induce mutual recognition of humanity. But visual arts provide additional avenues, as well as literature, cinema, and the dramatic arts when language is shared.

For the expressive performer, poetry, movement, and musical sound constitute an extrusion of the self—an aura or subjective corona extending beyond the physical body, interpenetrating with those of others, forming a quasi-independent intersubject, confirming to all who participate that participants are human.

Through lyrics, expression, and temporal-tonal patterning, music is highly affective—even when not understood or not understood in the same way—particularly in collective contexts where its emotional effect is not only direct but also reflective, derived from the perception of others' responses.

The affective power of sound is most intense in what Frishkopf terms *socio-sonic-visual resonance*: a collective cognitive-affective state resulting from communicative feedback, carrying, tuning, and amplifying musical meaning while gathering participants (Frishkopf in Rasmussen et al. 2019, 305–6; Frishkopf 2021, 2022).

Sound is particularly effective as it diffuses three-dimensionally, diffracting to pervade a performance space, masking competing dyadic communications, and demanding attention. Music enables mass participation while synchronizing and aligning participants through rhythm, melody, and harmony. Music provides, as Alfred Schutz (1951, 92) notes, the capability for social coordination, a "mutual tuning-in." Participants are unified by a common sensory focus. Music's sonic organization (temporal, spectral, and formal) connects participants by inducing social alignments (e.g., synchronized rhythm, call/response interactions, harmony). Over time, common feeling associated with a shared context leads to the sedimentation of shared meaning. All these factors induce social cohesion. At the same time, unlike the pragmatic functional language of quotidian interactions, poetry and music are inherently ambiguous, semantically powerful, symbols, "writerly" (Barthes 1990) and flexible in interpretation. Music may not be a "universal language," as was frequently claimed in the nineteenth century. Yet when participants all find music meaningful, albeit each in their own way, musical connections form that are far-reaching, flexible, and individualized and through which mutual humanity can be recognized in response.

But the role of arts is not limited to live interactions. Mediated interactions—through broadcasts or recordings, as well as through written literature—can also induce a sense of shared humanity, particularly when they form the basis for subsequent discursive interactions. Thus, people can watch the same TV drama, listen to the same radio-broadcast song, or read the same novel and derive a sense of connectedness not only to those who acted in, sang, or wrote a work but also to one another. Literature is particularly powerful in expressing experiences precisely, in a manner such that others can experience the same vicariously, even when such experiences are foreign to their actual lives.

Performing and mediated arts are not an unmitigated good, however. While powerful, they provide a collection of double-edged swords, ethically neutral tools of ambiguous moral value. For instance, while music might erase systemic barriers to humanization, the connections induced by musical participation may also exclude, hence divide, and even dehumanize, as in music supporting the social cohesion of extremist groups, such as neo-Nazis (thus Boko Haram has its recruitment music; Vladimir Putin his pro-war music), or even less virulent artistic nationalism. Even well-intentioned musical interventions require efficacious strategies in order to avoid possible divisiveness and realize ethical aims. Inclusivity is key.

There are other limitations too. None of the arts—even music and dance, often regarded as such—are truly universal, and by their very nature, arts tend to trace certain boundaries (e.g., of linguistic comprehension or social class). One cannot understand a novel without the requisite language, and literacy may also be a factor. A poem, whether in elevated language or idiosyncratic argot, may presume a requisite background, even given general linguistic competence. Levels of connection can, therefore, vary widely, and such selective participation—or implicit, even explicit, exclusion—may induce dehumanization of various degrees and kinds. The impact of the performing arts, in particular, can often be ephemeral when used as the sole basis for connection. After creating a sense of Durkheimian "effervescence," connecting participants through powerful shared experiences and emotions, and inspiring a sense of shared humanity, connections may quickly fade afterward if not supported by other more durable social structures undergirded by cognitive factors, such as a community association, a political party, or a religious group. Although expressive culture and the arts are not always practical for rehumanization—for example, one cannot hold a musical event in the midst of violent upheaval—they nonetheless provide useful tools for rebuilding connections and rehumanizing during the process of refugee resettlement in three directions. First, expressive culture helps refugees connect to one another, especially those arriving from the same geographical location, who share aspects of identity and culture—and perhaps language—to a great extent but do not know one another and would never have interacted in the homeland due to differences in language, locale, ethnic group, or social class. Such interactions regularly take place even in refugee camps, where "musicification" can serve as an effective tool for rehumanization (Frishkopf, Morgan, and Knight 2010; Morgan and Frishkopf 2011). Second, music helps refugees build connections to the wider host society (Frishkopf 2018), providing an effective catalyst for interactions in both professional and amateur contexts, with a variety of possible modalities for participation—especially for artists themselves, who begin to collaborate with their new fellow citizens. Third, music enables refugees to maintain connections to their homelands, ensuring that identities are not lost. These links may traverse vast distances. Indeed, live performances with members of their homelands may be impossible. But mediated artistic sharing—via books, newspapers, recordings, satellite broadcasts, or the internet—can still provide an important medium for connection. Ultimately, the arts help refugees—particularly those who have suffered through extreme trauma—effect the most critical form of rehumanization: that of the self.

We believe that the sections and chapters that follow contribute to the much-needed and largely absent dialogue across disciplines addressing the important question of how dehumanization can be reduced. The current global health and economic challenges have revealed how social injustices and socio-economic inequalities have unevenly affected marginalized populations. This has made the need for a dialogue on these salient topics urgent. The present-day protests across the world that erupted as a result of deeply rooted systems of oppression demonstrate that it is as important as ever to understand the impact of dehumanization. In recognizing the complexity of the contexts in which dehumanization occurs, the book offers potential strategies for resisting, minimizing, and potentially eradicating it.

References

Abu-Laban, Yasmeen. 2014. "Reform by Stealth: The Harper Conservatives and Canadian Multiculturalism." In *The Multiculturalism Question: Debating Identity in 21st Century Canada*, edited by Jack Jedwab, 149–72. Montréal: McGill-Queen's University Press.

Abu-Laban, Yasmeen. 2021. "Re-defining the International Refugee Regime: UNHCR, UNRWA and the Challenge of Multigenerational Protracted Refugee Situation." In *Research Handbook on the Law and Politics of Migration*, edited by Catherine Dauvergne, 310–22. Northampton and Cheltenham: Edward Elgar Publishing.

Ager, Alastair, and Alison Strang. 2008. "Understanding Integration: A Conceptual Framework." *Journal of Refugee Studies* 21 (2): 166–91.

Barthes, Roland. 1990. *Image, Music, Text*. Translated by Stephen Heath. London: Fontana.

Bilali, Rezarta, and Johanna R. Vollhardt. 2013. "Priming Effects of a Reconciliation Radio Drama on Historical Perspective-Taking in the Aftermath of Mass Violence in Rwanda." *Journal of Experimental Social Psychology* 49 (1): 144–51.

Brankamp, Hanno, and Yolanda Weima. 2021. "Introduction: Humanizing Studies of Refuge and Displacement?" *Refuge* 37 (2): 1–10.

Chwe, Michael Suk-Young. 2001. *Rational Ritual Culture, Coordination, and Common Knowledge*. Princeton, NJ: Princeton University Press.

Derrida, Jacques. 2000. "Hostipitality." *Angelaki-Journal of Theoretical Humanities* 5 (3): 3–18.

Dovidio, John F., Anja Eller, and Miles Hewstone. 2011. "Improving Intergroup Relations Through Direct, Extended and Other Forms of Indirect Contact." *Group Processes and Intergroup Relations* 14 (2): 147–60.

Esses, Victoria, Stelian Medianu, and Alina Sutter. 2021. "The Dehumanization and Rehumanization of Refugees." In *Routledge Handbook of Dehumanization*, edited by Maria Kronfeldner, 275–91. Abingdon-on-Thames: Routledge.

Freire, Paulo. 1972. "Education: Domestication or Liberation?" *Prospects* 2:173–81.

Freire, Paulo. 2000. *Pedagogy of the Oppressed*. Translated by M. B. Ramos. New York: Continuum.

Frishkopf, Michael. 2018. "Music for Global Human Development, and Refugees." *Ethnomusicology* 63 (2): 279–314.

Frishkopf, Michael. 2021. "Music for Global Human Development." In *Transforming Ethnomusicology: Political, Social & Ecological Issues*, edited by

Beverley Diamond and Salwa El-Shawan Castelo-Branco, 47–66. New York: Oxford University Press.

Frishkopf, Michael. 2022. "Music for Global Human Development: Participatory Action Research for Health and Wellbeing." *MUSICultures* 49:71–109.

Frishkopf, Michael, Samuel Morgan, and W. Andy Knight. 2010. "Sustainable Peacebuilding Through Popular Music." Conference paper, Pop Culture and World Politics 3, York University. http://yciss.info.yorku.ca/files/2012/06/PCWP3_program_oct291.pdf.

Ghosh, Ratna, and Ali A. Abdi. 2004. *Education and the Politics of Difference: Canadian Perspectives*. Toronto: Canadian Scholars' Press.

Halpern, Jodi, and Harvey M. Weinstein. 2004. "Rehumanizing the Other: Empathy and Reconciliation." *Human Rights Quarterly* 26 (3): 561–83.

Haslam, Nick, and Steve Loughnan. 2014. "Dehumanization and Infrahumanization." *Annual Review of Psychology* 65:399–423.

Hasmath, Reza, ed. 2011. *Managing Ethnic Diversity: Meanings and Practices from an International Perspective*. Burlington, VT, and Surrey, UK: Ashgate.

Hasmath, Reza. 2012. *The Ethnic Penalty: Immigration, Education and the Labour Market*. Burlington, VT, and Surrey, UK: Ashgate.

Heidegger, Martin. 2008. *Being and Time*. Translated by John Macquarrie and Edward Robinson. New York: HarperCollins.

Hollenbach, David. 2019. *Humanity in Crisis: Ethical and Religious Response to Refugees*. Threats to Humanity (1–12). Washington, DC: Georgetown University Press.

James, Carl. 2003. *Seeing Ourselves: Exploring Ethnicity, Race and Culture*. 3rd ed. Toronto: Thompson Educational.

Kirova, Anna. 2015. "Critical and Emerging Discourses in Multicultural Education Literature: An (Updated) Review." In *Multiculturalism in Canada: Theories, Policies and Debates*, edited by Shibao Guo and Lloyd Wong, 239–55. Rotterdam: Sense.

Klinenberg, Eric. 2018. *Places for the People: How Social Infrastructure Can Help Fight Inequality, Polarization, and the Decline of Civic Life*. New York: Broadway Books.

Kymlicka, Will. 2009. "The Current State of Multiculturalism in Canada." *Canadian Journal of Social Research* 2 (1): 15–34.

Levinas, Emmanuel. 1991. *Otherwise Than Being or Beyond Essence*. Translated by A. Ligins. Boston: Kluwer Academic.

Lund, Darren E. 2003. "Educating for Social Justice: Making Sense of Multicultural and Antiracist Theory and Practice with Canadian Teacher Activists 1." *Intercultural Education* 14 (1): 3–16.

Marx, Karl, and Friedrich Engels. (1845) 1998. *The German Ideology*. New York: Prometheus.

McKenzie, Jaffa, and Reza Hasmath. 2013. "Deterring the 'Boat People': Explaining the Australian Government's People Swap Response to Asylum Seekers." *Australian Journal of Political Science* 48 (4): 417–30.

Morgan, Samuel, and Michael Frishkopf. 2011. "Shadow and Music in the Buduburam Liberian Refugee Camp of Ghana." Michael Frishkopf. Vimeo, February 16, 2011. http://vimeo.com/20009721.

Nyers, Peter. 2019. "Humanitarian Hubris in the Global Compacts on Refugees and Migration." *Global Affairs* 5 (2): 171–78.

Oliver, Sophie. 2011. "Dehumanization: Perceiving the Body as (In)human." In *Humiliation, Degradation, Dehumanization: Human Dignity Violated*, edited by Paulus Kaufmann, Hannes Kuch, Christian Neuhäuser, and Elaine Webster, 85–97. Library of Ethics and Applied Philosophy 24. New York: Springer. https://doi.org/10.1007/978-90-481-9661-6_7.

Over, Harriet. 2020. "Seven Challenges for the Dehumanization Hypothesis." *Perspectives on Psychological Science* 16 (1): 3–13.

Pettigrew, Thomas F., Linda R. Tropp, Ulrich Wagner, and Oliver Christ. 2011. "Recent Advances in Intergroup Contact Theory." *International Journal of Intercultural Relations* 35 (3): 271–80.

Pitt-Rivers, Julian. 2012. "The Law of Hospitality." *HAU: Journal of Ethnographic Theory* 2 (1): 501–17.

Rasmussen, Anne K., Angela Impey, Rachel Beckles Willson, Ozan Aksoy, Denise Gill, and Michael Frishkopf. 2019. "Call and Response: SEM President's Roundtable 2016, 'Ethnomusicological Responses to the Contemporary Dynamics of Migrants and Refugees.'" *Ethnomusicology* 63 (2): 279–314.

Rector, John M. 2014. *The Objectification Spectrum: Understanding and Transcending Our Diminishment and Dehumanization of Others*. Oxford: Oxford University Press.

Saguy, Tamar, Hanna Szekeres, Rikki Nouri, Amit Goldenberg, Guy Doron, John F. Dovidio, Chaim Yunger, and Eran Halperin. 2015. "Awareness of Intergroup Help Can Rehumanize the Out-Group." *Social Psychological and Personality Science* 6 (5): 551–58.

Schafer, R. Murray. 1994. *The Soundscape: Our Sonic Environment and the Tuning of the World*. Rochester, VT: Destiny Books.

Schutz, Alfred. 1951. "Making Music Together: A Study in Social Relationship." *Social Research* 18 (1): 76–97.

Sidorkin, Alexander M. 1999. *Beyond Discourse: Education, the Self, and Dialogue*. Albany: SUNY Press.

Small, Christopher. 1998. *Musicking: The Meanings of Performing and Listening*. Hanover: University Press of New England.

Turner, Rhiannon N., Miles Hewstone, Alberto Voci, Stefania Paolini, and Oliver Christ. 2007. "Reducing Prejudice via Direct and Extended Cross-Group Friendship." *European Review of Social Psychology* 18 (1): 212–55.

Vaes, Jeroen, Maria Paola Paladino, and Nick Haslam. 2020. "Seven Clarifications on the Psychology of Dehumanization." *Perspectives on Psychological Science* 16 (1): 28–32.

van Manen, Max. 2014. *Phenomenology of Practice: Meaning-Giving Methods in Phenomenological Research and Writing*. Walnut Creek, CA: Left Coast Press.

Vezzali, Loris, Miles Hewstone, Dora Capozza, Gino Giovannini, and Ralf Wölfer. 2014. "Improving Intergroup Relations with Extended and Vicarious Forms of Indirect Contact." *European Review of Social Psychology* 25 (1): 314–89.

Volpato, Chiara, and Luca Andrighetto. 2015. "Dehumanization." In *International Encyclopedia of the Social and Behavioural Sciences*, edited by James Wright, 31–36. Vol. 6. 2nd ed. Amsterdam: Elsevier.

Wittgenstein, Ludwig. 2001. *Tractatus-Logico-Philosophicus*. London: Routledge.

Part I

The Role of Immigration Policies and the Media in the Dehumanization of Refugees

2 Dehumanizing or Humanizing Refugees?
A Comparative Assessment of Canada, the United States, and Australia

Yasmeen Abu-Laban

Although statistics can in and of themselves render actual human beings invisible and even dehumanized, it is nonetheless the case that they are helpful in drawing attention to changes we have been witnessing in the 2000s. On a global scale, the past decade has been dramatic in relation to forcibly displaced persons worldwide. The alarm clearly sounded by the then United Nations High Commissioner for Refugees (UNHCR) António Guterres in 2014 of the "mega crisis" stemming from rapidly increasing numbers of refugees from Iraq and Syria (Morello 2014) was the midpoint in a decisive trend of ever-increasing numbers over the 2010s. Thus, whereas in 2010 there were 41.1 million forcibly displaced persons worldwide, by the end of 2019, this number had nearly doubled to 79.5 million, amounting to one in every ninety-seven people worldwide (UNHCR 2020, 7–8). At the end of 2019, 26 million of the 79.5 million forcibly displaced persons were refugees, with 20.4 million falling under the mandate of the UNHCR and 5.6 million Palestine refugees falling under the mandate of the United Nations Relief and Works Agency (UNHCR 2020, 2). A further 4.2 million were asylum seekers who had submitted claims (UNHCR 2020, 2). A major concern buttressing these numeric trends has been the political conditions that sustain and foster the growth of refugees. These include the inability to solve the wars and conflicts that produce refugees, growing numbers of protracted refugee situations, and the limited number of refugees accepted for resettlement in host countries (UNHCR 2020, 11–12).

There is no doubt that the policy embrace of border closure as a common response across states to the COVID-19 pandemic further exacerbated the numeric trends, with clear evidence of dropping numbers of asylum applications in many jurisdictions (UNHCR 2020, 12). More broadly, speaking in September 2020, Francesco Rocca, the president of the International Federation of Red Cross and Red Crescent Societies, observed, "COVID-19 has been cruel for all of us. It has been catastrophic for migrants. They face even more restrictions in terms of accessing basic services in ways that contribute nothing to public health. They are disproportionately impacted by border closures. They face heightened risk of detention and deportation. *They are increasingly scapegoated for the pandemic*" (cited in International Federation of Red Cross and Red Crescent Societies 2020; my emphasis).

The speed with which migrants and refugees are blamed for public health concerns, such as the spread of COVID-19 during the pandemic, is notable (Banulescu-Bogdan, Benton, and Fratzke 2020; Varela 2020). Such a quick turn (or return) to presenting insecure refugees and migrants as threats—in this case, in the form of disease—raises questions about the tenacity of negative and dehumanizing tropes and how they are sustained.

Dehumanization can be defined as "denying humanness to others, introducing an asymmetry between people who have human qualities and people who are perceived as lacking these qualities" (Volpato and Andrighetto 2015, 31). Dehumanizing discourses are central to the drawing of boundaries between "in-groups" and "outgroups" and, at the extreme, can lead to violence and atrocities (Volpato and Andrighetto 2015, 31). Of course, dehumanizing language and actions can occur without an explicit disavowal of the "humanness" of those cast into outgroups (Smith 2016). For example, for some time, it has been noted that in public debates and media depictions in liberal democracies formally committed to human rights and the legal protection of asylum seekers, refugees and immigrants may be represented in dehumanizing ways. Refugees, and immigrants more generally, have been subject to zoological images (coming in "swarms"), botanical images (communities of refugees "mushrooming"), and water images (refugees "trickling" or even "flooding" in; Hintjens 1992, 13; see also Bender 2015, 35–58; Pruitt 2019). Additionally, in the post-9/11 environment, refugees have been subjected to discourses that construct them as a "threat" by stereotyping them as bogus, as carriers of disease, and as terrorists (Esses, Medianu, and Lawson 2013, 525–28). As well, similar to animals, refugees may also be presented as having high birth rates and lacking culture (Esses, Veenvliet, and Medianu 2012, 134).

The potential consequences of dehumanization in relation to refugees are substantial given what is potentially at stake. The nation-state is a historically specific form of human organization. Because humans have divided the planet into nation-states, holding citizenship is a basic criterion for membership in the modern world. Indeed, this is so central that Article 15(1) of the 1948 United Nations Universal Declaration of Human Rights holds that "everyone has a right to a nationality." Persecution resulting in the violation of basic human rights may cause people to flee a state. Because the international community has thus far failed to prevent the conditions that give rise to refugees in the first place, there is a strong case to be made for states having not only a legal responsibility toward refugees (as established through post–World War II refugee law) but also an ethical obligation. Put differently, the state system itself creates refugees, and therefore, this is one major component of an ethical obligation on the part of states to be responsive to refugees (see also Carens 1991). However, dehumanizing rhetoric may undermine support for policies reflecting such legal and ethical responsibilities toward refugees.

In this chapter, I focus on the policy responses and rhetoric of key leaders in three settler-colonial liberal democracies—Australia, Canada, and the United States—on refugees, with special reference to the period from 2015 to 2020. These countries share many features. What I argue is that each country exhibits elements of restrictiveness in refugee policy, but there are qualitative differences when it comes to the degree to which it impacts other categories of immigration, the party system, and the degree to which leaders employ discourses that humanize refugees. In making this argument, this chapter takes a threefold approach. First, I address how the countries are similar and useful for comparison. Second, I review recent developments in each country. Finally, I conclude with a discussion of the relevance of the findings for broader legal and ethical concerns as well as our understanding of dehumanization/humanization.

The Relevance of Empirical Comparison: Post-truth Politics, Settler Colonies, and Refugees

In an era that has been dubbed one of "post-truth politics" to characterize the way in which appeals to emotion may shape public opinion in liberal democratic countries more than actual facts (Oxford Dictionaries 2016), a lot is being said about immigrants and refugees in the media, in social media, and in popular conversations. As such, the five-year period spanning from 2015 to 2020 was remarkable for combining ever-rising numbers of forcibly displaced people and refugees worldwide alongside numerous examples of xenophobic populism and backlash to migrants and refugees. We know from some experimental studies in social psychology that negative and dehumanizing portrayals of migrants and refugees, however inaccurate, may drive support for restrictionist policies (Kteily and Bruneau 2017; Utych 2018). The work we do as social scientists and the work that is done by policy-makers and immigrant- and refugee-serving organizations is really at its best when it is informed by considerations of knowledge and evidence (Howlett 2009, 159). An international comparative lens is helpful to such efforts, and indeed, within the discipline of political science, comparative research has played a key role over the post–World War II period in terms of being a site for the production of empirically based theory building.

Canada, the United States, and Australia share a lot in common as countries with pre-existing and diverse Indigenous populations. Forged by settler colonialism and historically connected to Britain, all three countries were shaped by repeated waves of immigration and frontier expansion. The persistence of what might be called "settler privilege" continues to be in wide evidence (see, e.g., Battell Lowman and Barker 2015). Indeed, these three countries and New Zealand are referred to as the CANZUS countries by Indigenous scholars and activists because until recently, they were all holdouts to the 2007 United Nations Declaration on the Rights of Indigenous Peoples (UNDRIP). The conspicuousness of this reluctance on the part of the CANZUS states can be seen in the fact that the vast majority of world states voted in favour of UNDRIP in the UN General Assembly (Abu-Laban 2020). Only because the CANZUS countries were pushed by international organizations committed to human rights did they all come to belatedly endorse UNDRIP, but they also did so with caveats. Indigenous scholar Sheryl Lightfoot

(2012, 116–19) calls this process "selective endorsement" because it was a stance designed to quell international criticism but also avoid implementation.

This perspective is useful to keep in mind because it alerts us to the fact that there may be a contradiction in relation to how the settler colonies deal with Indigenous claims, especially when issues of sovereignty, resources, and power are at stake (Abu-Laban 2020). This contradiction finds parallels when we think of responses to migration in settler states like Canada, Australia, and the United States. As Shachar has observed, states engage in practices of inclusion and exclusion when it comes to human migration, making for a "potential contradiction between the sovereign power to exclude and the human need for inclusion in a political community that treats us as equal and worthy of respect and dignity" (2015, 1). It is refugees who represent "the embodiment of the paradox of a human rights discourse as they flee a persecutory nation state and lay their claims to rights derived from their shared, universal humanity at the feet of another nation state—concerned with its sovereignty and the rights of its citizens" (Fiske 2006, 223).

Of course, many other political scientists have not always explicitly dwelled on the settler-colonial foundations of countries like Canada, the United States, and Australia, instead classifying them as "liberal democracies" for their support of the individual rights of citizens and human rights. Even more specifically owing to their similar histories and electoral processes, they have also been dubbed the "Anglo American Democracies" (Alford 1963). All these distinctions matter as well. For example, part of the way the "human rights revolution" came to be expressed in these countries in the 1960s and 1970s was that all three countries formally moved away from the overtly racially discriminatory laws that marked their immigration intake in ways that favoured white British-origin Protestants historically. The United States did this by abandoning the 1924 National Quota (Johnson-Reed) Act in 1965, Canada did this with the adoption of a point system in 1967, and Australia did this by abandoning its graphically but tellingly dubbed White Australia policy, which barred various non-Europeans from the time of the 1901 Immigration Restriction Act until 1973. As well, Canada adopted an official policy of multiculturalism in 1971 for reasons relating to internal debates and especially a movement for an independent Québec, and Australia borrowed the lexicon from Canada and by 1977–78 had its own version of multiculturalism in the context of a growing intake of Indochinese refugees (Mann 2012). Both Canada and Australia are parties to the 1951 United Nations Convention Relating to the Status of Refugees and the 1967 Protocol Relating to the Status of Refugees, and the United States is a state party to the 1967 Protocol. In other words, all three countries have accepted legal obligations toward refugees as part of their human rights commitment.

Notwithstanding the relevance of liberal democratic norms and principles, it is also relevant to center the settle-colonial foundations of these three liberal democratic countries for a variety of reasons. First, all three countries continue to be challenged by Indigenous claims and relations as well as racism particularly directed at minorities of colour, reflecting on their shared historical status as "white settler colonies" that held a place of privilege in the British Empire (Abu-Laban 2020). Second, racialized and violent exclusion in immigration is not merely a feature of the past, and in particular, all three countries have also been implicated in trends reflecting on the criminalization of immigration and refugees, as they have all increasingly made greater use of practices of detention and deportation (see Kretsedemas and Brotherton 2017). Third, in the case of all three settler colonies, the sovereign power to exclude (or include) has largely denied Indigenous peoples a say in who immigrates and the terms, and this absenting is part and parcel of contemporary discussions of "reconciliation" between Indigenous and non-Indigenous peoples in countries like Canada (TRC 2015a, 2015b; Abu-Laban 2020).

The subject matter of political science as a discipline directs attention to issues of power and inequality, leadership and political parties, and conflict, contestation, and resistance, including resistance to dehumanization. Given the many similarities among the three countries, a key factor motivating interest in developing a comparative assessment of Canada, the United States, and Australia is the question of whether and how contemporary political leaders can be seen to contribute to the humanization or dehumanization of refugees and with what consequences for policy, political parties, and the broader society. For example, we know from the case of Denmark that in the face of restrictive asylum policies, individuals and groups may consciously resist what they see as dehumanizing policies toward asylum seekers through discourse and actions (Lassen 2018). By focusing on these similar countries, each case carries lessons for how we might think about dehumanizing and humanizing refugees.

The Settler-Colonial Liberal Democracies: Australia, Canada, and the United States Compared

Space limitations necessarily preclude a detailed description of all aspects of the discourse and policy of each of these countries. However, some key points can be drawn out to isolate key elements of the distinct features implicating the settler-colonial liberal democracies. In particular, while they all exhibit restrictiveness in refugee policy, there are also relevant qualitative differences when it comes to humanizing or dehumanizing refugees. Each will be briefly discussed in turn.

Australia

While geographically, Australia's island status might provide a convenient explanation for its well-known contemporary harsh treatment of asylum seekers arriving by boat, in point of fact, arrivals of primarily Vietnamese asylum seekers between 1976 and 1981 were largely met with sympathy from the government and Australian public (McKenzie and Hasmath 2013, 418). In this sense, geography is not inevitability. There is widespread agreement in the literature on Australia that the rise of Pauline Hanson's right-wing One Nation Party in 1998 marks a turning point in domestic politics because even though it was a fringe party in relation to votes, in criticizing multiculturalism and immigration, it had a major impact in making immigration an electoral issue (Wazana 2004; Pietsch 2013, 149; Maley 2016, 672–73). Specifically, One Nation presented refugee claimants arriving by boat as "queue jumpers" taking "pleasure cruises" to find a better country in which to live (Wazana 2004, 84). In this context, immigration—and particularly refugees—became a politicized issue that the mainline Liberal and Labor Parties did not want to lose votes on (Gale 2004; McKenzie and Hasmath 2013; Maley 2016), thereby encouraging a consensus around a policy of "deterrence" in relation to refugees arriving by boat.

Another point of agreement in the literature is that the *Tampa* crisis of late 2001 instigated the response of "deterrence" relating to how refugees arriving by boat are treated (Wazana 2004, 84; Gale 2004; McKenzie and Hasmath 2013, 418). The *Tampa* was a Norwegian freighter that rescued some 430 people, mostly refugees from Afghanistan, and entered Australian waters. Australia refused to let the *Tampa* dock even though the refugees were in desperate need of medical assistance and food. When the Norwegian captain attempted to dock the ship anyway, Australia responded with aggressive military commandos, and the refugees were transported to the small island nation of Nauru, where they were held in detention.

Notable as concerns a discussion of dehumanization is the fact that during this incident, the office of the Australian defense minister literally banned the release of any *"personalising or humanizing images"* of asylum seekers as part of Prime Minister John Howard's response (Maley 2016, 674; my emphasis).

As the *Tampa* crisis coincided with 9/11, the Australian public also tended to support government action, and this set forth a refugee deterrence policy based on declaring certain Australian external territories (such as Christmas Island and Cocos Islands) outside of Australia's migration zone and therefore not sites where a refugee claim could be made, intercepting boats militarily, and processing and detaining refugees in offshore facilities, particularly in Nauru and Papua New Guinea (McKenzie and Hasmath 2013, 418). Arguably, when we are talking about detention offshore on remote islands, we are talking about imprisoning people who are highly likely to be UN Convention refugees. Irrespective, in 2016, the Papua New Guinea Supreme Court itself ruled that Papua New Guinea's agreement with Australia to hold asylum seekers in a facility on Manus Island was in breach of its own constitutional provisions protecting personal liberty (Buchanan 2016).

The overall harshness of the deterrence response and the fact that it has been directed primarily at non-white asylum seekers have led some to liken it to a form of return to the White Australia policy of yore (Wazana 2004). Still others have suggested the policy harkens back to Nazi concentration camps in Europe, although as Amy Nethery notes, there are plenty of parallels that are actually specific to Australian history, including Indigenous reserves, quarantine stations, and enemy-alien internment camps (Nethery 2009, 66). What at base unites the various parallels and descriptions made to criticize the deterrence policy is the attention they have drawn to human rights abuses as well as the way humanity itself is seen to be at risk in the response of successive Australian governments to refugees arriving by boat since 2001 (Fiske 2006; Gosden 2006).

Australia is largely a two-party system that swings between the left-leaning Labor and right-leaning Liberal prime ministers. Overall, the debate between the mainline Liberal and Labor Parties is not on whether to continue the deterrence policy established from the response to the *Tampa* but rather on details of how it is best implemented (for example, debates on how much medical assistance detained people should get, with Labor favouring a more generous approach). Since 2015, Prime Ministers Malcolm Turnbull (2015–18) and Scott Morrison (2018–22) have hailed from the Liberal Party, and in both cases, they governed in a coalition with the National Party, another right-leaning party with support in rural areas. Both Prime Ministers Turnbull and Morrison supported deterrence of the sort established with the *Tampa*. Moreover, although the deterrence policy has drawn wide rebuke, including from the UNHCR, Morrison's prime ministerial office featured personal mementos and photos that included a metal replica of a migrant ship boasting "I stopped these," in reference to a previous stint in charge of immigration (Cave 2018). Hence, there is a consensus across the dominant parties to continue deterrence as concerns ships, although overall, this has not impacted other areas of immigration, including refugees accepted for resettlement from the UNHCR. Generally, Australia's immigration policy—until early 2018 with the introduction of new rules for admitting high-skilled workers and more recently with border closures inspired by the response to the COVID-19 pandemic (Wyeth 2020)—has placed an emphasis on attracting high-skilled immigrants (Boucher 2020).

Given the failure of the party system to be a site in which the refugee deterrence policy can be challenged, humanitarian and humanizing impulses have come from a flourishing of NGO groups and movements of Australians seeking to end dehumanized detention and welcome refugees (Fiske 2006; Gosden 2006). The impulse for change has also come from refugees themselves, including those who experienced detention. The world has heard the story now of Kurdish refugee Behrouz Boochani, who managed to eke out the award-winning international bestseller *No Friend but the Mountains* ([2018] 2019); the book's title is a reference to a Kurdish saying that highlights a sense of abandonment and betrayal by successive powers. Boochani's book details in prose and poem the experience of being incarcerated in the recently closed Australian-run detention center on Manus Island. This book was awarded Australia's top prize in literature, with the selection committee unanimously deciding to waive the requirement of being an Australian citizen, and in the words of Australian writer Bill Flanagan, it chronicles the five years Boochani spent on an island as a result of "policies in which both our major parties have publicly competed in cruelty" (Flanagan [2018] 2019, xi). In accepting the prize, Boochani claimed it is "a victory for human beings, for human dignity. A victory against a system that has never recognized us as human beings. It is a victory against a system that has reduced us to numbers" (Boochani 2019).

Canada

As a point of entry, it can be noted that Canada has a history of turning back ships as a result of its explicitly racist immigration policy. These include the *Komagata Maru*, containing persecuted migrants from India, held at shore for over two months in 1914 before being forced to return, with many passengers dying or being imprisoned, and the MS *St. Louis*, containing Jewish refugees fleeing Nazi persecution in 1939, many of whom perished in death camps after their return to Europe (see Bakan's chapter). However, as with Australia, there is nothing inevitable about how those arriving by boat (or at the border) are received, even by the same governmental administration. Hence, for example, in 1986, the Conservative government of Brian Mulroney welcomed a boatload of 155 Tamil refugees seeking entry into Canada (Anandasangaree 2016), but less than a year later, when a boat of 177 Sikhs arrived, the same government responded with an emergency recall of parliament and introduced Bill C-84, the Refugee Deterrents and Detention Bill.

From this period, appearing in the initial legislation was a provision to designate the United States as a "safe third country" in relation to asylum claimants arriving from or via the United States to Canada, although it ultimately did not get enacted (Bissett 2002, 36). However, both Liberal and Conservative governments favoured this plan, and thus after September 11, 2001, in the context of working out a "Smart Border Plan" to foster the continued flow of people and trade across the US-Canada border, Canadian officials were the ones to push for a provision relating to refugees (DeVoretz and Hanson 2003, 2). The resulting 2004 Safe Third Country Agreement (STCA), enacted under the Liberal government of Paul Martin, holds that an asylum seeker must make their claim in the country where they first arrive (i.e., Canada or the United States). The agreement applies to land ports of entry only, with certain specified exceptions (e.g., relating to a family member being present in the state where the claim is made or being an unaccompanied minor). Immediately and for many years thereafter, the STCA had the predicted effect of reducing the number of asylum claims in Canada in a way that was hard for the media or civil society groups to trace (Canadian Council for Refugees 2005; Alboim and Cohl 2012, 30).

This effect was predictable, since claims in the United States from asylum seekers arriving from Canada were negligible. For instance, in 2001, there were 13,497 claimants who arrived from or through the United States to Canada, in comparison with only a few hundred who came from Canada to make claims in the United States (DeVoretz and Hanson 2003, 4). Despite early attempts by the Canadian Council for Refugees, Amnesty International, and the Canadian Council of Churches to legally challenge the STCA on grounds that it violates the Canadian Charter of Rights and Freedoms by potentially denying refugees the right to make a claim in Canada, their case was not successful (Canadian Council for Refugees 2009). However, this agreement and a new legal challenge would come into sharp focus following the inauguration of US president Donald Trump in 2017, in the process highlighting the contradictions in the policy of the government of Liberal prime minister Justin Trudeau, one of the most publicly humanitarian and "pro-refugee" governments Canada has had (see also Ayres's chapter).

When Trudeau came to power in a surprise victory in 2015, he did so with a promise to immediately bring in twenty-five thousand Syrian refugees, a pledge aimed at countering the hostile and sluggish response of the reigning Conservative government of Prime Minister Harper specific to Syrian refugees. Recalling how Australia attempted to ban personalizing or humanizing images of refugees during the *Tampa* crisis helps us better understand the impact of the photo of Alan Kurdi that went viral. The image captured Kurdi, a lifeless three-year-old Syrian refugee, after he had drowned while trying to reach the Greek island of Kos. The image was called a "silent scream" by the journalist who had taken it (Virtue 2015). But the fact that Kurdi had a Canadian aunt who had been unable to bring Kurdi and his family to Canada made it a Canadian moral issue (Macklin 2015). This image literally impacted the Canadian media coverage of Syrian refugees in ways that made much more direct and explicit links between Syrian refugees alongside Canada and Canadians (Wallace 2018), and it also impacted the 2015 election in ways that were humanizing of Syrian refugees. Not only did it allow Trudeau to seize the popular imagination with his promise of bringing in twenty-five thousand Syrian refugees, but it created divisions in the Conservative Party, with people as high profile as former foreign minister in the Mulroney cabinet Barbara McDougall chastising the then prime minister Harper for his stance on Syrian refugees in an op-ed in a leading paper. In McDougall's words,

> He [Harper] surely does not want to go into history, whenever that may be, with the heartrending picture of a tragically drowned toddler at the top of his file. And it may well dominate, no matter what his accomplishments in government have been, unless he can find a way to *navigate the flood of sympathy now rightly being expressed by Canadians from all walks of life, including many Conservatives.* (McDougall 2015; my emphasis)

The Canadian party system and, in particular, the two mainline parties, the Liberals and Conservatives, have not thus far been impacted by a politicization of refugees that makes immigration policy restriction the main thing parties compete for. In fact, since Trudeau came to power, he made good on his 2015 campaign promise of bringing in Syrian refugees. In the process, he reactivated many civil society groups to support refugees through private sponsorship—a program first pioneered and developed by Canada involving the Canadian public along with various levels of government in supporting Indochinese refugees in the late 1970s (Molloy et al. 2017, 3–4). Overall, immigration levels have been higher, although like Australia, there is a solid preference for skilled immigrants (Harris, Hall, and Zimonjic 2017; Abu-Laban, Tungohan, and Gabriel 2023). Trudeau has also been colourful in his humanitarianism, with photo ops greeting Syrian refugees at the airport and tweets pronouncing Canada's openness to refugees. For example, when newly inaugurated President Trump announced the travel ban on select Muslim-majority states in January 2017, Prime Minister Trudeau tweeted, "To those fleeing persecution, terror and war, Canadians will welcome you regardless of your faith. Diversity is our strength" (Paling 2017).

At the same time, the Trudeau government clearly does not want to deal with refugee claimants showing up at the border, and the policies across successive governments since the 1980s have been geared at limiting this, culminating with the 2004 STCA. However, the gaps in the STCA became more visible early in Trump's presidency, when he threatened the withdrawal of protective measures extended to specific groups (ultimately rescinded in November 2017 for Haitians and January 2018 for Salvadorans). This led to a new surge of refugee claimants attempting perilous journeys from the United States to Canada, entering through unofficial points (Bilefsky 2018). Trudeau's then minister of immigration, refugees and citizenship, Ahmed Hussen, made it clear that these asylum claimants were not wanted, stating, "We don't want people to illegally enter our border, and doing so is not a free ticket to Canada. We are saying, 'You will be apprehended, screened, detained, fingerprinted, and if you can't establish a genuine claim, you will be denied refugee protection and removed'" (cited in Bilefsky 2018).

In December 2017, the Canadian Council for Refugees, the Canadian Council of Churches, and Amnesty International Canada announced that they would once again challenge the designation of the United States as a "safe third country" in the Federal Court, especially in light of Trump's policies (Canadian Council for Refugees 2017). In July 2020, the Federal Court ruled the STCA to be unconstitutional (and in violation of Section 7 on life, liberty, and security of the person) on the grounds that asylum claimants returned to the United States were very likely to be put in detention; however, the federal government appealed (Public Safety Canada 2020), achieving success on procedural grounds. That the decision was appealed is reflective of the contradictions involved in public humanitarianism underpinned by a settler-colonial sovereignty impulse aimed at control. The matter came before the Supreme Court of Canada in 2022.

That the Trudeau government used the border closure inspired by the COVID-19 pandemic to announce that asylum seekers entering at unofficial points of entry via the United States would be put in detention for fourteen days and then sent back to the United States or returned immediately to the United States is reflective of and related to this same impulse to control—one that has been criticized as a reversal that risks Canada not meeting its obligations under the UN Convention on Refugees and Protocol (see Ling 2020).

United States

Like Canada, the US impulse for immigration control has also been exerted in different periods. In terms of headline-grabbing attention in the two-party system of Republicans and Democrats, both parties have fixated more on the issue of undocumented immigration from Mexico than refugees per se, with the period preceding the passage of the 1986 Immigration Reform and Control Act marking one such period (Zolberg 1990) and with many more to follow, including the growing use of deportation by the Obama administration (Golash-Boza 2017). It is in the context of the focus on undocumented immigration that Trump's campaign kickoff speech in June 2015 needs to be situated. As Trump put the issue, "They're bringing drugs, they're bringing crime, they're rapists. I will build a great, great wall on our southern border. And I will have Mexico pay for that wall" (cited in Anderson 2017). In actual fact, while the wall has been a graphic and striking image suggestive of unchecked migration across America's southern border, contemporary figures show Mexicans only compose 26 percent of all US immigrants (down from 30 percent in 2000), and further, the emigration rate from Mexico has been fairly steadily low since the recession of 2009 (Zong, Batalova, and Hallock 2018, 8–9). Moreover, apprehension rates of unauthorized immigrants at the border were lower in 2015–16 than in the late 2000s, with Mexican nationals constituting about half (Zong, Batalova, and Hallock 2018, 21–22).

However, Trump's kickoff speech is a good point of entry into a distinct "post-truth" immigration politics. Trump's discourse was different in qualitative terms due to the repetitive nature of dehumanizing language in relation to immigrants and refugees as well as for ushering in a more radical shift in both refugee and immigration policy. These features make the contemporary US case stand out in relation to Australia and Canada as well as the Trump presidency stand out in relation to past US administrations. For example, on language, it is notable that Trump by far exceeds all presidential candidates in both the Democratic and the Republican Parties across the 2008, 2012, and 2016 elections for the sheer frequency with which he employed dehumanizing language in speeches on immigrants and refugees (Warnock 2019, 55). In terms of content, his speeches focused on refugees as a threat and included the dehumanizing injection of words like *pouring, flowing,* and *infiltrating* to illustrate their migration journey (Warnock 2019, 56).

In substantive terms, Trump also did a lot within the first days and year of his presidency. Analysts Pierce, Bolter, and Selee (2018) suggest that the August 2016 campaign speech given by Trump contains clues into ten key planks of his immigration policy. These are the following: (1) building the (southern) border wall; (2) ending so-called catch-and-release policies and practices allowing some unaccompanied minors and asylum seekers to be in the community as they await claims determination; (3) pursuing unauthorized immigrants who have committed crimes; (4) forcing compliance at local levels, especially vis-à-vis sanctuary cities; (5) ending the protection of some unauthorized immigration, especially ending the Deferred Action for Childhood Arrivals (DACA) and Deferred Action for Parents of Americans and Lawful Permanent Residents introduced by President Obama; (6) introducing a travel ban and extreme vetting; (7) making other countries take back deported nationals; (8) enhancing surveillance through a biometric entry-exit visa system; (9) limiting jobs and benefits to unauthorized immigrants and supporting the hiring of Americans; and (10) reforming the legal immigration system to emphasize "merit" (Pierce, Bolter, and Selee 2018).

These planks may be further summarized as border security, interior enforcement, and a merit-based system, with Canada's point system of selection favouring skilled migration being a model for determining merit (Dogherty 2018). Each one of these areas has carried consequences. For example, as Human Rights Watch drew attention to, while deportations at the southern border were down, at the interior of the country, immigration arrests and deportations of people who had never committed a crime tripled in the year 2017, when Trump came to office (Human Rights Watch 2017, 14), although ultimately, Trump's attempted cancellation of DACA, which protects nearly one million unauthorized young immigrants from deportation, was rejected by the US Supreme Court in June 2020. In the area of refugee intake, the impact of the Trump presidency has been decisive in creating massive reductions. In his first year of office, Trump reduced refugee intake by 50 percent and limited those coming from Chad, Iran, Libya, North Korea, Somalia, Syria, Venezuela, and Yemen (Zong, Batalova, and Hallock 2018). By the end of 2018, in a period of escalating global numbers of refugees, the United States had actually fallen behind Canada (with a population ten times smaller) in formal acceptances of refugees to be resettled and, under Trump, dramatically lowered the ceiling for refugee admissions to a record low for 2019 of 30,000 (in comparison with the 110,000 set by Obama for 2017; Blizzard and Batalova 2019).

A final point that can be made is that all these changes were accompanied by an "in-your-face" anti-humanitarianism during Trump's presidency. Everything from the decision of First Lady Melania Trump to wear clothing literally proclaiming she did not care en route to visit undocumented detained children separated from parents (Gambino and Laughland 2018) to Trump claiming that undocumented immigrants are "animals" (Korte and Gomez 2018) is a distinct form of the new mean-spirited politics of immigration (Dauvergne 2016). This is not about banning personalized or humanized stories but about overriding them with indifference. This has left it to courts, local-level leaders proclaiming "sanctuary cities," elected officials at all levels (particularly in the Democratic Party), civil society groups, and even leaders outside of the United States (such as Trudeau on occasion) to counter the dehumanizing rhetoric and impact of Trump on immigration.

Reflections on Dehumanization and Humanization

As this chapter has suggested, there are similarities among the three settler-colonial liberal democracies when it comes to their historical formation, their immigration histories, and their clear preference for the migration of "skilled" immigrants today. However, the extent to which leaders are employing humanizing versus dehumanizing discourse varies considerably, as does their overall impact on immigration policy as well as refugees. As this chapter has pointed out, there was both something distinct in the embrace of the US Trump administration for dehumanizing rhetoric and equally something distinct in the Trudeau administration for its humanizing language and performative embrace of refugees (albeit advanced in ways that are not always reflected in policy responses at the Canada-US border). Therefore, it underscores that there are language choices that implicate refugees and that choices that are dehumanizing may be linked to policies that exhibit greater restriction. Indeed, with the inauguration of Democrat president Joseph Biden in January 2021, changes in language and policy are already in evidence. In May 2021, Biden revised the refugee cap from its historic low of 15,000 to 62,500 for the fiscal year and also committed to a goal of 125,000 refugee admissions in the following fiscal year (Biden 2021). In Biden's words, "The United States Refugee Admissions Program embodies America's commitment to protect the most vulnerable, and to stand as a beacon of liberty and refuge to the world. It's a statement about who we are, and who we want to be" (Biden 2021). Likewise, in 2022, refugee advocates were encouraged by the willingness of Australia's newly elected majority Labour government led by Prime Minister Anthony Albanese to consider alternatives to detaining refugees (Karp 2022). However, Albanese has, rather paradoxically, pledged to be "strong on borders without being weak on humanity" by refusing permanent residence to those arriving by boat (quoted in Senanayake, Geeth, and Doherty 2022).

This discussion on the settler-colonial liberal democracies would be remiss without also stressing that the bulk of the world's refugees are from and located in the Global South. The Global Compact on Refugees agreed to in December 2018 by the UN General Assembly offers some hope that adequate responses to refugees can be done more predictably and equitably. There has been criticism of the compact for its non-binding character, lack of commitment to more resettlement on the part of northern states, and silence on the external forms of state intervention that create refugees (Chimni 2018). What might also be noted is that the three settler-colonial liberal democracies investigated in this chapter also responded to the Global Compact on Refugees differently. Hence while Canada played a lead role in developing the Global Compact on Refugees and agreed to it along with Australia, the United States, under Trump, quit the negotiations and refused to sign the compact because they saw it as interfering with American sovereignty. As a consequence, Trump's position in relation to multilateral agreements between states and in relation to basic human rights norms is one that is really standing as a new frontier to contemplate the question of humanizing refugees and raises both legal and ethical issues.

On a legal level, an alternative vision might come from revisiting the important 1948 Universal Declaration on Human Rights, which supports the idea that people can leave their country (i.e., the country where they hold nationality) but do not have a right to enter or stay in a different country. As Pierre Sané (2007, ix) has argued, "From a human rights point of view, we are faced with an incomplete situation that sees many people being deprived of their right to emigrate by an absence of possibilities to immigrate. It is therefore worth envisaging a right to mobility: in a world of flows mobility is a right to which everyone should have access."

The experience of refugees demonstrates that even with provisions specific to the rights of refugees, there continues to be a tension between sovereignty and human rights. In a world of nation-states that police borders and determine belonging and membership, ethical responses are ones in which refugees and their allies can all play a part in advancing through shared stories that challenge dehumanizing falsehoods and foster empathy and agential action. Part of that agency is also reflected in the words leaders (and people) choose to use in talking about refugees because what is said seems to be connected with what is done.

Acknowledgement

My thanks to co-editor Reza Hasmath as well as Ayelet Shachar and other colleagues in CIFAR's Boundaries, Membership and Belonging Program for comments on an earlier draft of this chapter.

References

Abu-Laban, Yasmeen. 2020. "Immigration and Settler-Colonies Post-UNDRIP: Research and Policy Implications." *International Migration* 30 (December): 12–28.

Abu-Laban, Yasmeen, Ethel Tungohan, and Christina Gabriel. 2023. *Containing Diversity: Canada and the Politics of Immigration in the 21st Century*. Toronto: University of Toronto Press.

Alboim, Naomi, and Karen Cohl. 2012. *Shaping the Future: Canada's Rapidly Changing Immigration Policies*. Toronto: Maytree Foundation.

Alford, Robert R. 1963. *Party and Society: The Anglo-American Democracies*. Chicago: Rand McNally.

Anandasangaree, Gary. 2016. "Accepting Tamils 30 Years Ago Changed Canada." *Toronto Star*, August 10, 2016. https://www.thestar.com/opinion/commentary/2016/08/10/accepting-tamils-30-years-ago-changed-canada.html.

Anderson, Jon Lee. 2017. "Can Mexico Come to Terms with Trump?" *New Yorker*, October 9, 2017.

Banulescu-Bogdan, Natalia, Meghan Benton, and Susan Fratzke. 2020. "Coronavirus Is Spreading Across Borders, but It Is Not a Migration Problem." Migration Policy Institute, Commentaries, March 2020. https://www.migrationpolicy.org/news/coronavirus-not-a-migration-problem.

Battell Lowman, Emma, and Adam J. Barker. 2015. *Settler Identity and Colonialism in 21st Century Canada*. Halifax: Fernwood.

Bender, Steven. 2015. *Mea Culpa: Lessons on Law and Regret in U.S. History*. New York: New York University Press.

Biden, Joseph. 2021. "Statement by President Joe Biden on Refugee Admissions." White House, Statements and Releases, May 3, 2021. https://www.whitehouse.gov/briefing-room/statements-releases/2021/05/03/statement-by-president-joe-biden-on-refugee-admissions/.

Bilefsky, Dan. 2018. "Migrants Fleeing to Canada Learn Even a Liberal Nation Has Limits." *New York Times*, January 14, 2018, 8. https://www.nytimes.com/2018/01/13/world/canada/quebec-immigrants-haitians.html.

Bissett, James. 2002. "A Defense of the 'Safe Country' Concept for Refugees." *Policy Options*, September 2002, 36–38.

Blizzard, Brittany, and Jeanne Batalova. 2019. *Refugees and Asylees in the United States*. Washington, DC: Migration Policy Institute. https://www.migrationpolicy.org/article/refugees-and-asylees-united-states-2018.

Boochani, Behrouz. (2018) 2019. *No Friend but the Mountains: Writing from Manus Prison*. Toronto: Anansi International.

Boochani, Behrouz. 2019. "Behrouz Boochani's Literary Prize Acceptance Speech—Full Transcript." *Guardian*, January 31, 2019. https://www.theguardian.com/world/2019/feb/01/behrouz-boochani-on-literary-prize-words-still-have-the-power-to-challenge-inhumane-systems.

Boucher, Anna Katherine. 2020. "How 'Skill' Definition Affects the Diversity of Skilled Immigration Policies." *Journal of Ethnic and Migration Studies* 46 (12): 2533–50.

Buchanan, Kelly. 2016. "Australia/Papua New Guinea: Supreme Court Rules Asylum-Seeker Detention Is Unconstitutional." Global Legal Monitor, May 2, 2016. https://www.loc.gov/law/foreign-news/article/australiapapua-new-guinea-supreme-court-rules-asylum-seeker-detention-is-unconstitutional/.

Canadian Council for Refugees. 2005. *Closing the Front Door on Refugees: Report on Safe Third Country Agreement 6 Months After Implementation*. Montréal: Canadian Council for Refugees.

Canadian Council for Refugees. 2009. "Supreme Court Denial of Leave on Safe Third Regretted." February 5, 2009. https://ccrweb.ca/en/bulletin/09/02/05.

Canadian Council for Refugees. 2017. "Why We Are Challenging the USA as a 'Safe Third Country' in the Federal Court of Canada." December 2017. http://ccrweb.ca/en/safe-third-country-challenge-explanation.

Carens, Joseph. 1991. "States and Refugees: A Normative Analysis." In *Refugee Policy: Canada and the United States*, edited by Howard Adelman, 18–29. Toronto: York Lanes Press.

Cave, Damien. 2018. "How Scott Morrison's Boat Trophy Burst into Public View—and Why It Matters." *New York Times*, September 19, 2018. https://www.nytimes.com/2018/09/19/world/australia/scott-morrison-boat-trophy-refugees.html.

Chimni, B. S. 2018. "Global Compact on Refugees: One Step Forward, Two Steps Back." *International Journal of Refugee Law* 30 (4): 530–634.

Dauvergne, Catherine. 2016. *The New Politics of Immigration and the End of Settler Societies*. Cambridge: Cambridge University Press.

DeVoretz, Don J., and Philip Hanson. 2003. *Sourcing Out Canada's Refugee Policy: The Safe Third Country Agreement*. Commentary Series No. 03-06. Vancouver: Vancouver Centre of Excellence for Research on Immigration and Integration in the Metropolis.

Dogherty, Michael. 2018. Talk delivered to the Plenary Panel on "Migration Policy in Canada, the USA and Mexico: Rethinking the Boundaries" by the Assistant Secretary for Borders, Immigration and Trade, Department of Homeland Security. Annual National Metropolis Conference, Calgary, March 22, 2018.

Esses, Victoria M., Stelian Medianu, and Andrea S. Lawson. 2013. "Uncertainty, Threat, and the Role of the Media in Promoting the Dehumanization of Immigrants and Refugees." *Journal of Social Issues* 69 (3): 518–36.

Esses, Victoria M., Scott Veenvliet, and Stelian Medianu. 2012. "The Dehumanization of Refugees: Determinants and Consequences." In *Social Categories in Everyday Experience*, edited by Shaun Wiley, Gina Philogène, and Tracey A. Revenson, 133–50. Washington, DC: American Psychological Association.

Fiske, Lucy. 2006. "Politics of Exclusion, Practice of Inclusion: Australia's Response to Refugees and the Case for Community Based Human Rights Work." *International Journal of Human Rights* 10 (3): 219–29.

Flanagan, Richard. (2018) 2019. Foreword to *No Friend but the Mountains: Writing from Manus Prison*, by Behrouz Boochani, ix–xii. Toronto: Anansi International.

Gale, Peter. 2004. "The Refugee Crisis and Fear: Populist Politics and Media Discourse." *Journal of Sociology* 40 (4): 321–40.

Gambino, Lauren, and Oliver Laughland. 2018. "Melania Trump Visits Child Detention Center as Fate of Families Remains Unclear." *Guardian*, June 21, 2018. https://www.theguardian.com/us-news/2018/jun/21/melania-trump-family-child-separation-detention-centre-visit-surprise.

Golash-Boza, Tanya. 2017. "Obama's Legacy as 'Deporter in Chief.'" In *Immigration Policy in the Age of Punishment: Detention, Deportation and Border Control*, edited by Philip Kretsedemas and David C. Brotherton, 37–56. New York: Columbia University Press.

Gosden, Diane. 2006. "'What If No One Had Spoken Out Against This Policy?' The Rise of Asylum Seeker and Refugee Advocacy in Australia." *PORTAL Journal of Multidisciplinary International Studies* 3, no. 1 (January): 1–21.

Harris, Kathleen, Chris Hall, and Peter Zimonjic. 2017. "Canada to Admit Nearly 1 Million Immigrants over Next 3 Years." CBC News, November 1, 2017. http://www.cbc.ca/news/politics/immigration-canada-2018-1.4371146.

Hintjens, Helen M. 1992. "Immigration and Citizenship Debates: Reflections on Ten Common Themes." *International Migration* 30, no. 1 (March): 5–17.

Howlett, Michael. 2009. "Policy Analytical Capacity and Evidence-Based Policy Making: Lessons from Canada." *Canadian Public Administration* 52, no. 2 (June): 153–75.

Human Rights Watch. 2017. *The Deported: Uprooted from the Country They Call Home*. New York: Human Rights Watch.

International Federation of Red Cross and Red Crescent Societies. 2020. "Migrants and Refugees 'Least Protected, Most Affected' in COVID Crisis Warns IFRC President." September 10, 2020. https://www.ifrc.org/press-release/migrants-and-refugees-least-protected-most-affected-covid-crisis-warns-ifrc-president#:~:text

=The%20report%20%E2%80%93%20Least%20protected%2C%20most,risks%20to%20health%20and%20safety.

Karp, Paul. 2022. "Refugee Advocates Encouraged as Albanese Government Considers Ways to Reduce Immigration Detention Backlog." *Guardian*, September 24, 2022. https://www.theguardian.com/australia-news/2022/sep/25/refugee-advocates-encouraged-as-albanese-government-considers-ways-to-reduce-immigration-detention-backlog.

Korte, Gregory, and Alan Gomez. 2018. "Trump Ramps Up Rhetoric on Immigration: 'These Aren't People. These Are Animals.'" *USA Today*, May 17, 2018. https://www.usatoday.com/story/news/politics/2018/05/16/trump-immigrants-animals-mexico-democrats-sanctuary-cities/617252002/.

Kretsedemas, Philip, and David C. Brotherton, eds. 2017. *Immigration Policy in the Age of Punishment: Detention, Deportation and Border Control.* New York: Columbia University Press.

Kteily, Nour, and Emile Bruneau. 2017. "Backlash: The Politics and Real-World Consequences of Minority Group Dehumanization." *Personality and Social Psychology Bulletin* 43 (1): 87–104.

Lassen, Inger. 2018. "Resisting Dehumanization: Citizen Voices and Acts of Solidarity." *Critical Discourse Studies* 15 (5): 427–43.

Lightfoot, Sheryl. 2012. "Selective Endorsement Without Intent to Implement: Indigenous Rights in the Anglosphere." *International Journal of Human Rights* 16, no. 1 (January): 100–122.

Ling, Justin. 2020. "The Dark Side of Canada's Coronavirus Response." *Maclean's*, March 20, 2020. https://www.macleans.ca/news/canada/the-dark-side-of-canadas-coronavirus-response/.

Macklin, Audrey. 2015. "Canadians Have a Decision to Make That Will Affect Syrian Refugees." *New York Times*, September 15, 2015. http://www.nytimes.com/roomfordebate/2015/09/15/what-can-countries-do-to-help-refugees-fleeing-to-europe/canadians-have-a-decision-to-make-that-will-affect-syrian-refugees.

Maley, William. 2016. "Australia's Refugee Policy: Domestic Politics and Diplomatic Consequences." *Australian Journal of International Affairs* 70 (6): 670–80.

Mann, Jatinder. 2012. "The Introduction of Multiculturalism in Canada and Australia, 1960s–1970s." *Nations and Nationalism* 18 (3): 483–503.

McDougall, Barbara. 2015. "Mr. Harper: This Refugee Crisis Should Be Your Moment." *Globe and Mail*, September 8, 2015. http://www.theglobeandmail.com/opinion/mr-harper-this-refugee-crisis-should-be-your-moment/article26259650/.

McKenzie, Jaffa, and Reza Hasmath. 2013. "Deterring the 'Boat People': Explaining the Australian Government's People Swap Response to Asylum Seekers." *Australian Journal of Political Science* 48 (4): 417–30.

Molloy, Michael J., Peter Duschinsky, Kurt F. Jensen, and Robert J. Shalka. 2017. *Running on Empty: Canada and the Indochinese Refugees, 1975–1980*. Montréal: McGill-Queen's University Press.

Morello, Carol. 2014. "Refugee Wave from Syria and Iraq Now a 'Mega Crisis' UN Official Says." *Washington Post*, November 17, 2014. http://www.washingtonpost.com/world/national-security/refugee-wave-from-syria-and-iraq-now-a-mega-crisis-un-official-says/2014/11/17/ebc5ee50-6eab-11e4-893f-86bd390a3340_story.html.

Nethery, Amy. 2009. "'A Modern Concentration Camp': Using History to Make Sense of Australian Immigration Detention Centres." In *Does History Matter: Making and Debating Immigration and Refugee Policy in Australia and New Zealand*, edited by Klaus Neumann and Gwenda Tavan, 66–80. Canberra: Australian National University E Press.

Oxford Dictionaries. 2016. "Oxford Dictionaries Word of the Year Is . . ." https://languages.oup.com/word-of-the-year/2016/.

Paling, Emma. 2017. "Trudeau Tells Refugees: Canada Will Welcome You." *Huffington Post*, January 29, 2017. https://www.huffingtonpost.ca/2017/01/28/trudeau-refugees_n_14461906.html.

Pierce, Sarah, Jessica Bolter, and Andrew Selee. 2018. *Trump's First Year on Immigration Policy: Rhetoric vs. Reality*. Washington, DC: Migration Policy Institute.

Pietsch, Juliet. 2013. "Immigration and Refugees: Punctuations in the Commonwealth Policy Agenda." *Australian Journal of Public Administration* 72 (2): 143–55.

Pruitt, Lesley J. 2019. "Closed Due to 'Flooding': UK Media Representations of Refugees and Migrants in 2015–2016—Creating a Crisis of Borders." *British Journal of Politics and International Relations* 21 (2): 383–402.

Public Safety Canada. 2020. "Government of Canada to Appeal the Federal Court Decision on the Safe Third Country Agreement." August 21, 2020. https://www.canada.ca/en/public-safety-canada/news/2020/08/government-of-canada-to-appeal-the-federal-court-decision-on-the-safe-third-country-agreement.html.

Sané, Pierre. 2007. Preface to *Migration Without Borders: Essays on the Free Movement of People*, edited by Antoine Pécoud and Paul de Guchteneire, ix–x. New York and Oxford: Berghahn and UNESCO.

Senanayake, Devana, Aliyar Mohammed Geeth, and Ben Doherty. 2022. "Exploited in a Crisis: Why Are Sri Lankans Getting on Boats Bound for Australia." *Guardian*, June 25, 2022. https://www.theguardian.com/australia-news/2022/jun/26/screened-out-before-arrival-questions-over-legality-of-australias-at-sea-asylum-seeker-rulings.

Shachar, Ayelet. 2015. "Introduction: Citizenship and the 'Right to Have Rights.'" In *Politics of Citizenship in Immigrant Democracies: The Experience of the United States, Canada and Australia*, edited by Geoffrey Brahm Levey and Ayelet Shachar, 1–11. London and New York: Routledge.

Smith, David Livingstone. 2016. "Paradoxes of Dehumanization." *Social Theory and Practice*. 42, no. 2 (April): 416–43.

TRC (Truth and Reconciliation Commission of Canada). 2015a. *Honouring the Truth, Reconciling for the Future: Summary of the Final Report of the Truth and Reconciliation Commission of Canada*. Winnipeg: TRC.

TRC. 2015b. *Truth and Reconciliation Commission of Canada: Calls to Action*. Winnipeg: TRC.

UNHCR (United Nations High Commissioner for Refugees). 2020. *Global Trends: Forced Displacement in 2019*. Geneva: UNHCR. https://www.unhcr.org/5ee200e37.pdf.

Utych, Stephen M. 2018. "How Dehumanization Influences Attitudes Toward Immigrants." *Political Research Quarterly* 7 (2): 440–52.

Varela, Julio Ricardo. 2020. "As He Bungles the Crisis, Trump Turns to a Familiar Scapegoat: Immigration." *Washington Post*, March 23, 2020. https://www.washingtonpost.com/opinions/2020/03/23/he-bungles-this-crisis-trump-turns-familiar-scapegoat-immigration/.

Virtue, Rob. 2015. "Photographer Behind Image of Dead Syrian Boy: 'I Wanted to Express His Silent Scream.'" *Express*, September 5, 2015. http://www.express.co.uk/news/world/603140/Aylan-Kurdi-photographer-speaks-out-about-syrian-dead-child-photo.

Volpato, Chiara, and Luca Andrighetto. 2015. "Dehumanization." In *International Encyclopedia of the Social and Behavioural Sciences*, edited by James Wright, 31–36. Vol. 6. 2nd ed. Amsterdam: Elsevier.

Wallace, Rebecca. 2018. "Contextualizing the Crisis: The Framing of Syrian Refugees in Canadian Print Media." *Canadian Journal of Political Science* 51 (2): 207–31.

Warnock, Amanda. 2019. "The Dehumanization of Immigrants and Refugees: A Comparison of All Candidates Across Three US Presidential Elections." *Journal of Purdue Undergraduate Research* 9 (Fall): 49–59.

Wazana, Richard. 2004. "Fear and Loathing Down Under: Australian Refugee Policy and the National Imagination." *Refuge* 22 (1): 83–95.

Wyeth, Grant. 2020. "COVID-19 Stalls Immigration to Australia." *Diplomat*, April 8, 2020. https://thediplomat.com/2020/04/covid-19-stalls-immigration-to-australia/.

Zolberg, Aristide R. 1990. "Reforming the Back Door: The Immigration Reform and Control Act of 1986 in Historical Perspective." In *Immigration Reconsidered:*

History, Sociology and Politics, edited Virginia Yans-McLaughlin, 315–39. New York and Oxford: Oxford University Press.

Zong, Jie, Jeanne Batalova, and Jeffrey Hallock. 2018. "Frequently Requested Statistics on Immigrants and Immigration in the United States." Migration Policy Institute, February 8, 2018.

3 Migrant and Refugee Precarity as a Double Movement

A Case Study of Dehumanization and Humanization in the Canada-US Borderlands

Jeffrey M. Ayres

On a Saturday afternoon in mid-October 2019, far-right and pro-immigration groups gathered along the Québec–New York border, engaging in competing protests near the Lacolle-Champlain border crossing. The location of the protests was not by chance: minutes away from this official border crossing is Roxham Road, an unofficial crossing that tens of thousands of asylum seekers for several years had been using to enter Canada from the United States. The far-right groups—who had instigated the demonstration—included members of Yellow Vests Canada, Storm Alliance, the People's Party of Canada, Groupe de Sécurité Patriotique, and the well-known white supremacist group Soldiers of Odin. Separated by a heavy presence of members of Sûreté du Québec, pro-immigration groups, including Bridges Not Borders (Créons des Ponts), Caring for Social Justice, Valleyfield, West Island refugee volunteers, and Unitarian Universalists from the Eastern Townships, held a press conference and displayed signs with pro-refugee messages to counter the far-right anti-immigration demonstrators (Campbell and Kovac 2019; Curtis 2019).

These duelling border protests—and the wider public debate and public policies they reflect—illustrate long-unfolding structural forces shaping the precarity of undocumented migrants, refugees, and asylum seekers, yet the protests also highlight the reformist potential of civil society, social movements, and contentious politics at a moment of overlapping global political, economic, and environmental crises. Moreover, this duality of migrant and refugee precarity—with multiple overlapping forms of vulnerability, anxiety, uncertainty, and deportability contrasted with civil society interventions and social movement mobilizations for human rights, economic wellbeing, and the right to claim asylum—provides insights into the conditions of globalization and contestation in the twenty-first century. Unpacking the processes that contribute to such precarity helps clarify the interdependence of policies, rhetoric, and actions that dehumanize refugee claimants with interventions, protests, and responses that seek to humanize refugees and migrants at a time of near-unparalleled crisis for displaced peoples globally. With the 2020 advent of the COVID-19 global pandemic and the resulting economic crisis of mass unemployment for hundreds of millions globally, these conditions of precarization have only deepened while nonetheless having been met by one of the largest US-centered transnational moments of contentious politics and social movement mobilization in decades (Kipfer 2020).

This chapter explores the appearance and consequences of the duality of migrant and refugee precarity along the Canada-US borderlands through the analytical lens of Polanyi's "double movement" (2001). Over the past several decades in the post–Cold War era, Polanyi's conceptual approach—originally applied to understand the transformative socio-political responses to the crisis of nineteenth-century civilization that resulted in the First World War—has been applied to explain a variety of countermovement reactions and responses to crises of twentieth-century civilization. Polanyi focused during his time on the so-called Great Transformation of the post–World War I era: the duelling fascist and socio-democratic responses to what he called the failed "utopian project" of founding a society on a self-regulating market (Desai 2020, 4). Yet Polanyian analysis is arguably just as potent today as it was a century ago, as the concept of the double movement has increasingly been drawn on by scholars and activists to place the spread of an extraordinary array of reactionary and progressive social movements today in a similar context: as diverse and socially protective responses and reactions to a similarly failed attempt to recreate another utopian project of a market society through neoliberal economic policies. From the alter-globalization movements of the 1990s culminating in the Seattle World Trade Organization (WTO) protests, to the post-Seattle contentious political cycle that produced variously the

World Social Forum, Occupy Wall Street, and global anti-austerity protests, to most recently the spread of populist, xenophobic reactionary movements countered by a revitalization of the Black Lives Matter movement, cycles of unrest and contentious political behaviour are linked to the neoliberal processes that have exacerbated global inequality and insecurity (Ayres and Macdonald 2019).

In short, I argue that we are currently witnessing the playing out of another Great Transformation, with the acceleration of the duality of migrant and refugee precarity an important part of this destabilized era. In this chapter, I first review the development of precarity as a hegemonic norm under neoliberalism, discussing briefly how neoliberal precarization has accelerated conditions that dehumanize life and labour for refugees and migrants. I then turn to a discussion of Trump administration executive orders, travel restrictions, and immigration bans that have exacerbated precarity, with a focus on the dehumanizing impact of these policies in the Canada-US borderlands region. In particular, I focus on the double movement of refugee and migrant dehumanization and humanization at Roxham Road, where tens of thousands of people have fled from the United States as irregular migrants seeking asylum and refugee status in Canada.

While expanded securitization by US Customs and Border Protection and anti-immigration protests notably on the Québec side of the border aggravated further the unpredictability of daily life for those seeking to cross into Canada, counterprotests, border solidarity actions, and humanitarian relief provided by civil society groups on both sides of the border suggest the possibility for an alternative, humanizing politics of refugee settlement and migration in a post-neoliberal era.

Precarity as a Hegemonic Norm in the Neoliberal Era

The past few years have marked a new era of mass migration, with hundreds of millions of people on the move globally due to an accumulation of crises and political conflicts. This trend of vast movements of people is linked to any number of challenges: state failure, civil war, human rights abuses, violence, transnational criminal activity, shifts in the global balance of power, environmental degradation, and accelerating climate change. The numbers are sobering; according to the International Organization for Migration (2020), 272 million people could be classified as migrants in 2019—3.5 percent of the world's population, with the global refugee population in 2018 at 25.9 million, internally displaced peoples at 41.3 million, and stateless peoples at 3.9 million. Less acute crises and more long-term economic, social, political, and technological transformations linked to post–Cold War globalization also have pushed and pulled people across the globe. Yet it is the neoliberal character of these globalization-induced transformations that is of particular relevance to understanding the precarization of migrant and refugee life and the accompanying countermovements that have reacted to it.

Neoliberalism has been described variously as an economic theory, political ideology, policy paradigm, and social imaginary (Evans and Sewell 2013). Whichever meaning is considered, the overriding theme is the dramatically increased role played by markets in shaping many of the most profound political, economic, and cultural changes of the post–Cold War era (Hall and Lamont 2013). Picking up steam dramatically in the early 1980s with the full support of key political leaders such as US president Ronald Reagan and British prime minister Margaret Thatcher, and to a lesser extent Canadian prime minister Brian Mulroney, neoliberal prescriptions such as deregulation, privatization, tax cuts, and the liberalization of trade and investment became embedded in national and international policies and regimes to legitimize a radical scaling back of the social welfare role played by governments and encouraged a dramatic change in prevailing views on the appropriate relationship between the public and private sectors (Hall and Lamont 2013). The impact of neoliberal ideas became especially identifiable in the emergence of free trade agreements such as the Canada-US Free Trade Agreement or the North American Free Trade Agreement (NAFTA), in the creation of the WTO, in the functioning logic of the World Bank and International Monetary Fund for dispensing loans across the developing world, and in the adoption of increasingly regressive income tax policies by states.

In addition to the obvious political and economic policy impacts, neoliberal ideas also have shaped what Hall and Lamont call the "collective imaginary" (2013, 4) of a society, and this rise in market fundamentalist ideologies has directly contributed to the growing precarious character of everyday life for so many in the twenty-first century. As Hall and Lamont argue, neoliberal ideas have contributed to the collective reimagining of those "overarching narratives that tell people what their society is about" so that national imaginaries have become neoliberalized: "Governments and international agencies were called upon to rethink their missions, and individuals faced profound redefinitions in the criteria for social worth, as economic performance and market status became more central markers for social and cultural membership" (4). Arguably, neoliberalism has brought not merely dramatic redistributive shifts—steadily rising levels of inequality within both developed and developing countries, contributing to a more precarious way of life (Evans and Sewell 2013)—but also profound shifts in those dominant scripts that previously might have been drawn on to legitimize government responses to counter widening material insecurity. And as the neoliberal script increasingly removed any role for the state, discouraging socially protective government interventions to counter growing income inequality and material insecurity within states, precarity has become a hegemonic norm embodying such market imperatives as efficiency, flexibility, unpredictability, and insecurity (Schierup, Alund, and Likic-Brboric 2014; Wise 2018).

The daily life experiences of migrants and refugees reflect a crossroads of precarity and intersecting and destabilizing crises—the migrant experience being the "quintessential incarnation" of precarity (Tsianos 2007, 192). As Paret and Gleeson argue, migrant experiences provide a critical and much broader lens for appreciating the origins and institutionalization of precarity over the past several decades (2016). While the condition and processes of precarity have become increasingly popular subjects of study in political economy and critical labour studies, focusing especially on the conditions of life and labour precarity, migrants experience precarity in multiple reinforcing ways with the added challenge of legal status/citizenship or precarity of place. Life precarity references a "situation in which persons do not have stable life conditions," implying existing in a "state of flux," while labour precarity "refers to a situation in which subjects are faced with flexible working conditions" (Biglia and Marti 2014, 1489). As Roy and Verdun point out, labour precarity focuses primarily on issues related to the insecurity of employment, whereas life precarity is linked to a much broader "feeling of vulnerability that could arise not just due to labour market conditions, but from various life experiences and prospects" (2019, 3). Added to these two precarious conditions is precarity of place or legal precarity, which Roy and Verdun argue is connected most closely to the migrant or refugee claimant experience: "precariousness around not having the correct legal documentation and status to reside lawfully in the country and/or to travel freely back to the mother country and to have the right to reenter after a short time away" (4). In other words, on top of the relentless uncertainty of having access to gainful employment or being able to coherently plan for a future, the migrant or would-be refugee experiences precarity of place in the day-to-day risk of being deported through a change in immigration or labour laws or through the general lack of state protection due to the status as a non-citizen of a given country.

Migrant and refugee precarity—in its life, labour, and legal dimensions—is further reinforced by state bordering practices that encourage reactionary movements no less shaped by neoliberal scripts that have redrawn the boundaries between public and private and accentuated clear lines between the included and excluded of a national community. Precarity as a hegemonic norm is therefore reinforced through processes of bordering, through which "territories and peoples are respectively included or excluded within a hierarchical network of groups, affiliations and identities" (Newman 2003, 13). As Black, Chattopadhyay, and Chisholm have noted, "The blatant hardening of borders through regulatory measures designed specifically to keep migratory labour cheap, disposable, and controllable, is not new. [. . .] In recent decades, the exploitation of global migrant populations has been fortified with increasingly technological sophistication, the spread of globalization, and the hegemony of neoliberalism" (2020, 6). In the nearly twenty years since the terrorist attacks on the United States on September 11, 2001, bordering processes are even less concentrated in central places along those territorial lines separating states and are, rather, more widely dispersed to serve surveillance, filtering, and sorting functions for the state. Law enforcement, the Department of Homeland Security (DHS), policing, Immigration and Customs Enforcement (ICE), and other agencies that exist to control and disaggregate have "delocalized" or gone "remote," operationalizing the neoliberal national imaginaries wherever authorities have deemed it necessary to protect community members from perceived dangers, such as asylum seekers, migrants, drug and sex traffickers, cheap labour, and undocumented workers. In short, remote and delocalizing bordering processes have exacerbated the precarious life, labour, and legal conditions facing migrants and refugees, with a political rationale that supports and sustains neoliberal norms: border regions are "decongested" to further liberalize and speed up cross-border trade, production, and tourism, while migrants and asylum seekers are intercepted, imprisoned, and deported prior to activating human rights, refugee, or citizenship claims (Walters 2006, 195), reinforcing a community that clearly demarcates between "us and them."

As much as several decades of neoliberal precarization processes today have exacerbated some of the more dehumanizing characteristics of this age—spiralling inequality, growing material insecurity, anxiety, vulnerability, and broadly shared feelings of despair—precarity also has been recognized for its dual significance: as a condition shaping social movement identity, contentious politics, and resistance (Schierup, Alund, and Likic-Brboric 2014, 51). This is where a Polanyian analysis is most instructive: the expectation that the movement toward neoliberal orthodoxy that has unfolded over the past several decades—commodifying work and life experiences, dis-embedding the market from government regulation, and accelerating the twenty-first-century norm of precarity—suggests the relevance of considering if neoliberalism would be met by countermovements of resistance seeking social protection from precarization. Critically, moreover, an accurate reading of Polanyi recognizes that these countermovements may take a variety of ideological and political forms; as fascist, socialist, and communist movements arose after the First World War competing for national and international dominance in the Great Transformation of Polanyi's time, today's countermovements against neoliberal precarity have demonstrated both reactionary and progressive characteristics. On the progressive, social justice, and emancipatory left, the past several decades have seen a number of challenges to neoliberal precarity: from the alter-globalization movement's campaigns opposing NAFTA and the WTO, to the global anti-capitalist World Social Forum, to Occupy Wall Street and anti-austerity protests and the Black Lives Matter movement. Yet, on the reactionary, xenophobic, and populist right, we have seen far different manifestations of socially protective impulses: the rise of a global white supremacy movement, the Tea Party, the 2016 "Make America Great Again" US presidential campaign, Brexit, and the spread of populist and authoritarian governments worldwide, couching socially and community-protective responses with anti-immigrant and racist delocalized bordering practices. The next section of this chapter looks to the Québec–New York–Vermont border region to illustrate this duality of precarity in its both dehumanizing and humanizing forms and highlights the potentials of migrant and refugee agency and civil society counter-hegemonic discourse and collective action to the precarization of life and work.

Exacerbating Migrant Precarity in the Borderlands

Clearly, the precarization of the average American played a crucial role in the election of Donald Trump, as the declining economic fortunes of Americans played a key role in the construction of negative and fearful frames of meaning about what life in the United States means today to Trump and his supporters. As many observers of the rise of Trump to the presidency have observed, Trump tapped into and exploited successfully a widespread shared sense of "cultural resentment" on the part of mostly white, working-class Americans, especially across Rust Belt states such as Wisconsin, Michigan, Ohio, and Pennsylvania (Cramer 2016; Campbell 2018), a population segment especially receptive to fearful rhetoric about a dangerous and unfair North America of violent immigrants and relentless job loss. A "profound and enduring connection" developed between Trump and his core voters, a connection based on grievance, where Trump met "his voters in a common perception (real or not) of being shunned, ignored and disrespected by 'elites'" (LeTourneau 2017). Trump's "Make America Great Again" campaign rallies provided a window into the depth of resentment, rage, and fear collectively shared by a large segment of the American population, with Trump's campaign and rhetoric exhibiting a collection of what were widely perceived as common-sense proposals to strengthen America's borders and protect its economy and its workers. Through his interactions with supporters at campaign rallies and through his rhetoric, fear and anxiety were fused in trade and security across the North American region, where the preoccupation with illegal immigration, fortifying the border, and building a wall were combined with the national security threat posed by both NAFTA partners, Canada and Mexico.

Executive Orders, Travel Bans, and Decreased Refugee Resettlement

The Trump administration wasted little time constructing a response to the precarious livelihoods of many Americans by developing policies and announcing proposals that contained racist and xenophobic overtones and served to exacerbate further the precarity of migrants, refugees, and undocumented workers in the United States. At times, President Trump was quite direct, attacking DACA (Deferred Action for Childhood Arrivals); complaining in 2018 that the United States had been accepting too many people from "shithole countries" from Africa, Haiti, and El Salvador (Sacchetti, Hauslohner, and Paquette 2020); or "scapegoating" almost a quarter of Africa's population with travel and immigration bans put in place ostensibly due to security risks in the vetting procedures in place in these countries (Tharoor 2020). Many of these policies created invisible walls and barriers to migration and clearly were designed to restrict immigration, reduce refugee resettlement, and deport people who did not fit the white nationalist imaginary that buttressed the Trump administration. In the days following his inauguration in January 2017, President Trump issued several executive orders, the results of which would have severely curtailed travel or migration from majority-Muslim or majority-non-white countries, including (1) Enhancing Public Safety in the Interior of the United States, (2) Border Security and Immigration Enforcement Improvements, and (3) Protecting the Nation from Foreign Terrorist Entry into the United States.

All three executive orders built upon the exclusionary campaign rhetoric to shape policies at the core of the Trump administration's nativist political project. The first two orders have had significant implications for securitized bordering and re-bordering along the US-Mexico and US-Canadian borders: the first ordered law enforcement agencies in the United States to aggressively act to remove all undocumented migrants, even those not previously convicted of a crime, which was a notable change from the emphasis on removal during the Obama administration, and the second focused on fulfilling Trump's central campaign promise of building a wall between the United States and Mexico, limiting the due process rights of asylum seekers, and broadening and expediting the detention of immigrants and removal with limited rights of appeal.

While the third executive order has gone through several changes and was ultimately upheld in revised form by the US Supreme Court in 2018, all three orders have significantly enhanced the deportation powers of key agencies within the DHS, including ICE and its key agency empowered with making arrests—Enforcement and Removal Operations (ERO)—and the Customs and Border Protection (CBP). Under Trump, over one hundred thousand people a year were arrested by the ERO—more arrests annually than are carried out combined by the FBI, the Marshals Service, and the Secret Service, with arrests skyrocketing by over 40 percent since the issuing of these executive orders (ICE 2018). The expanded arrests and deportations are linked to a more explicitly nativist political project and are also part of a much larger expansion of a US border control-security-industrial complex over the past several decades.

In addition to travel restrictions, immigration bans, and the elimination of visa lotteries, the Trump administration oversaw a dramatic curtailment in refugee resettlement in the United States. The 2017 Enhancing Public Safety in the Interior of the United States executive order suspended the settlement of Syrian refugees indefinitely and served as a harbinger of the administration's approach to refugee resettlement that was soon to follow: that same year, the administration capped resettlement at forty-five thousand—less than half the amount of refugee resettlement that occurred in the last year of the Obama administration and the first time in history that the ceiling was below sixty-seven thousand (Goudeau 2020). By 2018, Canada, with one-tenth the population, had surpassed the United States in total numbers of refugees resettled, and for the first time in the history of the United Nations Refugee Agency, the United States did not resettle the most refugees. Through 2019, with understaffing at the FBI, bureaucratic delays within the DHS, and relief agencies such as Catholic Charities and the International Rescue Committee closing offices, refugee resettlement continued to slow (Alvarez 2018), and the admission ceiling in 2020 was slashed again to a mere eighteen thousand.

Roxham Road and the Safe Third Country Agreement

The particular vulnerability and insecurity of undocumented migrants and asylum seekers—life, labour, and legal precarity—have been exacerbated by the functioning of the Canada-US Safe Third Country Agreement (STCA). The hostility, xenophobia, harsh rhetoric, and restrictive policies of the Trump administration toward migrants and potential asylum seekers have had a direct impact on the flow of people seeking to leave the United States for Canada. Since the beginning of the Trump administration in January 2017, over fifty-five thousand asylum seekers have entered Canada through land crossings, with long-time undocumented migrants in the United States pushed to the border due to increased fears of arrest, detention, and deportation. Many of these people overstayed visas or received a negative asylum decision, and while 60 percent purportedly always saw the United States as a "transit state" with the eventual goal of moving to Canada, 40 percent nonetheless felt threatened enough by the Trump administration's stance to uproot their lives and seek refuge in Canada (Keung 2019; Smith 2019).

Rural upstate New York, where Roxham Road dead-ends into the US-Canada border, is where over 90 percent of all crossings into Canada from the United States by undocumented migrants have taken place since 2016 (Banerjee 2018). What has encouraged undocumented migrants and refugee claimants to seek out Roxham Road is primarily the STCA—in addition to the anti-immigration and xenophobic stance of the Trump administration. Coming into effect in 2004, the STCA was designed to reduce so-called asylum shopping, forcing would-be refugee claimants to apply for status in whichever country they first landed in their official point of entry. The premise of the agreement is that both Canada and the United States are safe countries for people to make asylum claims, and the agreement mandates that anyone crossing at an official Canada-US land point of entry to seek asylum must be turned back to claim refugee status in their first country of entry. However, the unanticipated exception to the STCA is that people may try to cross at unofficial points of entry—such as Roxham Road—and while temporarily they may be detained, they may then pursue refugee status outside the parameters of the STCA. Granted, the STCA was initially negotiated at a time when few people were trying to cross dangerous and unofficial entry points between the United States and Canada. Yet by encouraging irregular crossing at an unofficial point in the border, the STCA exacerbates the already precarious livelihoods of undocumented migrants and asylum seekers: travel to and across the US-Canada border can be dangerous and risky, unscrupulous taxi drivers who drop people off at the end of Roxham Road have been known to charge exorbitant prices, and the experience of taking one's family to the border knowingly crossing at an unofficial site is extraordinarily anxiety producing, with uncertainty and fear over police treatment and an unknown time frame for asylum consideration awaiting (Wu, Reynolds, and Young 2020; Brown 2019). Moreover, negative and factually incorrect media portrayals of Canada "losing control" over its borders and being "invaded" by "bogus" refugee claimants oftentimes frame those crossing at Roxham Road as criminals or dangers to Canadian society rather than as individuals and families fearful of remaining in a hostile United States and desperate for refuge in Canada.

Re-bordering and Remote Control Beyond the International Border

Agents of the DHS currently are legally empowered to stop vehicles within one hundred miles of the border and search private land within twenty-five miles of the US-Canada border. Such practices illustrate the operationalization of "remote control"—where the expanded securitization functions of the border are increasingly delocalized and focused on policing, detaining, and relocating "mobilities" not in immediate proximity to the international legal border (Walters 2006). CBP officers have been known to board Greyhound busses without a warrant in Vermont and have stood outside bus doorways inquiring about citizenship status in Burlington, Vermont (a distance of less than fifty miles), prior to allowing passengers to board. The American Civil Liberties Union of Vermont (ACLU-VT) submitted a series of Freedom of Information requests in 2012 to federal agencies, discovering that the DHS had drawn up plans for creating an eight-acre stretch of permanent border control checkpoints, many as much as one hundred miles from the Canadian border, along the North-South interstates in Vermont, New Hampshire, and Maine (ACLU-VT 2013a). The following year, the ACLU-VT released a new study titled *Surveillance on the Northern Border*, which detailed the extensive way the newest surveillance technologies are being implemented to track the movements of citizens of Vermont (ACLU-VT 2013b). The ACLU-VT report noted that because over 90 percent of Vermonters live within the one-hundred-mile possible interior checkpoint zone, Vermont has become a "perverse Ground Zero in the accelerating surveillance society" (Picard 2013).

Relatedly, over the past several years, there has been a significant increase in the targeting, arrest, and detention of undocumented immigrants in the New York–Vermont border region by ICE and CBP agents, as reported by the Swanton Border Control Sector, an area from the eastern border of New York, across all Vermont, to the New Hampshire–Maine border. Importantly, the total number of people caught illegally crossing from Canada into the United States in the Swanton sector reached its highest level in the fiscal year 2018 since 2011: the CBP apprehended 736 people in the fiscal year 2018, up from 449 in the fiscal year 2017, including 142 families attempting to cross into the United States from Canada in the fiscal year 2018 (Norton and Rodrigues 2019). Yet in addition to this increase in the capturing and detention of immigrants attempting illegal border crossings from Canada into the United States, there has also been an increase in CBP and ICE arrests of undocumented immigrants in Vermont, with an increase in the Swanton sector from 291 to 449 for an increase of 54 percent in the fiscal year 2017 (Dilawar 2018). This increase in arrests of undocumented immigrants seems consistent with the Trump administration's 2017 executive order Enhancing Public Safety in the Interior of the United States, which eliminated the Obama-era focus on arresting undocumented immigrants with criminal convictions. Connected circumstantially to Vermont's status as a "sanctuary state" but more directly to recent political campaigns in Vermont designed to promote the human rights of undocumented immigrants, ICE and the CBP have appeared to target especially the state's population of immigrant dairy farm labourers. Workers and activists from the Vermont-based immigrant human rights group Migrant Justice have been detained, intimidated, harassed, and arrested conspicuously coinciding with three recent campaigns to improve the well-being of undocumented labourers in Vermont (True 2017; Dilawar 2020).

Anti-immigration Borderlands Protests

The most obvious signs of a reactionary countermovement that has exacerbated migrant and refugee precarity—especially due to the STCA and the resulting conditions and events transpiring at Roxham Road—are illustrated in the anti-immigration and right-wing protests that have been organized on the Québec side of the border over the past several years. Storm Alliance—an anti-immigration and anti-Muslim group formed in December 2016—has been a central player in organizing protests along the border and in Montréal and Québec City. Supporters of Storm Alliance broke from the white supremacist group Soldiers of Odin, which had emerged in Canada in 2015 and gained notoriety for the use of street patrols seen as an attempt to intimidate refugees and immigrants (Lamoureux 2017). Storm Alliance focuses explicitly on conditions in Québec and protests against the federal Liberal government's handling of the situation at Roxham Road. Members of Storm Alliance oppose what they perceive as illegal immigration flowing across the border and call for the federal government to reimburse Québec for the costs associated with handling the large influx of refugee claimants into the province, claiming that the needs of average Quebeckers are not being met (Olivier 2018). In addition to the "United to Protect Our Borders" rally in May 2018, Storm Alliance has also participated in so-called patrols of the Canada-US border—sometimes joined by the anti-Muslim group La Meute and members of other far-right and paramilitary organizations—to observe the Royal Canadian Mounted Police and the processing of asylum seekers crossing into Canada at Roxham Road. While not as overtly expressed through public policy and legislation, such concerns have echoed across the conservative political spectrum in Canada, as anxiety, fear, and anger over irregular border crossings have become features of political debate and rhetoric. In 2018, Michelle Rempel, a Conservative member of Parliament from Alberta, proposed turning the entire length of the Canada-US border into a formal point of entry, which would effectively block irregular border crossing to seek asylum; Jean-François Lisée, the Québec provincial Parti Québécois leader, called for a fence to be built at Roxham Road; and roughly timed with October 2019 border protests, former Federal Conservative Party leader Andrew Scheer sought to politicize the situation at Roxham Road to boost his party's fortunes in the October 21, 2019, federal election. This alarmist rhetoric coming from Canada's Conservative Party as well as the much more openly anti-immigrant People's Party has connected with the same theme of the "invasion of illegals" at the border espoused by right-wing protests, with concerns growing that Canada's Liberal Party and its immigration policy in turn are being influenced by these reactionary protests and concerns (Carbert 2019).

Challenging Migrant Precarity in the Borderlands

The precarious conditions experienced by undocumented migrants and asylum seekers in the Canada-US border region have a clear dual significance visible not merely in reactionary trends and actions but in solidaristic countermovements in support of migrants and refugees. Harsh US government policy and anti-immigrant rhetoric and executive orders have been met with and countered by pro-migrant borderlands protests. New civic organizations have emerged to provide humanitarian relief along the border in an attempt to reduce the levels of anxiety, life insecurity, and vulnerability experienced by individuals and families crossing into Canada at Roxham Road. Migrant groups have pushed back through protests and legal actions against the erosion of their collective agency and have demonstrated resiliency and solidarity in the midst of precarious life, labour, and legal conditions. All these initiatives suggest that neoliberal precarity and its particularly harsh effects on migrants and asylum seekers have been challenged by counter-hegemonic engagement and participation, highlighting that borderlands precarity is not just an inevitable and bleak condition but has become a rallying point for resistance. In short, while the Canada-US borderlands reveal the dangers and pressures associated with migrant precarity, this region has also become a space for a more progressive, human rights–oriented countermovement; a microcosm of broader challenges to neoliberal precarity; and a reference point and example for "social justice movements generating strategies and discourses of contestation in the name of human rights and universal citizenship" (Schierup, Alund, and Likic-Brboric 2014, 51). These elements are central to a more humanizing approach to migrants and refugees.

Border Solidarity and Humanitarian Relief

Concerned individuals on both sides of the Canada-US border have formed humanitarian-based organizations that focus on trying to improve the well-being and enhance the personal dignity of asylum seekers attempting to cross into Canada at Roxham Road. Both Plattsburgh Cares and Bridges Not Borders formed in 2017 in response to the increase in people streaming to the New York–Québec border in reaction to the tightening of US immigration and asylum policies. Plattsburgh Cares, based on the New York side of the border, and Bridges Not Borders, based on the Québec side, have both played important roles in distributing supplies, providing information, and dispelling misconceptions about asylum seekers and undocumented migrants crossing the border. Plattsburgh Cares has produced flyers explaining the STCA, helped people find local temporary housing, provided translators for immigration attorneys, given local presentations on the plight of migrants and refugees, rallied in support of DACA, and engaged particularly in everyday forms of humanitarianism at Roxham Road, providing water, food, clothing, crayons, and stuffed animals to asylum seekers and their families. The group also has built alliances and shared resources with other local organizations—such as Refugees Welcome International, Adirondack Friends of Refugees and Immigrants, and John Brown Lives—and enlisted local taxi drivers to more humanely and cost-effectively transport would-be refuge claimants from Plattsburgh to Roxham Road (Crête 2018; Plattsburgh Cares 2021).

There has been a similar trend toward networking and alliance building in support of refugee rights and to provide humanitarian relief on the Québec side of the border. Bridges Not Borders in Québec has engaged in similar small-scale relief actions to raise awareness of the challenges facing refugee claimants once they cross the border, including serving as a "peaceful and informed" presence at the border, providing meals and explaining the STCA to migrants, lobbying the federal and provincial governments to better protect and respect refugee rights, and meeting with members of Parliament and the

Quebec National Assembly to raise awareness about the conditions at Roxham Road and the trends forcing people to the border. Other organizations that have collaborated with Bridges Not Borders or are similarly engaged in collective actions and information raising on the precarious conditions facing the thousands of asylum seekers who have entered Canada include Foyer du Monde, Comité d'accueil des migrants du Haut-Saint-Laurent, Comité d'accueil des demandeurs d'asile au Québec, the Montréal-based office of the United Nations High Commissioner for Refugees, and Solidarity Across Borders, a migrant justice network based in Montréal and active since 2003, which is composed of both migrants and allies working to end deportations and detentions of asylum seekers (Bridges Not Borders 2020b). The different volunteer and citizens-based relief groups that have engaged in cross-border collaboration and increased their humanitarian efforts on behalf of migrants and refugees illustrate a type of "alternative politics of migration" (Alonso 2020, 73), mobilizing resources and raising awareness to change existing laws and policies that exacerbate migrant precarity and highlighting the violence, inequality, and poverty that have pushed and pulled people to travel tens of thousands of miles to seek refuge in Canada or even originally the United States. Promoting a different approach to migration policy and relief "from below"—as opposed to through top-down government proclamations or international agreements such as the STCA—these organizations serve as important countervailing forces against government policies at the federal, provincial, or state level that have proved not merely insufficient but harmful (ibid.).

Pro-immigration Borderlands Protests

Protests, campaigns, and other types of information-raising collective actions have emerged throughout the Canada-US borderlands region, complementing the relief efforts of the civil society organizations assisting people crossing the border into Canada. Again, Roxham Road has become a flashpoint for protest, with anti-immigration and pro-migrant protesters rallying peacefully but arrayed against each other, oftentimes separated by police in Québec. Bridges Not Borders joined Solidarity Across Borders in several counterprotests from 2017 to 2019 in Québec to counter the rallies organized by the Storm Alliance and other anti-immigrant and anti-Muslim groups. While these efforts have in part served to provide a counter-presence to the larger numbers of individuals participating in the anti-immigration rallies, Bridges Not Borders also has engaged in more everyday acts of micro-protest and humanitarianism, holding a press conference, hosting a picnic, and even hosting a tea party for news organizations to counter the "Secure Our Borders" demonstration in the Lacolle, Québec, border crossing in June 2018.

Other protests and demonstrations have occurred in the Montréal area at the proposed construction site in Laval for a new detention center for undocumented migrants while they await hearings on whether they will be allowed to remain in Canada. Anarchists and groups committed to the abolition of prisons have for several years organized protests on New Year's Eve at the Laval site, setting off fireworks and making noise through chants and music in solidarity with people already held in detention at the minimum-security federal training center (Milton 2019). Ni Frontières, Ni Prisons—an organization specifically devoted to halting the construction of the proposed new detention center—has targeted construction companies involved in the bidding process, while anti-capitalist groups framed the annual May 1 International Labour Day celebrations in 2019 around opposition to migrant detention and deportation (Earles 2019). Additionally, Solidarity Across Borders has organized marches in Montréal against the proposed detention center and kept the spotlight on the challenging conditions facing those individuals—detained or not—awaiting hearings to determine their refugee status.

Migrant Agency and Successful Organizing and Mobilization

There are many instances in the Canada-US borderlands region where people are mobilizing with some success against the precarious life, labour, and legal conditions they face as undocumented migrants, challenging trends, policies, and institutions that might otherwise erode their collective agency. Paret and Gleeson have referred to the "precarity-migrant-agency" nexus as situations where "migrants are building solidarity to push back against their precarity"—protesting against exploitation at work, exclusion from public services, and the ever-present threat of criminalization, deportation, and family separation (2016, 286). One of the more visible organizations that has engaged in a number of successful collective actions and mobilizations on behalf of undocumented workers and against the intersecting conditions of precarity facing migrants is Migrant Justice, based in the city of Burlington in northern Vermont. Similar in composition to Solidarity Across Borders in that its members are undocumented workers as well as local supporters, Migrant Justice has undertaken several campaigns that have targeted federal and state laws and corporate behaviour that exploits or destabilizes the daily lives of migrant workers in Vermont and across greater New England, including a mobilization to demand fair and impartial policing across Vermont as well as a campaign to demand that ICE stop targeting and arresting undocumented dairy workers in front of their homes.

A protest campaign in 2013 successfully pressured the Vermont General Assembly to approve legislation allowing migrants to gain access to a Vermont driver's license regardless of immigration status. In November 2018, Migrant Justice started a campaign against the Vermont Department of Motor Vehicles (DMV) and ICE, marching through downtown Burlington to the federal courthouse to announce a federal anti-discrimination lawsuit alleging that the DMV and ICE were collaborating to harasses and detain migrant workers. Specifically, Migrant Justice contended that the DMV was providing ICE with the personal information of undocumented workers who had applied for driver's licenses and had been involved in Migrant Justice human rights campaigns. The Vermont DMV and Migrant Justice reached a settlement in January 2020 that created new regulations that restricted communication and information sharing between federal immigration authorities such as ICE and the DMV (Blaisdell 2020). Migrant Justice's ongoing Milk with Dignity campaign highlights the benefits of targeting the market power and resources of companies to improve the labour and housing conditions of migrant workers. This campaign encourages dairy companies to commit to prioritizing the sourcing of milk from farms that enroll in the Milk with Dignity program so that the labour and housing conditions of migrant workers are improved in part through the commitment of farms employing undocumented workers but also by companies paying a premium to help raise wages and working conditions on the farms. The well-known socially conscious ice cream company Ben and Jerry's was the first to sign on to the Milk with Dignity campaign, reaching an agreement with Migrant Justice in October 2017. The agreement stipulated that 100 percent of Ben and Jerry's northeastern US dairy purchases and over 250 workers would be covered and protected by the agreement's code of conduct. Most recently, Migrant Justice has been targeting Hannaford, one of the largest supermarket chains in the northeastern United States, pressuring the chain to join the Milk with Dignity campaign through marches and protests outside individual stores (Migrant Justice 2020).

Challenging the Safe Third Country Agreement in the Era of COVID-19

In the absence of—or to some extent, because of—government action on immigration and refugees, civil society organizations in Canada decided to challenge the STCA in the Federal Court. The challenges posed by the STCA—increased fear, uncertainty, and vulnerability as tens of thousands of people crossed into Canada from the United States at Roxham Road—became impossible to ignore for social groups on the frontline of providing humanitarian relief to asylum seekers. As a result, in July 2017, six months after the inauguration of President Trump, the Canadian Council for Refugees, Amnesty International, and the Canadian Council of Churches joined an individual litigant and her children in a legal challenge, arguing that sending refugee claimants back to the United States violates their rights under the Canadian Charter of Rights and Freedoms (Canadian Council for Refugees 2018). Eventually joined by individuals from El Salvador, Syria, and Ethiopia, the challenge cited the Trump administration's hostility; growing restrictions on asylum seekers, visas, and immigration; removals of asylum seekers to unsafe countries; unlawful detention; barring of asylum claims based on gender and gang violence; criminalizing asylum at the border; and inconsistent access for asylum seekers to courts (Smith and Hofmann 2019). A federal court in Toronto eventually heard the challenge to the designation of the United States as a safe third country for refugees the first week of November 2019, with a supportive rally for refugee rights outside the courthouse in Toronto providing further grassroots support (Carbert 2019).

In the months following the November 2019 court hearing and the eventual decision against the STCA released in July 2020 by Justice Anne Marie McDonald, the COVID-19 pandemic swept through the world, dramatically exacerbating the precarious conditions facing migrants and would-be refugee claimants. Amid the surging global pandemic through the first six months of 2020, the Canadian and US governments put in place restrictive immigration and asylum policies that were not merely counterproductive in the fight against what had become a global health crisis but multipliers of the already existing life, legal, and workplace challenges facing migrants (Hsu 2020). Undocumented workers and asylum seekers were part of Québec's struggle with COVID-19: with hundreds working in long-term care homes in greater Montréal and fearing possible detention or deportation, many did not seek out treatment for COVID symptoms (Lowrie 2020). Compounding the challenges facing asylum seekers was the decision in March to close the border between Canada and the United States to all non-essential travellers, and any persons seeking asylum irregularly—at Roxham Road or any other unofficial border crossing—would be turned back to the United States. Closing the border effectively shut down what might be called the new underground railroad of largely racialized people fleeing the United States to Canada at Roxham Road, exposing asylum seekers now turned back to the hostile, xenophobic environment and threat of detention and deportation from the United States, with several dozen would-be refugee claimants turned away from the border at Roxham Road in April and May alone (Levitz 2020). In but just one desperate example, a thirty-two-year-old Vermont farmworker and Migrant Justice activist died of COVID-19 in Mexico in July 2020 after being deported by ICE in March despite having taken steps to apply for political asylum on the basis of "horrific and systemic violence that they experienced as a trans person in Mexico" (Brouwer 2020).

Nonetheless, the Federal Court ruling in July 2020 striking down the STCA, giving the federal government in Ottawa six months to respond to the decision, was particularly momentous for supporters of a new and more humanitarian approach to refugee resettlement in Canada. The ruling that the STCA is unconstitutional is seen as a major victory for refugee rights at a critical moment in the global COVID-19 pandemic. In the decision, Justice McDonald writes, "Security of the person encompasses freedom from the threat of physical and psychological punishment or suffering," noting in reference to those held in the United States, "The accounts of the detainees demonstrate both physical and psychological suffering because of detention, and a real risk that they will not be able to assert asylum claims" (Keung 2020). As the editorial board of the *Washington Post* notes in response to the ruling, "The question facing the administration of Prime Minister Justin Trudeau is whether its neighbor to the south still adheres to what Western democracies regard as the basic standards of dignity and decency on which the original treaty was based. [. . .] The evidence suggests it does not" (Editorial Board 2020). Regardless of the government's response, the challenge to the STCA demonstrates how important it is for countervailing forces to be brought to bear against government policies and institutions that have exacerbated migrant precarity for many years.

Toward a Progressive Agenda for Humanizing the Migrant and Refugee Experience?

This chapter has reviewed ways in which precarity—and especially migrant precarity—has developed into a flashpoint for social and political organization and collective action. Polanyi's concept of the double movement helps make sense of the decades-long unfolding of a neoliberal market orthodoxy that has exacerbated conditions of precarity for people around the world, who have experienced growing job insecurity, income inequality, accelerating day-to-day unpredictability, and feelings of vulnerability. For migrants and asylum seekers, neoliberal precarization has been accompanied by the added insecurity of precarity of place. In the Canada-US borderlands region of Québec–New York–Vermont, examples are widespread of countermovements of reaction and restriction slashing and sometimes overlapping with countermovements of agency and solidarity. Of course, what is playing out on this northern border of North America is taking place in different forms across Europe, Asia, Africa, and Latin America. Gramsci's concept of the "interregnum," which refers to moments between the breakdown of one political-ideological order and the emergence of a new one (Stahl 2019), is another tool for understanding what is happening. It seems clear that neoliberalism has been undermined—but not eliminated—by succeeding crises, from the 2008 financial crisis to the new global depression due to COVID-19. The world, in short, is ripe for a new successor to neoliberalism, but it is manifestly unclear whether that change and new order will be reactionary and dehumanizing or progressive and rehumanizing.

In reflecting on the precarity-migrant-agency nexus, Paret and Gleeson write, "We should celebrate acts of resistance, even when they are limited or largely symbolic [. . .] but we must also acknowledge the persistence of precarity and the structures that maintain it, whether institutional or ideological" (2016, 289). The challenges facing workers and people in their everyday lives, but especially the struggles of migrants and asylum seekers, are likely to carry on for the foreseeable future, with climate change, failing states, and deepening inequality characteristics of any post-COVID global order. Moments of agency and collective action help clarify the processes of social and political change, and any hopes for a trending toward a politics of migration that embraces a progressive push for the distribution of collective goods, inclusive national imaginaries, and greater equity will likely require a multi-scale countervailing front against precarity and its neoliberal scripts: everyday acts of humanitarianism, protests and collective action campaigns, and legal and institutional efforts brought by civil society interweave into larger progressive countermovement potentials. Polanyi's understanding effectively of the dual potential of the double movement is essential: today's reactionary and progressive bordering practices are historically and politically contingent, with political, cultural, economic, and discursive practices continually colliding and contesting to redraw extraterritorial borders to legitimize different social imaginaries and uncertain political outcomes. It is, however, the progressive practices that need to be capitalized on to push a humanizing agenda for asylum seekers and refugees at the 49th parallel.

References

ACLU-VT (American Civil Liberties Union of Vermont). 2013a. "Border Checkpoints That Aren't at the Border." September 24, 2013. https://www.acluvt.org/en/news/border-checkpoints-arent-border.

ACLU-VT. 2013b. *Surveillance on the Northern Border*. Montpelier: ACLU Vermont. http://www.vtlex.com/wp-content/uploads/2013/11/northern_border_report.pdf.

Alonso, Alexandra Delano. 2020. "Time for an Alternative Politics of Migration." *Current History*, February 2020.

Alvarez, Priscilla. 2018. "America's System for Resettling Refugees Is Collapsing." *Atlantic*, September 9, 2019. https://www.theatlantic.com/politics/archive/2018/09/refugee-admissions-trump/569641/.

Ayres, Jeffrey, and Laura Macdonald. 2019. "Transnational Protest and the New Global Protest Cycle." In *Protest and Democracy*, edited by Moises Arch and Roberta Rich, 47–70. Calgary: University of Calgary Press.

Banerjee, Sidhartha. 2018. "As Immigration Debate Heats Up, Quebec's Roxham Road Still Ground Zero." CBC News, December 19, 2018.

Biglia, Barbara, and Jordi Marti. 2014. "Precarity." In *Encyclopedia of Critical Psychology*, edited by Thomas Teo, 1488–91. New York: Springer.

Black, Johannah, Sutapa Chattopadhyay, and Riley Chisholm. 2020. "Solidarity in Times of Social Distancing: Migrants, Mutual Aid and COVID-19." *Interface: A Journal for and about Social Movements* 12 (1): 1–12.

Blaisdell, Eric. 2020. "DMV, Migrant Justice Settle Lawsuit." *Times-Argus*, January 15, 2020. https://www.timesargus.com/news/local/dmv-migrant-justice-settle-lawsuit/article_8a0dfca8-019f-5a77-a7b5-9f09afcfce40.html.

Brouwer, Derek. 2020. "Farmworker Activist Dies of COVID-19 Following Deportation." *Seven Days*, July 7, 2020.

Brown, Marcia. 2019. "An Imperiled Border Agreement Could Doom Canada's Welcoming Immigration Policy." *American Prospect*, July 3, 2019.

Campbell, Emily, and Adam Kovac. 2019. "Immigration Advocates, Far Right Groups Face Off near Roxham Road." CTV News, October 19, 2019.

Campbell, John. 2018. *American Discontent: The Rise of Donald Trump and the Decline of the Golden Age* New York: Oxford University Press.

Canadian Council for Refugees. 2018. *Why the US Is Not Safe for Refugees: Challenging the Safe Third Country Agreement Backgrounder.* Montréal: Canadian Council for Refugees. https://ccrweb.ca/en/why-US-not-safe-challenging-STCA.

Carbert, Michelle. 2019. "Trudeau Government's Tougher Line on Asylum Seekers a 'Dramatic Shift' in Policy, Says Amnesty International." *Globe and Mail*, April 29, 2019.

Cramer, Katherine. 2016. *The Politics of Resentment: Rural Consciousness in Wisconsin and the Rise of Scott Walker*. Chicago: University of Chicago Press.

Crête, Mylène. 2018. "Plattsburgh Flyer Tells Migrants How to Enter Canada Irregularly." *Montreal Gazette*, May 24, 2014.

Curtis, Christopher. 2019. "Far Right Groups, Counter-Protesters Face Off near Lacolle Border Crossing." *Montreal Gazette*, October 19, 2019.

Desai, Radhika. 2020. "Introduction: Karl Polanyi in the Twenty-First Century." In *Karl Polanyi and Twenty-First Century Capitalism*, edited by Radhika Desai and Karl Polanyi Levitt, 1–18. Manchester: Manchester University Press.

Dilawar, Arvind. 2018. "Border Patrol Arrests, Targeting of Immigrant Activists Rises Dramatically in Vermont." April 24, 2018. https://shadowproof.com/2018/04/24/border-patrol-arrests-targeting-immigrant-activists-rises-dramatically-vermont/.

Dilawar, Arvind. 2020. "Targeted, Imprisoned, Deported, Dead: How Ice's Detention Can Be Deadly to Migrants." *In These Times*, September 21, 2020.

Earles, David. 2019. "A New Migrant Detention Centre Is Being Built in Laval as Quebec Hardens Stance on Immigration." *Link* April 2, 2019.

Editorial Board. 2020. "The World Is Realizing the U.S. Is No Longer Committed to Basic Standards of Decency." *Washington Post*, July 27, 2020.

Evans, Peter, and William H. Sewell Jr. 2013. "Neoliberalism: Policy Regimes, International Regimes, and Social Effects." In *Social Resilience in the Neo-Liberal Era*, edited by Peter Hall and Michele Lamont, 35–68. Cambridge: Cambridge University Press.

Goudeau, Jessica. 2020. "Refugee Resettlement Is Close to Collapse. That Was Trump's Plan." *New York Times*, July 28, 2020.

Hall, Peter, and Michele Lamont. 2013. "Introduction: Social Resilience in the Neo-Liberal Era." In *Social Resilience in the Neo-Liberal Era*, edited by Peter Hall and Michele Lamont, 1–33. Cambridge: Cambridge University Press.

Hsu, Annie. 2020. "Canada Should Suspend Its Safe Third Country Agreement with the U.S. Amidst the COVID-19 Pandemic." *Sigma Iota Rho Journal of International Relations*, April 17, 2020.

ICE (Immigration and Customs Enforcement). 2018. "Features." https://www.ice.gov/features/ERO-2018.

IOM (International Organization for Migration). 2020. *World Migration Report 2020*. Geneva: IOM. https://publications.iom.int/system/files/pdf/wmr_2020.pdf.

Keung, Nicholas. 2019. "Hostile U.S. Refugee Policies Stoking Irregular Migration to Canada, Study Says." *Toronto Star*, October 25, 2019.

Keung, Nicholas. 2020. "Canada Cannot Turn a Blind Eye: Federal Court Says Safe Third Country Agreement with U.S. Violates Charter." *Toronto Star*, July 22, 2020.

Kipfer, Stefan. 2020. *The Naked City: Traversing Toronto in Pandemic Times*. The Socialist Interventions Pamphlet Series. Toronto: Socialist Project. https://socialistproject.ca/pamphlets/the-naked-city/.

Lamoureux, Mack. 2017. "An 'Ultranationalist' Group Is Patrolling Canada's Border with the U.S." *Vice*, May 23, 2017.

LeTourneau, Nancy. 2017. "What Can We Do About the Politics of Resentment?" *Washington Monthly*, April 14, 2017.

Levitz, Stephanie. 2020. "Asylum Seekers Continue to Cross into Canada Despite Border Shutdown." *Globe and Mail*, June 24, 2020.

Lowrie, Morgan. 2020. "Asylum Seekers on Front Line of Quebec's COVID-19 Battle in Care Homes." *Globe and Mail*, May 18, 2020.

Migrant Justice. 2020. "Campaigns." https://migrantjustice.net/campaigns.

Milton, Jon. 2019. "This Is a Prison, No Matter What You Call It." *Briarpatch*, June 25, 2019.

Newman, David. 2003. "On Borders and Power: A Theoretical Framework." *Journal of Borderlands Studies* 18 (1): 13–25.

Norton, Kit, and Felippe Rodrigues. 2019. "Family Border Apprehensions Reach Five-Year High in Swanton Sector." *VTDigger*, March 31, 2019.

Olivier, Annabelle. 2018. "Immigration Protestors and Counter-Protestors Rally near Lacolle Border." *Global News*, May 19, 2018.

Paret, Marcel, and Shannon Gleeson. 2016. "Precarity and Agency Through a Migration Lens." *Citizenship Studies* 20 (3–4): 277–94.

Picard, Ken. 2013. "ACLU-VT Maps Vermont's Vast 'Surveillance State.'" *Seven Days*, September 17, 2013.

Plattsburgh Cares. 2021. *For Asylum Seekers Crossing into Canada*. Plattsburgh, NY: Plattsburgh Cares. https://plattsburghcares.org/wp-content/uploads/2018/04/newenglish6.pdf.

Polanyi, Karl. 2001. *The Great Transformation: The Political and Economic Origins of Our Time, 2nd Edition*. Boston: Beacon.

Roy, Nilanjana, and Amy Verdun. 2019. "Bangladeshi Migrants of Italy and Their Precarity." *Social Sciences*, 8 (123): 1–15.

Sacchetti, Maria, Abigal Hauslohner, and Danielle Paquette. 2020. "Trump Expands Long-Standing Immigration Ban to Include Six More Countries, Most in Africa." *Washington Post*, January 31, 2020.

Schierup, Carl-Ulrik, Aleksandra Alund, and Branka Likic-Brboric. 2014. "Migration, Precarization and the Democratic Deficit in Global Governance." *International Migration* 53 (3): 50–63.

Smith, Craig Damian. 2019. "Changing U.S. Policy and Safe-Third Country 'Loophole' Drive Irregular Migration to Canada." Migration Policy Institute, October 16, 2019. https://www.migrationpolicy.org/article/us-policy-safe-third-country-loophole-drive-irregular-migration-canada.

Smith, Craig Damian, and Stephanie Hofmann. 2019. "Will Canada Suspend Its Safe Third Country Agreement with the United States?" *Foreign Policy*, November 6, 2019.

Stahl, Rune. 2019. "Ruling the Interregnum: Politics and Ideology in Nonhegemonic Times." *Politics and Society*, May 2019.

Tharoor, Ishaan. 2020. "Trump Scapegoats Almost a Quarter of Africa's Population." *Washington Post*, February 4, 2020.

True, Margaret. 2017. "ICE Detains Two More Migrant Justice Activists." *VTDigger*, March 17, 2017. https://vtdigger.org/2017/03/17/ice-detains-two-migrant-justice-activists/.

Tsianos, Vassilios. 2007. "Imperceptible Politics: Rethinking Radical Politics of Migration and Precarity Today." PhD diss., University of Hamburg.

Walters, William. 2006. "Border/Control." *European Journal of Social Theory* 9 (2): 187–203.

Wise, Raul Delgado. 2018. "Is There a Space for Counterhegemonic Participation? Civil Society in the Global Governance of Migration." *Globalizations* 15 (6): 746–61.

Wu, Grace, Johanna Reynolds, and Julie Young. 2020. "Refugee Stories Reveal Anxieties About the Canada-U.S. Border." *Conversation*, January 20, 2020.

4 Resisting Dehumanization Through Resettlement Based on Full Refugee Experiences

Fariborz Birjandian

In 1987, when I fled Iran as a refugee, there were 12.5 million displaced people in the world. In 2021, close to 90 million people around the globe have been forced to leave everything behind to seek refuge from war, persecution, or violence.

As the number of displaced people continues to rise, most countries are working to prevent refugees from crossing their borders. Fortunately, countries that have committed to resettling refugees are continuously exploring new strategies for ensuring that these vulnerable populations receive the support they need to thrive in their new homes.

When I left Iran, I came to Canada and embarked on a lifelong career in the settlement field, focusing on the policies and practices that impact the experiences and the long-term settlement and integration outcomes of refugees.

Although 145 countries are signatories of the United Nations High Commissioner for Refugees (UNHCR) 1951 Convention and 1967 Protocol, only about 25 are committed and active in the resettlement of refugees. As one of the signees, Canada has a rich history of welcoming refugees and has invested significant resources into refugee resettlement. The government continuously engages policy-makers, academia, community leaders, and refugees themselves in the formulation of policies and practices to ensure refugees enrich the fabric of Canadian society by successfully integrating into schools, workplaces, and communities.

While these efforts have been commendable, I personally believe that to fully achieve this goal, governments, policy-makers, agencies, and frontline workers involved in the resettlement and integration of refugees in Canada need to better understand the full spectrum relating to refugee experiences. From this vantage point of the full spectrum, the issue is not only resisting dehumanization but finding—or in other cases, rediscovering—faith in humanity.

Through my own life story and through my thirty-three years of involvement with refugee work on a local, national, and international scale, I've come to recognize that the reasons why people become refugees are varied, and the forced migratory experiences of refugees differ greatly, but resettled refugees typically undergo a similar process. This process includes experiences of negative or threatening conditions in the refugee's home country that ultimately lead to their decision to escape, the initial departure, the waiting period in the country of asylum, and then the arrival in the new home and the beginning of the long journey toward resettlement and integration.

For many refugees, this process is a harrowing and transformative experience that has long-lasting emotional, psychological, and even spiritual impacts. Many refugees experience trauma in their countries of origin and during the migratory process; many live under the threat of danger for prolonged periods of time, fearing for the safety of themselves and their families; and all are forced to leave behind friends, family members, careers, and homes to come to a new country. Because of what they have witnessed and experienced, many refugees arrive in their new homes with little hope and diminished faith in humanity.

In this chapter, I'll break down these different stages of the experience many refugees undergo, providing examples from my own story. I'll then share how, I believe, a better understanding of this kind of refugee experience (and its psychological, emotional, and spiritual impacts) is instrumental to informing and improving policies and practices related to refugee resettlement in Canada and around the globe.

The Decision to Escape

Individuals and families are forced to flee their home countries for many reasons. In most cases, people are at risk of persecution for their religious beliefs, political affiliations, gender identities, or sexual orientations. This persecution can take the form of restrictions imposed by authorities (such as taking away an individual's access to education, employment, ownership, or the right to vote), or it can take more even perilous forms, including the threat of arrest, imprisonment, torture, and execution. When individuals are identified as undesirable by authorities, their friends and relatives often distance themselves to avoid being seen as guilty by association. For many individuals, this period of ostracization and abandonment is when they begin to lose their faith in other human beings. For most people, the decision to flee comes when their lives in their home countries have changed irreparably and conditions have become unbearable.

My family and I were members of the Baha'i faith, a minority group in Iran. When we refused to convert, we lost our rights as citizens, our employment, and our properties. We were forced to forfeit our passports and were no longer allowed to enroll our children in the school system. Like many others, we did everything possible to live within the restrictions imposed upon us, but ultimately, the pressure became intolerable, and we chose to take the risk of becoming refugees, opting for an uncertain future in an unknown country over the ongoing threat of persecution.

The Initial Departure

For many refugees, the initial departure from their homes marks a moment of rupture in their lives. Between the decision to flee and the initial departure, there is a period of fear and extreme uncertainty. There are decisions to be made about who to leave behind, how to cover the cost of an illegal departure, where to go, and who to rely on for help. There is also the threat of discovery and punishment at the hands of the authorities for attempting to leave.

In my own case, I knew I had to take my elderly mother, my wife, and our two sons, who were six and four years old at the time. We had to come up with the money to pay smugglers by selling whatever we could, and we had to identify a route and a destination. During this period, I was confronted with so many fearful questions: How will I get the money? How can I entrust the lives of my loved ones to traffickers? What will happen if we get caught? How can I keep this secret from my own children and from my other family members?

In order to make our escape, I had to find a smuggler through a friend. I met this stranger on the street for ten minutes, handed him an envelope filled with cash, and listened carefully to his instructions, trying to remember every detail. Telling my wife and mother about the plan and seeing the fear in their eyes was an experience that has never left me. We had no contact with the smuggler again. We followed his instructions to leave Tehran and go to Isfahan, and from there to Zahedan, a border city with Pakistan. This journey was more than two thousand kilometres by bus. Every few hundred kilometres, revolutionary guards would come on board and question every passenger, especially the children, about their purpose in travelling to a border city.

At every checkstop, we listened as the guards questioned our boys and hoped they would repeat the same story we had asked them to memorize. Any wrong answer or suspicious move could have easily led to our arrest. When we finally reached the border town of Zahedan, a stranger approached us and asked a question. I gave the answer provided earlier by the smuggler and then put the lives of my loved ones in the hands of a total stranger. For the next three weeks, we stayed in dark and shabby places, walked through the desert, endured the cold at night, and were passed off between different groups of traffickers until we reached our final destination of Lahore, Pakistan.

Although I was a highly trained naval officer who had commanded ships during the Iran-Iraq War, I had never before experienced the fear that I felt during this journey with my family. After thirty-three years, I still experience sleeplessness every October, as I remember and relive our flight from Iran.

For many refugees, the trauma of the migratory experience has a lasting impact on their mental health and, without proper intervention and support, can impede their ability to move forward with their new lives.

The Waiting Period in the Country of Asylum

The experience of waiting in the asylum country is different for every refugee. For many, the initial arrival brings a sense of joy at having escaped unharmed; however, I've also witnessed people losing loved ones on their journey, leaving elders behind, or being mistreated by traffickers. In these cases, the relief of arriving in the country of asylum is tempered by the traumatic experiences of the journey it took to get there.

During this waiting period, new fears and uncertainties also arise. Refugees must secure essentials such as food and shelter for themselves and their families. To do so, they often have to rely on the generosity of strangers or, on rare occasion, find temporary employment. In camps, refugees often meet other individuals and families who arrived before them and can see the emotional and physical toll the waiting has taken on them. In the asylum country, many refugees also witness abuse on the part of locals, police, and other authorities. Again, seeing this type of mistreatment and lack of compassion is transformative for many refugees and can forever change their trust and faith in other human beings.

I was fortunate during this stage of my journey. I had lived in Pakistan for two years as a naval officer, so I felt comfortable with the environment and had connections to rely on. We also had the Pakistani Baha'i community, which, although small, was welcoming and supportive. Because of my experience living in Pakistan and my ability to speak English, I managed to secure a job as a teacher in an educational institution, with the help of a refugee advocate in Lahore. Two months after my arrival, I was invited to work for a joint initiative between the UNHCR and a Baha'i refugee support group to help the 1,800 Iranian refugees living in the area. This was the best thing that could have happened for me and my family. I could direct my anger and fear into something positive and productive, and this experience marked the beginning of my lifelong career assisting and advocating for refugees.

My experience during this waiting period was rare and fortunate. While I had the opportunity to work and my family received a great deal of kindness and generosity from the locals, I observed thousands of Afghani and Iranian refugees in the refugee camps in Lahore whose realities were much harsher.

The Arrival in the New Country and the Resettlement and Integration Process

I was also fortunate because my family eventually left Lahore and came to Canada to begin our new lives. As mentioned, close to ninety million people around the world have been displaced from their homes, but only a fraction (approximately fifteen out of every ten thousand refugees) will have a chance to resettle in a new country.

Although the numbers are small, the impacts of resettlement are significant. Here in Canada, we have had the opportunity to witness first-hand the profound effects of resettlement on refugees, host communities, and Canadian society at large.

Before the border closures in response to the COVID-19 pandemic, Canada allocated 10 percent of its total annual immigration target of 350,000 to humanitarian purposes. This meant approximately twenty to thirty thousand refugees were welcomed to Canada each year. (Approximately eight thousand of these individuals were government-assisted refugees, ten to twelve thousand were privately sponsored refugees, and the remaining number were refugee claimants or asylum seekers.)

Canada also has an impressive track record of resettling large numbers of refugees in response to global crises. Canada, for instance, played an important role in welcoming and resettling Vietnamese, Lebanese, Sudanese, former Yugoslavian, Kosovar, and more recently, Syrian and Yazidi refugees.

Overall, Canada has been highly successful in its resettlement efforts, and I believe that refugees who are selected to come to Canada are among the most fortunate. The government has demonstrated a long-term commitment to and investment in refugee resettlement; as such, Canadian settlement agencies have acquired many years of experience and expertise when it comes to supporting refugees and are able to deliver a spectrum of services to help these individuals and families as they progress on their resettlement and integration journeys. These services begin with airport reception and temporary accommodations for refugees immediately upon their arrival and extend to orientation to Canadian culture and society, long-term language learning, employment training, and support with labour market integration.

In Canada, we also see more community support for refugees than in any other country. We see this on an individual level (with scores of Canadians waiting at airports to welcome Syrian refugees, for example, and many more seeking volunteer opportunities with local settlement agencies) as well as on an institutional level (with, for instance, schools welcoming refugee children and designing customized programs to support their integration and meet their learning needs). Increasingly, there are also programs to facilitate better knowledge of Indigenous peoples through welcome events and the sharing of information, such as about treaties.

Although first-generation refugees often struggle with the trauma of their experiences, most refugees in Canada show great resilience and go on to learn one of the official languages if they do not have it already, secure rewarding employment, and become active and vital contributors within their communities. In turn, most Canadians have gained an appreciation of the challenges that refugees have overcome and the wealth of experiences and diversity they bring to Canadian culture and society.

Although my wife and I had many advantages (including education, professional backgrounds, and experience working and living in other countries), our initial settlement in Calgary was not without its challenges. We still had to learn about and adapt to life in Canada and make every effort to uncover opportunities and build our social capital. My first job, two months after our arrival, was at a pizza shop. Although I later secured employment as a settlement counsellor with the Calgary Catholic Immigration Society (CCIS), I needed to balance both jobs, working fifteen hours a day for two years, to maintain a reasonable standard of living. Again, however, I consider myself to be a fortunate refugee.

As noted, I had the honor of serving recently arrived refugees as a settlement counsellor with CCIS. In this role, I saw first-hand the multiple barriers that many refugees face upon their arrival. Many come to Canada with little formal education, limited work experience, little to no official language skills, and few financial resources, and as mentioned, many are facing and processing a great deal of trauma. Through this work, however, I also saw that Canada's resettlement program is on the right track, and many refugees are able to become contributing members of society.

Understanding and Addressing the Full Refugee Experience

By sharing my own story, I have tried to show that generally when refugees arrive in their destination country, they are typically midway through a challenging and transformative experience. They have completed the unsettling journey from their old lives to their new homes and are about to embark on the long pathway toward resettlement and integration. At this middle point, many refugees are at their most vulnerable. They have left behind everything that was familiar and are facing an unknown future in a country and culture where everything is strange and new. Many have also witnessed or experienced traumatic events that may have shaken their beliefs and values, impacted their mental and emotional health, and left them feeling very alone.

To date, resettlement and integration policies and processes in Canada have largely focused on addressing the immediate and basic needs of refugees upon their arrival. To fully support and expedite the resettlement and integration of refugees, however, I believe that policy-makers, practitioners, and host communities need to take into account what refugees have lived through and the impacts of these experiences. To improve resettlement outcomes, international, national, and local efforts should provide refugees with the customized resources and support they need to variously overcome past traumas, establish a sense of belonging in their new communities, rebuild their faith in humanity, and find and foster new hope for the future.

My journey led me from fleeing Iran as a refugee to ultimately becoming the chief executive officer of CCIS, a leading settlement organization in Calgary, Alberta. In this role, I've become an advocate for the development of policies and practices that recognize and address the full spectrum of refugee experiences. Within my own organization, my staff and I continuously work to design and deliver programs and services that not only address the immediate and basic needs of recently arrived refugees but recognize and respond to the emotional and psychological challenges many may face at the critical midpoint of their refugee journeys.

A key element of CCIS's work is helping refugees acknowledge and process their traumatic experiences. In 2017, CCIS opened the Centre for Refugee Resilience (CRR). To date, the CRR is the only initiative in southern Alberta that has been designed to address the unique needs of refugees who have experienced violence, torture, and trauma. The CRR provides accessible, culturally sensitive services, including individual therapy for children and youth, individual therapy for adults, parent support, psycho-education workshops for individuals and their families, and social support groups. CRR case managers also bridge the gap between refugees and the mainstream health care system by assessing the specific needs of refugee clients, developing customized care plans, and working with local health service providers to ensure that refugees access available mental health support.

It is also important to note that refugees process their experiences differently depending on their age, among other factors. At CCIS, we provide customized interventions to support refugee children and youth as they cope with issues related to experiences of trauma, migration, resettlement, acculturation, socio-economic barriers, and isolation. Recognizing that the best mental health intervention for children is play, we offer summer camps, recreational activities, and art therapy workshops. Moving forward, I believe the ideal to support the resettlement and integration of refugees of all ages is to develop customized policies, programs, and practices that can address the causes, impacts, and manifestations of trauma in each unique individual.

While these individual interventions are essential, it is also important that we address refugee trauma on a larger scale. Policies and practices must work to ensure that public institutions and the broader community are aware, compassionate, and responsive to the mental health challenges that many refugees face upon their arrival, throughout their resettlement and integration, and even at different life junctures. Here at CCIS, we work in close partnership with school boards, the health care sector, and other service providers to ensure a collaborative approach to fostering the mental, physical, emotional, and social well-being of refugees; this includes sharing information on how to recognize trauma, how to create trauma-sensitive environments, and how to provide trauma-informed services and care.

This leads to another key element in the successful resettlement and integration of refugees, which is the involvement of the greater community. In 2015, at the outset of the Syrian refugee crisis, CCIS (in partnership with many other organizations) began actively mobilizing the community, including the public and private sectors, to prepare for the resettlement of over four thousand Syrian refugees in a very short period of time. To achieve this daunting task, CCIS (as the lead organization) established a community-wide approach wherein a steering committee (and subcommittees dedicated to housing, community, education, language support, employment, initial settlement, and the law) was developed to identify the needs of incoming refugees and the best practices for supporting their resettlement. This close partnership among the settlement sector, school boards, the health care sector, the private sector, and other service providers and community services helped create a collaborative and holistic approach to facilitating the successful integration of Syrian refugees into schools, workplaces, and the community at large.

More importantly, it signalled to Syrian refugees that the community was coming together to welcome and support them. As I have mentioned, upon their arrival, many refugees feel disheartened and alone. Because of their experiences in their countries and throughout the migratory process, many have lost faith in human kindness. Policies and practices that call upon the engagement of the community are therefore fundamental to ensuring that all refugees feel strengthened and supported by others and are able to move into their futures with renewed optimism and hope.

At CCIS, like many other resettlement agencies across Canada, we design and deliver programs and services that focus on this key element of fostering welcoming, supportive, and engaged communities. On this note, I would like to share one more unique initiative that CCIS has developed to foster a sense of belonging among newly arrived refugees. CCIS was formed in the late 1970s when a small group of church volunteers came together to support Vietnamese refugees arriving in Calgary. Since then, we have recognized the powerful impact that local volunteers can have on the lives of newcomers, and for close to forty years, we have offered a host program through which community volunteers have welcomed refugees into their lives and homes and provided them with practical guidance for daily life in Canada, community orientation, social and emotional support, access to social and community events, and opportunities to practice their English skills.

Recently, CCIS introduced an additional, innovative concept to connect refugees with their new communities and homes. The Land of Dreams farm is located on eight hectares of farmland just outside of Calgary, for which we've secured a multi-year lease. The farm provides farming plots to refugee families, matches them with local farming mentors who teach them regenerative farming practices, and connects them with the Indigenous community to learn about the history of the land. At the farm, refugees are able to spend time in nature with their hands in the soil while gaining a sense of belonging, building self-sustainability, and connecting with their new homes. Visiting the farm and seeing refugees and Alberta farmers sharing stories, watching children playing, and seeing people from such diverse backgrounds and experiences coming together to plant and grow something new has been very healing for me personally. It has also shown me the profound role that community plays in fostering resilience among refugees and restoring their hope for the future.

Conclusion

As you can see from my personal story and my work, I firmly believe that the only way to completely and successfully support the resettlement and integration of refugees is to understand and address refugee experiences through a fuller spectrum that includes resisting dehumanization as well as ways to find or rediscover faith in humanity. This means that policy-makers and practitioners must take into consideration not only the physical journey that refugees undertake but also the emotional, psychological, and spiritual impacts of this journey. It means that we have to develop client-centered policies that not only address refugees' immediate and basic needs but also help them overcome their traumatic experiences and move forward with hope and optimism. It also means that we need to pay far more attention to the initial intervention for all categories of refugees to ensure that we are not adding to or prolonging the suffering and traumas they have experienced. Finally, we must collectively remember that resettlement is not only the responsibility of governments, policy-makers, or service providers. In fact, the successful resettlement and integration of refugees is only possible when the community comes together to create conditions where all refugees can heal and thrive.

A Note on COVID-19

Since I first agreed to write this chapter and share my thoughts on the refugee experience, the world has been profoundly shaken by the COVID-19 pandemic. Inevitably, questions have been raised about the impacts of this crisis on the resettlement and integration of refugees and how to support this vulnerable population through these unprecedented times. I would therefore like to share how my organization responded to the pandemic and what COVID-19 meant in the context of refugee experiences.

Like settlement agencies around the world, the primary concern for CCIS throughout the pandemic was mitigating the impacts of COVID-19 on the newcomer population, especially those who are most vulnerable. As I mentioned earlier, newly arrived refugees are typically at a critical midpoint in their journeys. They have transitioned from their old lives and are facing an unknown future. During this stage, many refugees feel fearful, disconnected, and very alone. The COVID-19 pandemic has had significant repercussions for most recently arrived immigrants and refugees. Hiring freezes, layoffs, school and daycare closures, and restrictions on in-person services at financial institutions and government and registry offices, for example, have stalled and disrupted many newcomers' settlement and integration processes. But for those refugees who have limited supportive networks, who are coping with trauma, and who are trying to transition into their new lives, COVID-19 has posed a myriad of critical challenges.

At the outset of the pandemic, CCIS questioned how our refugee clients with significant cultural and linguistic barriers would access and understand up-to-date pandemic information and directives for protecting their health and safety. We were concerned about their ability to advocate for themselves in unsafe workplaces; access relevant resources, benefits, and services; and acquire food and medication. We also knew the devastating effects that quarantine procedures and social distancing would have on refugees who were already processing experiences of ostracization and feelings of loneliness and disconnection, as well as those whose traumatic experiences were rooted in imprisonment and isolation.

In response to these concerns, CCIS compiled a list of close to five hundred families that we considered to be at risk. In collaboration with other agencies and community partners, CCIS developed a detailed protocol and the Crisis Response Team to identify and address the needs of these families on a case-by-case basis, ensuring that they had access to vital information, resources, and culturally sensitive support. Through a centralized intake, the Crisis Response Team conducted individual assessments and created coordinated service plans to address newcomers' immediate needs through direct resources, community referrals, and logistical support in the areas of family violence, mental wellness, health, housing, and food security.

The COVID-19 pandemic has only underscored the extreme vulnerability that typifies refugee experiences and the stages of their refugee journeys. In countries where refugees are resettled, I believe that one of the most important achievements is unquestionably the work done to ensure that, despite social distancing and isolation measures, refugees maintain a sense of community and connection and know that they are not alone.

5 Conflating Migration, Terrorism, and Islam

Mediations of Syrian Refugees in Canadian Print Media Following the 2015 Paris Attacks

Nariya Khasanova

A Syrian refugee "crisis" galvanized the attention of Canadian print media, with coverage alternating between "victimhood" and "violence" (Mustafa and Pilus 2020; Xu 2021; Tyyskä et al. 2018; Wallace 2018) and grounded in "asylum seeking being not a right, but rather a gesture of Western generosity" (Xu 2021, 672).[1]

Wallace's extensive and nuanced analysis of the "crisis" demonstrates that the media's representation of Syrian refugees in Canada was sporadic (see also Lawlor and Tolley 2017) and that framing varies, being largely responsive to events and their socio-political contexts. The coverage of international events—such as the September 2015 publication of Alan Kurdi's photo, followed by the horrific terrorist attacks in Paris two months later (both of which coincided with Canada's federal election and thus became subjects of political debates)—provides a good example of how quickly "humanizing depictions of refugees" can be replaced with conflict-driven representations (Wallace 2018, 207, 222).

---

1 For a critical discussion of this "crisis," see De Cleen, Zienkowski, Smets, Dekie, and Vandevoordt (2017); Sigona (2018); and Zaborowski and Georgiou (2016), as cited in Smetz and Bozdag 2018.

The terrorist attacks in Paris on November 13 and 14, 2015, and the discovery of a Syrian passport at the crime scene sparked emotional reactions in Canada, including hate crimes targeting Muslims in Ontario and divisive political rhetoric about the upcoming resettlement of refugees. The attacks became a pivotal moment for the securitization of refugees (see Hammerstadt 2014) by the media and politicians reviving the long-problematized linkage among migration, crime, illegality, and terrorism (see Benson 2013; Caviedes 2015; Lecheler, Matthes, and Boomgaarden 2019; Lawlor and Tolley 2017, as cited in Galantino 2020). The mere possibility that asylum seekers could be infiltrated by terrorists brought forward the discussion that terrorism is rooted in one's religious beliefs as opposed to extremist ideologies. Analyzing Canadian media in the aftermath of the Paris attacks, Wallace finds that "religious framing was largely used in conjunction with the 'conflict frame'" (2018, 222). These results are congruent with the findings of Lawlor and Tolley's study on the media's framing of refugees, concluding that the backgrounds of refugees often get scrutinized in the coverage of "focusing events" with an element of conflict (2017, 985–86).

Two other Western studies focused on the coverage of Syrian refugees in Swedish and US contexts find that it is through the media's representation of religion—and Islam in particular—that refugees get either "othered" or included (Abdelhady and Fristedt Malmberg 2018; Nassar 2020).

A six-country study employing human-validated sentiment analysis reveals that the combination of three topics—asylum seeking, terrorism, and Islam—results in more fear and lower levels of compassion toward refugees. In contrast, the coverage of refugees in isolation from Islam and terrorism is characterized by the lowest levels of fear and the highest levels of compassion (Chan et al. 2020).

Thus, through this discursive linkage of three topics grounded in an inaccurate and misguided representation of Islam, Syrian refugees, the majority of whom are Muslims or perceived as Muslims (Nassar 2020), are "cast as suspected community" (Chan et al. 2020, 3571) and get "othered" (Kumar 2010) and "dehumanized" (see Esses, Medianu, and Lawson 2013 and this volume's introduction). Being instrumental in shaping the beliefs and attitudes of the public, the Western media's framing of Islam as a global menace rooted in Huntington's (1996) idea of the clash of civilizations is deeply problematic. Moreover, it is affecting the daily realities of millions of Muslims, including those in Canada. For example, Kazemipur notes that compared to average

Canadians, Muslim Canadians have a two times higher chance of experiencing discrimination due to their ethnicity and culture and a more than four times higher chance of being discriminated against on the basis of their religion (Kazemipur 2018, 273).

While all studies of the Canadian media's treatment of the Syrian refugee "crisis" currently available address religious framing as an important dimension (in particular, see Tyyskä et al. 2018; Economou 2019), a deeper and more extensive analysis of the media coverage of Syrian refugees in relation to Islam can offer further insights into the inability of Canadian print media to differentiate three topics: asylum seeking, terrorism, and Islam. This task has become the inspiration and focus of my study.

More specifically, I will examine the media coverage of Syrian refugees in relation to Islam during the week following the 2015 Paris attacks. I will look at two English-language newspapers in Canada with high circulation rates: the *Globe and Mail* and the *National Post*. My research will be divided into three main sections: (1) a literature review of the Western media coverage of Muslims and Islam, (2) a presentation of the methodology and analysis, and (3) concluding remarks on the media's use of combined discourse toward Syrian refugees in the Canadian context.

Literature Review

Multiple studies have examined the media coverage of Muslims and Islam in the West post-9/11 (Abu-Laban and Trimble 2006; Baker, Gabrielatos, and McEnery 2013; Falah and Nagel. 2005; Karim 2000; Kazemipur 2014, 82–86; McCafferty 2005; Sultan 2016; Jaspal and Cinnirella 2010; Poole 2016; Tsagarousianou 2016, as cited in Smetz and Bozdag 2018, 293). Muslims are often represented as a group perpetrating violence and terror, unwilling to integrate, and engaged in "war" against the West. These anti-Islamic media portrayals are rooted in an Orientalist discourse of Islam as Other and a threat to Western civilization. Such a narrative is rooted in the deeply problematic idea of Muslims as "monolithic, violent, and irrational barbarians" and Islam as "the antithesis of the Western liberal values developed over the last three hundred years" (Karim 2000, 11–12).

Analyzing the coverage of Islam in the Western media as early as 1981, Edward Said, the author of the post-colonial critique *Orientalism*, states in his book *Covering Islam*, "In no really significant way is there a direct correspondence between the 'Islam' in common Western usage and the enormously varied life that goes on within the world of Islam, with its more than 800,000,000 people, its millions of square miles of territory principally in Africa and Asia, its dozens of societies, states, histories, geographies, culture" (1981, x). Addressing the most common stereotype of "Muslims being Arabs and Arabs being Muslims," McCafferty states that "Arabs don't number more than 12 percent of the world's Muslims" (2005, 20). Rane, Ewart, and Martinkus affirm that nearly 60 percent of all Muslims live in the Asia-Pacific region (2014, 180).

Edward Said aptly notes, Western "Islam" rooted in the generalization of monolithic and dangerous "Islamic mindset" has entered the consciousness of the people in the West due to its connection to sensational issues like the Iranian hostage crisis, Afghanistan, and terrorism (1997). While there are certain instances of "responsible media coverage" presenting Muslims as a diverse rather than a homogenous group and emphasizing that they are peaceful citizens, the bigger picture suggests a rather negative representation (see Ahmed and Matthes 2017 for a meta-analysis). Muslims are frequently mentioned in the context of war and conflict. More often, Muslims are portrayed as oppressive, anti-intellectual, restrictive, extremely dangerous, fundamentalist, and alien to democratic values. They are frequently brought to the attention of the public as involved in corruption or crime, fanatical, and threatening to liberal values (Akbarzadeh and Smith 2005). Another context in which Muslims often appear is the media coverage of political elections, where they are presented as voters with very different priorities from non-Muslims (Abu-Laban and Trimble 2006, 41; Baker et al. 2013, 18–19).

Such coverage feeds into public fears, lower levels of trust toward Muslims, and anti-Muslim sentiments. The culmination of these fears can be attributed to the post-9/11 period, as noted in Ahmed and Matthes's (2017) meta-analysis focused on the media coverage of Muslims and Islam from 2000 to 2015.

Multiple media studies examining the coverage of Islam and Muslims in the Western media context highlight 9/11 as an important milestone that has contributed to the intensification of Islamophobic media framing (Abu-Laban and Trimble 2006; Baker, Gabrielatos, and McEnery 2013; Falah and Nagel 2005; Karim 2000; McCafferty 2005; Sultan 2016). Such media framing is largely centered on a very dangerous and false narrative of "Islamic terrorism." In this narrative, there is no place for terror committed by non-Muslims. Referring to Western interventionism (the United States has invaded fourteen Muslim countries since 1980) in the Middle East as indicative of terror, Sultan aptly notes that this kind of discourse of terror is barely present or very unpopular in the media (2016, 4, 5). Aligned with the position of Sultan, Moore addresses this discursive construction of hypocrisy: "When we kill civilians we shouldn't call it 'collateral damage.' When *they* kill civilians we call it terrorism. But we drop bombs on Iraq, and more than 6,000 Iraqi civilians are slaughtered. We then apologize for the 'spillover'" (2003, 124). Nevertheless, the dominant discourse on terror is still built around the ideas of inherently violent Islam and Muslim/Islamic extremism. With the media painting Muslims as violent extremists committing suicidal acts "in the name of Allah," not surprisingly, the blame for all terrorist attacks immediately falls on Muslims, even if there is no evidence suggesting their involvement (Karim 2000, 79).

Another deeply problematic generalization widely present in the Western media coverage of Muslims is that Islam is inherently anti-Jewish.[2] As Karim (2000) notes in his book *Islamic Peril: Media and Global Violence*, this narrative of Muslims posing a threat to Jews helps divert attention from northern Christians' guilt for the Holocaust. He further brings the example of how when covering the Israeli-Palestinian conflict, the media compared Saddam Hussein with Hitler and Iraqi missiles holding poisonous gas with Nazi gas chambers. As Karim aptly notes, this coverage not only creates a false dichotomous relationship between Muslims and Jews but also perpetuates the idea of terrorist crimes against Jewish people being always committed by Muslims (110–12). Thus, the media's representation of Muslims is driven by three key narratives, including Islam as Other and versus the West, Islam as antisemitic, and Islamic/Muslim terrorism.

---

2 Such a generalization is often tied to the medieval times of Islamic rule. In accordance with the dominant academic and media discourse, this was a time when Jews were persecuted by Muslims. However, certain studies suggest that only one side of the story (Muslims victimized Jews and restricted them from practicing their religion) has been brought to the fore. The alternative viewpoint expressed in other scholarly works based on the translations of texts from medieval Jewish communities ("There was little compulsion upon Christians and Jews to convert"; "When the known facts are weighted, it can be revealed that the position of the non-Muslims under Arab/Islam was far better than that of Jewish in the Medieval Christian Europe") has been largely disregarded (Karim 2000, 107–10).

Methodology

My chapter examines coverage by the *Globe and Mail* and the *National Post* of Syrian refugees in relation to Islam during the week following the 2015 Paris attacks. Drawing my methodological approach from the studies of Akbarzadeh and Smith (2005) and Abu-Laban and Trimble (2006), my analysis is guided by the following research questions:

1. What portrayals of Syrian refugees in relation to Islam are most frequently propagated in the *Globe and Mail* and the *National Post*?
2. Are certain representations recurrent?
3. How does the media use the discursive opportunity to connect migration, terrorism, and Islam?
4. Does the media's use of combined discourse contribute to the "othering" and dehumanization or inclusion and rehumanization of refugees?

To complete my research task, I searched for articles mentioning "Syrian refugees" and "Muslims or Islam or Mosque." I limited my search to the period of November 13 to November 20, 2015 (a week after the series of Paris attacks). Besides constituting a pivotal moment for the securitization of refugees in Canada, these horrific terrorist attacks in France coincided with the Liberal plan to resettle twenty-five thousand Syrian refugees and the hate crime targeting Muslims when a mosque was set on fire in Peterborough on November 14, 2015.

The *Globe and Mail* and the *National Post* have been chosen for my analysis as two English-language newspapers in Canada with high circulation rates. To complete this analysis, I used Factiva, the database that provides full-text access to major Canadian newspapers, and entered the following search string: "Syrian refugees and (Muslims or Islam or Mosque)."

Analysis

My search yielded fifty-one entries that resulted in seventeen news articles after excluding duplicates and commentaries.

The co-occurrence of events—the horrific terrorist attacks in Paris and the upcoming arrival of Syrian refugees—provided the media with a discursive opportunity to link migration, terrorism, and Islam. The majority of the articles (fourteen) do reinforce this problematic linkage, and no article provides a voice to those most impacted by the discussion—refugees themselves. The act of vandalism that occurred in Canada the day after the Paris attacks when the mosque in Peterborough was set on fire received significantly less attention from both newspapers: only three articles within the period of November 13 to November 20, 2015, covered this egregious hate crime. The narratives surrounding this event will be explored further in my analysis too.

There is an obvious difference in how journalists from both newspapers present information. More specifically, it would not be an exaggeration to say that the *National Post*'s coverage of events in Paris is largely opinionated and clearly grounded in Orientalist discourse, whereas that of the *Globe and Mail* is mostly factual and based on statements from officials and politicians, as demonstrated in the examples below:

> Roosevelt's advice was followed until Obama determined that appeasement was a useful antidote to past American wrongdoing against Iran, Cuba, and the Palestinians, and very tentatively, at least certain varieties of Muslim terrorists. [. . .] The Syrian refugees, especially the very large proportion of them who are Christians, are unlikely to be jihadists. (Conrad Black, *National Post*, November 17, 2015)

> So it is somewhat worrying to see that Prime Minister Justin Trudeau's government continues to insist it will resettle 25,000 Syrian refugees by the end of the year, damn the torpedoes—and how many bien-pensant Canadians are absolutely certain this presents no risk whatsoever. (Chris Selley, *National Post*, November 18, 2015)

> Friday's bloody attacks in Paris have stirred concern among some Canadian politicians about the prime minister's pledge to welcome 25,000 Syrian refugees by the end of the year—with Saskatchewan's premier demanding the plan to be suspended to ensure Canadians aren't threatened by "malevolent" terrorists. (Mark Kennedy, *National Post*, November 17, 2015)

> Dr. Hoskins, who is co-chair of an ad hoc cabinet committee on the refugees with Immigration Minister Michael Chan, said Wednesday he is expecting to hear within days the federal government's plan, which will detail how many refugees are expected to arrive, the timing of the arrivals [how many each day, for example] and at which points of

> entry in the country. [...] Meanwhile, RCMP Commissioner Paulson, whose agency will conduct database checks on all refugees, said that all necessary security work can be quickly accomplished. (Daniel Leblanc and Jane Taber, *Globe and Mail*, November 19, 2015)

> In a letter to Mr. Trudeau Monday, Mr. Wall wrote that he is "concerned" that swiftly bringing large numbers of asylum seekers into the country "could severely undermine the refugee screening process." "The recent attacks in Paris are a grim reminder of the death and destruction even a small number of malevolent individuals can inflict upon a peaceful country and its citizens," he wrote. "Surely, we do not want to be date-driven or numbers-driven in an endeavour that may affect the safety of our citizens and the security of our country." (Andrian Morrow, Ingrid Peritz, and Steven Chase, *Globe and Mail*, November 17, 2015)

However, as some of such statements are dehumanizing and fearmongering and since oftentimes authors do not make much effort to refute them and engage the reader in critical thinking, both agencies can be blamed for the securitization and othering of Syrian refugees, albeit to varying degrees.

The media's representation of Syrian refugees in relation to Islam is prompted by the rise of an alleged Islamic State and the discovery of a Syrian passport at the scene of the Paris crime. The indication that a new terrorist entity called the Islamic State of Iraq and the Levant (ISIL) has nothing in common with Islam through either renaming it to "alleged" or "Islamist" or pointing otherwise is critical in shaping the opinions of those with a limited understanding of Islamic religion and history. Almost all the articles used the name as it is (see examples below), arguably giving legitimacy to this horrific group of "faux-religious sociopaths," as eloquently described by a journalist from the *National Post* in his article (Den Tandt 2015):

> Resettling Syrian refugees helps France and other countries in Europe and elsewhere cope with large numbers of displaced people, Ambassador Nicolas Chapuis said, and is part of the global struggle against the Islamic State. (Campbell Clark, *Globe and Mail*, November 18, 2015)

> The Paris attacks on Friday, for which the Islamic State claimed responsibility, left at least 129 people dead (Adrian Morrow, Ingrid Peritz, and Steven Chase, *Globe and Mail*, November 17, 2015)

> The English version of the audio statement released by the Islamic State of Iraq and Levant had terrorism experts wondering whether it had been voiced by someone who had learned the language in Canada or the northern United States. (Stewart Bell, *National Post*, November 16, 2015)

> Canada can't honestly claim, as Prime Minister Justin Trudeau did in his first statement the night of the attacks, to have offered France "all of our help and support" when his first order of business, even before formally taking office, was to announce that the six lousy jets which have been Canada's contribution to the US-led coalition, bombing Islamic State targets in Iraq and Syria, will be coming home. (Christie Blatchford, *National Post*, November 16, 2015)

Two authors—one from the *Globe and Mail* and another one from the *National Post*—abandoned this naming convention and began to call ISIL "so-called Islamic." The same could be noted about the discovery of a Syrian passport. The journalists were divided into those who chose to mention that the passport could have been fake, those who reported that one of the attackers had Syrian origin, and those who chose not to mention it whatsoever. The reporting of the Syrian passport by both newspapers is exemplified below:

> Reports that one Paris attacker carried a Syrian passport that was used by someone who landed in Greece fuelled concerns about potential Islamic State infiltrators, but French officials have suggested the passport might have been a forgery. (Campbell Clark, *Globe and Mail*, November 18, 2015)

> The promised resettlement of 25,000 Syrian refugees by Dec. 31 is being challenged by some provincial premiers, mayors and others after the discovery one of the Paris attackers entered Europe among the refugees carrying a fake Syrian passport. (Ian Macleod, *National Post*, November 18, 2015)

> Among the suspects in the bombings were two Palestinians and a Syrian. Police believe the attackers emerged from the Burj al-Barajneh refugee camp, where thousands of refugees from Syria's civil war now crowd in with generations of Palestinian refugees who fled here following the 1948 and 1967 Arab-Israeli wars. (Mark MacKinnon, *Globe and Mail*, November 14, 2015)

As can be noted from the text, the last statement is also entwined with the problematic narrative of "terrorists being produced in refugee camps":

> Assuming Canada resettles Syrian refugees holed up in Lebanese, Turkish and Jordanian camps, logic suggests there won't be scads of potential threats to weed out. But it would be foolhardy to be sanguine about it. (Chris Selley, *National Post*, November 18, 2015)

However, in my selection of articles, such a narrative was present only in two, and counter-narratives were provided at least once by both agencies in their reporting, with the *Globe and Mail* citing the former mayor of Calgary Naheed Nenshi:

> The mayor said Canada has a "tiny minority" of people who assume anyone who is a Muslim or an Arab "must be in cahoots with the terrorists that they are, in fact, actually fleeing from." He also questioned some of the terrorists-will-come logic being used in an attempt to thwart the Syrian refugee plan in this country. He said if he was organizing a plot to infiltrate Canada, he would consider the fact that terrorists were able to get people in France and Belgium to do horrible things inside their own countries. "If someone pulls out a French passport, they can be in Calgary in seven hours," the mayor said, "without checks of any kind. So why would I want to embed bad guys, put them on leaky boats where they could die, have them sit in a refugee camp possibly for 18 months, in the hopes they might end up in a country where they might want to do bad stuff? It's way easier to do bad stuff in other ways." (Gary Mason, *Globe and Mail*, November 19, 2015)

> For the truth is that conflating Islamic State of Iraq and the Levant terrorists with Syrian refugees does not bear scrutiny. It is belied by the fact that most of ISIL's victims are Muslim; that the refugees Canada seeks to rescue are already in camps administered by the United Nations High Commissioner for Refugees and have been for years; that the Paris terrorists held European Union passports, and thus could presumably have entered Canada simply by getting on a plane, had they wished to; and that the attacks in Canada last October were carried out by homegrown ISIL wannabes. (Michael Den Tandt, *National Post*, November 20, 2015)

It is through this conflation of migration, terrorism, and Islam that journalists discuss the necessity of "proper" and "thorough" screening of Syrian refugees. The division along ideological lines in this coverage is also clear.

The *Globe and Mail* is making every effort to ensure that "proper" screening of refugees is being considered, including Canada's selective policy of bringing in the most vulnerable, who bear fewer security risks. Most of the time, the journalists deliver these assurances by quoting official statements as opposed to providing their own opinion on the issue, as demonstrated in the following examples:

> Ontario Health Minister Eric Hoskins said Monday the province will stick to its commitment to bring in 10,000 Syrian refugees. He added that he trusts the federal government to do the proper security checks. Asked whether the Paris attacks changed the government's thinking on refugees, he said, "Not at all, and I don't think it changes the public's resolve, either." (Adrian Morrow, Ingrid Peritz, and Steven Chase, *Globe and Mail*, November 17, 2015)

> Mr. Goodale said that the first objective of the government's promise to take in 25,000 refugees is humanitarian, in order to "rescue people who are in terrible conditions and fleeing from the scourge that is [the Islamic State]," However, he added the government would meet its objective "without any diminution or reduction in our security work." The Public Safety Minister said federal officials would conduct database checks and biometrics tests to verify the ID of all refugees, in addition to submitting them to interviews. To do the task quickly, some officials from other agencies are being seconded to the operation, including border guards. The government will bring in many refugees who have been stuck in camps for years, Mr. Goodale added, giving a priority to those who are the most vulnerable and pose the least potential security risk. (Daniel Leblanc and Jane Taber, *Globe and Mail*, November 19, 2015)

> Public Safety Minister Ralph Goodale said the government was working across departments and with security services and other agencies to ensure the refugee screening process was "as thorough and competent and effective as possible. Can it be 100-per-cent foolproof? Well, nothing in life is 100 per cent," the minister said on CTV's Question Period. "But we're satisfied that the process is strong and robust." (Bill Curry, *Globe and Mail*, November 16, 2015)

Mr. Goodale said this country is better situated than Europe to carefully select those to allow entry. "We have the advantage of being able to plan the process, which we are trying to do. Whereas they [Europeans] were dealing with spontaneous, ad-hoc, unexpected chaos." (Adrian Morrow, Ingrid Peritz, and Steven Chase, *Globe and Mail*, November 17, 2015)

In its turn, the *National Post* is engaged in fearmongering tactics such as suggesting the possibility of these attacks in Canada, the perpetrators of violence having Canadian connections, and serious security risks in connection with Trudeau's decision to settle twenty-five thousand Syrian refugees. See the following examples:

Of course in every Western country more people die in car accidents. Calm and perspective are essential. But Canada's enviable position is nothing to take for granted. So it is somewhat worrying to see that Prime Minister Justin Trudeau's government continues to insist it will resettle 25,000 Syrian refugees by the end of the year, damn the torpedoes—and how many bien-pensant Canadians are absolutely certain this presents no risk whatsoever. Since Friday, a meme has made rounds on social media that of the hundreds of thousands of Muslim refugees resettled in the United States since 2001, none has faced terrorism charges. In fact, an Uzbek refugee was convicted of terrorism conspiracy charges in Idaho in August; in 2013 two Iraqi refugees pleaded guilty to trying to send money to al-Qaida; and the Boston Marathon bomber bombers are only not refugees on a procedural technicality. It's still a vanishingly low hit rate. But it doesn't take many baddies to do a lot of harm. (Chris Selley, *National Post*, November 18, 2015)

They've also been reviewing CSIS "target sets" of potential and suspected Islamic extremists in Canada, looking at their recent activities and trying to identify which individuals might be seriously thinking of violence, or those who associate with such people. A recalibration could produce new priorities on whom to watch most closely. (Ian Macleod, *National Post*, November 18, 2015)

But as Trudeau fights accusations his reaction to the Paris attacks is unserious, his government's continuing insistence on a wholly artificial deadline for resettling 25,000 refugees is a pointless and genuinely worrying fly in the ointment. Last week, Public Safety Minister Ralph Goodale even suggested some screening of refugees could be completed on Canadian soil, which is madness. Any Syrian citizen who lands on Canadian soil is here until Syria is safe to deport him to, and nobody seems to have a plan to make that so. (Chris Selley, *National Post*, November 18, 2015)

As can be seen from the previous analysis, combining three discourses is very prominent in the efforts of journalists from both newspapers to make their case either for allowing Syrian refugees or for barring "these people," "large numbers of displaced people," "malevolent terrorists," "ostensible refugees," and "desperate refugees." Here, the "masses" and "arrivals" are not provided a single chance to speak for themselves. Related to this security framing are very problematic narratives of Islam as Other and versus the West and Islam as antisemitic, propagated in the coverage of the *National Post*. Such representation is exemplified in problematic and divisive statements such as the following:

> A substantial part of the fundamental texts of Islam is violently hostile to non-Muslims, and to many categories of pallid Muslims also. ISIL is Islamic terrorism, and has no mitigating qualities. It is both evil and incapable and undesiring of coexistence with the West and its values, Judeo-Christian in origin, but of equal application to religious skeptics. (Conrad Black, *National Post*, November 17, 2015)

> Still, Paris invites many comfortable urban Westerners, certainly Canadians, to contemplate a whole new brand of unease. Terrorist logic can be perversely comforting, and we may yet learn of some in respect to Friday's attacks. Le Bataclan concert hall had received threats in the past on account of its longtime Jewish and pro-Israel owners. (Chris Selley, *National Post*, November 18, 2015)

> Maybe there's something there that Canadian officials can use in screening prospective refugees: How do you feel about Israel? How would you like to live among Jews? Ever chanted mort aux juifs? (Christie Blatchford, *National Post*, November 16, 2015)

One instance of using the Shia-Sunni divide as a pre-context for terrorism by a journalist of the *Globe and Mail* must also be noted. Although the author attempts to separate terrorism from Islam by using "so-called" in relation to ISIL, in the same sentence, he reinforces this linkage by suggesting that terrorism was inspired by the division along sectarian lines:

> In the immediate aftermath of Thursday's attack, Hezbollah issued a statement declaring itself enmeshed in a "long war" against the so-called Islamic State, the most extreme of an array of Sunni Muslim groups fighting Mr. al-Assad's regime, which is dominated by followers of an offshoot of Shia Islam. (Mark MacKinnon, *Globe and Mail*, November 14, 2015)

The unprecedented hate crime targeting Muslims immediately following the Paris attacks resulted in only three articles within the period of November 13 to November 20, 2015. Whereas both newspaper agencies condemned this act of violence and called Canadians to stand as one, the statements present in the coverage of two journalists deserve special attention. Their articles use the linkage of migration, Islam, and terrorism to de-securitize refugees and dismantle deeply ingrained stereotypes advanced by the media:

> And amid all this, a sizable portion of the West's Muslim minority was once more issued a set of reminders. When Republican presidential candidate Ted Cruz proposed accepting only Christian refugees from Syria because Christians do not commit acts of terrorism, it was a reminder. When an arsonist torched the only mosque in Peterborough, Ont., this weekend in a suspected hate crime, it was a reminder. The reminder is this: You do not belong here. You will never belong here. [. . .] The most existential threat to the Islamic State's aspirations is what the terror group calls the "Grey Zone." Within this zone reside all those who don't fit into the narrative of a polar world, eternally at war. Within this zone resides the author of this article, a Muslim man, Middle Eastern by birth, Canadian by citizenship and cultural inclination. Within this zone reside the members of the St. John's Anglican Church in Peterborough, who started a collection to help the city's torched mosque rebuild. (Omar El Akkad, *Globe and Mail*, November 17, 2015)

Naheed Nenshi can often speak eloquently about the pluralistic wonder he considers Canada. But as one of the most high-profile Muslim figures in the country, the Calgary mayor admits he has been "shaken" by the closed-minded, even racist nature of some of the debate over the Syrian refugee crisis. Anti-Muslim hate crimes since the terrorist attacks in Paris and Beirut have only added to the mayor's burden. And while he says he is not concerned about his personal safety amid the current backlash, he believes Canadians need to stand as one against the reprehensible conduct of a few. (Gary Mason, *Globe and Mail*, November 19, 2015)

Conclusion

Both newspapers engaged in perpetuating a combined discourse linking migration, terrorism, and Islam. Resorting to the narratives of Islamic terrorism, Islam as antisemitic, and Islam as Other and versus the West, Canadian print media reinforces the idea that migration poses threats to the host population.

Despite the positive intentions of some authors, mostly from the *Globe and Mail*, to challenge the sensational coverage of the Paris attacks, many of them seem to have failed to disconnect three topics supporting the "proper screening" discourse advanced by the politicians at that time. Congruent with the findings in previous studies, an extremely diverse and resilient group of people—with accomplishments, dreams, and ambitions for their future lives—is presented as either "dangerous" or "vulnerable" and turned into objects with no agency. Such representation contributes to the creation of in-group/outgroup boundaries and unsettled refugee identities, both imagined (as "others," unwilling and failing to adapt) and real (as subject to racial profiling, social exclusion, and discrimination).

However, separate instances of more responsible media coverage reflecting on the attackers having European nationality and on the unprecedented hate crime directed toward Canadian Muslims demonstrate that the same link of migration, terrorism, and Islam can be skillfully used to rehumanize refugees. Thus, the same combined discourse has a large potential to balance the discussion. Yet the media rarely uses this opportunity. A few thought-provoking contributions prompting readers to engage in more informed and critical thinking often get lost in the bigger picture, where boundaries between Muslim, Arab, Syrian, Islamist, extremist, and terrorist are blurred (Abu-Laban 2013, 2017).

References

Abdelhady, Dalia, and Gina Fristedt Malmberg. 2018. "Swedish Media Representation of the Refugee Crisis: Islam, Conflict and Self-Reflection." *Currents of Encounter* 58 (October): 107–36.

Abu-Laban, Yasmeen. 2013. "On the Borderlines of Human and Citizen: The Liminal State of Arab Canadians." Chap. 4 in *Targeted Transnationals: The State, the Media and Arab Canadians*, edited by Bassam Momani and Jenna Hennebry. Vancouver: University of British Columbia Press.

Abu-Laban, Yasmeen. 2017. "Building a New Citizenship Regime? Immigration and Multiculturalism in Canada." Chap. 14 in *Citizenship in Transnational Perspective: Australia, Canada and New Zealand*, edited by Jatinder Mann. London: Palgrave Macmillan.

Abu-Laban, Yasmeen, and Linda Trimble. 2006. "Print Media Coverage of Muslim Canadians During Recent Federal Elections." *Electoral Insight*, December 2006, 35–42. https://era.library.ualberta.ca/items/0d031ad2-e948-4643-8531-de4c14bbcb63/view/8f022c44-1bcb-4539-9775-8b1550acaf45/Insight_2006_12_e.pdf.

Ahmed, Saifuddin, and Jörg Matthes. 2017. "Media Representation of Muslims and Islam from 2000 to 2015: A Meta-Analysis." *International Communication Gazette* 79 (3): 219–44. https://doi.org/10.1177/1748048516656305.

Akbarzadeh, Shahram, and Bianca Smith. 2005. "The Representation of Islam and Muslims in the Media: (The Age and Herald Sun Newspapers)." School of Political and Social Inquiry, Monash University. https://www.academia.edu/8645594/The_Representation_of_Islam_and_Muslims_in_the_Media.

Baker, Paul, Costas Gabrielatos, and Tony McEnery. 2013. *The Representation of Islam in the British Press*. Cambridge: Cambridge University Press.

Benson, Rodney. 2013. *Shaping Immigration News: A French-American Comparison*. Communication, Society and Politics. Cambridge: Cambridge University Press.

Caviedes A.2015. "An Emerging 'European' News Portrayal of Immigration?" *Journal of Ethnic and Migration Studies* 41(6): 897–917.

Chan, Chung-Hong, Hartmut Wessler, Eike Mark Rinke, Kasper Welbers, Wouter Van Atteveldt, and Scott Althaus. 2020. "How Combining Terrorism, Muslim, and Refugee Topics Drives Emotional Tone in Online News: A Six-Country Cross-Cultural Sentiment Analysis." *International Journal of Communication*, June 2020, 3569–94. https://ijoc.org/index.php/ijoc/article/view/13247/3142.

Economou, Melina A. 2019. "Migration, Alterity and Discrimination: Media Discourse and Its Implications for Health Outcomes in Syrian Newcomers to Canada." Master's thesis, University of California, San Diego. https://escholarship.org/uc/item/8gk4812r.

Esses, Victoria M., Stelian Medianu, and Andrea S. Lawson. 2013. "Uncertainty, Threat, and the Role of the Media in Promoting the Dehumanization of Immigrants and Refugees." *Journal of Social Issues* 69 (3): 518–36. https://doi.org/10.1111/josi.12027.

Falah, Ghazi-Walid, and Caroline Rose Nagel. 2005. *Geographies of Muslim Women: Gender, Religion, and Space*. New York: Guilford Press.

Galantino, M. G. 2020. "The Migration–Terrorism Nexus: An Analysis of German and Italian Press Coverage of the 'Refugee Crisis.'" *European Journal of Criminology* 19 (2): 259–81. https://doi.org/10.1177/1477370819896213.

Hammerstadt, Anne. 2014. "The Securitization of Forced Migration." Chapter 21 in *The Oxford Handbook of Refugee and Forced Migration Studies*, edited by Elena Fiddian Qasmiyeh, Gil Loescher, Katy Long, and Nando Sigona. Oxford: Oxford University Press.

Huntington, Samuel P. 1996. *The Clash of Civilizations and the Remaking of World Order*. New York: Simon & Schuster.

Jaspal, R., and M. Cinnirella. 2010. "Media Representations of British Muslims and Hybridised Threats to Identity." *Contemporary Islam*, 4(3), 289–310. https://doi.org/10.1007/s11562-010-0126-7.

Karim, Karim H. 2000. *Islamic Peril: Media and Global Violence*. Montréal: Black Rose Books.

Kazemipur, Abdolmohammad. 2014. *The Muslim Question in Canada: A Story of Segmented Integration*. Vancouver: University of British Columbia Press.

Kazemipur, Abdolmohammad. 2018. "Religion in Canadian Ethnic Landscape: The Muslim Factor." Chap. 13 in *Immigration, Racial, and Ethnic Studies in 150 Years of Canada: Retrospects and Prospects*, edited by Shibao Guo and Lloyd Wong. Boston: Brill Sense.

Kumar, Deepa. 2010. "Framing Islam: The Resurgence of Orientalism During the Bush II Era." *Journal of Communication Inquiry* 34 (3): 254–77. https://doi.org/10.1177/0196859910363174.

Lawlor, Andrea, and Erin Tolley. 2017. "Deciding Who's Legitimate: News Media Framing of Immigrants and Refugees." *International Journal of Communication*, February 2017, 967–91. https://ijoc.org/index.php/ijoc/article/view/6273/1946.

Lecheler, Sophie, Jörg Matthes, and Hajo Boomgaarden. 2019. "Setting the Agenda for Research on Media and Migration: State-of-the-Art and Directions for Future Research." *Mass Communication & Society* 22 (6): 691–707. https://doi.org/10.1080/15205436.2019.1688059.

McCafferty, Heather. 2005. "The Representation of Muslim Women in American Print Media: The Case Study of the *New York Times*." Master's diss., Institute of Islamic Studies, McGill University. https://www.collectionscanada.gc.ca/obj/thesescanada/vol2/002/MR24894.PDF?is_thesis=1&oclc_number=435871168.

Moore, Michael. 2003. *Dude, Where Is My Country?* New York: Warner Books.
Mustafa, Manar, and Zacharia Pilus. 2020. "#Welcomerefugees: A Critical Discourse Analysis of the Refugee Resettlement Initiative in Canadian News." *GEMA Online Journal of Language Studies* 20 (4): 30–54. https://ejournal.ukm.my/gema/article/view/39958/11424.
Nassar, Rita. 2020. "Framing Refugees: The Impact of Religious Frames on U.S. Partisans and Consumers of Cable News Media." *Political Communication* 37 (5): 593–611. https://doi.org/10.1080/10584609.2020.1723753.
Poole, E. 2016. "The United Kingdom's Reporting of Islam and Muslims: Reviewing the Field." Chap. 2 in *Representations of Islam in the News: A Cross-Cultural Analysis*, edited by S. Mertens and H. de Smaele. Lanham: Lexington Books.
Rane, Halim, Jacqui Ewart, and John Martinkus. 2014. *Media Framing of the Muslim World: Conflicts, Crises and Contexts*. Basingstoke: Palgrave Macmillan.
Said, Edward W. 1981. *Covering Islam: How the Media and the Experts Determine How We See the Rest of the World*. New York: Pantheon Books.
Said, Edward W. 1997. *Covering Islam: How the Media and the Experts Determine How We See the Rest of the World*. Rev. ed. New York: Vintage Books.
Smetz, Kevin, and Cigdem Bozdag. 2018. "Editorial Introduction: Representations of Immigrants and Refugees: News Coverage, Public Opinion, and Media Literacy." *Communications* 43 (3): 293–99. https://doi.org/10.1515/commun-2018-0011.
Sultan, Khalid. 2016. "Linking Islam with Terrorism: A Review of the Media Framing Since 9/11." *Global Media Journal: Pakistan Edition* 9 (2): 1–10.
Tsagarousianou, R. 2016. "Muslims in Public and Media Discourse in Western Europe: The Reproduction of Aporia and Exclusion." Chap. 1 in *Representations of Islam in the News: A Cross-Cultural Analysis*, edited by S. Mertens and H. de Smaele. Lanham: Lexington Books.
Tyyskä, Vappu Blower Jenna, Deboer Samantha, Kawai Shunya, and Walcott Ashley. 2018. "Canadian Media Coverage of the Syrian Refugee Crisis: Representation, Response, and Resettlement." *Geopolitics, History, and International Relations* 10 (1): 148–66. http://dx.doi.org/10.22381/GHIR10120187.
Wallace, Rebecca. 2018. "Contextualizing the Crisis: The Framing of Syrian Refugees in Canadian Print Media." *Canadian Journal of Political Science* 51 (2): 207–31. https://doi.org/10.1017/S0008423917001482.
Xu, Man. 2021. "Constructing the Refugee: Comparison Between Newspaper Coverage of the Syrian Refugee Crisis in Canada and the UK." *Current Sociology* 69 (5): 660–81. https://doi.org/10.1177/0011392120946387.

Appendix: Newspaper Articles Resulting from Search

Bell, Stewart. 2015. "Voice on Terror Tape May Have Canadian Accent; Expert Opinion; Voice Sounds 'North American,' Says Professor." *National Post*, November 16, 2015, A4.

Black, Conrad. 2015. "'You Will Never Take Our Liberty'; France Must Lead ISIL Offensive." *National Post*, November 17, 2015, A1.

Blatchford, Christie. 2015. "We Have Much to Learn from Israel." *National Post*, November 16, 2015, A12.

Clark, Campbell. 2015a. "France's Ambassador to Canada Decries Backlash Against Syrian Asylum Seekers." *Globe and Mail*, November 18, 2015, A4.

Clark, Campbell. 2015b. "French Violence Makes Path Darker, More Tangled for the Rookie PM." *Globe and Mail*, November 16, 2015, A4.

Curry, Bill. 2015a. "Canada Stands with France, Trudeau Asserts." *Globe and Mail*, November 14, 2015, A13.

Curry, Bill. 2015b. "City of Light Mourns as Leaders Deliberate." *Globe and Mail*, November 16, 2015, A1.

Den Tandt, Michael. 2015. "Refugees an Opening for the Tories." *National Post*, November 20, 2015, A8.

El Akkad, Omar. 2015. "Anti-refugee Backlash Fuels Radicalization." *Globe and Mail*, November 17, 2015, A14.

Kennedy, Mark. 2015. "Wall Wants Refugee Plan Suspended; Terror Concerns." *National Post*, November 17, 2015, A4.

Leblanc, Daniel, and Jane Taber. 2015. "RCMP, CSIS Say Ottawa's Refugee Plan Is Feasible." *Globe and Mail*, November 19, 2015, A1.

MacKinnon, Mark. 2015. "Beirut Bombings Kindly Flames of Conflict." *Globe and Mail*, November 14, 2015, A6.

Macleod, Ian. 2015. "Go Slow on Changes to Anti-terror Law, Trudeau Warned." *National Post*, November 18, 2015, A8.

Mason, Gary. 2015. "As Racism Taints Debate, Nenshi Asks Canadians to Stand as One." *Globe and Mail*, November 19, 2015, A1.

Morrow, Adrian, Ingrid Peritz, and Steven Chase. 2015. "PM Faces Pressure at Home and Abroad." *Globe and Mail*, November 17, 2015, A1.

Selley, Chris. 2015. "Why Such Haste on Syrian Refugees?" *National Post*, November 18, 2015, A6.

Warnicka, Richard. 2015. "Neighbours Reach Out After Mosque Torched; Shock and Shame." *National Post*, November 17, 2015, A7.

Part II
The Role of Educational Institutions and Programs in the (De)humanization of Refugees

Part II

6 A New School and New Life
Understanding the Experiences of Yazidi Families with Children

Pallabi Bhattacharyya, Labe Songose, and Lori Wilkinson

While the trauma associated with the frightening events that precede refugees' resettlement is well researched, the trauma associated with the act of relocating to transition countries and the subsequent process of resettlement is still in need of further research. This chapter examines the experience of trauma in its entirety—from the pre-arrival, during the journey, and after the resettlement phases—addressing integration and resettlement using a trauma-informed lens. It addresses the question of how the health of the family influences the integration of Yazidi children and youth into Canadian schools. We were privileged to interview several Yazidi refugee families just shortly after their arrival in Canada. Some of these families continued to exhibit significant trauma related to their captivity, but the most pressing issue was the unknown status of family members who had "disappeared," been kidnapped, or been killed. This chapter is organized as follows. First, we review existing research on trauma and refugees, paying particular attention to the gaps in knowledge of how trauma may affect integration. We then briefly describe the methodology before examining the post-arrival integration experiences of refugee women and their children. We end the chapter with recommendations that we hope are useful to settlement provider experts, educators, and academics who study trauma and refugees.

As a distinct ethnic group, the Yazidi have lived primarily in Iraq but also have sizable communities in Turkey, Syria, Armenia, and Georgia (Tesch

2023). While the attacks perpetrated by Daesh in Iraq in 2014 garnered the most significant global attention to this ethnic group, the Yazidi have long been targets of persecution and expulsion because of their religious beliefs. Their religion adopts elements from Islam, Christianity, and Zoroastrianism (Arakelova 2010), and because they prefer to live in isolation and do not adhere to the dominant religion of the countries in which they live, the Yazidi have been religiously persecuted for centuries. The most recent attacks by Daesh in 2014 were particularly brutish, involving mass murders of men and boys and the sexual enslavement of women and girls. Nearly all Yazidi women and nearly three-quarters of their children either experienced or witnessed violence, which makes them exceptional among refugees who do not "normally" experience or witness violence to this degree (Abbott 2016). Canada was one of several countries that agreed to provide immediate assistance, given the extreme conditions that the Yazidi faced. What made this group of refugees different from others coming to Canada was that most of the newly arrived Yazidi had been released from captivity just weeks prior to their arrival in the country. This is in direct contrast to the arrival conditions of other refugees who often spend seven to nine years and as much as forty years in refugee camps prior to their arrival in Canada (Devictor 2019). More information about the culture, language, religion, and history of the Yazidi is located in Wilkinson et al. (2019).

The most recent group of Yazidi refugees arrived in Canada. Refugees are forced to flee their countries of origin because of several factors, with most of them experiencing some level of pre-flight trauma. Refugees' exposure to pre-flight and intergenerational trauma has been identified as a significant cause of psychological distress, especially among women and children (Sullivan and Simonson 2016). Women and children have experiences that are drastically different from men, and these experiences have been well documented (Callister 2016; Schweitzer et al. 2018). Whether en route or in camps, in their home countries or after arriving in their host countries, many have experienced rape, imprisonment, torture, separation from loved ones, and murder, leading to high rates of trauma (Bartolomei, Eckert, and Pittaway 2013). While much is known about pre-arrival trauma among refugees, much less is known about how it affects their post-arrival resettlement and integration or how traumas experienced after their resettlement may affect their longer-term outcomes. Following is just one tragic story of one woman's journey and how serious trauma can happen after arrival.

On June 19, 2019, a Yazidi refugee woman living in Winnipeg was charged for operating her vehicle without her three children properly restrained by seat belts and booster seats (MacLean 2019). She was involved in a minor collision that resulted in the death of her five-year-old daughter. Her two other children were seriously injured, as they too were not adequately restrained. She was driving the family van with only a learner's license without a supervising driver and was not aware of the traffic rules or the child safety rules in Canada. This event forever changed her family and has greatly affected her successful resettlement in Canada.

The family unit has been identified by researchers as a key protective factor that helps the well-being of all children in dealing with their emotional difficulties (Kalmanowitz and Lloyd 2005; Shafai-Palmer 1997; Akthar 2017). Unfortunately, since many refugee children and youth lose family members prior to arriving in their host countries, they also lose some of the psychological support and family bonding that can help mitigate prior traumas. Research conducted by Timshel, Montgomery, and Dalgaard (2017) identifies parental separation as a cause of depression, post-traumatic stress disorder (PTSD), and the physical ill health of isolated families. Family separation and uncertainty around the health and well-being of missing family members contribute to mental health illnesses and stress and can affect successful resettlement. Among the Yazidi, this issue is particularly acute given the brutality that this group experienced prior to their arrival in Canada (Cetorelli et al. 2017).

Trauma and Resettlement: What Is the Relationship?

Much is known about how trauma affects refugees in the short term. Robertson and her colleagues (2006) report that women who have larger families and who do not understand English or French upon arrival are among the group that takes the longest to integrate into their new societies. Bjørneseth and her colleagues (2019) find that newly arrived refugee women exhibit more significant and plentiful signs of trauma than their male counterparts immediately after their arrival in Greece. Women who head families with children experience the most trauma. The trauma experienced by refugee parents can also affect their relationship with their children. Sangalang, Jager, and Harachi (2017) conducted a longitudinal study on the effects of maternal traumatic distress on family functioning and child mental health outcomes among Southeast Asian refugee women and their adolescent children in the United

States. Their findings suggest that refugee parents' trauma can adversely affect the mental health of children even if they were not direct subjects of traumatic events. Parents' mental disorders can affect their communication with their children during resettlement. Research by Wood and her colleagues (2020) finds that families experiencing traumatic events are significantly more likely to experience intimate partner violence later during their resettlement in Canada.

Migrating into a new environment can also cause trauma, especially when the new environment has a very different culture. Because they are at different life stages, refugee parents and their children adapt to the new culture differently (Westermeyer 1991). Children can learn faster than their parents, and this makes the "speed" at which integration occurs very different between them. The accelerated pace of the integration of children and teens can bring tension between refugee parents and children, as parents feel they are losing their parental authority and control, especially when they must depend on their children for interactions or interpretations with settlement agencies (Ahearn and Athey 1991). This can lead to parents using violent actions to reinstate authority over their children. Wood and her colleagues (2020) find that about 45 percent of Cambodian refugees in psychiatric clinics reported becoming angry with their children, mostly because of language barriers, which also sometimes hinder the resolution of any conflict. Another study conducted on thirty-six Arabic-speaking refugee families from Iraq finds that the children of traumatized refugee parents are less psychologically well-adjusted than their Danish peers, which may show a general impact of parental trauma on non-trauma-exposed children's psychosocial adjustment (Dalgaard et al. 2016).

Previous research in Canada on other groups of refugees who have experienced war, trauma, rape, and loss shows that these events have a lasting impact on the ability of many people to learn the language, mainly because these traumatic experiences affect their memories (Beiser and Hou 2000). Low levels of education before their arrival also make it more challenging to learn a new language. Watt and Lake (2004) find that adult learners with no formal schooling have the most difficulty gaining a second language. PTSD, C-PTSD, anxiety, and depression interfere with language learning and cause memory loss, which increases with age, making language learning more difficult. For instance, Emdad, Söndergaard, and Theorell (2005) find that those with PTSD scored significantly lower on memory tests than those without PTSD.

Evidence from several countries, including Canada, shows that those who experience depression and PTSD and who are functionally illiterate at arrival have lower language-learning outcomes and take long periods of time to gain a new language proficiency compared to someone who has a few years of prior education (Wilkinson et al. 2019).

Among the Yazidi women in northeastern Iraq, murder, torture, and sexual slavery are common occurrences (Porter 2018; Vijanann 2017). As a result, refugee women and girls who survive enslavement and genocide arrive in Canada with significant mental illnesses. Over 80 percent of them are diagnosed with poor mental health upon their initial arrival, and 65 percent of the Yazidi children and adolescents suffer from various psychological problems (Ibrahim et al. 2018; Yüksel et al. 2018; Hosseini and Seidi 2018; Abbott 2016). Early reports from settlement agencies in Canada reveal that the high rates of trauma the Yazidi have experienced make their resettlement and integration very difficult (Wilkinson et al. 2019).

Psychologists and other specialists who work with traumatized refugee populations have all observed that the level of trauma experienced by recently arrived refugees in Canada is significantly higher and more prominent than what they have seen among previously resettled refugee populations (Hoffman et al. 2018; Hodes 2019). Its effects are lifelong and damaging, and if left untreated, they might be passed along to the next generation (Bourque, van der Ven, and Malla 2011). It is not surprising, then, that the effect of refugee children's and youths' exposure to war and conflict on their psychological well-being is also common among the Yazidi. For instance, trauma and perceived social rejection are common among Yazidi women and girls who survived enslavement and genocide. It becomes difficult for such a group to integrate well in any host country because of the state of their mental health.

A study in 2017 on refugees arriving in Canada reflects some of the mental health conditions of parents with young children (Wilkinson and Ponka 2017). It notes how during resettlement, the burden of caring for traumatized family members and their children falls on those who have fewer mental health problems. Similarly, another study shows that taking sole responsibility for traumatized family members creates depression and delays the overall integration process among other members of the family (Bjørneseth, Smidt, and Stachowski 2019). Although it is a common belief that refugees have more physical and mental health issues given the precarious situations they face before entering the host societies, the "majority of mental health problems among the newcomer population occur after their arrival and because of the uncertainties in the settlement process" (Wilkinson and Ponka 2017, 90).

Methodology

The research for the present study was conducted among the recently resettled Yazidi refugee populations living in Calgary, Winnipeg, Toronto, and London, the four cities where the largest populations of Yazidi resettled in Canada. A more detailed description of the methodology can be found in Wilkinson et al. (2019).

The Yazidi have been largely excluded from formal education in the countries in which they live. According to the United Nations High Commissioner for Refugees (UNHCR 2019), only 65 percent of Yazidi refugees are currently attending school. A majority of the Yazidi have not had the opportunity to attend or complete school in Iraq (IRCC 2017; Oliphant 2018). Given that school in Iraq is conducted in Arabic, a language most Yazidi do not commonly speak, it is not surprising that language and education levels are low among this population (Wilkinson et al. 2019). It is for these reasons that the researchers, in consultation with an advisory team of experts, decided against a survey and in favour of a more in-depth semi-structured interview.

The research team devised a draft interview guide that included the following themes: employment, childcare, wayfinding, housing, language, and the use of settlement services. Overlapping all these themes are the overarching issues of mental health and trauma. No aspect of the resettlement journey can be understood unless viewed through a trauma lens. Trauma is interwoven into all aspects of the integration process, so our discussion of challenges in finding a job, caring for children, wayfinding, and language/interpretation must be understood with this central concept in mind.

The advisory committee contributed to the development of the list of themes, the interview guide, and the analysis. The study was financially sponsored by Immigration Refugees and Citizenship Canada–Prairie and Northern Territories Region (IRCC-PNT). IRCC-PNT was represented on the advisory committee and was joined by settlement organizations from across Canada and by members of the Yazidi community already living in Canada.[1]

---

[1] Funding for this project was received from Immigration Refugees and Citizenship Canada–Prairies and Northern Territories Region. Support from an advisory

Although we used an interview guide, the last part of the interviews consisted of discussion and topics as suggested by the participants. A question at the end allowed the Yazidi to add more information if they liked. We expected that some of the Yazidi might have wanted to share their experiences at this time. We were surprised when all the participants shared their stories of pre-arrival trauma unprompted. This gave the research team valuable information about how trauma affected their integration experiences and how this affected their families. The resulting final report (Wilkinson et al. 2019) has been used by the government and settlement organizations to reorganize existing practices and introduce new ones.

The information we collected was from parents or guardians. The Psychology/Sociology Research Ethics Board at the University of Manitoba reviewed the study recruitment and methodological protocols and granted permission for the team to conduct the study. All identified data was kept separate from the interview materials and kept on a password-protected, encrypted computer. We endeavoured to keep the identities of the Yazidi participants confidential, so there were places where we purposely did not provide certain demographic or geographic characteristics. We gave each participant a Yazidi name as a pseudonym.

All interviews were conducted in Kurmanji, the primary language spoken by the Yazidi. Given that most of the people we interviewed had been in Canada for six months or less and none knew English or French, our selection of Kurmanji as the language for the interviews was our only option. We were aware of the cultural and political sensitivities of the Yazidi community, so we were careful to hire an interpreter who was not involved with political organizations or did not have leadership aspirations in any of the four study centers. The research team was very fortunate to identify a settlement service worker who was Yazidi herself, was fluent in Kurmanji, and did not live in one of the four selected cities. This proved to be a wise decision, as our participants commented to us that they felt at ease speaking to her and would often refer to her as "teacher," a term of respect.

In March 2018, our Kurmanji-speaking interpreter visited all four cities and conducted thirty-six interviews, representing thirty-six distinct

---

committee composed of settlement service providers in the four study cities is also gratefully acknowledged. Aryan Ghasemiyani and Khosrow Hakimzadeh provided translation support.

family units. The families and participants were identified by the Refugee Assistance Program funded by settlement service providers in each city. We ensured that a settlement service organization worker was on site to provide additional assistance should the participant experience trauma. We are pleased to report that no participant had to end the interview, but we did offer additional settlement assistance, as most of the participants had questions about the settlement process.

The process of translating the interview questions was conducted by a different Kurmanji speaker than the interviewer. The first version of the interview guide was then back translated by a third Kurmanji-speaking individual not connected with the project. This allowed us to check the consistency of the first translation. The transcripts were created first in Kurmanji, then translated to English. We took a sample of recorded interviews and had a second Kurmanji speaker listen to them and conduct a back translation—to ensure that the transcriptions were correct. We were extremely lucky to locate three Kurmanji-speaking individuals who were able to do this valuable translating work. Given the small population of more established Kurmanji speakers and the very high need for their services in the settlement organizations at that time, it was difficult for us to locate good translators.

Before detailing the findings, it is important to note the marital status of some of our participants. When we asked the women if they were married, all indicated that they were. However, it was clear throughout the interviews that most of their partners were not in Canada. When we asked about this, most of the women who indicated they were "married" actually did not know the whereabouts of their partners. We did not want to "pry," but it became clear through the information they graciously shared with the team that their partners had "disappeared," having been presumably kidnapped by Daesh. Since the women had heard nothing about the health and well-being of their partners and could not presume that they were dead, they described themselves as "married," a condition that the research team could not question. As a result, most of the women indicating they were married were actually in Canada alone and were hoping they would hear positive news about their partners someday.

Findings

The consequence of refugee trauma on children after they have been resettled is a varied and intricate matter that involves several aspects of their lives. Refugee children can experience substantial psychological, emotional, and social impacts as a result of forced migration, exposure to violence, displacement from their homes, and the difficulties of adjusting to a new environment. The following section discusses some of the major findings from our study reflecting how trauma among refugee parents impacts the overall integration of their children within Canadian society. The integration process of Yazidi women was particularly challenging compared to other refugee groups as a result of a mix of factors, including inadequate education or lack thereof in Iraq, the severe trauma inflicted upon them by Daesh, and the uncertainty surrounding their partners and children left behind in Iraq.

Finding Employment: Mental Health and Trauma Challenges

The challenge of coping with one's own trauma, in addition to integrating into a new society, can be overwhelming for caregivers. As mentioned above, those without mental health problems are often charged with assisting multiple family members overcome their trauma and loss at the same time as guiding their family through the integration process. This has damaging effects on the integration experience of the family members who must undertake this additional burden.

Battal is a father of five living in Toronto. He told us about the effect the trauma inflicted upon his family members has had on his ability to participate in essential language classes and to seek employment:

> I am not able to take any classes, my wife is sick, I must take care of the children, and I am also responsible for her mother and her three kids. It's very hard for me to go to school; my wife has a mental illness and has episodes of blacking out, even the cooking I am doing alone. At this point, my focus is to get help for my family and make sure my wife's sickness is dealt with.
>
> Interviewer: Are you willing to work anytime soon?
>
> Yes, I would love to work, but like I said, I am responsible for the kids, my wife, and her mother and her three children. I am unable to leave

them for a moment. Otherwise sitting in the house for anyone is bad. It makes you depressed and sad, and basically, you don't even feel like a human being after a while. —Battal

Sadly, Battal's situation is far from unique. Single parents, especially single female-headed families, face more challenges during resettlement, as Dema told us in the next paragraph. They need assistance on many measures, largely coming from male members from within their localities, to help them navigate through different resettlement resources in Canada.

How Trauma Influences Care for Children

As a result of a lack of need-based support during the resettlement process, families undergo more stress because of their past and current situation. Dema, a married mother of four, shared with us how her mental state prevents her from caring for her children:

> I have mental problems. I am not even able to take my daughter to school. And no, I haven't gone to school. I don't even know how to write my name. I haven't taken any classes, and I am not able to go to school because of my depression. I pass out and am unable to use the public transportations. When I found my house, I never had an interpreter. How is it that I am not able to get someone? The schools are far from me. I am not even able to walk my child to school; it's far. There is nothing we can do about buying a vehicle. I have a sister who's eleven years old; they [Canada Child Benefit] haven't even released her funds yet. I have asked the agency to get me an interpreter for the doctor's appointment, as I am unable to talk over the phone, and I am unable to eat properly. I've been forced to buy my own medication. I am tired of life, my head hurts, and Daesh has stricken me in the head several times. I've been asking for X-rays; nobody seems to be listening to me. —Dema

Parents with high levels of trauma find it difficult to take care of the needs of their own children and depend on others for help. Parental trauma therefore affects the health of children post-resettlement. In speaking about the problems she experiences accessing health care for herself and her children, Amira, a widowed mother of three, told us the following:

> Interviewer: What happens if you have a problem with your health? Has anyone provided you with any information?

> Participant: I have a child with Down's syndrome, and my child needs help. I don't know how to obtain help for my child. And no one has provided me with any information. I am always buying diapers for my daughter with Down's syndrome. I buy diapers for her that cost me CAD 30–40. She is unable to let me know she needs to use the washroom, so she just wets herself. —Amira

Because they are engrossed with caring for all their family members, the efforts of the main caregivers to integrate are often left aside. They cannot attend English-language classes because of mental health issues, and they are often entirely dependent on other Yazidi members from their communities to help them navigate the system, at least until they speak English. This dependency is not only because of their trauma but also because of the unavailability of settlement workers who speak Kurmanji. At the beginning of the project, the few Kurmanji-speaking settlement workers who were available to work faced enormous pressure and workloads. As a result, it was practically impossible to expect them to provide one-on-one attention to these families even though there was a significant need for this service. This scarcity of settlement workers not only makes the parents suffer but also affects the well-being of the children within these families.

Lack of Translation/Interpretation Services: Impacts on Integration

The process of recovering from trauma thus has effects on both survivors and their families or caregivers. Trauma makes it difficult for survivors and their family members to perform simple day-to-day activities, such as travelling to medical appointments, attending parent-teacher meetings, translating, reading, and interpreting official letters, among many other day-to-day tasks. Adults without family in Canada often approach their neighbours, mostly belonging to the Yazidi community, for help. Sadly, many of the Yazidi in Canada are already struggling. Some lack a good grasp of the English language and have difficulty understanding important letters or verbal sources of resettlement information. In one incident reported by a participant, a mother received a medical letter in English and asked a neighbour to translate. The translation given to her was that her youngest child had cancer. This participant was so distraught that she showed the original letter to our Kurmanji-speaking interviewer during the interview that took place approximately eight weeks later. The letter had been misinterpreted. The child *did not have cancer*, and there was no medical follow-up necessary. The community member who translated the letter misinterpreted the information, which caused additional distress to the mother. When we inquired why she did not approach the settlement center for an official translation of the letter, she mentioned that the only Kurmanji-speaking settlement worker was busy with other clients, and she had to depend on her community members for all these day-to-day needs. At the end of the interview, we ensured that this incident was reported to the settlement service organization, and they are now providing this family with additional translation assistance.

Wayfinding may be difficult for many refugees, as most lack proficiency in English or French. Many single female-headed families require constant company for wayfinding as well as communicating with others. Manal, a married mother of six, talked about how living with trauma and her inability to navigate her new environment using English make it difficult to care for her traumatized daughter who needs urgent health care:

> I don't know anywhere. I am always sick. My daughter is always sick and passes out from the trauma she experienced while in captivity by Daesh [ISIS]. My experience in getting health care is not the problem. My problem is I don't know how to get to my appointments without help. My daughter is impacted the most by what happened in the camps and hasn't received any emotional or physiological help. I need someone to be able to direct me and tell me what to do. We need the right interpreter present. —Manal

When asked further about who would be "the right interpreter," Manal had a strong preference for a female. This opinion was shared widely by the participants. Many of the families only felt comfortable sharing their experiences with a female, especially given the sexually based torture they endured and the need for mental health assistance that required that some details be divulged.

The availability of interpreters was also a problem. There were very few qualified Kurmanji-English-speaking interpreters available at the time the Yazidi arrived in Canada. Furthermore, for those who have experienced trauma, learning a new language is much more difficult and overwhelming. And for the Yazidi who were largely deprived of formal education, learning a new language when they are functionally illiterate in their mother tongue is even more challenging. Despite being in Canada for eight months, Gesa, a married mother of five, mentioned how she schedules her appointments according to the availability of one of the community members who have assisted her and her family since their time of arrival. Gesa shared with us the difficulties that refugee parents encounter because they are unable to communicate with their children's schoolteachers and how she depends on Uncle Zohan (a local Yazidi leader who speaks English; his name has been changed to protect his and Gesa's anonymity) to help her:

> Yes, we do need Uncle Zohan's [name changed] help because my sister and her children are sick. We don't know many people here. Daesh beat my sister's older children; we had a complaint from the teacher because both would pee themselves because they are easily frightened by loud noises, like if someone becomes loud with them. When Uncle Zohan accompanied us to talk to the teachers, they said, "Sorry, we didn't know," but they suggested to put diapers on them, and that's sorted now, thank God. —Gesa

Not only is it difficult for women with high levels of trauma to take care of themselves, but they are also unable to fulfil their children's basic needs.

Families with both parents and children who have trauma may find it very difficult to navigate through the new system—mostly because of language barriers—and cannot negotiate their living situations. In this scenario, everyone in the Yazidi family requires constant help and attention. Single female-headed families with mothers and children all facing mental health issues are unable to take advantage of the different settlement resources provided during the resettlement process. Their judgment is clouded by their physical and mental health conditions, which makes their resettlement experiences negative. Saadia, a widow with four children, described her unhappiness after moving to Canada. For her family, their basement unit is a terrifying reminder of the conditions in which they were held captive under Daesh:

> We currently live in a two-bedroom basement apartment. No, I am not happy there. It's expensive; we pay CAD 1,500 a month for rent, then we pay for electric and heat and water separately. If we are able to find a better place for that price, we will definitely move. My oldest son's school is very far for him. Like I said, he's not feeling well; he takes six medications a day to maintain himself. He was in captivity for two years. I would only see him once a month for a few hours, and they would take him away from me again. —Saadia

She could not remember the names of any refugee assistance centers, nor did she know about the 911 emergency number, despite living in Canada for eight months. She told us that she was mentally, emotionally, and physically abused and was still waiting to see a mental health professional. She also explained that she could not get doctor's appointments for her son for follow-up visits, as she had no transportation and not enough English for her to navigate the bus. Our interviewer reported that Saadia needed to see a counsellor, as she mentioned how she could not sleep at night and got continuous flashbacks of her traumatic experiences back home. At the conclusion of the interview, we directed the onsite service provider to make arrangements for Saadia to receive additional care.

Like Saadia, there were a few other refugee women who mentioned the problem of delayed appointments with various medical professionals because of the lack of interpreter availability. This delay with medical treatments lengthens the overall integration process, as women having mental health issues are unable to learn the language and look for jobs within the host society while dealing with health considerations. Language learning, additional schooling, and jobs come later, as Amal, a widow with six children, told us:

> I need to take care of my health problems first. Yes, I would join English-language classes once my health issues are taken care of and I am not so emotional. Like I said, we have seen too much with our bare eyes; we have seen people die in front of us. It's all taking a toll on the mind. The health care is too slow. It takes forever for us to be seen. Yes, my sisters have. They speak Arabic. Our interpreter is Arabic, so they talk to my sisters, and they interpret for me. And nothing is done; they're too slow. —Amal

Trauma and Learning a New Language

Trauma makes it more difficult to learn new skills as well as keep that knowledge for long. As Gesa, whose husband has "disappeared," indicated, it is more difficult to learn a new language for those who have had traumatic experiences in the past:

> When I first arrived, things were very hard for me. I am sick still. Daesh caused injuries to my head, and honestly, I am unable to process the language as fast as I had hoped or wanted to, but I am going to specialists. Maybe they will do further tests to help me. —Gesa

Sometimes, the presence of small children prevents women from attending language classes, as Zheyan, a married mother of four children, told us:

> The agency notified us about EAL [English as an additional language], and they gave us a literacy test and put my name on a waiting list. They've notified my husband, but he hasn't been able to go to school either because of his poor health.
>
> I also asked Imran [name changed] why isn't my name coming up to go to school. He replied, saying, "Your children are very young. That's why." I do have problems with processing English because of all the hardships we went through back home. My memory isn't so good. I have depression and anxiety. I saw my brother die buried under the house they were building. I am not attending school now, as my children are very young. Since I have been in Canada, I only attended school for one month. I have not been going to school, as I have young children and I have to breastfeed. —Zheyan

Some Yazidi were able to attend language classes despite dealing with trauma. They reported to us that learning is very difficult when they are in distress, and this affects their ability to retain information taught in class. Manal, a mother of six whose husband was still under Daesh captivity, told us the following:

> Yes, I am going to English-language classes, but it's hard for me to concentrate. You are aware of all that has happened to us. I am still thinking about those who are still in captivity; my two daughters, my husband, and my brother are still in captivity. No matter how much we're told, nothing is able to be processed. My thoughts are always with them. I am at level 0 at school right now. —Manal

Separation from family or not knowing what has happened to family members who have "disappeared" makes it extremely difficult to learn a new language. Like Manal, Sajda struggled with learning English and adapting to a new homeland, knowing that her five children remained unsafe in Iraq:

> Yes, it's hard for me to communicate with my neighbours. They don't come visit, and I don't go visit because we can't understand each other. I am attending [language classes] four days a week. And no, I can't be going full time. I must meet my son at his school bus drop-off; otherwise, he won't be able to get off the bus, and with all my stress and

health issues, it wouldn't be good for me right now. I am still in English classes; my progress isn't so good. Like I told you before, I lost my son and my husband, and I have also left five more children in the Iraq Kurdistan region with my father and mother. I am not able to process things well because I am always thinking about them. —Sajeda

Khalida, who was widowed with five children, also had difficulty adjusting to her new life in Canada. She constantly relived the trauma of losing her family and had just learned that one of her children had been released by Daesh but was still stuck in Iraq, while another child was still a captive. She explained that she was sick and that when having to deal with the uncertainty of her two remaining children in Iraq, it was difficult for her to integrate into her new home in Canada:

> No, I am not getting better, it seems. I was struck by a car while fleeing for safety. I was in captivity locked away for almost two and a half years. I am not well mentally. I was barely given a chance to see the light of the sun. My entire family was killed by Daesh. I am grateful to the Canadian government. They [Daesh] returned one of my sons recently, but my older son is still in captivity. I haven't heard back from him at all. It's hard to process information while you're under so much pressure and stress, worrying about my family and relatives and friends, knowing that most of them were killed by Daesh—some in front of you and others behind you. Yes, I would like to take care of my kids, but I need to learn the language, and when I went to welfare, they told me I am not able to work because of my children and my illness, so I am not sure what else I can do, but I will continue going to school. I want to be able to deal with my illness, then continue to learn the language and take care of my children. I am all they have, and they are all I have. —Khalida

In summary, the combination of poor or no schooling in Iraq, the brutality of the trauma inflicted upon them by Daesh, and the uncertainty about their partners and children left behind in Iraq made the initial integration process of the Yazidi women more difficult than for other refugee groups.

Discussion

In this study, all refugee adults, children, and youth have experienced prolonged and continuous separation from their immediate families. They have experienced and witnessed torture and other forms of violence, including murder, malnutrition, physical assault, and rape prior to their arrival in Canada. These events make it more challenging for young refugees and their families to successfully integrate into their host countries. Our findings support research studies by Kaplan and colleagues (2016) and Akthar (2017) indicating that pre-flight conflict and war have a significant influence on the traumatic experiences of refugee children and youth. According to Akthar (2017), the effect of trauma can undermine an individual's belief of how life unfolds, especially for children, as they are in the early stages of life.

According to our findings, trauma deeply affected the individuals' ability to learn a new language and integrate into their new societies, as was mentioned by many mothers in our study. Learning a new language is difficult for those who have no or little formal schooling in their mother tongue (Cummins 2001; Merisuo-Storm 2007). Some of the Yazidi we interviewed had never attended school, while most others had education that ended prior to high school (IRCC 2017), which is typical of some refugees (Provencher et al. 2017). Learning a new language, especially when it involves an entirely new alphabet and language structure, can pose challenges, as languages can differ in components such as the sounds of letters and rules by which sentences are constructed (Farran, Bingham, and Matthews 2012). This was also evident from our study. We characterized the participants in our study as functionally illiterate. According to UNESCO (1978, 183), "A person is functionally illiterate who cannot engage in all those activities in which literacy is required for effective functioning of his group and community and also for enabling him to continue to use reading, writing, and calculation for his own and the community's development." Because the Iraqi government, followed by Daesh, made it extremely difficult, if not impossible, for the Yazidi to attend school, their education as a community greatly suffered before they came to Canada. The fact that they were denied an education has made learning a new language even more difficult.

The fact that mothers, but occasionally other adults and young people, were often ill upon and after their arrival also makes it difficult for families to recover and integrate into their new societies. Often, the caregiver must put aside their own health issues, language learning, and job training to prioritize the health of children and teens. Yet by putting aside their own health and language training, the suffering of the entire family is prolonged. Without English-language skills, the family may find it difficult to navigate the public transportation system, meaning missed appointments with medical professionals. It also means increased dependency upon the few fully trained Kurmanji/English translators who work for settlement service providers or who volunteer with the community. Some of these volunteers are overwhelmed by requests for help, and their own health suffers as well.

It is not easy to adjust to a new life post-resettlement (Kirova 2019). As with the participants in this study, for refugee families with children of school age, the difficulties of resettlement might be magnified, since many of them have suffered trauma prior to migrating, such as "mass violence, living in extreme poverty, spending extended periods of time in refugee camps, etc." (1). No matter what direction a family chooses to take in their resettlement, the educational and psychological results of the children are profoundly affected by the parents' and caregivers' own pre-migration experiences (Kirova 2019; Chettleburgh 2008; Loewen 2003) and post-migration conditions. In addition to the effects of parental trauma on the children, the cognitive effects of complex trauma experienced by the refugee children themselves may have a significant impact on their academic performance (Tweedie et al. 2017). Adolescents who have spent their whole lives in continual danger and had their attention, energy, and resources focused only on survival may have trouble focusing their thoughts. Adolescents who have complex trauma may be hypersensitive to noises, touch, and light as a consequence of their over-responses to sensory stimuli as they developed when they were young. Children who have fled persecution may show the physiological consequences of tremendous stress when confronted with what is considered normal stress in a Canadian school, even sometimes "shutting down" completely (Tweedie et al. 2017; Downey 2008). In some Canadian classrooms, there are teachers who recognize their lack of trauma-informed teaching practices and refuse to accept a "deficit" perspective, either of refugee children as students or of themselves as educators. Unfortunately, trauma-informed educational practices are difficult to access, as they are not normally part of many educators' training (Stewart et al. 2019). Compulsory trauma-informed training should be part of pre-service teacher education programs.

Robertson and her colleagues (2006) find that families with more children take longer to fully integrate into Canadian society. Our study cannot confirm or deny this. Intuitively, however, it is easier to manage the integration, schooling, and language learning of a smaller rather than a larger number of family members. Extreme trauma experiences and the absence of missing family members further exacerbate the integration conditions of children and youth. While our research was not able to quantify the effects of trauma on any aspect of integration, we observed, based on our years of experience working with other refugee groups, that the extreme conditions experienced by Yazidi refugees appear to make it more difficult for them to integrate in a healthy, timely fashion. The fact that extreme trauma is experienced by mothers supports the findings of Bjørneseth and her colleagues (2019), who show that the burden of caring in the aftermath generally falls upon mothers. In the case of Yazidi refugees in Canada, however, not all these caregivers are female, so we would temper this observation with one that indicates that the burden of care tends to fall upon the caregiver who is most resilient to previous trauma. But the burden of care often means that the caregiver is the last person in the family to receive valuable integration and language training. In short, efforts to help newly arrived refugee families integrate should pay some attention to providing support to caregivers.

Often, the translation needs of trauma survivors are immediate, as in the incident where the mother was wrongly informed about the cancer diagnosis of her child. When they have to rely on other Yazidi members of the community for translation assistance, who themselves may have poor English-language skills, the results of inaccurate translations can be disastrous and induce additional stress. In addition to the availability of the interpreter, the person doing the translation must have the appropriate credentials for the job. This means having more than just a background in translation. Experience working in the refugee resettlement sector is key to understanding the context in which the families live and how they ask for assistance. In the case of the family with a child with Down's syndrome, having a settlement worker who understood that this family needed additional health and homecare support as well as additional financial considerations was important. Involving a team of educators, psychologists, and physicians in developing an individual learning plan for a child with special needs is key to that child's success in school. Trauma-informed practices require an understanding of how previous trauma can affect this family's integration experience. In summary, translation and interpretation must be paired with a specialized knowledge of human development as well as the role of resettlement services; otherwise, misunderstandings are more likely to occur.

Interpreters were needed in various environments but were not the only support necessary. Some caregivers could not attend school meetings because they were ill, they could not speak English or find a translator, or their family required additional social support. In short, the availability of interpreters was not the only problem. There needed to be a whole family support system available that could assist these families in multiple ways. Schools and other educational institutions must play a role in supporting refugee families so that the children in severely traumatized refugee families can thrive in various school contexts.

Conclusion

The Yazidi arriving in Canada represent a new type of refugee: sadly, one that will become more common as world conflicts arise more abruptly and war tactics become more brutalizing. They were resettled in Canada very quickly—some in a matter of weeks after their release from Daesh captivity. The "speed" at which they were brought to Canada and the brutal kidnapping and torture they faced have meant that mental health professionals, settlement service providers, and others who care for this population have witnessed acute trauma in ways that have not been experienced by many previously arriving refugees. Given the tactics of war and terrorism predominant in the twenty-first century, we are likely to witness more and more extremely traumatized refugee families.

So how can service providers such as settlement workers, school personnel, refugee support groups, and Canadian society at large better prepare for future emergency arrivals? In addition to providing more support to the families' primary caregivers, we can provide more one-on-one assistance in order to meet their settlement needs, including the educational needs of highly traumatized refugees and of children among refugee families, hence the need for education cultural brokers available in schools where there are traumatized refugees. This means substantial planning and investment prior to their arrival. Right now, there is a shortage of settlement service workers and qualified translators and interpreters. One of the reasons is that they are underpaid and work for community organizations that must rely on year-to-year funding, so there is little job security. While IRCC has increased its funding of agencies from three to five years, settlement organizations remain financially precarious and unstable. These are unattractive features for those future workers with the skills needed to become successful settlement workers and education brokers, especially introducing the latter in areas that do not have this type of assistance for children and youth. Counselling and support services, including guidance counsellors, should be culturally sensitive and knowledgeable about the experiences of refugee children, adolescents, and their families to better provide individualized support. The Settlement Worker in Schools (SWIS) program offers assistance to refugee and immigrant newcomer kids, as well as their parents and families, with the purpose of facilitating their integration into society, but not all schools have SWIS, hence the need to fund more such support services in schools. The current availability of professional training, which has recently emerged, should be supported by increased and continuous funding in this crucial area.

Obviously, there are gaps in addressing mental health issues within the larger Canadian health care system. These gaps are primarily discussed regarding mental health and all Canadians, but the problems with servicing refugees, particularly young refugees, are more difficult to address. Certainly, there is a need for mental health practitioners to speak the language of refugees or train interpreters from a cultural perspective to assist practitioners in working with refugees. Having training on refugee trauma may also assist some of the mental health workers in the work they do. Like settlement service providers, there are not enough experts for assistance, so refugee families wait a long time after their arrival before they become eligible to receive services. In addition, there is also a need for staff in schools trained on the best trauma-informed practices and how to handle issues relating to traumatized refugee children in schools.

The time between becoming eligible for services and actually receiving services is also a problem. It is often an "expectation" that the refugee families immediately enroll in a language class or meet with a teacher upon their arrival in Canada. For many traumatized families, that is not possible. Yet there is a clock ticking: refugees are only eligible for most services for three years after arrival. For many Yazidi, three years is not long enough considering that they must deal with their health problems before they can embark on language learning or finding a job. For extremely traumatized refugees, it may take many months before they are healthy enough to learn a new language.

The number of refugees worldwide is growing. In 2015, 19.5 million refugees were looking for a safe place to live. By 2020, that number was 26.4 million (UNHCR 2019). The refugee population is also young; 60 percent of refugees arrive in their new host countries on or before their twenty-ninth birthdays. This means that educational institutions will become a major site for the integration and resettlement of a large number of newcomer families. Given the extreme tactics used by militias and terrorists, we can only expect that the levels of trauma experienced by young refugees and their families arriving in the future will be severe and widespread. This means that the Yazidi are the first of many who will be arriving in Canada under more challenging circumstances, and these investments are worthwhile from a future planning and human rights perspective. In mid-2021, the Liberal government announced that it would be accepting the resettlement of at least twenty thousand Afghan nationals to Canada as part of their emergency evacuation after the Taliban takeover of the country (IRCC 2021). Like the Yazidi, they too will have very little time between their initial displacement and their resettlement in Canada. There is reason to expect that these emergency-type evacuations will continue into the twenty-first century, which means that large numbers of future refugees to Canada will be arriving with acute trauma needs that the settlement community and Canadian society must acknowledge and treat.

References

Abbott, Alison. 2016. "The Troubled Minds of Migrants." *Nature* 538 (7624): 158–60.

Ahearn, Frederick L., Jr., and Jean L. Athey, eds. 1991. *Refugee Children: Theory, Research, and Services*. Baltimore: Johns Hopkins University Press.

Akthar, Zahra. 2017. "Giving a Voice, Healing Trauma: Exploring the Usefulness of Art Therapy with Refugee Children." Master's thesis, University of Chester, United Kingdom. http://hdl.handle.net/10034/621114.

Arakelova, Victoria. 2010. "Ethno-religious Communities: To the Problem of Identity Markers." *Iran and the Caucasus* 14 (1): 1–17. http://web.b.ebscohost.com.uml.idm.oclc.org/ehost/pdfviewer/pdfviewer?vid=1&sid=d8b98e35-d62e-4d6e-9282-fd3ed0d7990c%40sessionmgr102.

Bartolomei, Linda, Rebecca Eckert, and Eileen Pittaway. 2013. "'What Happens There . . . Follows Us Here': Resettled but Still at Risk: Refugee Women and Girls in Australia." *Refuge* 30 (2): 45–56. https://doi.org/10.25071/1920-7336.39618.

Beiser, Morton, and Feng Hou. 2000. "Gender Differences in Language Acquisition and Employment Consequences Among Southeast Asian Refugees in Canada." *Canadian Public Policy* 26 (3): 311–30. https://doi.org/10.2307/3552403.

Bjørneseth, Frida, Martin Smidt, and Jakub Stachowski. 2019. "Gender, Parenthood and Feelings of Safety in Greek Refugee Centres." *Journal of Refugee Studies* 32, special issue 1: 163–179. https://doi.org/10.1093/jrs/fez039.

Bourque, François, Elsje van der Ven, and Ashok Malla. 2011. "A Meta-analysis of the Risk for Psychotic Disorders Among First- and Second-Generation Immigrants." *Psychological Medicine* 41 (5): 897–910.

Callister, Lynn Clark. 2016. "Refugee Women and Children: What Can I Do?" *MCN: The American Journal of Maternal/Child Nursing* 41 (5): 309. https://doi.org/10.1097/NMC.0000000000000266.

Cetorelli, Valeria, Isaac Sasson, Nazar Shabila, and Gilbert Burnham. 2017. "Mortality and Kidnapping Estimates for the Yazidi Population in the Area of Mount Sinjar, Iraq, in August 2014: A Retrospective Household Survey." *PLoS Medicine* 14 (5): e1002297. https://doi.org/10.1371/journal.pmed.1002297.

Chettleburgh, Michael. 2008. *Now Is the Time to Act: Youth Gang Prevention in Ottawa*. Richmond Hill, ON: Astwood Strategy Corporation. https://youthrex.com/wp-content/uploads/2019/02/Now-is-the-time-to-Act-_FINAL-REPORT.pdf.

Cummins, Jim. 2001. "Bilingual Children's Mother Tongue: Why Is It Important for Education." *Sprogforum* 7 (19): 15–20. http://www.iteachilearn.com/cummins/mother.htm.

Dalgaard, Nina Thorup, Brenda Kathryn Todd, Sarah I. F. Daniel, and Edith Montgomery. 2016. "The Transmission of Trauma in Refugee Families: Associations Between Intra-family Trauma Communication Style, Children's Attachment Security and Psychosocial Adjustment." *Attachment & Human Development* 18 (1): 69–89.

Devictor, X. 2019. "2019 Update: How Long Do Refugees Stay in Exile? To Find Out, Beware of Averages." World Bank, December 9, 2019. https://blogs.worldbank.org/dev4peace/2019-update-how-long-do-refugees-stay-exile-find-out-beware-averages.

Downey, Laurel. 2008. "Calmer Classrooms: A Guide to Working with Traumatised Children." *Journal of the Home Economics Institute of Australia* 15 (1): 33–42.

Emdad, Reza, Hans Peter Söndergaard, and Töres Theorell. 2005. "Learning Problems, Impaired Short-Term Memory, and General Intelligence in Relation to Severity and Duration of Disease in Posttraumatic Stress Disorder Patients." *Stress, Trauma, and Crisis* 8 (1): 25–43. https://doi.org/10.1080/15434610590913612.

Farran, Lama K., Gary E. Bingham, and Mona W. Matthews. 2012. "The Relationship Between Language and Reading in Bilingual English-Arabic

Children." *Reading and Writing* 25 (9): 2153–81. https://doi.org/10.1007/s11145-011-9352-5.

Hodes, Matthew. 2019. "New Developments in the Mental Health of Refugee Children and Adolescents." *Evidence-Based Mental Health* 22 (2): 72–76. https://doi.org/10.1136/ebmental-2018-300065.

Hoffman, Joel, Belinda Liddell, Richard A. Bryant, and Angela Nickerson. 2018. "The Relationship Between Moral Injury Appraisals, Trauma Exposure, and Mental Health in Refugees." *Depression and Anxiety* 35 (11): 1030–39.

Hosseini, Seyedeh Behnaz, and Pegah AM Seidi. 2018. "A Study of Psychological Problem in Yazidi Children and Adolescents." *Journal of Kermanshah University of Medical Sciences* 22 (1). https://doi.org/10.5812/jkums.68968.

Ibrahim, Hawkar, Verena Ertl, Claudia Catani, Azad Ali Ismail, and Frank Neuner. 2018. "Trauma and Perceived Social Rejection Among Yazidi Women and Girls Who Survived Enslavement and Genocide." *BMC Medicine* 16 (1): 1–11.

IRCC (Immigration, Refugees and Citizenship Canada). 2017. *Population Profile—the Yazidis*. Ottawa: IRCC. http://www.rstp.ca/wp-content/uploads/2016/07/Yazidi-Population-Profile-February-2017.pdf.

IRCC. 2021. *Canada Expands Resettlement Program to Bring More Afghans to Safety*. News release. Ottawa: IRCC. https://www.canada.ca/en/immigration-refugees-citizenship/news/2021/08/canada-expands-resettlement-program-to-bring-more-afghans-to-safety.html.

Kalmanowitz, Debra, and Bobby Lloyd, eds. 2005. *Art Therapy and Political Violence: With Art, Without Illusion*. London and New York: Routledge.

Kaplan, Ida, Yvonne Stolk, Madeleine Valibhoy, Alan Tucker, and Judy Baker. 2016. "Cognitive Assessment of Refugee Children: Effects of Trauma and New Language Acquisition." *Transcultural Psychiatry* 53 (1): 81–109. https://doi.org/10.1177/1363461515612933.

Kirova, Anna. 2019. "Introduction: Syrian Refugees' Encounters with the Education System in Their Initial Resettlement in Canada." *Journal of Contemporary Issues in Education* 14 (1). https://journals.library.ualberta.ca/jcie/index.php/JCIE/article/view/29369/21370.

Loewen, Shawn. 2003. "Second Language Concerns for Refugee Children." In *Educational Interventions for Refugee Children: Theoretical Perspectives and Implementing Best Practice*, edited by Richard Hamilton and Dennis Moore, 49–66. London: RoutledgeFalmer.

MacLean, Cameron. 2019. "Girl Who Died After Dalhousie Drive Crash Was Yazidi Refugee, Community Member Says." CBC News, June 21, 2019. https://www.cbc.ca/news/canada/manitoba/girl-who-died-in-crash-was-yazidi-refugee-1.5185121.

Merisuo-Storm, Tuula. 2007. "Pupils' Attitudes Towards Foreign-Language Learning and the Development of Literacy Skills in Bilingual Education." *Teaching and Teacher Education* 23 (2): 226–35. https://doi.org/10.1016/j.tate.2006.04.024.

Oliphant, Robert. 2018. *Road to Recovery: Resettlement Issues of Yazidi Women and Children in Canada*. Ottawa: House of Commons, Canada.

Porter, Catherine. 2018. "Canada Struggles as It Opens Its Arms to Victims of ISIS." *New York Times*, March 18, 2018. https://www.thestar.com/news/world/2018/03/17/canada-struggles-as-it-opens-its-arms-to-yazidis-victims-of-daesh-brutality.html.

Provencher, Claudine, Anne Milan, Stacey Hallman, and Carol D'Aoust. 2017. "Report on the Demographic Situation in Canada. Fertility: Overview, 2012 to 2016." Statistics Canada, 2017. https://www150.statcan.gc.ca/n1/pub/91-209-x/2018001/article/54956-eng.htm.

Robertson, Cheryl Lee, Linda Halcon, Kay Savik, David Johnson, Marline Spring, James Butcher, Joseph Westermeyer, and James Jaranson. 2006. "Somali and Oromo Refugee Women: Trauma and Associated Factors." *Journal of Advanced Nursing* 56 (6): 577–87. https://doi.org/10.1111/j.1365-2648.2006.04057.x.

Sangalang, Cindy C., Justin Jager, and Tracy W. Harachi. 2017. "Effects of Maternal Traumatic Distress on Family Functioning and Child Mental Health: An Examination of Southeast Asian Refugee Families in the US." *Social Science & Medicine* 184 (2017): 178–86. https://doi.org/10.1016/j.socscimed.2017.04.032.

Schweitzer, Robert D., Lyn Vromans, Mark Brough, Mary Asic-Kobe, Ignacio Correa-Velez, Kate Murray, and Caroline Lenette. 2018. "Recently Resettled Refugee Women-at-Risk in Australia Evidence High Levels of Psychiatric Symptoms: Individual, Trauma and Post-migration Factors Predict Outcomes." *BMC Medicine* 16 (1): 1–12. https://doi.org/10.1186/s12916-018-1143-2.

Shafai-Palmer, Afsaneh. 1997. "Trauma of Displacement: Art Therapy with Children from Refugee Families (Based on Workshop Presented at CATA Conference, Toronto, 1996)." *Canadian Art Therapy Association Journal* 11 (1): 29–37.

Stewart, Jan, Dania El Chaar, Kari McCluskey, and Kirby Borgardt. 2019. "Refugee Student Integration: A Focus on Settlement, Education, and Psychosocial Support." *Journal of Contemporary Issues in Education* 14 (1). https://journals.library.ualberta.ca/jcie/index.php/JCIE/article/view/29364.

Sullivan, Amanda L., and Gregory R. Simonson. 2016. "A Systematic Review of School-Based Social-Emotional Interventions for Refugee and War-Traumatized Youth." *Review of Educational Research* 86 (2): 503–30. https://doi.org/10.3102/0034654315609419.

Tesch, N. 2023. S.v. "Yazidi Religious Sect." *Encyclopedia Britannica*, October 19, 2023. https://www.britannica.com/topic/Yazidi.

Timshel, Isabelle, Edith Montgomery, and Nina Thorup Dalgaard. 2017. "A Systematic of Risk and Protective Factors Associated with Family Related Violence in Refugee Families." *Child Abuse & Neglect* 70 (2017): 315–30. https://doi.org/10.1016/j.chiabu.2017.06.023.

Tweedie, M. Gregory, Carla Belanger, Kimberley Rezazadeh, and Karen Vogel. 2017. "Trauma-Informed Teaching Practice and Refugee Children: A Hopeful Reflection on Welcoming Our New Neighbours to Canadian Schools." *BC Teal Journal* 2 (1): 36–45. https://doi.org/10.14288/bctj.v2i1.268.

UNESCO. 1978. *Records of the General Conference, 20th Session, Paris.* Vol. 1: *Resolutions.* Paris: UNESCO. https://unesdoc.unesco.org/ark:/48223/pf0000114032.

UNHCR (United Nations High Commissioner for Refugees). 2019. *COI Note on the Situation of Yazidi IDPs in the Kurdistan Region of Iraq.* New York: UNHCR. https://www.refworld.org/pdfid/5cd156657.pdf.

Vijanann, M. 2017. "Helping Traumatized Yazidi Refugees Requires a Different Kind of Care." TVO, April 18, 2017. https://www.tvo.org/article/helping-traumatized-yazidi-refugees-requires-a-different-kind-of-care.

Watt, David L. E., and Diedre M. Lake. 2004. *Benchmarking Adult Rates of Second Language Acquisition: How Long and How Fast?* Edmonton: Alberta Learning, Language Training Programs and Citizenship and Immigration Canada.

Westermeyer, Joseph. 1991. "Psychiatric Services for Refugee Children: An Overview." In *Refugee Children: Theory, Research, and Services,* edited by Frederick L. Ahearn Jr. and Jean L. Athey, 127–62. Baltimore: Johns Hopkins University Press.

Wilkinson, Lori, Pallabi Bhattacharyya, Annette Riziki, and Abdul-Bari Abdul-Karim. 2019. *Yazidi Resettlement in Canada—Final Report 2018.* Ottawa: Immigration, Refugees and Citizenship Canada.

Wilkinson, Lori, and David Ponka. 2017. "Mental Health of Immigrants and Refugees in Canada." In *Migration, Health and Survival: International Perspectives,* 88–109. Northampton and Cheltenham: Edward Elgar Publishing.

Wood, Sara, Kat Ford, Katie Hardcastle, Joanne Hopkins, Karen Hughes, and Mark Bellis. 2020. *Adverse Childhood Experiences in Child Refugee and Asylum Seeking Populations.* Cardiff: Public Health Wales NHS Trust. https://www.wmsmp.org.uk/wp-content/uploads/ACEs-in-Child-Refugee-and-Asylum-Seekers-Report-English-final.pdf.

Yüksel, Sahika, Suzan Saner, Ayse Devrim Basterzi, Zerrin Oglagu, and Israfil Bülbül. 2018. "Genocidal Sexual Assault on Women and the Role of Culture in the Rehabilitation Process: Experiences from Working with Yazidi Women in Turkey." *From Sexualized Torture and Gender-Based Torture to Genderized Torture: The Urgent Need for a Conceptual Evolution* 28 (3): 124.

7 "Where Are You From?"
A Personal Perspective on the Struggles of Youth Living Between Two Cultures

Jwamer Jalal

For many second- or even third-generation immigrants, the journeys embarked on by their ancestors were presumably to provide them with greater opportunities for success. The upheavals experienced by their parents or grandparents may have been motivated by various factors, perhaps most notably armed conflict, poverty, limited financial opportunity, or political instability. Rarely would one seek out the risk and adversity synonymous with restarting their life in another country, particularly one with foreign languages and customs, if not pressured by necessity. Despite this necessity, the nature of these decisions means that the children of these immigrants are thrust unwittingly into a purgatory of identity, one in which they do not entirely belong to their cultural heritage or to the dominant culture of their host country. The question "Where are you from?" is the launch pad to ground my personal experiences as a first-generation immigrant who grew up in Canada. These experiences serve as anecdotal evidence that I situate within some relevant academic studies.[1] In doing so, I also discuss selected harmful discourses and policies that may contribute to the tension (or "othering") felt

---

1 Although I use academic research to support points of contention or to bolster the discussion in this chapter, my primary desire is to embody the voice of these children of immigrants and to share my own story. As a result, large portions of this chapter are primarily rooted in narrative.

by immigrant children and their desire for belonging through obtaining legal citizenship. I conclude by considering potential solutions to these adversities that could foster a movement toward inclusiveness and belonging.

Where Are You From?

"Where are you from?" This is a question immigrant children face ad nauseam. The first time I can remember being asked this question was during a routine grocery trip with my mother. We were refugees in Turkey, mere hours away from our native Kurdistan, from where we had fled. I have faint memories at four years old of a Turkish officer bending over to ask me the question, and I remember the tension radiating from my mother as her grip on my hand tightened.

This was in the late 1990s, amid ongoing conflict between those of Kurdish heritage and the government of Turkey. The Treaty of Sèvres in 1920 potentially provided for a Kurdish territory and the self-determination of Kurdish peoples for the first time in modern history. However, the Turkish War of Independence (1919–23) led to the treaty being superseded by the Treaty of Lausanne (1923), in which there was no provision for a Kurdish state. The result was that the Kurds, along with the Assyrians, were divided among Turkey, Iraq, Syria, and Iran, and conflict is ongoing to this day.

In hindsight, the encounter with the Turkish officer was an incredibly difficult situation for my mother, who did not speak the language and barely understood it, having only been in Turkey for six months. By this point, as children often do, I had learned the language almost fluently from cartoons and from other children in the old, run-down apartment complex where we shared a two-bedroom apartment with another Kurdish family. My mother would take me on grocery trips to translate for her. The task of translating for parents and older relatives is one that many newcomer and refugee youth can relate to. With parents desperate to understand the new language but without the capacity to do so, it falls to the children to navigate conversations that are perhaps much more mature than they're ready for.

"Where are you from? What's your name?" I was confused by the questions and intimidated by the officer staring down at me, waiting intently for my answers. I am not sure why, but during our time in Turkey, I had taken a particular liking to Turkish pop sensation Tarkan, Turkey's equivalent to Michael Jackson or Justin Timberlake. So, with all the confidence and imagination of a four-year-old whose main source of entertainment had been watching a shirtless Turkish man strut across a TV, I answered, "I'm Tarkan!" The officer paused for a moment, then laughed loudly, patting me on the head and eventually leaving my mother and me to our shopping.

"Where are you from?" That question is a complicated one because it is difficult for the asked to know the intention of those asking. Are they merely trying to learn more about you, to empathize with you? Or is it, as I feared it may have been in the case of the Turkish officer, an interrogation, an inquisition, a question with a presupposed answer that will allow those asking it to categorize or even perhaps to antagonize you?

In 1997, after nine months in Turkey, my family was granted refuge through the UN to resettle in Canada. Months into our settlement in our new home, I had come to expect that question nearly anytime I met someone new: curious teachers, inquisitive classmates, and new friends and their parents alike. However, for a routine question that I had come to expect, I never nailed down the perfect response. At that point, not many people knew where or what Kurdistan was, so I learned that when I answered "Kurdistan," it would encourage more questions, ranging from "Where is that?" to "Do you mean Dagestan/Afghanistan/Pakistan?" or any other "stan" they could think of. So rather than explaining it, I simply began to say "Iraq"—the country to which my part of Kurdistan was assigned. This was an answer that allowed me to mostly avoid any further inquiry in a conversation that had become incredibly tedious to me. Iraq was a country, unlike Kurdistan, and it was at least recognizable to most people in Canada.

Then, in 2003, the United States began its campaign against the Iraqi Ba'aths. It soon became clear that I could no longer answer that question with "Iraq" to avoid an extended conversation. Although my parents tried to shield me from the media coverage of the war, I inevitably saw clips of missile strikes and the frontline combat between Iraqi forces and the American military. Sentiment about Iraq had changed drastically, and the few times when I did claim to be from there, I was met with looks of concern and apprehension.

Certainly, I did not want to be associated with the Iraqi regime, the very regime that had taken so much from my family by way of decades of Iraqi genocide and the suppression of Kurdish people. My own father, a poet and scholar in Kurdistan, had been jailed by the Ba'ath party for his writing, which they believed promoted Western ideology. The Iraqi regime was the very reason we had fled our homeland in the first place.

"Well, I'm from Kurdistan," I'd say. "You see, it's in Iraq, but we're actually enemies of Saddam too!" Was I trying to reassure my friends at ten years of age that geopolitical jockeying made me an ally of the good guys, not one of the "villainous terrorists" many of them had seen fighting against the liberation of Iraq? Or was this my attempt to justify my identity, a subconscious plea for acceptance of aspects of myself that I could never change?

After the terrorist attacks of 9/11, there was a rise in anti–Middle Eastern sentiment, with the FBI reporting 481 hate crimes against Muslims in 2001, compared to only 28 in the year 2000 (Ser 2016). The invasion of Iraq by the Western coalition led by the United States only served to amplify this sentiment. One could tune in to the evening news and witness rallies calling for the bombing of the countries many Americans believed to be responsible for the attack on the United States.

Following the war, with the Ba'ath party now overthrown, my family could travel back to Kurdistan for the first time since arriving in Canada. So, in 2004, my mother, my two older sisters, and I took the two-day trip by plane, then bus, back to Kurdistan, and I was reunited with cousins, aunts, uncles, and grandparents I had not seen for over six years. Even at ten years of age, this visit brought with it an incredible feeling of relief, as I did not need to engage in long explanations of my past or my birthplace, and I did not need to worry that others might judge parts of my identity as offensive due to circumstances I could not control. I was around people who *knew* me.

About three weeks into the trip, my aunt gave me a few extra dinars to buy some snacks for myself and my little cousin. I walked to the corner shop about thirty seconds from my grandma's house and picked out a few bags of likely expired chips and a knock-off Kinder chocolate egg. As I handed the clerk my money, he stared at me with the same sort of gaze I had become so familiar with in Canada. Looking back, I think part of me almost knew what he was going to ask next.

As he handed back my change, he asked me in Kurdish, "Where are you from?" This time, more than any other, I was confused—confused by the question, confused by what sort of answer to give. I felt his eyes gazing down at me, waiting for a response. "Here," I answered in Kurdish, "I'm from here."

His pursed lips changed into a mischievous grin, and I could tell he was not satisfied with my response. "Well, I suppose, but where are you actually from? You don't sound or look like a kid from Kurdistan."

I stood still for a moment, then picked up the bagged snacks from the counter and whispered, "Canada."

"Aha! Canada! I once had a neighbour whose brother moved to Canada! Do you know him? His name's Rawaz. I think he's in Detroit!"

"No," I answered, heading quickly for the exit.

On the way home, I began re-examining my trip. I remembered that my cousins had asked all sorts of questions over the past few weeks: questions about my clothes, my life in Canada, the video games I had brought with me. I remembered that occasionally they would laugh when I used the wrong word in Kurdish, and I remembered how they had made fun of me when I had cried to my mom about having sore legs from the squatting toilets in Kurdistan. Perhaps I was not old enough to articulate it or understand what I was feeling, but it *felt* like I was in limbo, in a purgatory of identity between two parts of myself that I accepted but that did not reciprocate that acceptance to me.

Back at my grandmother's house, I sat silently on the couch, staring at a counterfeit Kinder egg that did not quite seem so appealing anymore.

My story may be unique in its details, but for children born in Canada to immigrant parents or immigrant children who have, like me, come to Canada at a young age, it is a familiar one. The motivation behind the question "Where are you from?" is often innocent, even well intended and caring: it came from teachers who took an interest in me or from friends who wanted to know more about me. But what can I possibly do to meet their expectations when I struggle for the answer myself? How can I provide a short but positive answer that gives a glimpse into the story of "me" when the very question asked is the subject of so much inner monologue and turmoil, when the question itself strips from me the ability to represent myself wholly in the way I want to be seen—as a person defined by my character, my interests, or even my motivations, not by my birthplace or my place of residence?

I do not intend to frame the motivations behind the question "Where are you from?" as malicious; I know very well they were often not. I simply mean to illuminate the struggles of a child, a youth, growing up between two cultures that share many similarities but many beautiful differences as well. For us, the children of immigrants and immigrant children, the weight of those differences walks with us in every step, and the feeling that we do not entirely fit into either side pursues us like a shadow we can never leave behind.

Peeled Labels

It seems that by nature, and almost entirely subconsciously, humans label and sort things into categories. Foroni and Rothbart (2013) posit that labelled categories such as race, ethnicity, gender, and religion all function as psychological "equivalence classes" and affect our perception and our judgments of the categories' members. I am intrigued by an experiment they conducted that showed that once someone was given a subjective label, the subsequent removal of the label and even challenges to its validity had no effect on its overriding categorization effects. According to this study, "The perseverative effects observed here have direct implications for social perception. The link between the perseverative effects of category labels and the de-individualization of group members is an important one and deserves further investigation" (131). This finding supports the notion that once a person has been labelled or miscategorized, not only is it incredibly difficult to shed that label (regardless of its accuracy), but the label will directly infringe on the person's ability to represent themselves independently of it. This study's findings make it clear that as immigrant and refugee children, both first and second generation and beyond, we have little control over the narratives that surround our labels. Being asked where we are from is just one way in which we are asked to neatly fit ourselves into those labels; we also face potential categorization by our food, dress, religious markers, or culturally shaped behaviours.

While the question "Where are you from?" asks the individual to accept that there is a label that identifies them as "other" and therefore from somewhere else, incidents of misrecognition can indicate deliberate attempts at using these labels to fuel racial and cultural intimidation, which has seen a resurgence in the last decade. This trend is apparent in the province of Alberta, according to a 2019 report from the Organization for the Prevention of Violence, which states, "Since 2014 there has been a steady rise in police-reported hate crimes in the province. From 2014 to 2015 Alberta experienced a 40 per cent increase in this area. More recently, from 2016 to 2017 the rate of police-reported hate crimes increased by a further 38 per cent" (17). Likewise, at a national level, a viewer poll conducted by Global News in 2019 revealed that 37 percent of Canadians believed that immigration was a threat to them personally (Abedi 2019).

Labels can be used to promote hostility toward minorities, as the trends at the start of the COVID-19 pandemic demonstrated. For example, the misrecognition that has arisen from ignorance surrounding the recent coronavirus outbreak has profoundly affected children in Asian communities. On May 8, 2020, United Nations Secretary-General António Guterres said that "the pandemic continues to unleash a tsunami of hate and xenophobia, scapegoating and scare-mongering" (1) and urged governments to "act now to strengthen the immunity of our societies against the virus of hate" (3).

Unfortunately, these labels are often perpetuated by those in positions of the most power. The former American president Donald Trump promoted the use of the term *China virus*, and a member of the Canadian embassy in China embroidered shirts that spelled out *Wuhan Virus* in stylized text, fuelling the animosity toward Asian communities in both the United States and Canada. The Vancouver Police Department documented a "significant" increase in reports of hate crimes against people of Chinese, Korean, and Japanese descent in Vancouver in 2020 (Xu 2020).

For me and many others, the weight of these labels, particularly those that explicitly vilify minorities, creates a resentment of our cultural identity because of the barriers it seemingly imposes on our ability to simply fit in as normal persons. In my case, questions about cultural identity seemed to always move me farther away from fitting into a simple or singular category. In more troubling situations, labels put children of immigrants and refugees on the defensive and perhaps even make them targets of racial abuse, often asking them to answer for the behaviours, ideologies, or beliefs of groups with which they have no association.

Due to this misrecognition and under the perceived threat of vilification, I did not see my culture as empowering. I saw it as a constant barrier between myself and the acceptance I longed for growing up in Canada. Rather than my cultural identity being a part of who I was, among various character and personality traits, I saw it as a restrictive barrier that limited who I could be in the eyes of my peers. The assigned label felt like a restriction, hindering my ability to surpass the definitions or expectations imposed based on my heritage, whether accurate or not.

My mother and father embody the story of many migrants who, due to threats to their lives, have left behind careers, homes, and families to work multiple jobs in a country where they struggle with the language, do not have a full understanding of the systems, and have yet to achieve the level of familiarity with everyday life that they had "back home." The sacrifices these immigrants made and continue to make are the foundation on which we, their children, build our lives. While growing up as children of immigrants, though, we do not quite understand the world on those terms. At times, we feel beholden to this eternal debt. We see our parents' sacrifices etched into every new wrinkle on their faces, every grey hair that seems to multiply by the week, month, year. Already struggling with the pressures of belonging, we witness first-hand as our parents struggle under the weight of providing us with opportunities to succeed. Yet their sacrifices don't make our journey to success any easier. Even when we speak the language without an accent, are educated entirely in the Canadian education system, and have a very good understanding of the systems and institutions in Canada, we continue to be defined by the labels placed on our parents, which are based on markers of difference that seem to keep us apart from "native-born" Canadians, the majority of whom are white and monolingual (Statistics Canada 2016, 2017). This can manifest, as I know it did with me, into further complicating the relationship with our racial and cultural identity. We long for the natural sense of belonging that our "truly Canadian" friends feel. We crave the stability that comes from having parents and a cultural background firmly established in what we're told, both implicitly and explicitly, are the genuine customs, traditions, and identity of our new home.

To make our situation more difficult, rarely do those other responsible adults in our lives whom we rely on for guidance within the dominant culture even attempt to understand our struggle. For instance, in grade seven, a math teacher told me I should "lighten up" after I explained an incident at recess when kids were throwing erasers at me, pretending they were bombs. In grade ten, a coach I had never met before thought he was complimenting me by saying I played like a "little terrorist" during a rugby tryout. These sorts of incidents are not unique. They are echoed in the stories of nearly all multicultural youth in Canada.

The False Promise of Being a Brown Citizen

Since the government began collecting population data in 1871, Canada has never seen a higher proportion of foreign-born residents (Statistics Canada 2017). With immigration come significant increases in Canada's diversity. By 2036, 80 percent of Canada's population growth will come from migration (Statistics Canada 2017). And in the Prairie provinces, where my family and I live, the share of recent immigrants has more than doubled over the past fifteen years. For these newcomers, not unlike my family's experience, one of the greatest concerns is obtaining Canadian citizenship—the ultimate in-group legal status recognition.

In the first few years in Canada, my family and many other Kurdish families we knew were deeply concerned about citizenship. I remember the day we received our citizenship in the town hall and how excited my entire family was to finally be officially Canadian. As an immigrant youth, I distinctly remember being incredibly proud of finally becoming Canadian upon receiving my citizenship. I have a photo from that day with a mini Canadian flag in hand and a large grin on my face, holding my official documents. But in hindsight, I wonder about my fascination with immigration status as a child who knew little about settlement laws or even deportation. Looking back, it seems to me that my fascination with citizenship, like that of so many immigrant children, revolved around that same longing for belonging. So, for immigrants like us, citizenship affirms that we truly belong to our new home and collective.

Examining more analytically numerous broad and legal definitions, citizenship seems to consistently reference a relationship that is accompanied by rights, privileges, and duties. Those who are undertaking citizenship presumably opt into those duties in exchange for the rights and privileges afforded to them. If so, how can we explain the discrimination faced by immigrants who have become citizens and dutifully fulfill their obligations? They should be shielded from discrimination as full-fledged members of the collective, but in practice, not much changes with the acquisition of official citizenship.

Rogers Brubaker (2010) suggests that citizenship laws are heavily influenced by whatever conception of national identity has historically formed the state. Peter O'Brien (2016), in his analysis of the various immigration policy changes of numerous liberal democracies within the last twenty years, states, "Virtually every national government has revisited and revamped its immigration and naturalization laws—some toward greater exclusivity [...] others toward greater inclusivity" (66). Some nations, such as Germany, that have embraced a more inclusive policy have established through voting processes that this "belonging" should be extended—in theory—but what of countries, such as France, that have opted for more exclusivity? O'Brien writes that "Muslim immigrants in particular tend to experience higher levels of exclusivist discrimination when applying for citizenship" (72). Taking Brubaker's evaluation and applying it to O'Brien's data, we begin to understand how a higher refusal rate for Muslim immigrants may suggest a refusal to accept their belonging within the French national identity, even on a surface or legal level.

This knowledge may help us understand why, in countries such as Canada and Germany, many newcomers continue to feel like aliens even after citizenship is awarded. From a legislative standpoint, Canada disagrees with France regarding designating citizenship; however, it would be naïve to assume that immigrants who are of different backgrounds and cultures are seamlessly accepted as "belonging." While white immigrants from western Europe have accents that may differ from Canadian-born speakers' or may have different cultural habits or mannerisms, they often fit what seems to be the standardized image of a "teammate." Similarly, many political leaders in Germany, Britain, and France have been critical of multiculturalism, publicly denouncing it as a disaster (Citrin, Johnston, and Wright 2012), but have been silent in any criticism of immigrants from the United States or Canada, for example. The assertion seems to be that patriotism or even contribution toward a collective good is only accessible by those who share similar cultural and ethnic identities and habits, perpetuating exclusion regardless of legal citizenship. Indeed, citizenship alone is not a remedy for the alienation we as immigrants feel. In fact, on its own, it may reinforce the perception of a split identity among immigrant youth when recognition as a legal citizen does not come with recognition as a peer or a member of the "team."

Resilience: A Way Out of Identity Purgatory

Feelings of ostracization experienced by immigrant youth in schools and elsewhere deeply impact youth in racialized and minoritized communities and serve as invisible barriers to well-being. Strong evidence points to racism as a social determinant of mental and overall health, with a recent meta-analysis concluding that "racism is significantly related to poorer health, with the relationship being stronger for poor mental health" (Paradies et al. 2015, 15). Systemic/structural racism is often invisible to actors within the dominant culture's institutions, meaning that schools and even supportive programming are underequipped to deal with the fallout (18). These factors add to the challenges racial and ethnic minority youth already face as they seek to develop a healthy sense of their cultural identity, develop their strengths, and build a strong social network. When youth must shoulder family stresses, navigate relationships with parents, and deal with racism and bullying at school in addition to the typical adolescent challenges of struggling with schoolwork and finding employment, these intersecting pressures can quickly derail mental health and resiliency.

Among culturally diverse youth, resiliency has been predicted by (1) the capacity of the individual to navigate through health-sustaining resources, including finding opportunities in which they have positive experiences, and (2) the capacity of the individual's family, community, and culture to provide these health resources and positive experiences in a way that is culturally meaningful for the individual (Ungar 2008). With proper support, immigrant youth and their communities can be equipped to foster resiliency and deal with adversity.

In retrospect, this is exactly what my sister tried to help me do. In 2007, she dragged me kicking and screaming to the youth group she created with support from an organization called Multicultural Health Brokers Cooperative (MCHB Cooperative; https://mchb.org/). The program, which was funded by Alberta Health Services' Addiction and Mental Health Branch, brought together not only Kurdish youth but other ethno-cultural youth from all over Edmonton. These children, like me, were living in identity purgatory. I had little interest when my sister and the other youth leaders approached subjects about our Kurdish identity. By this point, in my early teens, I was not particularly interested in being once again boxed into identifiers associated with my culture. Nor was I particularly interested in the traditional dance, arts, and clothing we were required to interact with or try on during these sessions. I remember insisting that the food, prepared by a local Kurdish women's group, was inedible and demanding a burger or fries on the way home. I had experienced too much trauma with my Kurdish identity. I didn't want to experience that identity anymore. I just wanted to be a "normal" Canadian kid.

What I did have an interest in, what I grew to love, were the connections I made with kids who were just like me. I also loved the soccer time they used to bargain with us in exchange for an hour of Kurdish-related activities, which featured folk stories and occasionally learning the Kurdish alphabet. Over time, though, it became more difficult to tune out the barrage of facts, history lessons, and mythologies about the place where I was born. Day by day, I found myself listening more intently when we talked about Kurdistan. I found myself more interested in our struggle for independence and feeling how unfair it was that we still did not have our own country. When I was growing up, my mom and dad had tried to tell me stories about Kurdistan, but I rarely listened. Now, with the support of other Kurdish youth and mentors who made my own culture interesting to me, I felt more empowered as I learned more about my Kurdish identity.

To my surprise, this newly acquired interest in Kurdistan did not make me feel any less Canadian, nor did it mean I could no longer identify with my friends who were not Kurdish. It simply alleviated bit by bit a path of self-destruction I was pursuing in the desire to be white or to elevate my social, political, and cultural status in proximity to whiteness. By the time I was in university, the youth group, through years of meaningful involvement, had tricked me into loving my Kurdish self. The experience had such a profound effect on me that when my sister decided it was time for her to move on with her career, I offered to become the youth leader of the Kurdish group.

This new role connected me to what I found out was a chain of youth groups, all supported by the MCHB Cooperative, representing sixteen different ethno-cultural communities. I found similar success stories in other communities that had little in common with my own except for one factor—the active youth and community leaders who had experienced (and to some extent still did) the immigrant youths' cultural context in a way that other support groups could not fully understand. These leaders were able to make time to develop individual connections with youth whom they knew had histories of difficult experiences surrounding their identity. The community groups recognized that building relationships with youth is a process of building trust, so as the programs have grown, youth who were once participants struggling with their circumstances, such as myself, are now helping their communities' leaders run the programs or have taken over the programs as leaders themselves. I believe the key to these programs' success is the culturally rooted, responsive, and supportive care they provide. According to Alberta Health Services' (2015) anchoring document *Foundations of Caregiver Support*, "It is critical that children be immersed in their culture so that they can internalize a healthy self-concept and positive cultural identity" (3). If a host country such as Canada is to adequately support struggling immigrant youth, this philosophy must be integrated universally into intervention programs.

Just under twenty years ago, Dr. Tara Yosso (2005) from the Graduate School of Education at the University of California discussed the "cultural wealth" of racialized and immigrant children. To summarize, Yosso examined the cultural wealth that minority students leverage to bolster their resiliency in the competitive schooling environment. Simply put, she interviewed graduate students who were children of immigrants who did not come from privileged backgrounds, and she found that although many of these students did not have the same financial security as their peers, they brought talents, strengths, and experiences with them to their college environment that were fostered by their family relationships. Their parents, grandparents, aunts, and uncles—all these relationships armed them with forms of capital that Yosso describes as including but not limited to linguistic capital (the ability to speak more than one language) and aspirational capital (the ability to maintain hope and dreams for the future in the face of real and perceived barriers). These forms of capital were essential in their ability to traverse the university landscape, and they also added diversity of thought to the students' environment, which was crucial in their own learning and that of their peers.

While responsive interactions are key to alleviating the struggle immigrant youth undergo, I believe that support for them needs to be culturally rooted, culturally safe, and interculturally competent to be effective. Too often, service providers and others from the dominant culture, albeit with the best of intentions, intervene with cultural minority children and their families in ways that increase, rather than prevent or bridge, the painful cultural gaps that often exist in immigrant children's ability to develop healthy bicultural, bilingual identities. This failure is often a result of ignoring the cultural contexts in which the youth live and approaching their support within a rigid Eurocentric framework that inevitably positions them as "other."

Despite the hope that culturally rooted programs bring to their communities, such programs are profoundly lacking in funding, support, and resources. Programs like the youth groups rely on year-to-year funding and often are put in competition against one another. This funding shortfall sends the message that this programming is non-essential, despite the profound effect it has had on many youths. And because immigration patterns have changed dramatically over the last century, there is a great need to prioritize these programs. The increase in immigrant populations, combined with limited resources and the inability to provide proper support, has the potential to result in many kids being left behind, struggling with a fragmented sense of identity.

Concluding Thoughts: From Identity Purgatory to Cultural Wealth

Although many immigrant children had no say in the circumstances that led to their arrival in Canada, they are faced with the repercussions that accompany their resettlement. Their sense of identity is often split between their ancestral identity and the dominant cultural identity they do not operate in. Often, this fragmented identity creates a tension that the youths are forced to deal with regularly—for example, when questions such as "Where are you from?" lead to stereotypes and negative labels. A common response in such instances is to distance themselves from their own cultural identity in pursuit of belonging to the dominant culture, which may manifest itself in the desire for citizenship as a pathway to belonging. Immigrant youths' embrace of the dominant culture may further alienate them when they discover that citizenship alone is not a remedy for the "othering" they experience. To foster an inclusive environment and to limit the struggles of these youth, there should be a concentrated effort to tap into their cultural wealth through community-based programming. This programming should also be supported by policy and resources—namely, funding—to allow it to empower youth within their own cultural identities.

Working with the MCHB Cooperative, now as the coordinator for community-led youth programming, I know that my experiences are not unique to me. They are echoed by the over 650 youth we work with annually. I also know that allowing youth space to explore their cultural identity and connecting them with support tailored by their own community can play a vital role in relieving the anxiety of struggling with their own identity. I now know that my story, like the stories of so many immigrants like me, is a story not just of struggle but of perseverance. Examining our communities from a lens of appreciation reveals the cultural capital embedded within them, not just in the contributions immigrants can make to all facets of Canadian society, economically and culturally, but in their resilience and courage. With evidence gathered over sixteen years of youth-focused programming, we also now know that youths who are connected to support systems that understand their struggles and are embedded in their communities can build their resilience and thrive.

As immigrants, our cultural heritage identity is inescapable. Often, it is etched in the colour of our skin, the smell of our food, and the traditions we carry from those who came before us. There is value in that culture, and youth must be reminded that their unique identity is another piece of the beautiful mosaic of our society. And some of us who now support other immigrant youth can make it clear to them that their feelings are mentionable and manageable. By doing so, we will have done a great service not only for them but for ourselves.

References

Abedi, Maham. 2019. "37% in Ipsos Poll Say Immigration Is a 'Threat' to White Canadians—What's the Threat?" Global News, May 22, 2019. https://globalnews.ca/news/5288135/immigration-threat-canadians-poll/.

Alberta Health Services. 2015. *Foundations of Caregiver Support: Government of Alberta*. Edmonton: Alberta Health Services. https://alignab.ca/wp-content/uploads/2016/10/Foundations-of-Caregiver-Support-June-2015-Final.pdf.

Brubaker, Rogers. 2010. "Migration, Membership, and the Modern Nation-State: Internal and External Dimensions of the Politics of Belonging." *Journal of Interdisciplinary History* 41, no. 1 (Summer): 61–78. https://www.jstor.org/stable/40785026.

Citrin, Jack, Richard Johnston, and Matthew Wright. 2012. "Do Patriotism and Multiculturalism Collide? Competing Perspectives from Canada and the United States." *Canadian Journal of Political Science* 45 (3): 531–52. https://www.jstor.org/stable/23320998.

Foroni, Francesco, and Myron Rothbart. 2013. "Abandoning a Label Doesn't Make It Disappear: The Perseverance of Labeling Effects." *Journal of Experimental Social Psychology* 49 (1): 126–31. https://doi.org/10.1016/j.jesp.2012.08.002.

Guterres, António. 2020. "Plan of Action on Hate Speech." United Nations. https://www.un.org/en/coronavirus/we-must-act-now-strengthen-immunity-our-societies-against-virus-hate.

O'Brien, Peter. 2016. "Citizenship." In *The Muslim Question in Europe: Political Controversies and Public Philosophies*, 65–103. Philadelphia: Temple University Press. https://www.jstor.org/stable/j.ctt1kft8dx.6#metadata_info_tab_contents.

Organization for the Prevention of Violence. 2019. "Building Awareness, Seeking Solutions." https://preventviolence.ca/publication/building-awareness-seeking-solutions-2019-report/.

Paradies, Yin, J. Ben, N. Denson, A. Elias, N. Priest, A. Pieterse, A. Gupta, M. Kelaher, and G. Gee. 2015. "Racism as a Determinant of Health: A Systematic Review and Meta-Analysis." *PLoS ONE* 10 (9): e0138511. https://doi.org/10.1371/journal.pone.0138511.

Ser, Kuang Keng Kuek. 2016. "Data: Hate Crimes Against Muslims Increased After 9/11." *World*, September 12, 2016. https://theworld.org/stories/2016-09-12/data-hate-crimes-against-muslims-increased-after-911.

Statistics Canada. 2016. "Census Profile, 2016 Census." https://www12.statcan.gc.ca/census-recensement/2016/dp-pd/prof/details/page.cfm?Lang=E&Geo1=PR&Code1=01&Geo2=PR&Code2=01&Data=Count&SearchText=canada&SearchType=Begins&SearchPR=01&B1=All&TABID=1.

Statistics Canada. 2017. *Immigration and Diversity: Population Projections for Canada and Its Regions, 2011 to 2036*. Ottawa: Statistics Canada. https://www150.statcan.gc.ca/n1/pub/91-551-x/91-551-x2017001-eng.htm.

Ungar, Michael. 2008. "Resilience Across Cultures." *British Journal of Social Work* 38, no. 2 (February): 218–34. https://doi.org/10.1093/bjsw/bcl343.

Xu, Xiao. 2020. "Data Shows an Increase in Anti-Asian Hate Incidents in Canada Since Onset of Pandemic." *Globe and Mail*, September 13, 2020. https://www.theglobeandmail.com/canada/british-columbia/article-data-shows-an-increase-in-anti-asian-hate-incidents-in-canada-since/.

Yosso, Tara J. 2005. "Whose Culture Has Capital? A Critical Race Theory Discussion of Community Cultural Wealth." *Race, Ethnicity and Education* 8 (1): 69–91. https://doi.org/10.1080/1361332052000341006.

8 Precarious Inclusion
Refugees in Higher Education in Germany

Encarnación Gutiérrez Rodríguez

In September 2020, a petition calling for the immediate evacuation of Moria revealed the disastrous and inhumane conditions of the refugee camps on the Greek island of Lesbos.[1] Designed for 2,500 inhabitants, the camp housed approximately 13,000 women, men, and children. It was set on fire—most likely by right-wing extremists—on the night of September 8, 2020, forcing 13,000 refugees waiting for their asylum applications to be processed to sleep on the streets. Families, children, and elderly people found themselves in a desperate situation: they were often subjected to racist attacks but were prevented by the police from going to the hospital in Mytilene. In response to this dire situation, a request was made to the European Union (EU) to provide immediate humanitarian assistance. During the first weeks of September 2020, the EU debated the possibility of offering shelter to unaccompanied minors. On September 11, 2020, the German internal affairs minister announced that four hundred unaccompanied children would be relocated to the Greek mainland.[2] As an EU member state, Germany called on other EU countries to participate in a rescue action that would provide shelter for refugees in Moira. Most of the states either hesitated or refused outright to take in refugees. Countries such as Hungary and Poland, but also Austria and Sweden, openly expressed

---

1 See International Movement for the Evacuation of Moria (2020).
2 See Deutscher Bundestag (2020).

their unwillingness to shelter refugees in crisis conditions, while countries like Spain, Italy, and Greece drew attention to the numerous refugee camps they already provide and their role as European border guards, preventing refugees from venturing any further into EU territory (Hess and Petrogiannis 2020). The German government reacted to this crisis by agreeing to receive 1,500 refugees from Greece.

Asylum and migration policies within the EU are marked by political conjunctures: the rise of extreme right-wing political forces and the COVID-19 pandemic have accelerated and accentuated the restrictive nature of these policies. It is against this backdrop that the discussion about the access of persons seeking asylum in Germany is set. The prevention of access to education for refugees applying for asylum is a symptom of the inhumane character of this process. This chapter engages with the project Branch Out: Initial Support for Transcultural Learning, which took place at Justus-Liebig-University (JLU) in Giessen between 2016 and 2018 and attempted to create spaces of access to post-secondary education where none existed before. However, the structural ability of this project to dismantle the barriers to post-secondary education for refugees has been very limited. In this chapter, I discuss the paradox of attempting to provide a certain degree of access to university while being confronted with unyielding barriers to post-secondary education for refugees. The discussion of the project Branch Out that follows illustrates the inhumane living conditions of persons seeking asylum in Germany while offering immediate provisional suggestions on how to deal with this problem. The lack of institutional support for projects like this one, as our discussion will also show, demonstrates the need for universities to create access to post-secondary education for those seeking asylum—and for refugees as a whole. I will first embed this question within the analytical framework of the asylum-migration nexus by engaging with EU asylum policies. I will then discuss access to post-secondary education for students seeking asylum by focusing on Germany, in particular on the Branch Out project. Within this context of asylum seeking, I will look at the potential and limits of transcultural learning. Finally, I will end with some observations and concluding remarks about how to build an anti-racist intersectional university.

Coloniality of Migration, Asylum, and Access to HEIs

Research on access to post-secondary education for refugees conducted in the last few decades highlights the dynamics of exclusion and inclusion in universities (see Dryden-Peterson and Giles 2012). Khalid Arar, Yasar Kondakci, and Bernhard Streitwieser (2020) note that studies on displaced people, particularly refugees, have been neglected by research on international student migration. The inclusion of displaced people, undocumented migrants, and refugees in post-secondary education requires further research to provide a better understanding of the relationship between asylum and migration policies and inclusion in higher education institutions. Existing research draws attention to questions of social justice by emphasizing education as a human right (Smith 2004). However, Sarah Dryden-Peterson and Wenona Giles (2012, 3) observe that education "is not often included in humanitarian responses" to refugees' needs. The 1951 Refugee Convention "recognizes the fundamental rights of refugees to access education, earn a livelihood, and seek justice when wronged" (ibid.). Free access to primary education is guaranteed to children, but access to post-secondary education is seldom mentioned in relation to the educational inclusion of refugees in Europe. Notably, the United Nations' (1989) Convention on the Rights of the Child emphasizes that this right should also include access to post-secondary education. As Dryden-Peterson and Giles (2012) argue, post-secondary education for refugees is a sustainable resource for society as a whole and a stepping stone for the development of universal quality education. This claim is particularly important when we consider migration policies as framed within what I call the coloniality of migration (Gutiérrez Rodríguez 2018, 2023). Migration control and management policies, seen from the perspective of the coloniality of power (Quijano 2000), exert mechanisms of colonial differentiation inserted in classification systems that produce and mark social hierarchies. Embedded in a human/non-human dichotomy, migration policies lead to the creation of societal positionalities framed by processes of dehumanization. This is particularly true when it comes to the negation of basic human and citizenship rights such as access to secondary and post-secondary education. My discussion of the situation of refugees in German higher education institutions (HEIs) in this chapter addresses these inhumane conditions while also following local and timely attempts at minor destabilization or collective strategies that challenge this situation—namely, the pilot project Branch Out: Initial Support for Transcultural Learning in HEIs.

Research on access to post-secondary education for refugees in the EU has primarily been conducted in the United Kingdom (Stevenson and Willott 2007), followed by Germany (cf. Blumenthal et al. 2017; Lambert, Blumenthal, and Beigang 2018) and Austria (Atanasoska and Proyer 2018). Between 2015 and 2017, German society experienced "the long summer of migration" (Kasparek and Speer 2015). This term describes the developments following the September 2015 march of thousands of refugees from the Keleti railway station in Budapest toward Austria, Germany, and other parts of western Europe. During this time, diverse social actors reacted positively to this movement by supporting the arrival of refugees locally. There were numerous initiatives in neighbourhoods, villages, towns, and cities to welcome refugees and promote their inclusion. Promoted by the regional state of Hesse and JLU in Giessen, the project Branch Out: Initial Support for Transcultural Learning was founded at the university. Drawing upon this experience, this chapter reflects upon the potentiality and limitations of current programs on refugees' access to post-secondary education.

From Exile to Refugees: The Asylum-Migration Nexus

After World War II, most countries in Europe committed to the individual right to asylum for those fleeing war, political persecution, and authoritarianism. Until 1993, this individual right to asylum was the legal basis for acquiring political refuge. After the unification of the German Democratic Republic (GDR) and the Federal Republic of Germany (FRG) in 1989, German nationalism re-emerged, and racial myths about the so-called German Volk reappeared; both manifested on the street as racist attacks against refugees and migrants. Media and political debates played an important role in this political conjuncture: racist images of "overburdening refugee boats" heading toward Europe were disseminated by newspapers and television news. Refugees were constructed in the media not as needing shelter but as "invaders." Those seeking asylum in Europe, particularly in Germany, were suspected of making bogus asylum claims. Thus, the human right to asylum was turned into a state regulatory device, subjected to political conjunctures, no longer based on individual entitlement to sanctuary or shelter for persons fleeing violence and persecution. Since the change of the asylum law in Germany in 1993, the individual right to asylum has been restricted. Asylum claims are decided on the basis that the countries are considered by the German state as "unsafe" or "safe" countries in regard to human rights infringements. Currently, persons fleeing war or political, religious, gendered, or sexual persecution are able to apply for asylum, with the outcome dependent on the specific facts of their case within their countries' capacity of state protection. Asylum laws, however, are constantly modified and tightened, and the state's goal is to process asylum applications as quickly as possible. The number of deportations of people whose petitions for asylum have been rejected is steadily increasing (Pro Asyl 2021).

In 2020, the EU enforced migration containment through the implementation of the New Pact of Asylum and Migration (NPAM).[3] This pact's neoliberal rhetoric introduces terms such as *responsibility*, *solidarity*, *talent*, and *resilience*, appealing to a discourse of protection of refugees and balanced, fair decision-making. According to the European Commission (2020),

> Migration is a complex issue, with many facets that need to be weighed together. The safety of people who seek international protection or a better life, the concerns of countries at the EU's external borders, which worry that migratory pressures will exceed their capacities and which need solidarity from others. Or the concerns of other EU Member States, which are concerned that, if procedures are not respected at the external borders, their own national systems for asylum, integration or return will not be able to cope in the event of large flows. Based on a holistic assessment, the Commission is proposing a fresh start on migration: building confidence through more effective procedures and striking a new balance between responsibility and solidarity.

While this rhetoric seems to guarantee the well-being of refugees, we would be mistaken in this assumption. The "new balance between responsibility and solidarity" addresses the need for cooperation among EU member states for implementing measures and policies on the national level to foster the control of the union's external borders, coordinating asylum application proceedings, and fostering effective policies of deportation throughout the EU. The use of the term *solidarity* is contemptuous and self-serving—its

---

3 See European Commission (2020).

goal is to monitor the entry of refugees to EU territory based on national labour market demands and economic interests. In other words, what is meant here is solidarity among EU countries rather than global solidarity and responsibility. The costs should be evenly shared across EU member states. Words like *flexibility* and *resilience* allude to the implementation of measures to monitor and regulate migration into the EU in times of so-called crisis. The respective measures are subsumed under the labels of "preparedness and crisis blueprint" and "effective crisis response"—in the latter, "solidarity mechanisms" outline "relocation and return sponsorships." EU member states are asked to equitably participate in the "relocation" or distribution of refugees among individual countries or to help with what is euphemistically called the "responsibility of returning"—that is, the deportation of those with no legal residence in any member state. For countries opposed to hosting refugees, like Hungary or Poland, this "fair share of responsibilities" would mean "sponsoring" the deportation of refugees in Greece or Italy. Creating an effective and speedy decision-making process as well as an acceleration of deportation measures, the cooperation among the EU member states contributes to fostering the control of Schengen and the EU's external borders. After several political debates and submission to extreme right-wing and conservative forces within the EU, the New Pact on Migration and Asylum was agreed upon by the European Parliament and the Council in December 2023. The agreement addresses five main areas of regulation within the EU:

- **Screening Regulation:** Creating uniform rules concerning the identification of non-EU nationals upon their arrival, thus increasing the security within the Schengen area.
- **Eurodac Regulation:** Developing a common database gathering more accurate and complete data to detect unauthorised movements.
- **Asylum Procedures Regulation:** Making asylum, return and border procedures quicker and more effective.
- **Asylum Migration Management Regulation:** Establishing a new solidarity mechanism amongst Member States to balance the current system, where a few countries are responsible for the vast majority of asylum applications, and clear rules on responsibility for asylum applications.

- **Crisis and Force majeure Regulation:** Ensuring that the EU is prepared in the future to face situations of crisis, including instrumentalisation of migrants. (European Commission 2023[4])

Since 2020, the New Pact has delivered various outcomes regarding the control of EU borders and the deportation of refugees. It established "warning and forecasting systems allowing prompt identification of migration situations" (ibid.) and a common European deportation system through the EU Return Coordination, established on March 2, 2022. Besides the control of borders and the reduction of asylum claims, the NPAM outlines the need to reform and revise migrant labour recruitment policies within the EU under the point "skills and talents." The NPAM has defined four tasks:

- reform of the EU Blue Card for highly skilled workers;
- revision of the Single Permit Directives enabling low and medium-skilled workers to regularize their employment on an individual basis;
- revision of the Long-Term-Residence Directives addressing the mobility of EU citizens within the EU; and
- the creation of a talent pool for the recruitment of international specialized workers based on national employment demands. European Commission (2020[5])

Considering this new EU development, the post-secondary educational inclusion of refugees seems to be a remote endeavour. The NPAM rhetoric of integration—prominently established in EU pacts on migration and asylum in the late 1990s and the beginning of the millennium—is rather silent when it comes to HEI access for persons seeking asylum. Equally absent is the human right of asylum: the offer of shelter for people suffering displacement or persecution or escaping from war and conflict zones. What is never mentioned is Europe's own participation in and responsibility for the creation of global inequalities.

The analysis of global migratory movements from former European-colonized territories as well as territories at the center of international political conflicts where the EU plays a significant role calls to mind Anibal Quijano's (2000, 2008) framework of the coloniality of power, which has

---

4 See European Commission (2023).
5 See European Commission (2020).

informed my own work on the coloniality of migration (Gutiérrez Rodríguez 2016, 2018, 2023). We cannot discuss contemporary asylum and migration control rhetoric and policies without acknowledging the modern colonial entanglement from which they surface. Drawing upon Quijano's analysis of the coloniality of power, the coloniality of migration refers to new forms of racism, producing a nomenclature of racial differentiation, categorization, and classification developed through migration and asylum policies. These policies degrade and dehumanize persons with regulations that attempt to govern their lives and attack their subjectivity. Encompassing different social sites, asylum and migration policies aim to hinder movement and impose restrictions on individual autonomy and agency. Among those sites regulated by asylum and migration policies is post-secondary education.

During the application process, asylum seekers have a limited right to work and no rights when it comes to their educational goals, besides being obliged to participate in German courses and so-called integration classes. If not granted asylum, they will be given permission to remain in the country for a specific period of time. In general, the right of asylum has become a device in migration control policies. As I argued in my article on the coloniality of migration (Gutiérrez Rodríguez 2018) following Stephen Castles's (2006) paradigm of the migration-asylum nexus, the humanitarian goal of asylum policies has become connected to the labour market demands of nation-states. In the twenty-first century, asylum in the Global North has become a field of governance shaped by utilitarian nation-state approaches mediated by global economic and political conjunctural governance strategies and interests. It is necessary, then, to acknowledge the field of asylum as an entry point for the control and management of migration and to focus on the link between national asylum policies and migrant labour recruitment strategies.

The asylum-migration nexus draws attention to the global historical and contemporary economic and political entanglement (Gutiérrez Rodríguez 2021) in which humanitarian migratory movements are nationally administered through devices attached to the political governance of asylum. Focusing on the governance of asylum makes us aware of its political implications: asylum is related to other fields of global governance linked to development policies, integration, and public security practices. The field of public security has especially been the subject of political attention since the turn of the century, with 9/11 inaugurating a new period in the governance of asylum and migration, shaped by the introduction of increasing control and surveillance measures linked to political threat and terrorism addressed by nation-states and regional international organizations.

The asylum-migration nexus is mediated through the political conjuncture of security practices on three levels. First, it is managed in connection to the "collateral damage" caused by global wars and political conflicts. Second, it is related to the surveillance and control of national and regional borders and the production of bordering and border control devices and rhetoric. This positioning reproduces the refugee and migrant as the racialized other of Europe, constructed in popular media and political debates as a potential threat to the nation's social cohesion. Third, asylum and migration configure institutional semantic fields, producing a nomenclature of hierarchical differentiation and categorical classification of causes, patterns, and trajectories that serve as rationales for the refusal of asylum. These circumstances undermine the ethical obligation of states to offer asylum as a universal human right.

Asylum policies are also governed by the integration aims of nation-states. Refugee access to the labour market has been at the forefront of nation-state integration agendas. As the Socio-Economic Panel at the German Institute for Economic Research (DIW Berlin) demonstrated in its 2019 study *IAB-BAMF-SOEP Survey of Refugees in Germany*, 43 percent of male refugees who arrived in Germany in 2015 found employment (DIW Berlin 2022). Regarding those from Syria, although two-thirds were highly educated, they were unable to find employment commensurate with their educational qualifications. The study notes that refugee women have not experienced the same degree of inclusion into the labour market as men. Furthermore, refugees were generally paid less than their German counterparts for similar jobs. While the integration of refugees into Germany's labour market has received attention, their inclusion within post-secondary education has been scarcely studied.

Access to Post-secondary Education for Students Seeking Asylum

In 2018, the Federal Office for Migration and Refugees estimated that there were 1.5 million refugees in Germany, with more than two-thirds of them arriving in 2015. In 2019, 71,000 adults applied for asylum in Germany—12,000 of them Syrian, 7,500 Turkish, and 6,000 from Iran (Brücker et al. 2019). Half of all applicants were younger than thirty years old, 47 percent were married, and 60 percent self-defined as men. Most of the women—56 percent—came from Syria. Twenty-four percent of all applicants had obtained a university degree, 19.9 percent had secondary education, 29.8 percent had attended a middle school, and 17 percent had received primary education. The applicants with the highest educational level came from Iran, followed by Turkey (Bundesamt für Migration und Flüchtlinge 2020). These figures demonstrate that a large percentage of persons in the asylum application process could be enrolled in post-secondary institutions, but how are these institutions responding to this reality?

There are at least three entry points to post-secondary educational institutions for refugees in Germany. First, on arrival, school-age refugee children are integrated into the German primary and secondary school system. Research in this area demonstrates that more than 90 percent of children who arrived since 2015 have completed a German-language proficiency course. These children accessed regular German schools, continuing to post-secondary education after receiving their *Abitur*. Yet, as recent research (de Paiva Lareiro 2019) on refugees in secondary education demonstrates, a large percentage of school students who entered the country as refugees attend the vocational secondary school (*Hauptschule*), with only a small percentage attending the intermediate secondary school (*Realschule*) or the college preparatory school (*Gymnasium*). The German education system streams students, based on their grades, to either an academically oriented education (Gymnasium), where students enroll in an Abitur program,[6] or a vocational route with a shorter educational period (Hauptschule), or a mix of both (Realschule) that lasts one year longer than the Hauptschule but does not offer an Abitur. This three-tier system reflects deep social inequalities based on class and migration background. The Hauptschule has a high percentage of working-class children, largely from migrant and refugee families, while the Gymnasium remains the stronghold of the white German middle classes. Students in the Hauptschule and Realschule need to obtain qualifications equivalent to the Abitur to access post-secondary education.

The integration of students from refugee families into post-secondary educational institutions, such as research-intensive universities or more vocationally oriented schools, has been channelled through their integration into the primary and secondary education system and through the efforts of several

---

6 The Abitur is the German access exam for university.

civil institutions and actors since the summer of migration. Alarmist political debates and media reports about the influx of migrants in 2015 marked the summer of migration with the trope "refugee crisis." Part of German civil society reacted to the new arrivals with hospitality, or what the Merkel government termed at that time *Willkommenskultur* (welcome culture). Local initiatives emerged, such as Teachers on the Road, an association of teachers and educators offering free German courses to refugees in refugee camps and elsewhere. Civic institutions such as trade unions, workers' associations, and churches also organized social assistance and support for refugees, providing a broad range of additional services, including accompanying refugees to doctors or bureaucratic meetings (Karakayali 2016). This volunteerism (Yurdakul et al. 2018) was not new, however. It resulted from the anti-racist refugee social movements and their advocacy groups beginning in 2013 (see also Doppler 2021), which drew attention to their situation in Germany but also other parts of Europe, such as Austria, Belgium, and France. As Bernhard Streitwieser and Lukas Brück (2018, 43) note, this "level of civil society engagement became a critical bridge" in organizing the arrival of refugees. Some critics (Schmitz 2016) have pointed out that while motivated by political conviction and compassion, this work risked being patronizing and racist by infantilizing or exoticizing refugees as revolutionaries or treating them as inferior to the presupposed "modern European subject." Nevertheless, between 2015 and 2017, this culture of "hospitality" opened new possibilities for the creation of support networks, providing local access to medical, health, education, work, and housing facilities.

Some of these refugee advocacy groups became active in universities, creating pathways to post-secondary education (Steinhardt and Eckhardt 2017; Streitwieser et al. 2017). At this time, most refugees had just arrived and were still in the process of applying for asylum—a status that does not confer the right to post-secondary education. The requirements for entry to post-secondary education can be summarized in three routes: (1) higher secondary education qualification, (2) German-language proficiency, and (3) proof of sufficient financial means for the course of study, including health insurance. Following university registration, international students need to apply for an international student visa in order to obtain fixed-term study residency status in Germany. The third route (point 3) to post-secondary education applies to recently arrived refugees with secondary school education qualifications equivalent to the German Abitur or who have attended university in their countries of origin.[7] This last route drew the attention of the Federal Ministry of Education and Research (BMWF) between 2015 and 2018.

Refugees could not officially apply for regular admission to university. However, most post-secondary educational institutions offered a guest-student status for refugees, allowing them to audit courses while applying for asylum. Many of the refugees who took advantage of this offer held high school diplomas and had begun university or already earned a degree in their countries of origin (Brücker, Rother, and Schupp 2016). The German federal government, in turn, implemented a funding program for prospective students seeking asylum. Funded by the BMWF, this program provided universities and preparatory colleges (*Studienkollegs*) with administrative support in creating additional preparatory courses (Grüttner et al. 2018). By 2016, a large number of German post-secondary institutions had partially introduced German-language preparatory courses, audit study programs, and German courses for refugees (see Streitwieser and Brück 2018). In total, eleven of the sixteen German *Länder* (states) launched BMWF-funded programs to promote refugees' access to post-secondary education between 2016 and 2017. These initiatives addressed (a) the establishment of personal support through buddy or tandem programs, (b) additional German courses, (c) social interaction activities between local and international students, and (d) the creation of access routes for refugees to guest-student programs, bridging courses, or other measures aimed at preparing refugees for regular study programs (Schammann and Younso 2017; Steinhardt and Eckhardt 2017).

The BMWF worked closely with the German Academic Exchange Service (DAAD) and other research-funding bodies, such as the Humboldt Foundation and the Volkswagen Foundation, and the funding institutions affiliated with political parties, such as the Hans Böckler,[8] Rosa Luxemburg,[9] and Heinrich Böll[10] Foundations. All of them established scholarships for at-risk

---

7 Among recently arrived refugees, 17 percent have started a post-secondary degree, 11 percent have completed a post-secondary degree, 44 percent aspire to complete a secondary degree, and 68 percent are interested in a professional or academic career (see DIW Berlin 2022).

8 See home page: https://www.boeckler.de/de/index.htm.

9 See home page: https://www.rosalux.de/.

10 See home page: https://www.boell.de/en/startpage.

students and academics fleeing war zones, authoritarian regimes, and political persecution. Furthermore, the DAAD assisted university international offices in providing audit study programs and offering German-language courses (Fourier et al. 2017). Between 2015 and 2019, the DAAD made €100 million available to implement the Integra program. As the DAAD notes, the Integra program financially supports DAAD measures "to help academically qualified refugees" access German universities "by offering language instruction and subject-specific preparatory courses" (DAAD, n.d.).

All these programs offered some access to education by enabling students with refugee status to audit courses and enroll in German courses, with the possibility of attending regular information events on campus. However, not all programs led to full access to post-secondary education. Some universities—such as the University of Applied Sciences in Magdeburg, the University of Saarbrücken, the University of Osnabrück, and the University of Göttingen—developed programs enabling students with refugee status to enroll as first-time university students or continue the studies they had initiated in their home countries. These programs provided access to specific areas of study, particularly mathematics, informatics, hard science, and technology. Other universities did not develop this access route to post-secondary education for students in the process of seeking asylum; instead, they provided an advocacy and volunteering structure that supported students seeking asylum with German classes and audit programs. Among these universities was JLU. In response to the BMWF call, and mediated through the Hessian Ministry of Higher Education and the Arts (HMWK), several projects received funding between 2016 and 2017 for initiatives that supported access for students seeking asylum. Among them was Branch Out.

Branch Out: Initial Support for Transcultural Learning

Branch Out: Initial Support for Transcultural Learning provided a teaching module in the Bachelor of Arts in Social Sciences at the JLU Institute of Sociology between 2016 and 2018. Other projects funded by HMWK at the JLU Faculty of Social and Cultural Studies trained education students by promoting their intercultural skills or supported students working with refugee families and children. Established in the Professorship of General Sociology, Branch Out was interested in bridging connections between JLU students and individuals who had recently arrived in Giessen and applied for asylum and who wanted to initiate or continue their studies in Germany. To realize this aim, the Professorship of General Sociology collaborated with the Giessen refugee advocacy group an.ge.kommen e.V.[11] on the Branch Out project. Established at the beginning of the summer of migration, an.ge.kommen e.V. offered support, along with German courses, and functioned as a social, cultural, and political hub for persons arriving as asylum seekers and their supporters in Giessen. Operating as a link between the university and people seeking asylum, the aim of an.ge.kommen e.V. was to work not *on* but *together with* refugees.

Branch Out was built on this conviction with the following goals: (a) to be a bridge between the university and persons seeking asylum in Giessen, (b) to offer asylum seekers introductory access to the university, and (c) to establish a transcultural learning space for major and minor students pursuing bachelor's degrees in social sciences and asylum seekers enrolled in this program (Theuerl 2021). As part of the project, a one-year research-oriented course where students could develop a small student-led ethnographic project was established. This course was integrated into an existing third-year module in the social sciences bachelor's program: the *Lehrforschungsprojekt* (fieldwork research course). The Branch Out course was offered in English and consisted of one year of fieldwork research on the topic of "arrival, city, and migration." The course was capped at thirty students and offered twice during 2016 and 2018. A half-time lecturer—a doctoral candidate in sociology and a co-founder of an.ge.kommen e.V.—was employed for two years to run the course with HMWK funding. The course was advertised as a regular course in the social sciences bachelor's program, and an.ge.kommen e.V. disseminated this information in their advocacy networks working with persons seeking asylum in Giessen. In response, approximately twenty people applying for asylum expressed interest in the course, with ultimately ten of them enrolling. At that time, persons seeking asylum in Hesse were transferred to the main reception center for refugees, located in Giessen. The refugee reception center—actually a refugee camp—is situated on the outskirts of town behind the main train station. Established in 1946 for German expellees from Eastern Europe, followed by displaced persons between the 1950s and 1980, the camp housed refugees from the Soviet zone and the

---

11 See web page: http://angekommen-giessen.de.

GDR (van Laack 2017). In the 1990s, it was then transformed into the central reception center for asylum seekers in Hesse.

Between 2015 and 2017, the number of refugees arriving in Hesse increased rapidly, and the center reached full occupancy. New arrivals were thus sent to provisional camps (*Lager*) consisting of tents or former military barracks. Participants in the Branch Out course lived in the refugee center in Giessen or in one of the regional Lager. To ensure course attendance, funding was made available for bus and train tickets, as attendees were not registered as regular JLU students because of their legal status and were not eligible for student tickets. Branch Out worked with asylum seekers who wanted to study in Giessen. The students who were asylum seekers participated in the course through the university audit program for refugees.

Despite legal barriers for students seeking asylum, Branch Out offered them the opportunity to gain some insight into how the university functioned while also allowing interested social sciences students to meet colleagues in other disciplines, such as global health or law. These opportunities were supported by a group of teaching assistants (TAs) funded by HMWK who worked with the convenor of the Branch Out course. The TAs were last-year BA students in social sciences and education with a specific profile—namely, (a) a social science background with a focus on migration and diaspora studies, (b) experiences working with refugees and migrants, (c) transcultural competence, and (d) multilingual skills. All the TAs were active in refugee and migrant advocacy groups; came from families who had arrived in Germany as migrants or refugees from Afghanistan, Iran, or Turkey; and spoke a variety of languages such as Arabic, Farsi, Urdu, Spanish, and German. As a result, the Branch Out classroom environment was multilingual. Furthermore, because the course was offered in English rather than German, it attracted major and minor social sciences BA students, international exchange students, and ERASMUS students.[12] The ERASMUS students came from countries such as Spain, Italy, and Turkey, while the international students were from South Africa or Ukraine. Some of the BA students also had experience studying abroad or were from families who had experienced migration.

Besides multilingual skills, class participants also brought a variety of viewpoints to the question of migration, both from their own experiences

---

12 ERASMUS is a European Union student exchange program that takes place between European universities.

and from having attended lectures or classes on this topic. While the German students were pursuing their regular study program, the international and ERASMUS exchange students were on their year abroad. Some of the German students had spent a year abroad at another European university. Thus, the students, the TAs, and the lecturer all shared the experience of mobility, though in very different forms: exile, migration, or spending some time abroad. While the experience of not knowing the language and being new to a place was something they all shared, only the asylum seekers had experienced dangerous, life-threatening situations during their journey, after experiencing violence, the loss of loved ones, and the destruction of their homes. These heterogeneous, sometimes conflicting experiences were productive on both methodological and conceptual levels.

These different perspectives on migration and exile were approached by forming small student working groups that developed research projects and conducted place-based ethnography by contacting initiatives and organizations that served as points of contact for newcomers to Giessen, including German organizations (for example, Caritas) working with refugees and migrants, a Kurdish organization, and neighbourhood initiatives. During this year, students reviewed the literature on migration and exile while examining methodologies such as urban ethnography, walking methods (Racleş 2021), and place-based research. They presented their research projects during the last class. Branch Out's aims were tailored to the students' needs. While the German and international students pursued their regular course units, for those in the asylum process, the course gave them access to the university and the city's support structures in regard to education, health care, the job market, religion, childcare, and social activities. A safe space was created for those seeking asylum with the aim of offering support, "partial allyship" (Sempértegui 2019), and practical solidarity (Garbe 2021). Efforts were made to create an inclusive, non-discriminatory classroom.

In summary, there were three elements in the goals of this class: (a) immediate access to the university for persons seeking asylum, (b) cooperative learning for all participants, and (c) place-oriented fieldwork for all participants. Branch Out drew on the buddy model by establishing partnerships between local students and newly arrived persons but went beyond by fostering common transcultural learning practices drawing on experiential and placed-based knowledge (Theuerl 2021). This was achieved by creating small working groups of social sciences students, asylum seekers, and ERASMUS and international exchange students. The Branch Out classroom was a microcosm that could be described using Mary Louise Pratt's (1991) concept of contact zones: social spaces "where cultures meet, clash and grapple with each other, often in contexts of highly asymmetrical relations of power, such as colonialism, slavery, or their aftermaths as they are lived out in many parts of the world today" (34). In the Branch Out microcosm, teaching and learning evolved transculturally, demonstrating the potential, but also limits, of creating access to the university for persons seeking asylum.

The Limits and Potential of Transcultural Learning Within the Context of Asylum Seeking

Branch Out operated under the assumption that the classroom is a site of transcultural encounters and disencounters (Ortiz 1995) that occur on the grounds of antagonistic relationships shaped by entangled global inequalities (Gutiérrez Rodríguez and Reddock 2021). Drawing on Pratt (1991) and Ortiz (1995), Branch Out considered the university as a transcultural contact zone, a perspective that framed the learning and teaching approach. Within JLU as a transcultural contact zone, four issues had to be navigated: (a) power relations in the classroom, (b) the diverse entry points to learning, (c) multilingualism, and (d) the structures of individual and class support.

Research conducted by the groups introduced local and newly arrived students to the university and the support infrastructure in Giessen. Furthermore, while becoming acquainted with support networks and institutions, students took courses in sociological qualitative and ethnographic research, exploring stories of escape and migration. However, despite this common learning course, students did not meet on equal terms. Their educational, economic, institutional, and cultural lives differed. Thus, while the German and international students were completing their majors or minors in the social sciences bachelor's program, the persons seeking asylum had only partly completed their bachelor's degrees, mainly in areas not related to social sciences. Their interest in this course emerged from their aim to access the university, and this particular course offered partial access to it through its audit program. Even course attendance did not provide them with regular student status. Access to student status was tied to German university requirements, German-language proficiency, recognition of their acquired school and study degrees abroad, basic income, and proof of local accommodation (Weiser

2016). For persons seeking asylum or in the status of *Duldung* (a limited legitimation of the right to remain that is given to persons who cannot be deported based on health issues or personal vulnerabilities), these requirements were hardly achievable, as very often they lacked German-language proficiency, their degrees were not homologized, and their income and housing facilities were precarious. Undocumented migrants do lack any legal access to education.

In addition to limited access to post-secondary education, Branch Out attendees also experienced economic hardship and transportation problems. As applicants for asylum, they were obliged to live in initial reception facilities for six weeks to a maximum of twenty-four months, though this time period was often exceeded. These housing facilities were composed of old military barracks, abandoned buildings, or emergency tent compounds on the outskirts of villages or towns. The participants of Branch Out lived under these circumstances. As already mentioned, most of them lived in the refugee camp in Giessen or other nearby Lager; their travel to the university was organized through crowd-funding support because they did not receive any financial support at all. As they did not have student identification cards because they were not registered as regular students, they could not access the basic infrastructure providing IT facilities, housing, and access to student cafeterias or sports facilities. Branch Out was able to facilitate limited access to the library, the cafeteria, and e-class facilities while voicing concerns about these limitations in the university-created network for refugee affairs, which operated from 2015 to 2019. As a result, temporary access to some of the university's facilities was made available during this time. However, no institutional changes were made to provide refugees enrolled with audit status permanent access to the broader university infrastructure.

On the cultural level, language was a major barrier, as German was the language of instruction for most courses, with very few offered in English. Furthermore, proficiency in languages other than German and previous academic training of class members varied according to their class and educational background. In terms of gender, although the class as a whole was composed of an equal number of self-identified women and men, most of the refugee students were men. This in part reflected the fact that there were fewer women among the refugees who arrived in Giessen. Nevertheless, this fact does not deter from the need to develop a tailored approach toward women in the refugee camps, including mothers, as refugee political self-organised groups such as Women in Exile e.V.[13] and International Women* Space[14] do. As research on this question demonstrates (Negin and Dryden-Peterson 2017), childcare provision as well as the inclusion of digital education might open other avenues to facilitate the participation of refugee women in post-secondary education, considering that this group shows a high educational achievement profile (Brücker et al. 2019).

Despite these institutional limitations, Branch Out created an interactive space of communal learning and teaching. While some of the refugee students did not know when their applications for asylum would be processed or how long they would live in Giessen or Germany, they were still able to establish relationships of trust and reliance with their peers. The inequalities structuring the classroom were determined by the impact of asylum and migration policies on the students subjected to these regulations, in particular those seeking asylum. The students with German passports or passports from other EU member states had not experienced personal harm caused by asylum and migration control policies. However, Europeans, particularly German students racialized as Black, persons of colour, or migrants, though they had legal residency status as citizens, shared some of the experiences of everyday institutional racism at the university. These experiences of othering and racism were reflected upon in the classroom.

Some of the refugee students were not able to continue with Branch Out because they were moved to other refugee camps in other parts of Germany or their attendance was interrupted due to the schedule and demands of the bureaucracies processing their applications for asylum. Despite the barriers to entering the university that students seeking asylum encountered, Branch Out facilitated access to the university. Out of the group of refugee students attending the course, three were able to enroll in master's courses at German universities following the approval of their asylum applications. In general,

---

13 The organization Women in Exile e.V. visits and supports the organization of refugee women in the Lager. They work on empowerment strategies for refugee women and their access to health, education, and politics. See https://www.women-in-exile.net.

14 The organization International Women* Space is actively engaged in the self-political organizing of Black refugee and migrant women against border and migration necropolitics. They work on access to health, education, and politics for refugees. See https://iwspace.de.

all the students gained insight into the support structure for new arrivals to the city of Giessen. For the BA students at JLU, this course was unique: their learning practices connected with their immediate lives. The place-based ethnography enabled them to reflect on the immediate historical entanglements shaping their lives and to understand society through this angle. Migration was no longer an abstract concept in a textbook or on the news but became a lived experience connected to their own lives. For the ERASMUS and international students, this course helped them understand the global character of a local phenomenon. They often compared the situation in Germany with their countries of origin, introducing a comparative perspective on the subject of migration. The course also offered the students applying for asylum the possibility to connect to other working groups and networks at JLU, such as the Research Network on Human Rights and Migration. The Branch Out experience was shared with colleagues in the JLU task force group on refugees and in Germany-wide networks of universities working with refugees coordinated by the Berlin Center on Integration and Migration.

From a short-term perspective, Branch Out as a pilot project was unique in its approach to heterogeneous learning backgrounds and place-based analysis. It also succeeded in creating a classroom that challenged the nation-state border logic by admitting students whose regular access was denied by asylum policies. For a module in sociology, this was an extraordinary experience and opened up the possibility for universities to actively take part in challenging the space of learning by beginning to transform the classroom and thus contribute to the creation of an inclusive, anti-racist society. However, the university was unable to continue with the project due to a lack of funding. By autumn 2015, the welcoming political climate of the summer of migration had abruptly veered in the opposite direction. Following the 2015 New Year's Eve incident in Cologne, racist imaginaries went viral, fuelled by rapidly growing hostility against refugees among certain segments of the German population (Carastathis et al. 2018). This expression of anti-refugee racism also became evident in the national elections of 2017, where the extreme right party received an increase in votes. The models of anti-racist inclusive classrooms in post-secondary education trialled in the wake of the summer of migration did not result in any lasting institutional commitments on the level of anti-discrimination strategies in German universities. Given these circumstances, concrete measures for building the anti-racist intersectional university require further consideration.

Conclusion: Building the Anti-racist University—an Ongoing Project

In this chapter, I have discussed the relationship between refugees and post-secondary education in Germany using the case of the pilot project Branch Out. Focusing on the broader engagement of German universities in providing access to post-secondary education between 2015 and 2018, I have discussed the specific characteristics of Branch Out and its potential to delineate a new learning horizon by creating a multilingual transcultural classroom. I have also critiqued the lack of institutionalization of inclusive intersectional transcultural learning projects in German post-secondary education. Following other researchers in the field, I assert that this recent development of access to post-secondary education for refugees in Germany has been unique and needs to be further developed. To enable this development, as other researchers (Jungblut, Vukasovic, and Steinhardt 2020) argue, several criteria for controlling access to post-secondary education in Germany need to be reformed.

First, the requirement for German-language proficiency needs to be adjusted. Due to the demand for German-language proficiency, refugee students who participated in pathway programs to gain access to the university were not able to complete this program because they could not meet the language requirements (Aver 2018; Fourier et al. 2018; Schiffauer, Eilert, and Rudloff 2017; Trautwein 2015). The German-language proficiency requirement, currently C1, should be lowered or replaced by a subject-specific language proficiency (Unangst 2019). Second, potential health problems related to depression and trauma should be taken into account. Third, financial hurdles to university study need to be considered (Stifterverband 2017). If these barriers are addressed, as some researchers note, the German experience can represent "a chance for universities to scale up services for all students" and enable refugee students' access to higher education (Streitwieser and Unangst 2018, 16). As the DAAD's programs Integra and Welcome have shown, providing refugees with German-language and preparatory university courses, along with offering alternative routes to higher education via credential assessment and subject matter competency testing, might represent some valid options (ibid.). Furthermore, as Bernhard Streitwieser and Lisa Unangst (2018, 16) note, universities need to address equality-sensitive aspects because "refugees have to work through socioemotional trauma, asylum uncertainty, and a societal backlash."

If the anti-racist, intersectional, and inclusive work conducted in universities does not translate into institutional changes, then well-intentioned inclusion offers no more than empty promises. As Bernhard Streitwieser and Lukas Brück (2018, 44) note, these inclusion measures can "set up unrealistic expectations for some refugee students" by creating the impression that they have been enrolled or accepted as students; however, auditing courses offers them only temporary and limited access to the university. On another level, researchers have proposed that a change be made to the admission criteria level access mark (*Numerus Clausus*) for refugee students, and all students in general, and have called for emergency funds for housing, transportation, food, and books as well as fellowships for refugees. In the case of Branch Out, the university's general audit study program focused only on refugees with a fixed status, while those in the process of seeking asylum were not included. However, Branch Out worked with persons seeking asylum and communicated this to the international office, creating an exception to the audit program for Branch Out participants. A long-term engagement with a transcultural model of education enabling access for persons wishing to complete their studies in Germany while seeking asylum requires further institutionalization. Programs addressing the needs of women seeking asylum need to be considered within established gender equity and promotion policies and processes in universities. Branch Out argued for the need to develop inclusion strategies in the university for all refugees irrespective of gender identity and those seeking asylum by supporting their access to post-secondary education. As Dryden-Peterson and Giles (2012) argue, access to post-secondary education for refugees is a tool to achieve autonomy and agency. Furthermore, the Branch Out experience argues for the incorporation of anti-discrimination awareness and transcultural learning/teaching methods as pillars of the curriculum and classroom levels in universities.

On a more general level, inclusion in post-secondary education provides all citizens with the potential for social transformation and is a vital tool in decolonizing the university. This means that, first and foremost, migration and border control policies that subject human beings to administrative devices, preventing them from accessing basic human rights such as the right to education, need to be abolished. Everyone, despite their legal residency status, should have access to education, including post-secondary education. Refugees having started their studies in their countries of origin previous to their leaving should have immediate access to their careers. It is incomprehensible, for example, to publicly state that there is a shortage of doctors in Germany, while medical school students from Afghanistan, Iran, Syria, and Egypt are not allowed to study while they are in the process of applying for asylum.

Considering the abolition of migration and asylum control policies as instruments of dehumanization, deployed against persons seeking refuge and a better life, represents the first step in the project of decolonizing the university. Decolonizing the university means here striving for racial, gender, economic, and social justice. This is an urgent task in order to work through Europe's complicity in the creation of global inequalities that are rooted in its colonial, settler-colonial, and imperial activities and contemporary political and economic interests. The conversation on reparations for European atrocities committed during colonialism in Africa, for example, remains an open question in Germany. Why do we not think about these reparations from the angle of the asylum-migration nexus and what it would mean in regard to the provision of post-secondary education access for refugees?

Acknowledgement

I would like to thank Anna Kirova for her insightful comments and Michele Faguet for her thorough reading of this chapter.

References

Arar, Khalid, Yasar Kondakci, and Bernhard Streitwieser. 2020. "Higher Education for Forcibly Displaced Migrants, Refugees and Asylum Seekers." *Higher Education Policy* 33:195–202.

Atanasoska, Tatjana, and Michelle Proyer. 2018. "On the Brink of Education: Experiences of Refugees Beyond the Age of Compulsory Education in Austria." *European Educational Research Journal* 17 (2): 271–89. https://journals.sagepub.com/doi/10.1177/1474904118760922.

Aver, Caner. 2018. "Beteiligung von Bildungsinländer*innen mit Migrationshintergrund an der Hochschulbildung in Nordrhein-Westfalen Zusammenfassung." ResearchGate, December 2018. https://www.researchgate.net/publication/337244613_Beteiligung_von_Bildungsinlanderinnen_mit_Migrationshintergrund_an_der_Hochschulbildung_in_Nordrhein-Westfalen_Zusammenfassung.

Blumenthal von, Julia, Steffen Beigang, Katja Wegmann, and Valentin Feneberg. 2017. *Forschungsbericht. Institutionelle Anpassungsfähigkeit von Hochschulen.* Berlin: Berliner Institut für empirische Integrations und Migrationsforschung.

Brücker, Herbert, Johannes Croisier, Yuliva Kosyakova, Hannes Kröger, Giuseppe Pietrantuono, Nina Rother, and Jürgen Schupp. 2019. "Zweite Welle der IAB-BAMF-SOEP-Befragung. Geflüchtete machen Fortschritte bei Sprache und Beschäftigung." Bundesamtes für Migration und Flüchtlinge, 2019. https://nbn-resolving.org/urn:nbn:de:0168-ssoar-67577-1.

Brücker, Herbert, Nina Rother, and Jürgen Schupp, eds. 2016. *IAB-BAMF-SOEP-Befragung von Geflüchteten. Überblick und erste Ergebnisse.* Berlin: Berliner Institut für empirische Integrations und Migrationsforschung.

Bundesamt für Migration und Flüchtlinge (National Ministry for Migration and Refugees). 2020. *Migration Report 2018.* Berlin: Bundesamt für Migration und Flüchtlinge. https://www.bamf.de/SharedDocs/Anlagen/EN/Forschung/Migrationsberichte/migrationsbericht-2018.html?nn=1018856.

Carastathis, Anna, Natalie Kouri-Towe, Gada Mahrouse, and Leila Whitley. 2018. "Introduction: Intersectional Feminist Interventions in the 'Refugee Crisis.'" *Refuge: Canada's Journal on Refugees* 34 (1): 3–15.

Castles, Stephen. 2006. "Global Perspectives on Forced Migration." *Asian and Pacific Migration Journal* 15:17–28.

DAAD (German Academic Exchange Service). n.d. "Integrating Refugees in Higher Education—the 'Integra' Funding Programme." Accessed November 1, 2023. https://www.daad.de/en/information-services-for-higher-education-institutions/further-information-on-daad-programmes/integra/.

de Paiva Lareiro, Cristina. 2019. *Ankommen im deutschen Bildungssystem. Bildungsbeteiligung von geflüchteten Kindern und Jugendlichen.* Ausgabe 02/2019 der Kurzanalyse des Forschungszentrums Migration, Integration und Asyl des Bundesamtes für Migration und Flüchtlinge. Nürnberg: Bundesamt für Migration und Flüchtlinge.

Deutscher Bundestag. 2020. "Konsequenzen aus dem Brand im Flüchtlingslager Moria auf Lesbos verlangt." 2020. https://www.bundestag.de/dokumente/textarchiv/2020/kw37-de-moria-791342.

DIW Berlin (German Institute for Economic Research). 2022. "IAB-BAMF-SOEP Survey of Refugees in Germany." November 29, 2022. https://www.diw.de/en/diw_01.c.538695.en/projects/iab-bamf-soep_survey_of_refugees_in_germany.html.

Doppler, Lisa. 2021. *Widerständiges Wissen. Herbert Marcuses Protesttheorie in Diskussion mit Intellektuellen der Refugee-Bewegung der 2010er Jahre.* Bielefeld, Germany: Transcript.

Dryden-Peterson, Sarah, and Wenona Giles. 2012. "Higher Education for Refugees." *Refuge* 27 (2): 3–9.

European Commission. 2020. "Pact on Migration and Asylum." September 2020. https://commission.europa.eu/system/files/2020-09/new-pact-on-migration-and-asylum-package_1.pdf.

European Commission. 2023. "What Is the New Pact on Migration and Asylum of the EU." https://home-affairs.ec.europa.eu/policies/migration-and-asylum/new-pact-migration-and-asylum_en.

Fourier, Katharina, Linn Hildebrandt, Julia Kracht, and Katharina Latsch. 2018. *Zukunftswege: Erfolge und Herausforderungen bei der Integration von Geflüchteten ins Studium*. Bonn: Deutscher Akademischer Austauschdienst / German Academic Exchange Service. https://www2.daad.de/medien/der-daad/zukunftswege_barrierefreie_version.pdf.

Fourier, Katharina, Julia Kracht, Katharina Latsch, Ulrich Heublein, and Carolin Schneider. 2017. *Integration von Flüchtlingen an Deutschen Hochschulen: Erkenntnisse aus den Hochschulprogrammen für Flüchtlinge*. Bonn: Deutscher Akademischer Austauschdienst / German Academic Exchange Service. https://www.daad.de/medien/der-daad/studie_hochschulzugang_fluechtlinge.pdf.

Garbe, Sebastian. 2021. *Weaving Solidarity. Decolonial Perspectives on Transnational Advocacy of and with the Mapuche*. Bielefeld, Germany: Transcript.

Grüttner, Michael, Jana Berg, Stefanie Schröder, and Carolin Otto Stefanie. 2018. "Refugees on Their Way to German Higher Education: A Capabilities and Engagements Perspective on Aspirations, Challenges, and Support." *Global Education Review* 5 (4): 115–35.

Gutiérrez Rodríguez, Encarnación. 2016. "'Flüchtlingskrise,' Kolonialität und Rassismus—eine andere Grammatik der Krise des Kapitalismus denken." *Das Argument* 319 (58): 1–18.

Gutiérrez Rodríguez, Encarnación. 2018. "The Coloniality of Migration and the 'Refugee Crisis': On the Asylum-Migration Nexus, the Transatlantic White European Settler Colonialism-Migration, and Racial Capitalism." *Refuge* 34 (1): 16–28. https://doi.org/10.7202/1050851ar.

Gutiérrez Rodríguez, Encarnación. 2021. "Temporal-Spatial Entanglements of Global Inequalities: On Care and Domestic Work in Western Europe." In *Decolonial Perspectives on Entangled Inequalities: Europe and the Caribbean*, edited by Encarnación Gutiérrez Rodríguez and Rhoda Reddock, 77–96. New York: Anthem.

Gutiérrez Rodríguez, Encarnación. 2023. *Decolonial Mourning and the Caring Commons: Migration-Coloniality Necropolitics and Conviviality Infrastructure*. Anthem Studies in Decoloniality and Migration. New York: Anthem.

Gutiérrez Rodríguez, Encarnación, and Rhoda Reddock, eds. 2021. *Decolonial Perspectives on Entangled Inequalities: Europe and the Caribbean*. Anthem Studies in Decoloniality and Migration. New York: Anthem.

Hess, Sabine, and Vasileios Petrogiannis. 2020. *Border Experiences and Practices of Refugees: Comparative Report*. Working Papers on Global Migration: Consequences and Responses, 2020/62. Göttingen University and Uppsala University: RESPOND: Multilevel Governance of Migration in Europe and Beyond.

International Movement for the Evacuation of Moria. 2020. "Moria: Immediate Evacuation | Evacuation Immediate | Sofortige Evakuierung." Change.org, September 12, 2020. https://www.change.org/p/moria-immediate-evacuation-evacuation-immediate-άμεση-εκκένωση-sofortige-evakuierung-evacuación-inmediata?recruiter=1148573462&recruited_by_id=7df6a760-f510-11ea-a496-cb041e322c32&utm_source=share_petition&utm_medium=copylink&utm_campaign=petition_dashboard.

Jungblut, Jens, Martina Vukasovic, and Isabel Steinhardt. 2020. "Higher Education Policy Dynamics in Turbulent Times—Access to Higher Education for Refugees in Europe." *Studies in Higher Education* 45 (2): 327–38.

Karakayali, Serhat. 2016. "Practicing Willkommenskultur: Migration and Solidarity in Germany Intersections." *East European Journal of Society and Politics* 2 (4): 69–86.

Kasparek, Bernd, and Marc Speer. 2015. "Of Hope. Hungary and the Long Summer of Migration." Translated by Elena Buck. bordermonitoring.eu, September 9, 2015. https://bordermonitoring.eu/ungarn/2015/09/of-hope-en/.

Lambert, Laura, Julia von Blumenthal, and Steffen Beigang. 2018. *Flucht und Bildung: Hochschulen*. State-of-Research Paper 8b, Verbundprojekt, Flucht: Forschung und Transfer. Osnabrück: Institut für Migrationsforschung und Interkulturelle Studien der Universität Osnabrück; Bonn: Internationales Konversionszentrum Bonn.

Negin, Dahya, and Sara Dryden-Peterson. 2017. "Tracing Pathways to Higher Education for Refugees: The Role of Virtual Support Networks and Mobile Phones for Women in Refugee Camps." *Comparative Education* 53 (2): 284–301.

Ortiz, Fernando. 1995. *Cuban Counterpoint: Tobacco and Sugar*. Durham, NC: Duke University Press.

Pratt, Mary Louise. 1991. "Arts of the Contact Zone." *Profession*, 1991, 33–40.

Pro Asyl. 2021. "Thema, Fakten, Zahlen." https://www.proasyl.de/thema/fakten-zahlen-argumente/statistiken/.

Quijano, Anibal. 2000. "Coloniality of Power, Eurocentrism, and Latin America." *Nepantla: Views from South* 1 (3): 533–80.

Quijano, Anibal. 2008. "Coloniality of Power, Eurocentrism, and Social Classification." In *Coloniality at Large: Latin America and the Postcolonial Debate*, edited by Mabel Moraña, Enrique D. Dussel, and Carlos A. Jáuregui, 181–224. Durham, NC: Duke University Press.

Racleş, Andreea. 2021. *Textures of Belonging. Senses, Objects and Spaces of Romanian Roma*. New York and Oxford: Berghahn.

Schammann, Hannes, and Christin Younso. 2017. "Endlich Licht in einer dunklen Ecke? Hürden und Angebote für Geflüchtete im tertiären Bildungsbereich." *Zeitschrift für internationale Bildungsforschung und Entwicklungspädagogik* 40 (1): 10–15.

Schiffauer, Werner, Anne Eilert, and Marlene Rudloff, eds. 2017. *So Schaffen Wir Das: Eine Zivilgesellschaft im Aufbruch. 90 wegweisende Projekte mit Geflüchteten*. Bielefeld, Germany: Transcript.

Schmitz, Markus. 2016. "Das Begehren der >Flüchtlinge<. Überlegungen zur Psyho(patho)logie der deutschen Flüchtlingsdebatte nach dem Märchen grenzenloser Hilfsbereitschaft." *Das Argument* 319, 58 (5): 694–706.

Sempértegui, Andrea. 2019. "Indigenous Women's Activism, Ecofeminism, and Extractivism: Partial Connections in the Ecuadorian Amazon." *Politics & Gender* 17 (1): 1–28.

Smith, Merrill. 2004. "Development Without Refugee Rights? A Civil Society Response." *Fordham International Law Journal* 28 (5): 1479–1503. https://core.ac.uk/download/pdf/144225862.pdf.

Steinhardt, Isabel, and Lukas Eckhardt. 2017. "'We Can Do It': Refugees and the German Higher Education System." In *Refugees Welcome? Recognition of Qualifications Held by Refugees and Their Access to Higher Education in Europe: Country Analyses*, edited by Jens Jungblut and Karolina Pietkiewicz, 25–42. Brussels: European Students' Union.

Stevenson, Jacqueline, and John Willott. 2007. "The Aspiration and Access to Higher Education of Teenage Refugees in the UK." *Compare* 37 (5): 671–87.

Stifterverband. 2017. *Hochschulbildungsreport 2017*. Essen: Edition Stifterverband.

Streitwieser, Bernhard, and Lukas Brück. 2018. "Competing Motivations in Germany's Higher Education Response to the 'Refugee Crisis.'" *Refuge* 34 (2): 38–51.

Streitwieser, Bernhard, Lukas Brueck, Rachel Moody, and Margaret Taylor. 2017. "The Potential and Reality of New Refugees Entering German Higher Education: The Case of Berlin Institutions." *European Education* 49 (4): 231–52.

Streitwieser, Bernhard, and Lisa Unangst. 2018. "Access for Refugees into Higher Education: Paving Pathways to Integration." *International Higher Education* 95 (Fall): 16–18.

Theuerl, Marah. 2021. "Transforming Education: Reflections on the Potential and Future of Transcultural Spaces and Learning in Higher Education." In *Decolonial Perspectives on Entangled Inequalities: Europe and the Caribbean*, edited by Encarnación Gutiérrez Rodríguez and Rhoda Reddock, 219–36. New York: Anthem.

Trautwein, Peggy. 2015. *Heterogenität als Qualitätsherausforderung für Studium und Lehre: Ergebnisse der Studierendenbefragung 2013 an den Hochschulen Sachsen-Anhalts (HoF-Arbeitsbericht 1'2015)*. Halle-Wittenberg: Institut für Hochschulforschung (HoF) an der Martin-Luther-Universität.

Unangst, Lisa. 2019. "Refugees in the German Higher Education System: Implications and Recommendations for Policy Change." *Policy Reviews in Higher Education* 3 (2): 144–66.

United Nations. 1989. *Convention on the Rights of the Child*. New York: United Nations. https://www.ohchr.org/en/professionalinterest/pages/crc.aspx.

van Laack, Jeannette. 2017. *Einrichten im Übergang: Das Aufnahmelager Gießen (1946–1990)*. Frankfurt am Main: Campus.

Weiser, Barbara. 2016. *Recht auf Bildung für Flüchtlinge*. Berlin: Informationsverbund Asyl und Migration. https://www.nds-fluerat.org/wp-content/uploads/2017/02/Recht-auf-Bildung-für-Flüchtlinge.pdf.

Yurdakul, Gökce, Regina Römhild, Anja Schwanhäußer, Birgit zur Nieden, Aleksandra Lakic, and Serhat Karakayali, eds. 2018. *Witnessing the Transition: Moments in the Long Summer of Migration*. E-book project of Humboldt University students. Berlin: Berliner Institut für empirische Integrations und Migrationsforschung.

9 (Not) Meeting the Needs of Refugee Students
Toward a Framework for the Humanization of Education

Anna Kirova

In 2019, Save the Children International published a report titled *Stop the War on Children: Protecting Children in 21st Century Conflict*. The report eloquently captures the current state of the world: "Right now, across the world, millions of children are caught up in conflicts they played no part in creating. Often their rights are violated with total impunity" (9). The report points to the disproportional suffering children endure in contemporary wars that tend to last longer and are fought in urban areas with a high density of civilian population, leading to a higher number of deaths and injuries.

Since the publication of the report, two major wars have erupted, continuing these brutal trends—the ongoing war in Ukraine that began with the invasion of Russia on February 24, 2020, and the Israeli-Hamas war that followed the attack of Hamas on Israeli civilians on October 7, 2023, that is affecting predominantly the Palestinian civilians in Gaza. Thousands of children have been killed, severely injured, abducted, displaced, or left orphans as a result of the armed conflicts in the Middle East in the last several decades and, most recently, in the two on-going wars that have led to multiple humanitarian crisis. The reports on children being killed as a result of the indiscriminate bombing or who have died because of the lack of health care or medications or because of the infectious diseases that spread out quickly in the affected territories that lack basic sanitation show an alarming rising trend.

Although absolutely staggering, the unprecedented numbers of people, including children, being killed, injured, or displaced in recent wars cannot capture the scale of human suffering. The images of the complete obliteration of homes, roads, hospitals, schools, and human activities that are shared on a daily basis convey better what life is like for millions of civilians. Yet neither numbers nor images can make those of us who are not in these war/conflict zones feel what it is like to be haunted by the unmistakable stench of decaying human flesh under the rubble, to go for days without food or with very little water, to have no place to sleep, or, for a child, to hold their parent's guiding hand as they make their way through the rubble. Finding an improvised temporary shelter where a hospital or school once stood is a rare, usually very short-lived respite from the immanent dangers of the surrounding world that only a few can find. With more than half of Gaza in ruins, schools are one of the few places where the displaced can take temporary refuge, but the long-term consequences of the total devastation of children's lives—including the loss of family, community, and a place to call home or a place to learn—are yet to be seen.

Iman Farajallah (2023), a psychologist who was born and raised in Gaza and now lives in California and who traveled to Gaza to interview children about their experiences during the previous round of fighting between Israel and Hamas in 2016, offers a glimpse of what some of the consequences of these children's experiences of trauma could be on their emotional and cognitive behavior as well as their ability to function at school and home. She states that the results of two months of the latest Israeli attacks could damage an entire generation of children in Gaza.

As the world celebrates the seventy-fifth anniversary of the Universal Declaration of Human Rights (UN General Assembly 1948), almost sixty-five years since the adoption of the UN Declaration of the Rights of the Child by the UN General Assembly (1959), and almost thirty-five years since the UN Convention of the Rights of the Child (UN General Assembly 1989), it is hard not to agree with the main argument made in the 2019 Save the Children report: "Children suffering in conflict today are not primarily suffering from a deficit of identified rights. Rather, they are suffering from a crisis of compliance with those rights" (10).

It seems that as a whole, the world leaders not only failed miserably to secure children's "inherent right to life" (UNCRC Article 6.1) or protect them from "all forms of physical or mental violence, injury or abuse, neglect or negligent treatment, maltreatment or exploitation, including sexual abuse" (UNCRC Article 19.1), but that the intensified global and local geo-political tensions have created conditions that cause harm in a scale not seen since the second world war.

While the children's right to protection is violated on a daily basis in war and conflict zones, children's rights to education (UNCRC Articles 12, 13, 14, 29, and 30), and more specifically their right to participate in their education is violated even after their resettlement in their host countries often after a long period of living in refugee camps or on the road as their parents or surviving relatives make a long journey to a "safe haven" such as Canada. This begs the question, How do refugee children experience school in Canada?

Niga Jalal shared, "By the time I was five years old, I had survived two wars and a year and a half in a refugee camp, but the hardest thing I had to do was to adjust to school in Canada" (personal communication). This recollection of the first year in elementary school is that of a young woman who came to Canada as a refugee in 1999 because of the ongoing war in Kurdistan. It is the harshest and perhaps the most honest judgment I have come across that reveals the (in)ability of Canada's education system to meet the complex needs of refugee children. It is also one of the most compelling "calls to action" to make changes in the education system so that those who come to Canada as refugees not only find refuge but also fulfill their dreams and aspirations for brighter futures.

One may ask how—in a country of immigrants like Canada, which prides itself on being welcoming and accommodating diversity, a country that, by the time Niga arrived as a child, had more than twenty-five years of multiculturalism as its federal policy—a refugee child could have a more difficult school experience than surviving two wars and living in a refugee camp. Unfortunately, Niga's experience in school is not unique. Refugee students are often dealing with feelings of grief and loss that make it difficult to thrive in school (Celik at al. 2019; Coelho 2004; Elsayed et al. 2019). As a result, the school experience can be a difficult transition for refugee children. Traumatic experiences that children have gone through or witnessed can manifest as troubled behaviour (Eruyar, Maltby, and Vostanis 2018; Strekalova and Hoot 2008). These behaviours may include explosive anger that is inappropriate to a situation, rule testing, problems with authority, age-inappropriate behaviour, an inability to concentrate, withdrawal, and lower academic achievement (Ayoub 2014; Blackwell and Melzak 2000; Strekalova and Hoot 2008).

Providing refugee students with a safe and welcoming environment is critical not only for school success but also for healing. However, providing such an environment largely depends on teachers' training, values, and attitudes (Cummins 2001; Frater-Mathieson 2004; Kaplan et al. 2016). As noted by teachers and school leaders who participated in a recent study conducted in Canada, the lack of appropriate training prevents them from responding to refugee students' needs, or they may respond to behaviours "that could be potentially misunderstood, such as unknown cultural differences or a child becoming aggressive out of fear for personal safety" (Stewart at al. 2019, 65). In some cases, teachers can even contribute to the problem of creating an unsafe environment for refugee students. In my own experience as a political refugee who came to Canada in 1990 with my family, including my five-year-old son, the lack of understanding on the part of some teachers and administrators of my child's experiences had a detrimental impact on his behaviour, learning, and overall attitude toward school.

My son's experiences in elementary school in Canada motivated me to explore childhood loneliness and isolation in school, which became the topic of my second PhD, completed at the University of Alberta in 1996. The methodology I used in that dissertation was hermeneutic phenomenology (van Manen 1994), which concerns itself with subjective lived human experience. The notion of the lifeworld—the world of everyday experience (Husserl [1936] 1970)—is taken as the beginning of the phenomenological understanding of what it means to be human. Jennifer Skuza (2007) argues that phenomenology allows for humanizing the understanding of acculturation experiences. This argument prompts me to ask in this chapter, What does humanizing the educational experiences of refugee students mean? And has the education system concerned itself with the humanization of refugee/immigrant students?

In unpacking these questions, I first provide a brief critical overview of the promises and failures of multicultural and anti-racist education, particularly in regard to their essentialism and assumptions of normalcy. I then define dehumanization and trace its roots in educational theory and practice back to the seventeenth century, when the universal benchmarks for a "civilized" modern human were created and since then have positioned those who are different as less than human. I also provide examples of the impact of dehumanizing practices such as homogenization, "schooling the body," objectification, stereotyping, and racism on multiply minoritized and racialized students, many of whom are also refugees/immigrants and

English-language learners. Finally, I explore the concept of alterity as a key concept in intercultural philosophy and its potential to develop a framework for the humanization of education.

Being Concerned with Humanization

To humanize, according to the *Cambridge Dictionary* (2020), is to "make something less unpleasant and more suitable for people." This everyday understanding of the verb *to humanize* is exemplified in numerous academic and practitioner-oriented publications devoted to making the educational experiences of refugee and immigrant children—most of whom are from ethnic, cultural, racial, and linguistic minority groups—more suitable for their needs. However, Reza Hasmath (2012) found that most teachers' awareness of ethnic differences appears to be at a superficial level. Joanne MacNevin (2012) found that teaching refugee students requires educators to (1) become proficient with different teaching skills, (2) overcome challenges that exist in supporting children emotionally, (3) include refugee students socially and academically in all aspects of the classroom, and (4) build on students' prior experiences.

Although recognizing the experiences refugee students have had when they arrive at school seems to be the logical first step that teachers can take to effectively meet their needs, Jan Stewart (2012) suggests that complications often arise in schools because educators are not fully aware of the complexity of students' migration experiences. Teachers' approaches to inclusion are based on an assumption that all immigrants have had similar pre-migration experiences and therefore would benefit from a similar exercise that fosters diversity and inclusion. For example, in a twenty-five-page booklet, *Dream Big Together*, developed by the Canadian Teachers' Federation in response to a large number of Syrian refugees who arrived in Canada, educators and school administrators in Canadian secondary schools are encouraged to "ignite a dialogue on cultural diversity within the school setting." While the activities proposed in the booklet "encourage students to understand and respect cultural differences and to appreciate similarities with other young Canadians" (Canadian Teachers' Federation 2015), the difference between "immigrant," "refugee," and "ethnic minority" is blurred. Many educators see these measures as pathways to achieving equal accessibility and eliminating discrimination. The uncritical multicultural values fostered in many schools not only do not distinguish between immigrant and refugee experiences, but they also emphasize celebrating differences on special occasions or dates, typically accomplished as an add-on to the regular curriculum, as well as an increased effort to reduce prejudice and promote cultural awareness and knowledge. While these measures leave the status quo intact (see, e.g., Barton and Tan 2020; Giroux 1993; McLaren 1995), it can be argued that they result in pockets of transformative teaching and learning experiences that are "humanizing," in the dictionary definition of the term, for those involved. But has the education system truly concerned itself with humanizing refugee/immigrant students' experiences?

In the most general sense, to "be concerned with humanization is to uphold a particular view or value of what it means to be human, and furthermore to find ways to act on this concern" (Todres, Galvin, and Holloway 2009, 69). In the case of Canada's education system, it seems that being concerned with humanization means that educational institutions act on the values inherent in the Canadian Charter of Rights and Freedoms (Department of Justice Canada 1982), the Canadian Multiculturalism Act (Department of Justice Canada 1988), and the UN Convention on the Rights of the Child (1989) and form standards. However, scholars such as Maria Kronfeldner (2018) have noted that theories of human rights could be conceptualized as resting on a normative conception of human nature that is based on an incomplete set of essentialist assumptions regarding the causal importance of nature in development and evolution. In analyzing the current discourse of inclusion as a framework for providing high-quality learning opportunities for all students, for example, Angela Barton and Edna Tan (2020, 434) argue that such a framework is grounded in the extension of a set of static rights as well as responsibilities "regarding who one is and must become."

In regard to Canada's federal multiculturalism policy, multiple scholars have pointed out that a major problem with its implementation in education is the "lack of federal control over education, and provincial legislation in general, [which] has limited federal ability to influence education in this direction to any meaningful degree" (Ghosh and Abdi 2004, 45). Almost forty years ago, Margaret Gibson cautioned that the general field of multicultural education theory "abounds with untested and sometimes unsupportable assumptions regarding goals, strategies, and outcomes" (1984, 109). Indeed, she suggested that "unless these assumptions are made more explicit and educational practices embody these assumptions, multicultural education as a whole risks being dismissed not only as ineffective but as potentially encouraging of even greater educational inequalities" (as cited in Hoffman 1996, 546). In their review of critical perspectives on multicultural education, Boyle-Baise and Gillette remark on multicultural education's disconnect from its transformative, emancipatory roots in the civil rights movement, noting that it "has been co-opted and redefined within schools, textbooks and teacher education programs as attitudinal, tolerance-oriented, sensitivity training" (1998, 20; see also Sleeter and Delgado Bernal 2004). Its power to promote transformative change has been dulled.

In the past couple of decades, concerns have become stronger among the general public, ethno-cultural communities, and practitioners that schools are poorly equipped to cope with increased diversity and that, instead of facilitating equity and belonging, they foster isolation and replicate racialized forms of injustice (Wideen and Barnard 1999). Such inequalities and injustices are experienced as acts of dehumanization: a process through which some groups are ejected from the category of the human (Abdi 2012; Caraballo and Souto-Manning 2017).

Defining Dehumanization

In her recent book *What's Left of Human Nature? A Post-essentialist, Pluralist, and Interactive Account of a Contested Concept*, Maria Kronfeldner defines dehumanization as "an evaluative stance (merely cognitive or also behavioural) toward other humans that consists in drawing the line between individuals or groups (as in-group/out-group) according to an assumed concept of what it means to be human" (2018, 18). Steffen Herrmann identifies three different ways in which social exclusion as a form of dehumanization can be explained: "as a form of special separation, a lack of participation, or as emanating from practices of misrecognition" (2011, 133; italics in original). Charles Taylor connects identity to recognition or its absence; he states that because our identities are also often shaped "by the misrecognition of others" (1992, 25), a person or group of people can suffer real damage, real distortion, if the people or society around them mirror back to them a confining, demeaning, or contemptible picture of themselves. Nonrecognition or misrecognition can inflict harm and be a form of oppression, imprisoning someone in a false, distorted, and reduced mode of being (25).

Dehumanization is demonstrated in practices such as racism, sexism, classism, and ableism, among others. Nick Haslam (2006) cites Jahoda's historical catalogue of ways in which ethnic and racial others have been represented not only in popular culture but also in scholarship: "as barbarians, who lack culture, self-restraint, moral sensibility, and cognitive capacity" (252). These representations, he argues, have become normalized. Mariana Souto-Manning and Ayesha Rabadi-Raol (2018), in their review of quality in early childhood education over the past thirty years, identify three assumptions about multiply minoritized and racialized children on which the discourse on early childhood education quality was constructed: inferiority, deficit, and cultural difference. They explain these assumptions as follows:

- Inferiority: Children from multiply minoritized backgrounds have been seen as biologically inferior—as having smaller brains and lower IQs than White children, who have been seen as racially superior.
- Deficit: Children from multiply minoritized backgrounds have been seen as experiencing poor upbringings in their homes and communities and developing a deficit—whether linguistic or cultural—for example, having a word gap, being at risk, or needing a head start to succeed in schools and schooling. (These assumptions are grounded in the desirability of colonial monocultural, monolingual norms that have been imposed ethnocentrically and violently onto them.)
- Cultural difference: Children from multiply minoritized backgrounds have been seen as different from the colonial monocultural, White, monolingual norm. (Souto-Manning and Rabadi-Raol 2018, 205–6)

Beyond early childhood, Angela Barton and Edna Tan (2020, 433) provide examples of multiple oppressions "minoritized youth experience through the regularities of classroom practice, including otherization, conditional participation/belonging, and dehumanization." Educational practices informed by these discourses that are based on outdated essentialist ideologies should be understood as dehumanizing, since they position multiply minoritized and racialized children, including refugee/immigrant children, as less than human.

Othering as a Persistent Problem in Educational Theory and Practice

The systemic injustices that manifest themselves through the practice of othering those who are different and therefore presented as less than human have been a persistent problem in educational theory and practice (Kirova 2013; Kirova and Prochner 2015). As Carmen Mills and Julie Ballantyne (2016) argue, inequalities are (re)produced through the social structures of schooling, including assumptions embedded in models of teaching and learning, assessment, and management. In order to understand the historical roots of these inequality-producing social structures, we need to trace them back to the publication of Johan Comenius's *Orbis Sensualium Pictus* (*The Visible World in Pictures*) in 1666.

The Creation of Universal Benchmarks for a "Civilized" Modern Human

Orbis Sensualium Pictus, translated shortly afterward into all official European languages, promoted a particular vision of order, an order presented as "normal" to humankind. This order "privilege[d] some things in particular, and at the same time, through processes of exclusion, segregate[d] that which [was] considered different, foreign, of less value or simply incapable of integration" (Lippitz 2007, 5). As a result, the everyday life of the underclass, unable to fit into the perfectly ordered (divine) structure of the world that was desired, was made invisible.

The underclass's way of living and being was thus excluded; it was seen as a kind of foreignness—that is, a "type of 'sickness' or 'sinfulness' that can always be healed in the great beyond" (Lippitz 2007, 4). The book used the concepts of being human and of human nature for social demarcation. The "civilizing" process of the modern individual/human through the creation of order in schooling has since had an impact on pedagogical theory and practice in many ways, including generalizing the manners and customs of the higher class (in terms of such things as cleanliness and order) as a universal benchmark for a civilized modern individual/human (Lippitz 2007).

The practices of labelling and "fixing" children from certain groups who were deemed different and therefore deficient/other/abnormal (Kirova and Prochner 2015) have persisted. In Canada in 1879, for example, the journalist and newspaper publisher Nicolas Flood Davin (later the member of

Parliament for Assiniboia West) proposed a residential school system for Indigenous children modelled on the Indian industrial schools in the United States and aimed at assimilating "Indians" and "half-breeds" into Canadian society (Prochner 2020). The premise of the residential school system was that "young children could be saved from their lifestyle and become productive citizens of the state and fully assimilate into the dominant society" (Nishnawbe Aski Nation, n.d., quoted in Elementary Teachers' Federation of Ontario 2017, 49). Currently, millions of Roma children in Europe are subjected to similar kinds of dehumanization through the system of segregated schools, despite the European Union's attempts to end such practices (Lambrev, Kirova, and Prochner 2019).

Homogenization: Becoming "One of a Type"

In addition to civilizing or fixing children of lower socio-economic classes or those of non-European descent, the school's role has been (and still is) to socialize all children into the world outside the home, a world that Clinton Collins calls "the third-person world of political life" (1974, 149), a world where people—children, teachers, administrators, and parents—relate to one another on the basis of shared expectations about their respective roles. The role of a child in school is different from their role at home, and the goal of schooling is "to make students out of children" (Lippitz and Levering 2002). Martin Packer and Jessie Goicoechea (2000) suggest that becoming a student requires an ontological change; in contrast to the home, a child in school is asked to become one of a type: a student who is expected to have the same kind of relationship with each teacher based on designated school rules. Or, as Alfred Schütz put it in 1964, students are expected to conduct themselves "in the manner of the anonymous type" (102). This practice of homogenization deemphasizes each person's uniqueness in favour of how they fit the characteristics of a student.

If the experience of schooling can be described as a "foreign imposition" (Lippitz 2007, 7) on all children that results in their becoming cultural hybrids, how is this otherwise for children who are (im)migrants, refugees, or newcomers to the school? In other words, what makes the experience of schooling different for immigrant/refugee children?

Schütz's description of a stranger as a "marginal man, a cultural hybrid on the verge of two different patterns of group life, not knowing to which of them he belongs" (1964, 104) is helpful in understanding immigrant children's experiences of schooling. Although all children are in some sense strangers to schooling, immigrant and refugee children are also strangers in that their history or past experiences are not shared by others in the school. In this sense, the description of a stranger as "a person without a history" (97)—that is, with no shared experiences with others in the school—makes the experience of schooling even more alienating for immigrant children. The accelerated rate of change brought about by the migration experience presents a challenge to refugee/immigrant children as they struggle to recreate a personal history in which past, present, and future make it possible for them to experience continuity and consistency in their sense of being in the world. Refugee and immigrant children's embodied sense of belonging to the homeworld (both the family home and the cultural homeworld) is shaken because they can no longer rely on their tacit knowledge or their language to navigate their journey in the world. As the world remains foreign both inside and outside the school, the sense of dislocation can be overwhelming.

Limiting Human Agency: Schooling the Body

While school rules in most countries in the world concern students' bodily activities (e.g., ways of walking, talking, playing, using equipment), discipline at school differs from school to school and culture to culture. In addition to being unfamiliar with the school spaces in the new country, "learning the ropes" of the school culture can overwhelm the newcomer child. For Iris Marion Young, the requirement to assimilate is unjust because it "always implies coming to the game after it is already begun, after the rules and standards have been set, and having to prove oneself accordingly" (1990, 165). School rules are abstractions sustained by the school/classroom community and by the requirement that students relate to the world in a way that is sanctioned by these rules. However, those who are historically marginalized in schooling, as Barton and Tan (2020, 435) state, "are expected to reconfigure themselves towards the dominant White, patriarchal, English-speaking culture, regardless of the real or symbolic violence such acts require." Particularly insightful here is Michel Foucault's (1977) concept of the necessity of "docility-utility," which was an essential quality of the urban citizenry in capitalist democracy in general and to the smooth and efficient management of institutions such as schools in particular. Brenda Simpson states that "the underlying intent of the school curriculum is to ensure that schools are inhabited by 'docile bodies'" (2000, 63). She argues that the overarching goal of the curriculum is to order children's spatial and temporal lives. Thus, school rules such as the timetable and differentiation of school spaces aim not only to determine the location of all students, individually or in cohorts, at all times (i.e., the "time-space path"; Gordon et al. 1999) but also to determine the correct kind of embodiment acceptable in that place and at that time. While these school rules seem to be in contradiction with the United Nations Convention on the Rights of the Child (UNCRC Article 15; freedom of association), learning the "curriculum of the body" (Lesko 1988, 123) is indeed a difficult task for newcomer students whose daily lives might have been governed by the need to survive or, at best, to get by unnoticed by the authorities.

Lunchtime Routine

A specific example of immigrant and refugee children's struggle with learning foreign rules and acquiring the correct kind of embodiment is the lunchtime routine (Kirova, Mohamed, and Emme 2006). Historically, the purpose of mealtime rules was to socialize children into "proper" behaviour. According to Luis Cantarero, this may be because commensality is seen as the "symbolic manifestation of humanization" (2001, 4). Pierre Bourdieu (1986) points to the competitive dimension of taste and how eating practices are used to establish and reproduce distinctions between social classes.

Meal planning in schools usually favours foods from the dominant culture (Morrison 1996). In relation to Foucault's notion of docility-utility, a dietary regime is a form of schooling bodies (Kirk 2004). Thus, the selection of foods in general and of foods on school menus is based on the ideology of caring for students' health. Outlining a "political anatomy" of the body, Felicity Armstrong (1999) argues that children's bodies are increasingly subjected to pedagogical and medical surveillance. Cultural tensions between private (home) and public (school) views regarding appropriate and nutritious foods can clash in the case of refugee/immigrant families when the food choices are subjected to control and educational guidance on the part of the school.

A clash can also be experienced in the lunchroom, where being rejected by peers based on how food looks or smells or how it is eaten can be a dehumanizing experience for some refugee/immigrant students. A geography of the lunchroom can emerge where particular groups sit in certain locations

(Thorne 1993). The lunchroom geography exemplifies how food choices and practices can serve to regulate social inclusion and exclusion based on divisions between ethnic groups. Barrie Thorne writes that "eating together is a prime emblem of solidarity, and each day there is a fresh scramble as kids deliberately choose where, and with whom, to eat" (1993, 42). The prestige that comes with being part of a social grouping at lunchtime may lead some children to bring "desirable" foods such as candy and chips to use in negotiating a higher position for themselves in the social lunchtime hierarchy. Moreover, navigating through lunch alone without friends can be a painful experience.

Objectification

While school rules and food regulations can negatively affect refugee/immigrant children's self-confidence and self-esteem as a necessary condition of self-realization (Honneth 1996), learning the new language, as the main symbolic system refugee/immigrant children need to master in order to succeed in school, has a much more forceful impact on their identity and overall well-being. If we take Martin Heidegger's (1982) notion that language is the house of being, refugee and immigrant children's initial inability to speak the language of the new world of school is more than an inconvenience. Students whose first language is not the dominant language in school report feeling stupid, laughed at, and embarrassed (Kirova 2007). These experiences also bring feelings of being excluded or rejected. Remedial (English/French) language classes are often held in segregated environments in or outside the school building, which creates and reinforces boundaries between the students in the classes and the rest of the people in the school. The creation of the category "second-language learner" that is also associated with a "code" for funding purposes is an example of a dehumanizing process of objectification. Students labelled as belonging to this category are made into objects by the diagnostic system, which emphasizes the distance between them and "native speakers" of English/French and both solidifies the boundaries between these groups and positions the non-native speakers as inferior and as outsiders.

Language-based discrimination is exacerbated by adding the designation "at risk" to the label "second/additional-language learner." Built on the normativity attached to the concept of human nature, the "at risk" category of students and their families subjects students to a number of intervention programs that they often experience as humiliating as well as useless in terms of meeting their social and academic needs. The proliferation of such programs today indicates that the discourses of cultural and linguistic inferiority according to white monolingual and monocultural norms still perpetuate the colonial values and beliefs firmly grounded in cultural and linguistic normativity. These values inform practices that violate linguistic minority children's right "to use his or her own language" (UNCRC Article 30) and thus to participate meaningfully in their education.

Loss of Meaning

While the different explanations of the relationship between language and meaning offered by different philosophical traditions are beyond the scope of this chapter, under the influence of Wittgenstein, Winch, and Kuhn, among others, the linguistic turn in social science is associated with the view that social life and language are interwoven (Hughes and Sharrock 1997). From this perspective, practices, things/objects, and events in the world are inseparable from language, and the primary means of understanding among members of a society is their everyday language. What children know and can do as they begin formal school is related to their families' and communities' everyday lives and practices. Children's development of everyday concepts is based on the "families' cultural practices associated with their experiences with objects outside of an integrated system of knowledge" (Hedegaard 2007, 248). Cultural diversity in symbols leads to differences across cultures in the way that members of a culture think and express themselves. However, school rules require students to relate to the world by mastering symbolic forms—such as the (Latin) alphabet, numbers, musical notes, and so forth—to represent their knowledge and relationship to the self, others, and the world around them. In contrast to learning at home, scientific concepts are connected to children's activities in settings with conventional symbolic systems the children learn at school. Scientific concepts are organized in an integrated system of knowledge in relation to other concepts about academic disciplines (Kirova, Prochner, and Massing 2019). Thus, school not only necessitates an ontological change in children but also imposes a particular (scientific) epistemological construction of their knowledge of and about the world, which may or may not be similar to the everyday epistemology of their homes (Lippitz 2007). In some cases, it can even contradict their families' worldviews. This may lead to children's inability to exercise their right to form and express their own views (UNCRC Article 12.1). It also violates that child's right to freedom of expression, including "freedom to seek, receive and impart information and ideas of all kinds, regardless of frontiers, either orally, in writing or in print, in the form of art, or through any other media of the child's choice" (UNCRC Article 13.1). Such violations of children's rights can lead not only to internal tension but to the loss of meaning in life. The dehumanization of non-Europeans by the school system worldwide based on the Western worldview has positioned those who speak minority languages and/or have non-Western worldviews as lesser humans, as "barbarians"—a word that literally means, in ancient Greek, those without language or civilization (Kronfeldner 2018, 29).

Stereotyping: Who Is a "Good" Person?

As already discussed, the concept of human / being human can be used for inclusion in or exclusion from groups as well as for respective normative judgments about being a good person / good human. Judgments, according to Young, "are made unconsciously [. . .] and these judgements often mark stereotype, devalue, or degrade some groups" (1990, 133). Venus Nicolino defines stereotypes as "faulty generalizations [that] frequently serve as mental shortcuts" (2006, 17). Stereotyping is a form of dehumanization founded on the belief that certain groups (e.g., Jews or Muslims) are evil people. Assumptions about Muslims, for example, are mostly developed before non-Muslims and Muslims encounter each other and are often based on the negative media projection of Muslims as terrorists, which creates and reinforces stereotypes about them (McCoy, Knight, and Kirova 2011; Zine 2004). These stereotypes support the difference of the other and therefore increase the social distance between the host/dominant society and Muslims. Because of their unfamiliarity with or stereotypical beliefs regarding certain groups, mainstream classroom teachers often underestimate Muslim students' learning abilities and interact differently with them (Barrera 1995; Berhanu 2008; Zine 2006). Goli Rezai-Rashti (1994) criticizes the Eurocentric focus of Canadian education because it often clashes with Muslim students' cultural and religious beliefs. She writes, "In dealing with teachers, students and administrators I find their interaction with Muslim students to be based largely on stereotypes of Muslims that are reminiscent of a long-gone colonial era" (37). Thus, teachers can contribute to escalating anti-Muslim sentiments and behaviours in school. A student in Afshan Amjad's 2016 study, for example, reported that her teacher "showed [the class] a movie about the Holocaust and afterwards said that if a holocaust ever happened again, it would happen to Muslims" (125). As a result, the student had difficulty sleeping for many days, waking up several times during the night because she was having bad dreams about a holocaust for Muslims. In this case, the teacher, in the authority vested in her by the school as a government-funded institution, failed to respect the right of the child to preserve her identity, including nationality and religion (UNCRC Article 8.1).

Racism

Researchers (e.g., Nicolino 2006; Ridley 1995) have found that stereotypes affect the attitudes and behaviours of one group toward another and usually become a major reason to promote the dehumanizing practices of racism. Peers' racist views can result in jokes students make about racialized minority students or even physical attacks (Zine 2008). Kanu (2008), MacNevin (2012), and Stewart (2012) have all identified teachers' attitudes and knowledge levels as factors contributing to racism and discrimination against refugee students. Racism can also become the reason children from certain groups or classes are excluded and can marginalize the competencies of children who have different norms of competence than the dominant society (Ghosh and Abdi 2004). However, Pérez and Saavedra (2017, 5) argue that the so-called achievement gap for students of colour and Indigenous students exists only when education is enacted from three perspectives, as summarized below:

- One rooted in colonization—the epistemological global north belief in the inherent (genetic) deficiency and inferiority of people of colour from the global south or those who have global south positionings within the global north
- The superiority and standardization of global north knowledge
- The corporatization of education through sweeping reforms, neoliberal public policy, and accountability systems

Education enacted from these perspectives positions minoritized children as "less than" from birth (Delpit 2012).

What Can Be Done?

So far, this chapter has explored the dimensions of dehumanization found in educational theory and practice and has demonstrated how the image of a normalized child has been legitimized and widespread through Western onto-epistemological dominance that has had devastating consequences for multiply minoritized and marginalized children, including refugees. These dimensions violate many of the articles of the UNCR and serve as barriers to the humanizing potential of education, especially in the case of students from refugee backgrounds who have already been subjected to the most severe forms of dehumanization—war, genocide, and other forms of violence—because of who they are. So what can be done? What would the educational experiences of refugee students look like if the education system concerned itself with humanization? Kronfeldner writes, "From the social point of view, dehumanization itself is the challenge: it needs to be overcome because it conflicts with basic ideas about equality, human rights and justice. Given that normalcy assumptions and essentialism make dehumanization stronger, the challenge becomes one of minimizing dehumanization as much as possible by getting rid of the normalcy assumptions and essentialism" (2018, 5).

Going back to the potential of multicultural education to serve as a source of values that should increase the humanizing potential of education, one would expect that because multicultural education rejects the assimilationist agenda, promotes respect for human dignity, and advocates for social justice and greater equity within society (Bennett 2001), it should reduce discrimination, promote enhanced self-understanding through expanding one's cultural lens, and liberate individuals from the restraints of cultural boundaries (Banks 2008; Eckermann 1994). However, multiple authors (e.g., Gosine 2002; Kirova 2015) point out that by emphasizing exoticized, knowable (other) cultures, multicultural education has instead solidified the boundaries between majority and minority cultures.

In sum, the current multicultural education practices based on ethno-racial distinctions (e.g., curricula that essentialize knowledge about other cultures and celebrate them) have not contributed to eliminating racism or the unequal treatment of minority, non-white students. Nor have they led to a critical examination of the dominant white, middle-class, Eurocentric culture. Therefore, although multicultural efforts that take the form of curricular add-ons about the "Cultural Other" (Montecinos 1995) take steps toward challenging and altering the mainstream curriculum, they have their own hidden curriculum, a major outcome of which is reinscribing essentialized notions of culture and essentialized representations of the members of cultural groups. Furthermore, as Kevin Gosine (2002) argues, not only multicultural but also anti-racism education oversimplifies the dynamics of cultural diversity and racism because both emphasize the defensively situated collective identities, or essentialisms, that racialized communities construct in relation to a dominant culture that represents them in homogeneous and stigmatized terms and fails to adequately consider the multifaceted subjectivities such seemingly homogeneous identities often mask. Thus, although anti-racism represents a leap forward in the fight against racism and racial inequality, in the past decade, scholars (e.g., Yon 2000) have critiqued the anti-racism movement for what they see as an uncritical reliance on essentialized or homogeneous conceptions of racialized communities.

Toward a Framework for the Humanization of Education: Alterity

In contemplating the possibility of developing a values framework for humanizing health care, Todres, Galvin, and Holloway (2009) identified eight dimensions that are essential constituents of humanization in relation to caring. In their view, "each dimension is heuristically expressed as a continuum stretching from the term that characterizes humanization in a positive sense; through to the term that characterizes the barrier to such possibility" (69). The conceptual framework they developed is presented in table 9.1.

I do not suggest here that health care and education systems are identical; however, I find it alarming how many of the dehumanizing practices or barriers to humanization identified in the literature briefly discussed so far are similar in both contexts. It might be valuable for education theorists to explore existing humanizing practices that, based on Todres, Galvin, and Holloway's (2009) suggestion, can be seen as being on the "opposite" ends of a continuum (e.g., from passivity to agency, from dislocation to a sense of place, or from isolation and rejection to belonging and togetherness).

In terms of education's humanizing potential, alterity as a key concept in interculturalism should be examined (Abdallah-Pretceille 2004). Although there are various conceptualizations of interculturalism with subtle differences, the intercultural perspective derives its foundations from the principles

Table 9.1. Todres, Galvin, and Holloway's (2009, 70) conceptual framework

Forms of Humanization	Forms of Dehumanization
Insiderness	Objectification
Agency	Passivity
Uniqueness	Homogenization
Togetherness	Isolation
Sense-making	Loss of meaning
Personal journey	Loss of personal journey
Sense of place	Dislocation
Embodiment	Reductionist body

of liberalism and hermeneutics. At its core, intercultural philosophy highlights the importance of understanding through intercultural dialogue; however, understanding and agreement are not synonymous. Intercultural education involves open, respectful dialogue among cultures, which is believed to promote cross-cultural sensitivity and increased understanding not only about diverse cultures encountered but about one's own and the general influence of culture on how we perceive and interact in the world (Kirova and Prochner 2015).

The term *alterity* derives from the Latin word *alter*, which means "other." Although *Other* was used most often in the late 1990s, *alterity* seems to be the preferred term today. The central question governing philosophical discussions of alterity is not that of who the Other is but that of our access to alterity. Martine Abdallah-Pretceille (2004) argues that the question of who the Other is leads to the reification of culture and should be avoided. She points out the interdependence of the concepts of self and the Other as represented by the paradox "l'identité de l'un exige la reconnaissance de l'Autre comme Je" (the identity of one requires the recognition of the Other as I; 42).

From this perspective, knowledge of the Other as other is experienced as a process in which one needs to remain open to the Other's perspectives as a possibility for questioning one's own. The goal, therefore, is "disturbing the totalizing system of knowledge which assimilates the Other into being the same" (Kemp 1992, as cited in Dahlberg, Moss, and Pence 2007, 39). Claire Kramsch (1993) maintains that when engaging in a "third space" at the interstices between cultures, individuals must name and interpret the world in alternative ways, leading to novel understandings about their own culture and the culture(s) of their partner(s) in dialogue. Thus, intercultural interaction is a unique process for every individual because the third space will be variously located depending on the context and the interpretive frame of the interactors.

When the intercultural interaction is seen as a dialogic process rather than a product, culture is understood as a cultural frame that influences how people perceive and interact in the world while they develop the ability to operate in multiple cultural settings. It seems that because schools are sites of active cultural reconstitution, not just exchange, where children engage in both the ongoing reproduction of the classroom community and its transformation, they can also change the adults in the community. Our pedagogical understanding of children as strangers in school shows us that the simple fact that we are never really able to understand who the children are opens the possibility of pedagogy as an ethical means to renew our world. In other words, seeing children as strangers whom we can never fully understand can allow us to get "rid of the normalcy assumptions and essentialism," as Kronfeldner (2018, 5) asserts, and make a shift from "grasping the other to respecting the other" (Dahlberg, Moss, and Pence 2007, 39). Only then can educators attempt to transgress the deeply entrenched norms, rules, and codes meant to assimilate the Other into a homogeneous same and instead enact alterity as a movement toward the richness and brilliance of the heterogeneous Other and bear responsibility for who they are. Only then can schools become sites where the educational experiences offered to all children, including those who come from refugee backgrounds, truly respect the alterity of the Other. The education system has a long way to go before making this shift. Although pockets of practice attend to the humanization of refugee students, without a concerted and systematic approach, such isolated practices may remain piecemeal and will likely not result in systemic changes that are overdue.

References

Abdallah-Pretceille, Martine. 2004. *L'éducation interculturelle*. 2e édition mise à jour. Paris: PUF.

Abdi, Ali A., ed. 2012. *Decolonizing Philosophies of Education*. Rotterdam: Sense.

Amjad, Afshan. 2016. "Multicultural Education and Immigrant Children: The Case of Muslim Children in Canadian Schools." PhD diss., University of Alberta. https://era.library.ualberta.ca/items/a35034f9-48f9-4d03-a291-a515645e0acf.

Armstrong, Felicity. 1999. "Inclusion, Curriculum, and the Struggle for Space in School." *Inclusive Education* 3 (1): 75–87.

Ayoub, Mohamad Najib. 2014. "An Investigation of the Challenges Experienced by Somali Refugee Students in Canadian Elementary Schools." Master's thesis, University of Windsor. https://scholar.uwindsor.ca/etd/5120.

Banks, James A. 2008. *An Introduction to Multicultural Education*. 4th ed. Boston: Pearson.

Barrera, Isaura. 1995. "To Refer or Not to Refer." *New York State Association for Bilingual Education Journal* 10 (Summer): 54–66.

Barton, Angela, and Edna Tan. 2020. "Beyond Equity as Inclusion: A Framework of 'Rightful Presence' for Guiding Justice-Oriented Studies in Teaching and Learning." *Educational Researcher* 49 (6): 433–40.

Bennett, Christine. 2001. "Genres of Research in Multicultural Education." *Review of Educational Research* 71 (2): 171–217.

Berhanu, Girma. 2008. "Ethnic Minority Pupils in Swedish Schools: Some Trends in Over-Representation of Minority Pupils in Special Educational Programs." *International Journal of Special Education* 23 (3): 17–29.

Blackwell, Dick, and Sheila Melzak. 2000. *Far from the Battle but Still at War: Troubled Refugee Children in School*. London: Child Psychotherapy Trust.

Bourdieu, Pierre. 1986. "The Forms of Capital." In *Handbook of Theory and Research for the Sociology of Education*, edited by John G. Richardson, 241–58. Westport, CT: Greenwood.

Boyle-Baise, Marilynne, and Maureen Gillette. 1998. "Multicultural Education from a Pedagogical Perspective: A Response to Radical Critiques." *Interchange* 29 (1): 17–32.

Cambridge Dictionary. 2020. S.v. "Humanize." https://dictionary.cambridge.org/dictionary/english/humanize.

Canadian Teachers' Federation. 2015. "Dream Big Together: Engaging Dialogue on Cultural Diversity with Immigrant Families." December 10, 2015. https://www.ctf-fce.ca/blog-perspectives/dream-big-together-a-practical-resource-to-welcome-refugee-students-to-our-canadian-high-schools/.

Cantarero, Luis. 2001. "Eating in a Home for Children. Food Resistance in the Residence." *Anthropology of Food*, no. 0 (April). https://journals.openedition.org/aof/1024.

Caraballo, Limarys, and Mariana Souto-Manning. 2017. "Co-constructing Identities, Literacies, and Contexts: Sustaining Critical Meta-Awareness with/in Urban Communities." *Urban Education* 52 (5): 555–60. https://doi.org/10.1177/0042085915618726.

Celik, Rukiye, Naime Altay, Selverhan Yurttutan, and Ebru K. Toruner. 2019. "Emotional Indicators and Anxiety Levels of Immigrant Children Who Have

Been Exposed to Warfare." *Journal of Child and Adolescent Psychiatric Nursing*, no. 32, 51–60. https://doi.org/10.1111/jcap.12233.

Coelho, Elizabeth. 2004. *Adding English: A Guide to Teaching in Multilingual Classrooms*. Toronto: Pippin.

Collins, Clinton. 1974. "The Multiple Realities of Schooling." In *Existentialism and Phenomenology in Education*, edited by David E. Denton, 139–58. New York: Teachers' College Press.

Cummins, Jim. 2001. *Language, Power, and Pedagogy: Bilingual Children in the Crossfire*. Clevedon, UK: Multilingual Matters.

Dahlberg, Gunilla, Peter Moss, and Alan Pence. 2007. *Beyond Quality in Early Childhood Education and Care: Languages of Evaluation*. New York: Routledge Taylor and Francis Group.

Delpit, Lisa. 2012. *"Multiplication Is for White People": Raising Expectations for Other People's Children*. New York: New Press.

Department of Justice Canada. 1982. "The Canadian Charter of Rights and Freedoms." https://www.justice.gc.ca/eng/csj-sjc/rfc-dlc/ccrf-ccdl/.

Department of Justice Canada. 1988. "Canadian Multiculturalism Act." https://laws-lois.justice.gc.ca/eng/acts/c-18.7/page-1.html.

Eckermann, Anne-Katrin. 1994. *One Classroom, Many Cultures: Teaching Strategies for Culturally Different Children*. St. Leonards, Australia: Allen & Unwin.

Elementary Teachers' Federation of Ontario. 2017. *First Nations, Métis, and Inuit Education Resource: Engaging Learners Through Play*. Toronto: Elementary Teachers' Federation of Ontario.

Elsayed, Danah, Ju-Hyun Song, Eleanor Myatt, Eleanor Colasante, and Tina Malti. 2019. "Anger and Sadness Regulation in Refugee Children: The Roles of Pre- and Post-Migratory Factors." *Child Psychiatry & Human Development* 50 (5): 846–55. https://doi.org/10.1007/s10578-019-00887-4.

Eruyar, Seyda, John Maltby, and Panos Vostanis. 2018. "Mental Health Problems of Syrian Refugee Children: The Role of Parental Factors." *European Child & Adolescent Psychiatry* 27 (4): 401–9. https://doi.org/10.1007/s00787-017-1101-0.

Farajallah, Iman. 2023. "A Palestinian Psychologist Reckons with the Trauma Gaza Children Face After Two Months of Attacks." CBC, December 9, 2023. https://www.cbc.ca/player/play/2290701891701.

Foucault, Michel. 1977. *Discipline and Punish*. New York: Allen & Unwin.

Frater-Mathieson, Kaaren. 2004. "Refugee Trauma, Loss, and Grief: Implications for Interventions." In *Educational Interventions for Refugee Children: Theoretical Perspectives and Implementing Best Practice*, edited by Richard Hamilton and Dennis Moore, 12–34. London: RoutledgeFalmer.

Ghosh, Ratna, and Ali A. Abdi. 2004. *Education and the Politics of Difference: Canadian Perspectives.* Toronto: Canadian Scholars' Press.

Gibson, Margaret. 1984. "Approaches to Multicultural Education in the US: Some Conceptions and Assumptions." *Anthropology of Education Quarterly* 15 (1): 94–119.

Giroux, Henry A. 1993. *Living Dangerously: Multiculturalism and the Politics of Difference.* New York: Peter Lang.

Gordon, Tuula, Elina Lahlma, Pirkko Hynninen, Tuija Metso, Tarja Palmu, and Tarja Tolonen. 1999. "Learning the Routines: 'Professionalization' of Newcomers in Secondary School." *Qualitative Studies in Education* 12 (6): 689–705.

Gosine, Kevin. 2002. "Essentialism Versus Complexity: Conceptions of Racial Identity Construction in Educational Scholarship." *Canadian Journal of Education* 27 (1): 81–100.

Haslam, Nick. 2006. "Dehumanization: An Integrative Review." *Personality and Social Psychology Review* 10 (3): 252–64. https://doi.org/10.1207/s15327957pspr1003_4.

Hasmath, Reza. 2012. *The Ethnic Penalty: Immigration, Education and the Labour Market.* Burlington, VT, and Surrey, UK: Ashgate.

Hedegaard, Mariane. 2007. "The Development of Children's Conceptual Relation to the World, with a Focus on Concept Formation in Preschool Children's Activity." In *The Cambridge Companion to Vygotsky*, edited by Harry Daniels, Michael Cole, and James V. Wertsch, 246–76. Cambridge: Cambridge University Press.

Heidegger, Martin. 1982. *On the Way to Language.* New York: Harper & Row.

Herrmann, Steffen K. 2011. "Social Exclusion: Practices of Misrecognition." In *Humiliation, Degradation, Dehumanization: Human Dignity Violated*, edited by Paulus Kaufmann, Hannes Kuch, Christian Neuhäuser, and Elaine Webster, 133–50. New York: Springer.

Hoffman, Diane M. 1996. "Culture and Self in Multicultural Education: Reflections on Discourse, Text, and Practice." *American Educational Research Journal* 33, no. 3 (Autumn): 545–69. https://www.jstor.org/stable/i248888.

Honneth, Axel. 1996. *The Struggle for Recognition: The Moral Grammar of Social Conflicts.* Cambridge, MA: MIT Press.

Hughes, John, and Wes Sharrock. 1997. *The Philosophy of Social Research*, 3rd ed. London: Addison Wesley Longman.

Husserl, Edmund. (1936) 1970. *The Crisis of European Sciences and Transcendental Phenomenology: An Introduction to Phenomenological Philosophy.* Translated by David Carr. Evanston, IL: Northwestern University Press.

Kanu, Yatta. 2008. "Educational Needs and Barriers for African Refugee Students in Manitoba." *Canadian Journal of Education* 31 (4): 915–40.

Kaplan, Ida, Yvonne Stolk, Madeleine Valibhoy, Alan Tucker, and Judy Baker. 2016. "Cognitive Assessment of Refugee Children: Effects of Trauma and New

Language Acquisition." *Transcultural Psychiatry* 53 (1): 81–109. https://doi.org/10.1177/1363461515612933.

Kemp, Peter. 1992. *Emmanuel Levinas: En introduction* [*Emmanuel Levinas: An Introduction*]. Göteborg, Sweden: Daidolos.

Kirk, David. 2004. "Beyond the 'Academic' Curriculum: The Production and Operation of Biopower in the Less-Studied Sites of Schooling." In *Dangerous Coalitions? The Uses of Foucault in the Study of Education*, edited by Bernadette M. Baker and Katharina E. Heyning, 117–35. New York: Peter Lang.

Kirova, Anna. 2007. "Moving Childhoods: Children's Lived Experiences with Immigration." In *Global Migration and Education: Schools, Children, and Families*, edited by Leah Adams and Anna Kirova, 185–99. Mahwah, NJ: Lawrence Erlbaum.

Kirova, Anna. 2013. "A Foreigner Among Strangers: The Lived World of a Newcomer Child in School." *Educational Research* 4:127–37.

Kirova, Anna. 2015. "Critical and Emerging Discourses in Multicultural Education Literature: An (Updated) Review." In *Multiculturalism in Canada: Theories, Policies and Debates*, edited by Shibao Guo and Lloyd Wong, 239–55. Rotterdam: Sense.

Kirova, Anna, Fauza Mohamed, and Michael Emme. 2006. "Learning the Ropes, Resisting the Rules: Immigrant Children's Representation of the Lunchtime Routine Through Fotonovela." *Journal of the Canadian Association for Curriculum Studies* 4 (1). https://jcacs.journals.yorku.ca/index.php/jcacs/article/view/16997.

Kirova, Anna, and Larry Prochner. 2015. "The Issue of Otherness in Pedagogical Theory and Practice: The Case of Roma." *Alberta Journal of Educational Research* 61, no. 4 (Winter): 381–98.

Kirova, Anna, Larry Prochner, and Christine Massing. 2019. *Learning to Teach Young Children: Theoretical Perspectives and Implications for Practice*. London: Bloomsbury.

Kramsch, Claire. 1993. *Context and Culture in Language Teaching*. Oxford: Oxford University Press.

Kronfeldner, Maria. 2018. *What's Left of Human Nature? A Post-essentialist, Pluralist, and Interactive Account of a Contested Concept*. Cambridge, MA: MIT Press.

Lambrev, Veselina, Anna Kirova, and Larry Prochner. 2019. "Education Reforms for Inclusion? Interrogating Policy-Practice Disjunctions in Early Childhood Education in Bulgaria." *Education Inquiry* 11 (2): 126–43.

Lesko, Nancy. 1988. "The Curriculum of the Body: Lessons from a Catholic High School." In *Becoming Feminine: The Politics of Popular Culture*, edited by Leslie G. Roman, Linda K. Christian-Smith, and Elizabeth A. Ellsworth, 123–42. London: Falmer.

Lippitz, Wilfried. 2007. "Foreignness and Otherness in Pedagogical Contexts." *Phenomenology and Practice* 1 (1): 76–96.

Lippitz, Wilfried, and Bas Levering. 2002. "And Now You Are Getting a Teacher with Such a Long Name . . ." *Teaching and Teacher Education* 18 (2): 205–13.

MacNevin, Joanne. 2012. "Learning the Way: Teaching and Learning with and for Youth from Refugee Backgrounds on Prince Edward Island." *Canadian Journal of Education* 35 (3): 48–63.

McCoy, John S., W. Andy Knight, and Anna Kirova. 2011. "Xeno-Racism in Canada? Patterns of Exclusion and Integration." Paper presented at Global Governance: Political Authority in Transition, annual conference of the International Studies Association, Le Centre Sheraton Hotel, Montréal, Québec, March 16, 2011.

McLaren, Peter. 1995. *Critical Pedagogy and Predatory Culture: Oppositional Politics in a Postmodern Age.* New York: Routledge.

Mills, Carmen, and Julie Ballantyne. 2016. "Social Justice and Teacher Education: A Systematic Review of Empirical Work in the Field." *Journal of Teacher Education* 67 (4): 263–76. https://doi.org/10.1177/0022487116660152.

Montecinos, Carmen. 1995. "Culture as an Ongoing Dialog: Implications for Multicultural Teacher Education." In *Multicultural Education, Critical Pedagogy, and the Politics of Difference*, edited by Christine E. Sleeter and Peter L. McLaren, 291–307. Albany: SUNY Press.

Morrison, Marlene. 1996. "Cross-Cultural Perspectives on Eating: A Hidden Curriculum for Food." In *Reshaping Education in the 1990s: Perspectives on Primary Schooling*, edited by Rita Chawla-Duggan and Christopher J. Poole, 89–103. London: Falmer.

Nicolino, Venus M. 2006. "The Relationships Between Racism, Islamophobia, Religious Dogmatism, and Attitudes Toward War." PhD diss., Alliant International University.

Packer, Martin, and Jessie Goicoechea. 2000. "Sociocultural and Constructivist Theories of Learning: Ontology, Not Just Epistemology." *Educational Psychologist* 35 (4): 227–41.

Pérez, Michelle S., and Cinthya Saavedra. 2017. "A Call for Onto-Epistemological Diversity in Early Childhood Education and Care: Centering Global South Conceptualizations of Childhood/s." *Review of Research in Education* 41 (1): 1–29. https://doi.org/10.3102/0091732X16688621.

Prochner, Larry. 2020. "'Placing a School at the Tail of a Plough': The European Roots of Indian Industrial Schools in Canada." In *From Disconnection to Reconciliation: Indigenous Education in Canada*, edited by Sheila Carr-Stewart, 26–53. Vancouver: Purich Books.

Rezai-Rashti, Goli. 1994. "Islamic Identity and Racism." *Orbit* 25:37–38.

Ridley, Charles R. 1995. *Overcoming Unintentional Racism in Counseling and Therapy: A Practitioner's Guide to Intentional Intervention.* Newbury Park, CA: SAGE.

Save the Children. 2019. *Stop the War on Children: Protecting Children in 21st Century Conflict.* London: Save the Children. https://resourcecentre.savethechildren.net/pdf/report_stop_the_war_on_children.pdf/.

Schütz, Alfred. 1964. "The Stranger: An Essay in Social Psychology." In *Collected Papers II*, edited by Arvid Brodersen, 91–105. The Hague: Martinus Nijihoff.

Simpson, Brenda. 2000. "Regulation and Resistance: Children's Embodiment During the Primary-Secondary School Transition." In *The Body, Childhood, and Society*, edited by Alan Prout, 60–77. London: Macmillan.

Skuza, Jennifer A. 2007. "Humanizing the Understanding of the Acculturation Experience with Phenomenology." *Human Studies* 30 (4): 447–65.

Sleeter, Christine E., and Dolores Delgado Bernal. 2004. "Critical Pedagogy, Critical Theory, and Antiracist Education: Implications for Multicultural Education." In *Handbook of Research on Multicultural Education*, edited by James A. Banks and Cherry A. McGee-Banks, 240–58. San Francisco: Jossey-Bass.

Souto-Manning, Mariana, and Ayesha Rabadi-Raol. 2018. "(Re)centering Quality in Early Childhood Education: Toward Intersectional Justice for Minoritized Children." *Review of Research in Education* 42:203–25.

Stewart, Jan. 2012. "Transforming Schools and Strengthening Leadership to Support the Educational and Psychosocial Needs of War-Affected Children Living in Canada." *Diaspora, Indigenous, and Minority Education* 6 (3): 172–89. https://doi.org/10.1080/15595692.2012.691136.

Stewart, Jan, Dania El Chaar, Kari McCluskey, and Kirby Borgardt. 2019. "Refugee Student Integration: A Focus on Settlement, Education, and Psychosocial Support." *Journal of Contemporary Issues in Education* 14 (1): 55–70.

Strekalova, Ekaterina, and James L. Hoot. 2008. "What Is Special About Special Needs of Refugee Children? Guidelines for Teachers." *Multicultural Education* 16, no. 1 (Fall): 21–24.

Taylor, Charles. 1992. *Multiculturalism and the Politics of Recognition.* Edited by Amy Gutmann. Princeton, NJ: Princeton University Press.

Thorne, Barrie. 1993. *Gender Play: Girls and Boys in Schools.* New Brunswick, NJ: Rutgers University Press.

Todres, Les, Kathleen T. Galvin, and Immy Holloway. 2009. "The Humanization of Healthcare: A Value Framework for Qualitative Research." *International Journal of Qualitative Studies on Health and Well-Being* 4:68–77.

UN General Assembly. 1948. *The Universal Declaration of Human Rights.* New York: United Nations. https://www.un.org/en/about-us/universal-declaration-of-human-rights.

UN General Assembly. 1959. *Declaration of the Rights of the Child*. New York: United Nations. https://archive.crin.org/en/library/legal-database/un-declaration-rights-child-1959.html#:~:text=The%20child%20shall%20be%20entitled,a%20name%20and%20a%20nationality.&text=The%20child%20shall%20enjoy%20the,natal%20and%20post%2Dnatal%20care.

UN General Assembly. 1989. *Convention on the Rights of the Child*. New York: United Nations. https://www.ohchr.org/en/instruments-mechanisms/instruments/convention-rights-child.

van Manen, Max. 1994. *Researching Lived Experience*. London, ON: Althouse Press.

Wideen, Marvin, and Kathleen A. Barnard. 1999. *Impacts of Immigration on Education in British Columbia: An Analysis of Efforts to Implement Policies of Multiculturalism in Schools*. No. RIIM WP 99-02. Vancouver: Vancouver Centre of Excellence, Research on Immigration and Integration in the Metropolis.

Yon, Daniel A. 2000. *Elusive Culture: Schooling, Race, and Identity in Global Times*. Albany: SUNY Press.

Young, Iris Marion. 1990. *Justice and the Politics of Difference*. Princeton, NJ: Princeton University Press.

Zine, Jasmin. 2004. "Anti-Islamophobia Education as Transformative Pedagogy: Reflections from the Education Frontlines." *American Journal of Islamic Social Sciences* 21 (3): 110–18.

Zine, Jasmin. 2006. "Unveiled Sentiments: Gendered Islamophobia and Experiences of Veiling Among Muslim Girls in a Canadian Islamic School." *Equity and Excellence in Education* 39 (3): 239–52.

Zine, Jasmin. 2008. *Canadian Islamic Schools: Unravelling the Politics of Faith, Gender, Knowledge, and Identity*. Toronto: University of Toronto Press.

Part III
Countering Dehumanization
State Apologies and New Approaches

10 When the State Says "Sorry"
Jewish Refugees to Canada and the Politics of Apology

Abigail B. Bakan

In an age of pandemic, past inequalities weigh heavily on current realities. A microscopic virus that respects no human or geographic boundaries most severely impacts communities rendered the most vulnerable due to socially, politically, and economically structured oppressive practices. It is—perhaps now more than ever—a time to revisit such inequities and to consider past practices that have shaped them. Significantly, we live in an era where state redress for past wrongs is increasingly common internationally, often referred to as an "age of apology" (Thompson 2000; Gibney and Roxstrom 2001; Rotberg 2006; Gibney et al. 2008; Nobles 2008; Kampf and Lowenheim 2012; Augoustinos, Hastie, and Wright 2011; James and Stanger-Ross 2018).

Canada has been no stranger to the process. This is marked by the state apology in 2008 to survivors of the foundational residential school system, under the Conservative administration of then prime minister Stephen Harper (James 2018). As discussed further in the next chapter, in the name of education, the widespread institution of residential schools rendered an entire Indigenous population the subject of "cultural genocide," as identified in the report of the Truth and Reconciliation Commission (TRC 2015). Another example of state apology in Canada is the 1988 redress settlement negotiated by the federal government with the National Association of Japanese Canadians. This was intended as part of the process of compensation to Japanese Canadians for violent racist internment between 1941 and 1949, when this community was profiled and charged with being a threat to security (Kobayashi 1992; Miki 2005; Wood 2014). Other apologies include the 2016 Liberal government apology to Canada's Sikh community for the 1914 refusal, on an overtly racial basis, to welcome the passengers of the *Komagata Maru* ship to Canada's shores (Johnston 2014; Dhamoon et al. 2019).

Consistent with this pattern is an apology offered by Liberal prime minister Justin Trudeau on November 7, 2018, on behalf of the government, to the 1939 passengers of the MS (*Motorschiff*; or SS, steamship) *St. Louis*. The passengers were Jewish refugees fleeing Nazi Germany who had been refused entry and asylum to Canada (Canada 2018b). The apology, which notably followed a US apology in 2012 (Eppinger 2012), was significant. From the standpoint of advancing human rights for a refugee community and their descendants and humanizing the inhuman, it was and is welcome. It marked a major acknowledgement of the history of antisemitism, or anti-Jewish racism, in Canada. It was also highly relevant for addressing antisemitism in the present. In this regard, however, the apology was tainted and can be seen to bear the characteristics of a poisoned gift. The narrative of apology for refusing asylum to Jewish refugees from Nazi Germany aboard the MS *St. Louis* tragically asserted a certain common, but very dangerous and unhelpful, definition of antisemitism in the process. In the apology, antisemitism was described as centrally including legitimate criticism of the state of Israel and also conflated defense of Palestinian rights by specifically targeting the Boycott, Divestment and Sanctions (BDS) movement against Israel (Canada 2018b).

In an apparently bold move on behalf of the Canadian government to humanize Jewish refugees and Jewish immigrants and citizens in Canada, the apology for the crimes associated with the MS *St. Louis* simultaneously enforced the dehumanization of Palestinians. This dehumanization is ongoing and includes generations—past and present—of Palestinian refugees. It is this conflation and the implications of such an asserted definition of antisemitism subsumed in the apology for the refusal to welcome the passengers of the MS *St. Louis* that animate this chapter. The conflation, I argue, is inaccurate regarding the nature of antisemitism—a term and an experience that is all too often used without clarity or context. The absence of clarity bears serious consequences regarding redress and the humanization of a dehumanizing reality of occupation and anti-Palestinian abuse of human rights characteristic of the state of Israel.

Antisemitism as a term can suggest multiple meanings, including anti-Judaism (based on religious or theological beliefs), anti-Jewish racism (the commonly held meaning in the context of human rights; the meaning adopted in this chapter), or inaccurately, legitimate criticism of policies and practices of the state of Israel, particularly regarding the violation of the rights of Palestine and Palestinians (Bakan 2014; Abu-Laban and Bakan 2020). Tying the apology to a pledge to challenge antisemitism in the present and then conflating such a pledge with opposition to the BDS movement dangerously condemned a progressive, non-violent campaign for solidarity for Palestinian rights. The BDS campaign, significantly, includes Jewish participation among multiple communities within Canada, as well as in Israel and internationally (see IJV 2021). Therefore, while claiming to apologize to the Jewish community, in fact, Trudeau's statement selectively apologized only to a portion of this community—those who adhere to the policies of the state of Israel and deny Palestinian claims to human rights as recognized by international policy and as delineated in the demands of the BDS call.

The example of Canada's 2018 apology indicates that political context matters. The implications of states saying "sorry" need to be considered on a case-by-case basis. There are certain embedded meanings in politically complex motivations and interests associated with state apologies, including some interests that are not associated with sincerely redressing harm. Significantly, as the last chapter suggests, most state apologies are about redeeming the legitimacy of the state rather than providing meaningful redress toward those the state has harmed. In the case addressed in this chapter, the apology demonstrates that such moments can serve to extend a poisoned gift. The 2018 apology is framed as a poisoned gift to the Jewish community, selectively apologizing to only some and implicitly condemning others for current political views. Here the focus on the history of Jewish refugees needs to be delinked from the present-day realities of Israel/Palestine and the fraught context of global solidarity as expressed in the BDS movement.

The remainder of this chapter proceeds in three sections. First, the story of the MS *St. Louis* and the historical context of antisemitism in Canada are outlined. Second, the discussion turns to a close look at the discursive content, context, and multiple meanings of Trudeau's apology regarding the MS *St. Louis* from this analytical lens. Third, the analytical frame is extended to consider racism and human rights, in particular regarding the conflation of antisemitism with the divergent experiences of Jewish refugees fleeing Nazism and the BDS movement. The chapter concludes with a brief statement regarding the positionality of the author and revisiting the politics of apology from a wider perspective.

The MS *St. Louis* and Jewish Refugees

The transatlantic ocean liner set sail from Germany with more than nine hundred Jewish passengers, most of whom were fleeing Nazi Germany. It was owned by the Hamburg America Line and heading for Havana, Cuba, "a popular stopover for refugees seeking to immigrate to the United States" (Tikkanen 2019). Though the ship was known as a luxury liner, the passengers were hardly on a relaxing tour, as indicated in the following description:

> The black and white ship with eight decks held room for four hundred first class passengers (800 Reichsmarks each) and five hundred tourist-class passengers (600 Reichsmarks each). The passengers were also required to pay an additional 230 Reichsmarks for the "customary contingency fee" which was supposed to cover the cost if there was an unplanned return voyage. As most Jews had been forced out of their jobs and had been charged high rents under the Nazi regime, most Jews did not have this kind of money. Some of these passengers had money sent to them from relatives outside of Germany and Europe while other families had to pool resources to send even one member to freedom. (Jewish Virtual Library 2020)[1]

Originally, passengers had obtained landing certificates to Cuba, where they anticipated entry while awaiting US visas. In early May (shortly before the ship departed on May 13), however, then Cuban president Federico Laredo Brú declared invalid previously issued landing certificates. The details of this reversal are unclear. However, rumours—"which some believe were spread by Nazi agents on the island"—circulated in Cuba "that the Jewish passengers were communists and criminals," and a large antisemitic rally held in Havana on May 8 certainly fuelled the Cuban decision (Tikkanen 2019, 2). Ultimately, Cuba allowed entry for only twenty-seven passengers, with the remainder

---

1 The monetary unit of Germany was changed in June 1948 to the *Deutschmark*, where 1 *Deutschmark* equals 10 *Reichsmark*. In January 1940, 1 *Reichsmark* was worth approximately USD 2.50.

forced to depart. As Abella and Troper explain, "Argentina, Uruguay, Paraguay, and Panama were approached in vain, by various Jewish organizations. Within two days all the countries of Latin America had rejected entreaties to allow these Jews to land. On 2 June the St. Louis was forced to leave Havana harbor. The last hope seemed to be either Canada or the United States" (1979, 179).

The ship changed course for Florida, United States, but to no avail. The United States did not even send a reply to the desperate request for entry. Canada was the country of final hope for a safe destination, but the response from the government of the day was unequivocal. Notably, "On June 7, 1939, Prime Minister Mackenzie King was in Washington. His response mirrored America's when he stated he was 'emphatically opposed to the admission of the *St. Louis* passengers'" (R.W. 2007, 13).

This was not an aberrant response. The refusal to allow the MS *St. Louis* passengers fleeing Nazi Germany to enter Canada was not an exception but consistent with Canadian and global public policy, ideology, and practice. An international conference that had taken place earlier specifically to address the challenge of Jewish refugees—in Evian, France, in 1938—indicated that Canada's position, along with those of the United States and every other major country, was clear. King had stated, "The admission of refugees perhaps posed a greater menace to Canada in 1938 than Hitler" (R. W. 2007, 13). The position was consistent with the advice of Charles Frederick Blair, then director of the Immigration Branch of the Department of Mines and Resources, who asserted the view of the Canadian state on the acceptable number of Jewish refugees was that "none is too many" (Abella and Troper 2012). Antisemitism was a recognized feature of border control, but it was also deeply entrenched in civil society and daily public life in both English Canada and Québec.

The context for refugees seeking humanity included the flight from inhumanity. The fate of the Jewish refugees was not in doubt. The ship departed from Germany on May 13, 1939, approximately six months after Kristallnacht (November 9–10, 1939), the Nazi massacre of Jewish persons and property—or pogrom—organized by the Nazi regime in Germany and Austria. The event left 1,400 synagogues and 7,000 businesses destroyed, 30,000 Jews arrested and taken to concentration camps, and almost 100 Jews killed (USC Shoah Foundation 2013). This was also two months before the official start of World War II (September 1, 1939). The experience of the MS *St. Louis* passengers became known as the *Voyage of the Damned*, popularized in a 1974 book and 1976 film with this title (Thomas and Morgan-Witts [1974] 2010; Rosenberg 1976). The events took place in a context when antisemitism was widely legitimated in state policy and practice as well as among civil society. In the lead-up to and outbreak of World War II, Germany was an extreme version of state-sponsored antisemitism, but liberal democratic states were not innocent in the process, forwarding eugenic conceptions of the "nation" and various stereotypes and practices expressed in bordered restrictions. These were policies that often led to death. There is now an extensive literature documenting Canada's normalized antisemitism, including a text cited in Trudeau's apology, *None Is Too Many: Canada and the Jews of Europe, 1933–1948* (Abella and Troper 2012; also see Bialystok 2000; Cassara 2017; Vincent 2011; Ogilvie and Miller 2006; Klein 2012). Abella and Troper (2012, i) summarize the global context:

> One fact transcends them all. The Jews of Europe were not so much trapped in a whirlwind of systemic mass murder as they were abandoned to it. The Nazis planned and executed the Holocaust, but it was made possible by an indifference to the suffering of the victims which sometimes bordered on contempt. Not one nation showed generosity of heart to those who were doomed, not one made the Jewish plight a national priority and not one willingly opened its doors after the war to the surviving remnant of the once thriving Jewish community. Rescue required sanctuary, and there was none.

The Jewish refugees from Nazi Germany on the MS *St. Louis* returned across the ocean to Europe, landing in Antwerp on June 17, 1939. After three days of negotiations, carried out with the intervention of the American Jewish Joint Distribution Committee (JDC), a Jewish advocacy organization, the passengers were allowed to disembark and resettle variously in England, France, Belgium, and the Netherlands. Of the 907 passengers who were on the ship as it docked in Europe, 255 were killed, the majority in Nazi concentration camps. It is in this context that the apology from the government of Canada needs to be considered.

The Apology: Justin Trudeau's Discursive Message

The 2018 state apology for the treatment of Jewish refugees in Canada in general and the passengers of the MS *St. Louis* in particular was, arguably, long overdue. The conditions surrounding the exact timing of the apology are hard to determine. It was presented to coincide with the eightieth anniversary of Kristallnacht. The statement also followed the October 27, 2018, violent attack on Jewish community members at the Tree of Life synagogue in Pittsburgh, Pennsylvania, where an armed man shot and killed eleven and injured six (Ortiz 2019). However, there is little doubt that the exposure of the details of the voyage and Canada's response is significant, largely the result of the 1983 publication of *None Is Too Many: Canada and the Jews of Europe, 1933–1948*, by historians Irving Abella and Harold Troper.

The apology was stated and elaborated extensively. Trudeau apologized with compassion and a sense of deep sincerity. This merits citing the text at length:

> Today I rise in the House of Commons to issue a long overdue apology to the Jewish refugees Canada turned away. We apologize to the 907 German Jews aboard the MS St. Louis, as well as their families. We also apologize to others who paid the price of our inaction, whom we doomed to the ultimate horror of the death camps. We used our laws to mask our anti-Semitism, our antipathy, our resentment. We are sorry for the callousness of Canada's response, and we are sorry for not apologizing sooner. We apologize to the mothers and fathers whose children we did not save, and to the daughters and sons whose parents we did not help. We apologize to the imprisoned Jewish refugees who were forced to relive their trauma next to their tormentors. To the scientists, artists, engineers, lawyers, businessmen, nurses, doctors, mathematicians, pharmacists, poets and students, to every Jew who sought safe haven in Canada, who stood in line for hours and wrote countless letters, we refused to help them when we could have.
> We contributed to sealing the cruel fates of far too many at places like Auschwitz, Treblinka and Belzec. We failed them and for that we are sorry. Finally, we apologize to the members of Canada's Jewish community whose voices were ignored, whose calls went unanswered. We were quick to forget the ways in which they had helped build this country since its inception, quick to forget that they were our friends and neighbours, that they had educated our youth, cared for our sick and clothed our poor. Instead, we let anti-Semitism take hold in our communities and become our official policy. We did not hesitate to circumvent their participation, limit their opportunities and discredit their talent. They were meant to feel like strangers in their own homes,

aliens in their own land. We denied them the respect that every Canadian, every human being, regardless of origin, regardless of faith is owed by their government and by their fellow citizens. When Canada turned its back on the Jews of Europe, we turned our back on Jewish Canadians as well. It was unacceptable then and it is unacceptable now. The country failed them, and for that we are sorry. (Canada 2018b)

While Jewish organizational advocacy for the original refugees has been consistent, the motivations of such advocacy have changed significantly over time. Since the 1930s, Jewish advocacy organizations have evolved and changed. Most significantly, these organizations have increasingly linked domestic Jewish interests to foreign policy aims specifically associated with defending the practices of the state of Israel. This has not been a simple or linear process (Freeman-Maloy 2006). Originating as movements grounded in advocating for Jewish rights and equality, often as aspiring or recent immigrants or refugees, the most established Jewish advocacy organizations have over time transformed into apparatuses closely linked politically and financially to the interests of the Israeli state. Relatedly, these organizations have become closely embedded in Canadian foreign and domestic policies that advance Israeli interests in the Middle East. While this is a global phenomenon, organizations in Canada have been major players in both the national and international arenas (see Freeman-Maloy 2006; Abu-Laban and Bakan 2020, 81–108).

Each state apology has its own history, context, and implications. Though the tragedy of the MS *St. Louis* took place many years ago, the calls by MPs have moved relatively swiftly over recent years. Both Conservative and Liberal MPs have advocated for an apology for those turned away on the MS *St. Louis*. Prime Minister Justin Trudeau announced his intention to apologize on behalf of the Canadian state in May 2018 at a fundraising event for the March of the Living program's thirtieth anniversary gala (Canada 2018a). The March of the Living is a highly contested program, where the experience of the Holocaust in Poland is explicitly linked physically and emotionally to the establishment of the state of Israel in 1948 and related interests (Peto 2010).

On September 7, 2018, Trudeau forwarded in the House of Commons the date of November 7, 2018, for the apology (Dangerfield 2018). Tories and Liberals have competed for favour among multiple constituencies, and the demonstration of a willingness to apologize for the MS *St. Louis* tragedy was not exempt from political claims. The recent calls for apology were first led by the late Deepak Obhrai, Tory MP for Calgary Forest Lawn, Alberta. In June 2016, Obhrai made his first call for a state apology at a World Refugee fundraising event addressing the Canadian Humanitarian Coalition on Parliament Hill. Speaking to the *Canadian Jewish News*, Obhrai stated that while an exhibit about the MS *St. Louis* had been established in Halifax, Nova Scotia, at the Canadian Museum of Immigration, the need for an apology remained (Lungen 2016). A long-standing conservative MP with roots in the far-right Reform Party, Obhrai was first elected in 2004 and re-elected in 2006, 2008, 2011, and 2015; he failed to secure leadership of the Conservative Party of Canada in 2017 and died suddenly in 2019. Obhrai served in Stephen Harper's Conservative Party government as parliamentary secretary to the minister of foreign affairs for international human rights.[2] His advocacy for an apology was consistent with the Tories' ongoing efforts to align with the most pro-Israel and conservative wing of the Jewish advocacy community in Canada. The call for a state apology was later taken up in January 2017, however, and now by a Liberal MP, Anthony Housefather. This was during an emergency debate in the House of Commons regarding the US suspension of immigration from seven predominantly Muslim countries (Arnold 2017). Housefather, MP for Mount Royal, Montréal, was elected in 2015 and 2019. From 2015 to 2019, Housefather served as chair of the Justice and Human Rights Committee; he has a background in law and business, mayoral politics, and advocacy for English-speaking rights in Québec. He also self-identifies as Jewish and boasts of being a competitive swim champion in the Israeli Maccabiah Games (2013; see Housefather 2021).

Trudeau's apology was forwarded explicitly not only to remedy a past wrong but also to indicate a present promise to eradicate antisemitism as he chose to define it. The linking of the apology to a very specific association with the state of Israel is explicit. Moreover, the apology makes a point to condemn the BDS campaign, which has been advanced to recognize international law as applied to the Palestinian population (see Abu-Laban and Bakan 2020, 147–76).

Consideration of the text of the apology in further detail is helpful in explaining this context. The story Trudeau relayed aloud on November 7, 2018, drawn from a carefully prepared text to the House of Commons, was

---

2 Deepak Obhrai was an immigrant to Canada from Tanzania and the first and only Hindu MP in Canada. He died on August 2, 2019, following a diagnosis of cancer.

compelling and delivered with appropriate sincerity. First, Trudeau set the stage for the refugees' departure from Germany on the MS *St. Louis*:

> On May 15, 1939, more than 900 German Jews boarded an ocean liner known as the St. Louis. The passengers had been stripped of their possessions, chased out of their homes, forced out of their schools and banned from their professions by their own government. Their synagogues had been burnt. Their stores raided. Their clothing scarred with yellow stars, they had been forced to add "Israel" or "Sarah" to the names they had known their whole lives. Women and men who had once contributed so much to their country had been labelled as aliens, traitors and enemies—and treated as such. Persecuted, robbed, jailed and killed because of who they were. Nazi Germany had denied them their citizenship and their fundamental rights. And yet, when the St. Louis set sail from Hamburg that fateful Monday, the more than 900 stateless passengers onboard considered themselves lucky. Lucky because they each carried on board an entrance visa to Cuba, a rare chance to escape the tyranny of the Nazi regime under Adolf Hitler. (Canada 2018b)

Then, Trudeau listed the failures of the Cuban and American governments to allow the refugees to disembark and the plan to seek permission to land in Canada. Trudeau did not shy away from the implications of the consequences:

> But by the time the ship docked in Havana Harbour, things would take a turn for the worse. The Cuban government refused to recognize their entrance visas and only a few passengers were allowed to disembark. Even after men, women and children threatened mass suicide, entry was denied. And so continued their long and tragic quest for safety. They would request asylum from Argentina, Uruguay, Paraguay and Panama. Each said no. On June 2, the MS St. Louis was forced to leave Havana with no guarantee that they would be welcomed elsewhere. And after the Americans had denied their appeals, they sought refuge in Canada. But the Liberal government of Mackenzie King was unmoved by the plight of these refugees. Despite the desperate plea of the Canadian Jewish community, despite the repeated calls by the government's two Jewish caucus members, despite the many letters from concerned Canadians of different faiths, the government chose to turn its back on these innocent victims of Hitler's regime. At the time, Canada was home to just 11 million people, of whom only 160,000 were Jews. Not a single Jewish refugee was to set foot—let alone settle—on Canadian soil.

The MS St. Louis and its passengers had no choice but to return to Europe, where the United Kingdom, Belgium, France and Holland agreed to take in the refugees. And then when the Nazis conquered Belgium, France and Holland, many of them would be murdered in the gruesome camps and gas chambers of the Third Reich. (Canada 2018b)

Trudeau went further, indicating that the refusal was "not an isolated incident." He elaborated on the historical context, asserting that "Jews were viewed as a threat to be avoided, rather than the victims of a humanitarian crisis" (Canada 2018b).

All this, notably, is about history. But it is history viewed from the standpoint of a different present. The refusal to admit Jewish refugees fleeing almost certain death was perceived as something that merits shame—a political expression of an emotion commonly associated with state apologies (Ahmed 2004). As Trudeau noted, "The story of the *St. Louis* and the ill-treatment of Jews before, during and after the Second World War should fill us with shame. Shame because these actions run counter to the promise of our country. That's not the Canada we know today—a Canada far more generous, accepting and compassionate than it once was" (Canada 2018b).

Trudeau's contemporary iteration of Canadian multiculturalism, we are informed, includes Jewish refugees. Here, however, the poison in the gift of the apology is made clear.

The Poisoned Gift: History Reframed

The distinction between then and now is a point the prime minister forcefully and clearly reiterated:

Of all the allied countries, Canada would admit the fewest Jews between 1933 and 1945. Far fewer than the United Kingdom and significantly less per capita than the United States. And of those it let in, as many as 7,000 of them were labelled as prisoners of war and unjustly imprisoned alongside Nazis. As far as Jews were concerned, none was too many. (Canada 2018b)

The distance between then and now is a point of emphasis in Trudeau's apology. He condemned the Canadian government's knowledge of Jewish victimization during the war:

The plight of the *St. Louis* did not lead to a significant change in policy, nor did alarming reports from across Europe or the gruesome details of a coordinated effort to eliminate Jews. When the Allies caught wind of the concentration camps, they did not bomb the rail lines that led to Auschwitz, nor did they take concrete action to rescue the remnants of Europe's Jewish community.

The distinction between a historic wrong and a contemporary right regarding Jewish citizenship in Canada is important in explaining the nature of the apology. It marks a transformation of Jewish experience and related targeted racism from the late 1930s to the early twenty-first century and is one of the most significant and dramatic examples of minority integration in modern history. Again, on this point, Trudeau is explicit. These were "good" refugees, but a prior governmental regime conceived of them, wrongly, as "bad" refugees (regarding the political and social construction of "good" versus "bad" Muslims, see Mamdani 2004). To the government of the day, Jews were among the least desirable immigrants; their presence on Canadian soil had to be limited. The government imposed strict quotas and an ever-growing list of requirements designed to deter Jewish immigration. Trudeau outlined the government's response:

> As the Nazis escalated their attacks on the Jews of Europe, the number of visa applications surged. Canadian relatives, embassy officials, immigration officers, political leaders—all were flooded with calls for help. Wealthy businessmen promising job creation. Aging parents vowing to take up farming. Pregnant women begging for clemency. Doctors, lawyers, academics, engineers, scientists imploring officials and the government to let them serve our country. They offered everything they owned, promising to comply with Canada's every request. These refugees would have made this country stronger, and its people proud. But the government went to great lengths to ensure that their appeals went nowhere. (Canada 2018a)

The details of this transition in the status of Jews in the post-war period are significant, especially notable in the case of the United States, but take us beyond the scope of the current discussion (see, for example, Brodkin 1998; Bakan 2014). The specific relevance here can be summarized briefly, exemplified in a change in the racialization of Ashkenazi (or European) Jews in North America, moving from a condition of "less than white" (Brodkin 1998) to what I term "whiteness by permission" (Bakan 2014). Such permission is granted from a hegemonic, or dominant, Anglo-Christian state, where a new "Judeo-Christianity" is incorporated into the state multicultural project. The text of the apology indicates the explicit logic. Regarding the experience of Jews at home and abroad, the Canada of today, we are told, is different from the Canada of the past. Canada today is a different place: a place where citizenship is first defined, apparently, by principles and ideals, not by race or faith (Canada 2018b). Moreover, Jewish Canadians and Jews internationally are credited with helping advance Canadian multiculturalism. Trudeau stated,

> This change in attitudes, this shift in policy was no accident. It was the work of Canadian men and women who dedicated their lives to making this country more equal and more just. Men and women who were children of the Holocaust, Jewish refugees, or descendants of the oppressed. These Jewish men and women took part in social struggles for fairness, justice, and human rights. At home, they furthered the great Canadian causes that shaped this country—causes that benefitted all Canadians. Abroad, they fought for democracy and the rule of law, for equality and liberty. The scope of their impact should not only be recognized, but celebrated. They were scientists and activists; ministers and singers; physicists and philanthropists. They were and continue to be proudly Jewish—and proudly Canadian. They helped open up Canada's eyes and ears to the plight of the most vulnerable. They taught us *Tikkun olam*—our responsibility to heal the world. (Canada 2018a)

This marks a new "true patriot love," as the Canadian national anthem, "O Canada," so clearly identifies.[3] Importantly, however, this is not an unconditional love; instead, it is given on certain terms and can therefore also be withdrawn. Enter Canada's close relationship with Israel, a state where all the major political parties are committed to the politics of Zionism.[4]

---

3 "O Canada" is the official anthem of Canada, sung in English and French. The English lyrics are the following: "O Canada! Our home and native land! True patriot love in all of us command. With glowing hearts we see thee rise, the True North strong and free! From far and wide, O Canada, we stand on guard for thee. God keep our land glorious and free! O Canada, we stand on guard for thee. O Canada, we stand on guard for thee." See Canada (n.d.).

4 Zionism is a political orientation, not a religion or theology, that insists that Jews can only live in peace, free of antisemitism, in a separate state that is defined by

The relationship to the state of Israel is identified and named in the apology as a key factor in changing Canada's relationship to its Jewish immigrants and citizens. Trudeau noted, "It would take new leadership, a new world order, and the creation of the State of Israel, a homeland for the Jewish people, for Canada to amend its laws and begin to dismantle the policies that had legitimized and propagated anti-Semitism" (Canada 2018b).

Other refugee groups, then as now, have not been offered such a warm welcome to Canada, even retroactively. And significantly, neither have Palestinian refugees to Israel or to Canada ever been afforded such humanitarian praise and recognition. Indeed, Canada has a long-standing alliance with Israel. And even in terms of minimal recognition of the rights of Palestinians regarding the land from which they have been exiled since 1948, there is at best a checkered and inconsistent history (see Abu-Laban and Bakan 2020; Freeman-Maloy 2011).

Trudeau quite rightly and legitimately stated in the apology that antisemitism, while differing historically, is a thing not only of the past but of the present. But in referencing Canada's close alliance with Israel, there is a nearly explicit assumption that criticism of Israel is equivalent to antisemitism. This is not only inaccurate; it is dangerously misleading and carries serious and contemporary political consequences. The apology targeted the BDS movement, adding poison to the gift of the apology. Trudeau said, "Holocaust deniers still exist. Anti-Semitism is still far too present. Jewish institutions and neighbourhoods are still being vandalized with swastikas. Jewish students still feel unwelcomed and uncomfortable on some of our college and university campuses because of BDS-related intimidation" (Canada 2018a).

The BDS movement is based on a call for the implementation of three demands regarding the rights of Palestinians, all of which are named in United Nations policies (Masri 2017). It was originally advanced in 2005 following a unified call of 170 diverse Palestinian organizations and has widely resonated in Canada and internationally, including among many Jewish organizations. The call is based on three central demands of the state of Israel, as follows:

1. Ending its occupation and colonization of all Arab lands and dismantling the Wall;
2. Recognizing the fundamental rights of the Arab-Palestinian citizens of Israel to full equality; and

---

ethnicity. See Bakan 2014; Abu-Laban and Bakan 2020.

3. Respecting, protecting and promoting the rights of Palestinian refugees to return to their homes and properties as stipulated in UN resolution 194. (BDS 2005)

The conflation of a movement for Palestinian rights with contemporary and historic antisemitism marks a dangerous minimization of Nazi terror and exposes the selective humanitarianism of the apology for the refusal to accept refugees on the MS *St. Louis*.

Moreover, there is a significant presence of Jewish Canadians in the BDS movement, whose presence is also obfuscated in the apology. For example, Independent Jewish Voices (IJV), a pan-Canadian Jewish organization, has explicitly adopted and campaigns to support the BDS call (IJV 2021). However, such Jewish Canadians were apparently to be written out of the apology for the antisemitic crimes of Canada's past and present. Indeed, upon the announcement of the apology, IJV released a statement challenging the manipulation of historic injustice against Jewish refugees while Canada continued to deny refuge to others in desperate need of humanitarian asylum:

> While Trudeau's apology is a welcome step towards righting a historic wrong, such words ring hollow in light of Canada's continued harmful practices toward migrants, refugees and asylum seekers and its active role in perpetuating mass forced migration in the first place. This apology comes within a week of an announcement by the Canadian Border Services Agency (CBSA) of plans to substantially increase deportations of migrants by 25–35%. IJV is dismayed that the Liberal government would apologize for wrongs committed in the past, yet commit to increasing such practices today, many of which have resulted in torture and sometimes death in recent years. (IJV 2018)

The IJV statement also challenged Trudeau's claimed adherence to Jewish spiritual and moral tradition and the associated hypocrisy:

> Within the Jewish Tradition, there is a concept called *T'shuvah*, or "making amends." This concept is prefaced on the immediate halting of the harmful action followed by concrete, tangible steps to rectify it, including a steadfast commitment not to repeat such harms in the future. For Trudeau's apology to be meaningful, he must commit to ending the ongoing detention of migrants, that sees thousands of people—including children—jailed in immigrant detention centers each year, at times indefinitely, on stolen Indigenous land. (IJV 2018)

Other statements similarly objected to the way the apology was framed and forwarded by the Trudeau government. One of these was offered by Canadians for Justice and Peace in the Middle East (CJPME), a national organization that also supports BDS among multiple justice campaigns. While delivering this long-overdue apology, Trudeau shifted the conversation to condemn Canadians who support BDS and legitimate criticism of Israel. CJPME stated, "BDS is a legitimate non-violent movement designed to put economic pressure on the Israeli government until it respects Palestinian human rights. [. . .] Indeed, the objectives of BDS are fully aligned with official Canadian foreign policy and international law and condemn unjust behavior" (2018).

Further, a letter was sent to Trudeau by over two hundred university and college faculty in Canada:

> This letter concerns Canada's recent apology for turning away the MS St. Louis in 1939. First, thank you for acknowledging Canada's complicity in the murder of hundreds of Jewish refugees fleeing the Holocaust. On the 80th anniversary of Kristallnacht, and after the recent terrorist attack on a Pittsburgh synagogue, it is more important than ever to pay close heed to Canada's own history of bigotry and to recommit to preventing such tragedies from ever happening again. For this reason, we must register our deep disappointment with your apology's inclusion of condemnation for the Boycott, Divestment, Sanctions movement (BDS) and your equation of BDS with the worst kind of hate crimes. (Ghabrial and Raziogova 2018)

The letter continues to note that actual antisemitism remains unabated, while the apology misrepresents as a threat "peaceful advocacy for Palestinian human rights." The signatories identify how the prime minister has in fact helped "perpetuate a chilling, anti-democratic climate on campuses, one in which dissenting voices and peaceful protest are not welcome" (Ghabrial and Raziogova 2018). These challenges to the apology indicate a perception that it was insincere and inauthentic in both content and tone. These challenges also indicate that the apology suggested the Liberal administration used the opportunity to advance its own political aims. This was indicated by associating the tragedy of the MS *St. Louis* incident—for which the Canadian state was directly complicit—with contemporary alliances and interests in the Middle East.

Conclusion

In concluding, a note on my positionality is in order. I am Jewish. Both of my late parents were born and raised in New York City and were the children of Polish and Russian refugees who fled violent racist programs in their home countries. Our relatives who were unable to leave Eastern Europe are unaccounted for, assumed to have died in the camps. My namesake, my aunt Basha, is only known to me as someone who died in Hitler's gas chambers. My parents changed their last name—from Bakanofsky to Bakan—and spoke Yiddish to each other as a secret form of communication. We understood that Yiddish was a kind of special code between our parents, a way to keep their six children from understanding private conversations. However, on reflection, the fact that as children we did not learn to speak fluent Yiddish served to limit the visible and audible markers of our Jewish family in public life. My parents hoped we would grow up in a world where we could avoid the daily experiences of antisemitism with which they and their parents were painfully familiar.

I am also an active supporter of the BDS movement. I supported in 2005 the founding in Toronto of the Coalition Against Israeli Apartheid, an organization that advanced the BDS call in Canada. Trudeau's apology, for those of us who support the BDS movement, is no comfort. Instead, it comes as a poisoned gift, a dangerous endorsement of the dehumanization of Palestinian and other refugees wrapped in the sorrows and tears of past injustices of those close to my own history, cynically manipulated to provide a shiny exterior. There is a context of poisoned gifts—from the biblical story of Adam and Eve to the fairy tale of Snow White. There are, however, few lessons inspired by the endings that emerge from religious texts or mythical tales. There is no Almighty God or the kiss of a prince that will reverse or redress either the historical or the present realities of Canada's denial of the rights and claims of refugees for humanity, compassion, and solidarity.

State apologies generally, and the apology for refusing to grant asylum to the passengers of the MS *St. Louis* specifically, remain an important part of the current political landscape. We need to study them collectively and separately but in so doing attend to the details of context. Such apologies have important implications beyond the specific historical events and the painful experiences of the harmed populations. If offered with sincerity and authenticity, state apologies can serve, at least theoretically, to warn against harmful actions toward vulnerable populations in the present and future. These vulnerable groups include refugees and those living with precarious immigration status—groups deserving of and demanding human rights. But tragically, with each step forward, there can also be a step back.

In the case of the Jewish question, the complexities of Israel/Palestine need to be addressed and named. The BDS movement, condemned widely by Liberals and Tories alike (see Abu-Laban and Bakan 2020) and so dangerously targeted by Trudeau in this apology, is not only in no way antisemitic—it is an inspiring movement of solidarity. The movement, grounded among and led by Palestinians, has successfully forged a broad, diverse, and effective international campaign to advance the human rights of Palestinians. The BDS movement also has the potential to inspire real and lasting peace in a newly imagined Middle East. The threat to the existing powers that this social movement has garnered, forged from grassroots organizing and public education, can be read perhaps as a tribute to its effectiveness. We can learn from these moments of apology, even in the form of a poisoned gift, to find inspiration in the words unspoken and search for hope of some real redress.

References

Abella, Irving, and Harold Troper. 1979. "'The Line Must Be Drawn Somewhere': Canada and Jewish Refugees, 1933–9." *Canadian Historical Review* 60 (2): 178–209.

Abella, Irving, and Harold Troper. 2012. *None Is Too Many: Canada and the Jews of Europe, 1933–1948*. Toronto: University of Toronto Press.

Abu-Laban, Yasmeen, and Abigail B. Bakan. 2020. *Israel, Palestine and the Politics of Race: Exploring Identity and Power in a Global Context*. London: I.B. Tauris.

Ahmed, Sara. 2004. *The Cultural Politics of Emotion*. New York: Routledge.

Arnold, Janice. 2017. "MP Asks Canada to Apologize for 1939 Refusal of Jewish Refugees." *Canadian Jewish News*, February 7, 2017. https://www.cjnews.com/news/canada/mp-asks-canada-apology-refusing-ms-st-louis.

Augoustinos, Martha, Brianne Hastie, and Monique Wright. 2011. "Apologizing for Historical Injustice: Emotion, Truth and Identity in Political Discourse." *Discourse and Society* 25 (5): 1–25.

Bakan, Abigail. 2014. "Race, Class and Colonialism: Reconsidering the 'Jewish Question.'" In *Theorizing Anti-racism: Linkages in Marxism and Critical Race Theories*, edited by Abigail B. Bakan and Enakshi Dua, 252–79. Toronto: University of Toronto Press.

BDS (Boycott, Divestment and Sanctions). 2005. "Palestinian Civil Society Call for BDS." July 9, 2005. https://bdsmovement.net/call.

Bialystok, Franklin. 2000. *Delayed Impact: The Holocaust and the Canadian Jewish Community*. Montréal: McGill-Queen's University Press.

Brodkin, Karen. 1998. *How Jews Became White Folks: And What That Says About Race in America*. New Brunswick, NJ: Rutgers University Press.

Canada. 2018a. "Prime Minister Announces St. Louis Apology." News Release, May 8, 2018. https://pm.gc.ca/en/news/news-releases/2018/05/08/prime-minister-announces-st-louis-apology.

Canada. 2018b. "Statement of Apology on Behalf of the Government of Canada to the Passengers of the MS St. Louis." Speeches, November 7, 2018. https://pm.gc.ca/en/news/speeches/2018/11/07/statement-apology-behalf-government-canada-passengers-ms-st-louis.

Canada. n.d. "National Anthem of Canada." National Anthem and Symbols of Canada. Last modified October 4, 2023. https://www.canada.ca/en/canadian-heritage/services/anthems-canada.html.

Cassara, Catherine. 2017. "To the Edge of America: U.S. Newspaper Coverage of the 1939 Voyage of Jewish Refugees Aboard the MS St. Louis." *Journalism History* 42 (4): 225–38.

CJPME (Canadians for Justice and Peace in the Middle East). 2018. "CJPME: Trudeau Smear on BDS Totally Inappropriate." November 8, 2018. https://www.cjpme.org/pr_2018_11_08.

Dangerfield, Katie. 2018. "Trudeau Sets Date to Apologize for 'Absolute Moral Failure' of Turning Away Jewish Refugees." Global News, September 7, 2018. https://globalnews.ca/news/4433267/justin-trudeau-apologizes-jewish-refugees/.

Dhamoon, Rita Kaur, Davina Bhandar, Renisa Mawani, and Satwinder Kaur Bains, eds. 2019. *Unmooring the Komagata Maru: Charting Colonial Trajectories*. Vancouver: UBC Press.

Eppinger, Kamrel. 2012. "State Department Apologizes to Jewish Refugees." SS St. Louis Legacy Project, SHFWire, September 26, 2012. https://stlouislegacyproject.org/2012/09/26/state-department-apologizes-to-jewish-refugees-2/.

Freeman-Maloy, Dan. 2006. "AIPAC North." Parts 1, 2 and 3, ZNet, June 26, 2006. https://zcomm.org/znetarticle/aipac-north-by-dan-freeman-maloy/.

Freeman-Maloy, Dan. 2011. "Israeli State Power and Its Liberal Alibis." *Race and Class* 52 (3): 61–72.

Ghabrial, Sarah, and Elena Raziogova. 2018. "Justin Trudeau Conflating BDS with Anti-Semitism Is Dangerous." *HuffPost Canada*, November 15, 2018. https://www.huffingtonpost.ca/sarah-ghabrial/bds-anti-semitism-trudeau-holocaust_a_23590519/.

Gibney, Mark, Rhoda E. Howard-Hassmann, Jean-Marc Coicaud, and Niclaus Steiner, eds. 2008. *The Age of Apology, Facing Up to the Past*. Philadelphia: University of Pennsylvania Press.

Gibney, Mark, and Erik Roxstrom. 2001. "The Status of State Apologies." *Human Rights Quarterly* 23 (4): 911–39.

Housefather, Anthony. 2021. "Anthony Housefather. Member of Parliament for Mount-Royal." https://anthonyhousefather.libparl.ca/.

IJV (Independent Jewish Voices). 2018. "IJV Statement on MS St. Louis Apology." November 7, 2018. https://www.ijvcanada.org/ms-st-louis-apology/.

IJV. 2021. "About IJV." https://www.ijvcanada.org/about-ijv/.

James, Matt. 2018. "Narrative Robustness, Post-apology Conduct, and Canada's 1998 and 2008 Residential Schools Apologies." In *The Palgrave Handbook of State-Sponsored History After 1945*, edited by B. Bevernage and N. Wouters, 833–49. Houndmills: Palgrave Macmillan.

James, Matt, and Jordan Stanger-Ross. 2018. "Impermanent Apologies: On the Dynamics of Timing and Public Knowledge in Political Apology." *Human Rights Review* 19:289–311.

Jewish Virtual Library. 2020. "U.S. Policy During the Holocaust: The Tragedy of the S. S. St. Louis." https://www.jewishvirtuallibrary.org/the-tragedy-of-s-s-st-louis.

Johnston, Hugh J. M. 2014. *The Voyage of the Komagata Maru: The Sikh Challenge to Canada's Colour Bar*. Vancouver: UBC Press.

Kampf, Zohar, and Nava Lowenheim. 2012. "Rituals of Apology in the Global Arena." *Security Dialogue* 43 (1): 43–60.

Klein, Ruth, ed. 2012. *Nazi Germany, Canadian Responses: Confronting Antisemitism in the Shadow of War*. Montréal: McGill-Queen's University Press.

Kobayashi, Audrey. 1992. "The Japanese-Canadian Redress Settlement and Its Implications for 'Race Relations." *Canadian Ethnic Studies* 24, no. 1 (January): 1–19.

Lungen, Paul. 2016. "Tory MP Calls on Government to Apologize for St. Louis." *Canadian Jewish News*, June 24, 2016. https://www.cjnews.com/news/canada/tory-mp-calls-government-apologize-st-louis.

Mamdani, Mahmood. 2004. *Good Muslims, Bad Muslims: America, the Cold War, and the Roots of Terror*. New York: Random House.

Masri, Mazen. 2017. *The Dynamics of Exclusionary Constitutionalism: Israel as a Jewish and Democratic State*. Oxford: Hart.

Miki, Roy. 2005. *Redress*. Vancouver: Raincoast.

Nobles, Melissa. 2008. *The Politics of Official Apologies*. Cambridge: Cambridge University Press.

Ogilvie, Sarah A., and Scott Miller. 2006. *Refuge Denied: The St. Louis Passengers and the Holocaust*. Madison: University of Wisconsin Press.

Ortiz, Jorge L. 2019. "Tree of Life Massacre: A Year Later, US Jewish Communities Still Facing 'Significant Threats.'" *USA Today*, October 27, 2019. https://www.usatoday.com/story/news/nation/2019/10/27/tree-life-year-after-pittsburgh-attack-u-s-jews-threatened/2451390001/.

Peto, Jennifer. 2010. "The Victimhood of the Powerful: White Jews, Zionism and the Racism of Hegemonic Holocaust Education." Master's thesis, University of Toronto. https://tspace.library.utoronto.ca/handle/1807/24619.

Rosenberg, Stuart, dir. 1976. *Voyage of the Damned*. London: ITC Entertainment.

Rotberg, R. 2006. "Apologies, Truth Commissions, and Inter-State Conflict." In *Taking Wrongs Seriously: Apologies and Reconciliation*, edited by E. Barkan and A. Karn, 33–49. Stanford, CA: Stanford University Press.

R. W. 2007. "Moment: June 7, 1939: Prime Minister Mackenzie King Turns Away Jewish Refugees on Board the *SS St. Louis*." *Beaver*, June–July 2007, 12–13. https://www.canadashistoryarchive.ca/canadas-history/the-beaver-jun-jul-2007/flipbook/12/.

Thomas, Gordon, and Max Morgan-Witts. (1974) 2010. *Voyage of the Damned: A Shocking True Story of Hope, Betrayal and Nazi Terror*. New York: Skyhorse.

Thompson, Janna. 2000. "The Apology Paradox." *Philosophical Quarterly* 50, no. 201 (October): 470–75.

Tikkanen, Amy. 2019. S.v. "MS St. Louis." *Encyclopedia Britannica*. https://www.britannica.com/topic/MS-St-Louis-German-ship.

TRC (Truth and Reconciliation Commission of Canada). 2015. *Honouring the Truth, Reconciling for the Future: Summary of the Final Report of the Truth and Reconciliation Commission of Canada*. Winnipeg: TRC.

USC (University of Southern California) Shoah Foundation. 2013. "Remembering Kristallnacht." https://sfi.usc.edu/exhibits/remembering-kristallnacht-0.

Vincent, C. Paul. 2011. "The Voyage of the St. Louis Revisited." *Holocaust and Genocide Studies* 25, no. 2 (Fall): 252–89.

Wood, Alexandra L. 2014. "Rebuild or Reconcile: American and Canadian Approaches to Redress for World War II Confinement." *American Review of Canadian Studies* 44 (3): 337–65.

11 State Apologies and the Rehumanization of Refugee, Indigenous, and Ethnic Minority Groups

Reza Hasmath, Benjamin Ho, and Solomon Kay-Reid

It is quite frequently the case that when nation-states apologize for their past transgressions, the outcome of the apology is to redeem the apologizer—that is, the state. In fact, research suggests that the general focus of an apology is to rehumanize the apologizer after they have committed a transgression and have temporarily been "Otherized" in the eyes of the victimized party or wider community (Gobodo-Madikizela 2002; Marrus 2007). In effect, by apologizing, the transgressor is attempting to redeem themselves while restoring their trustworthiness. This strategy is clearly exemplified in Bakan's chapter, whereby she analyzes Canadian prime minister Justin Trudeau's apology for turning away Jewish refugees who were fleeing persecution in Europe just before and during World War II.

In some rare cases, however, state apologies are employed to rehumanize the apologized party—the refugee, Indigenous, or ethnic minority group(s). That is to say, in these instances, the apology serves to bring voice and recognition to the grievances suffered by the victimized party, even perhaps psychologically healing the aggrieved individuals or social group(s) affected. Examples of apologies that at least partially address rehumanizing the apologized group include Canada's apologies to Chinese Canadian immigrants for the Head Tax and Indigenous groups for residential schools or South Africa's apologies to non-white ethnic groups for apartheid. This is not to imply that such apologies served no other purpose; in most cases, they did, but they are noteworthy for their focus on the apologized party.

In contrast, other state apologies—for example, Germany's role in the Holocaust—have primarily been about atonement for the nation-state. Similar to acts of ritual purification, the apology serves to cleanse the state and the people it represents and, in the process, rehumanize them. Moreover, in these cases, the grievances and lingering trauma of the victimized party often remain insufficiently addressed as to meaningfully benefit them socially and psychologically (Halpern and Weinstein 2004).

To best evaluate this discord between apologies aimed at rehumanizing the apologizer instead of the apologized party, this chapter bridges insights from the literature about apologies, which has focused on how apologies function, and the literature about truth and reconciliation, which has focused on rehumanization. It poses the following analytical queries: How are apologies different toward refugee, Indigenous, or ethnic minority group(s) when the goal is to rehumanize the apologized party and not the apologizer? What happens to the apologizer in such apologies? What can be learned by jointly considering the apology and truth and reconciliation literature on how to make an effective apology? This chapter will show that while the function of an apology is often to rehumanize the apologizer, paradoxically, an apology is really only effective if the intent is to rehumanize the victim, the apologized party.

Framework

The conventional and popular understanding of apologies, inclusive of state apologies, is fairly straightforward. An individual, group, or organization commits a transgression, breaching the accepted current social norms or even laws of their community; in doing so, trust is broken between the transgressor and the aggrieved party. Moreover, in some cases, the transgressor's social standing becomes diminished in the eyes of their community, potentially to the point of being ostracized. In an effort to repair this broken trust and potentially restore their reputation for trustworthy behaviour in the present day, the transgressor will apologize for their past actions.

One way to conceptualize the efficacy of apologies is through signalling theory. Signalling theory explains how information between different parties in cases of information asymmetry is communicated (or signalled) and how that signal is interpreted (Connelly et al. 2011). In our context, a transgressor's apology signals their fitness to be restored to the in-group. More acutely, apologies signal two things: they are an acknowledgement of shared values and norms that the transgressor violated through prior action and an implicit or explicit promise that in the future the behaviour will be different (Ho 2012; Ohtsubo et al. 2012).

Not all apologies are created equal. But what makes an effective apology, which properly signals what it is intending to the receiver, and what makes these signals costly to the apologizer? There is a significant degree of consensus in the literature regarding the bare minimum elements for an apology to be effective. As Marrus (2007, 79) suggests, there are four key elements for an apology to be deemed complete:

1. An acknowledgement of a wrong committed, including the harm that it caused.
2. An acceptance of responsibility for having committed the wrong.
3. An expression of regret or remorse both for the harm and for having committed the wrong.
4. A commitment, explicit or implicit, to reparation and when, appropriate, to non-repetition of the wrong.

Much of the literature on apologies builds upon these essential four elements. Diers-Lawson and Pang (2016), drawing up the ethics of care and atonement theory, suggest an ethical apology framework (EAF), which could be used to categorize apologies as ethical or not. The EAF includes all four of the aforementioned components of a complete apology but also proposes that for an apology to be ethical, it must be delivered early, evolve over time to reflect changes in the situation, be consistent across sources and contexts, listen to those affected, and expressly seek forgiveness.

Research in political science has emphasized the dangers that state apologies can have on the domestic political situation. According to Mihai (2013), discussing the state's past injustices can be particularly concerning for those people who strongly identify with their nationality. These individuals are likely to object to the state apologizing, and their criticism can often undermine the effectiveness of the apology in the eyes of the victimized community, as was the case with Japan's apologies to China and South Korea. Wohl et al.'s (2013) research helps further reinforce this. He found that in the aftermath of a state apology, the victimized community tends to expect better treatment from the dominant community. For this reason, Mihai (2013, 203) suggests that "broadening the basis of support for the apology is crucial both in terms of its democratic legitimacy—the more support for the apology, the more legitimate the apology—but also in terms of its effectiveness." To resolve this problem, the state can demonstrate how apologizing actually has a positive impact on the national image. For instance, in the case of liberal democracies, Mihai argues, "Living up to the principles that define 'us' as liberal democrats implies acknowledging wrongs done to specific groups among 'us.' 'We' are the best that 'we' can be when 'we' look to our fundamental normative commitments and take responsibility for past suffering" (215).

This is similar to Blatz, Schumann, and Ross's (2009) codification of praising the majority and the present system.

Ho (2012) provides a way to frame these guidelines for best practices through an economic taxonomy of apologies, where the apology's efficacy is measured by the cost associated with it. That is, the costlier the signal, the more effective it is likely to be. He distinguishes among five types of apologies: tangible cost apologies, a commitment to improved conduct, a loss of status, an admission of incompetence, buck-passing apologies, and partial apologies.

Tangible cost apologies are those that either include some type of material restitution or expose the transgressor to potential material liability. These apologies can include monetary reparations to the victims of past transgressions or, in some cases, their family members. Most commonly, reparations occur in state apologies, such as those given to the living victims of residential schooling in Canada. Sometimes, monetary reparations can also comprise funds spent on community-wide social projects, such as those devoted to educating the public about a past transgression. Tangible costs can further include the potential for exposing the apologizer to legal liability in a lawsuit. In effect, the apology can be viewed as an admittance of wrongdoing and could be used by the apologizer to seek financial compensation in court.

The apologizer promising to do better in the future can serve as an extremely effective signal; implicitly, the apologizer is accepting that they will be held to a higher standard compared to those who did not apologize (Ho 2012). That is, a promise to do better ups the ante for the apologizer in the future, and if they transgress again, they can expect to be punished more, relative to those who have not apologized. This can apply not just to the apologizer's exact transgression but to all future transgressions affecting the same group (Wohl, Hornsey, and Philpot 2011). For this reason, promises to do better can be highly risky for state institutions if they cannot guarantee that transgressions will not reoccur. This form of apology overlaps with two of the elements found in state apologies by Blatz, Schumann, and Ross (2009). That is, in praising the present system and disassociating the past injustice from the present system, there is an implication that the past transgression could not occur now and will not occur in the future.

All full apologies—differentiated from partial/weak apologies, which will be discussed next—contain some element of status loss as well. By its nature, apologizing is an admittance of fault that an action performed was incorrect. Clearly, there is a range to this behaviour; someone voluntarily lowering themselves by admitting to "being such an idiot" or statements of a similar nature represent a greater loss of status than merely apologizing (Ho 2012). Chaudhry and Loewenstein (2019) suggest there is a warmth-competence trade-off; in effect, apologies increase perceptions of warmth but decrease perceptions of competence. This loss of status can prove to be a costly signal, especially for those groups who tend to put a premium on status (Ho 2012). There is also overlap here with Mihai's (2013) work in that state apologies can represent a loss of national status, impacting those who have strong affinities with their nationality.

Evidently, all the signals identified by Ho (2012) can be incorporated into an apology; however, it is analytically useful to delineate them. Weak apologies are those that do not contain a cost associated with them; instead, the apologizer makes excuses for the transgression. By shifting the blame onto external circumstances, the apologizer avoids the penalties associated with the previously mentioned apologies, which has obvious appeal; however, it greatly weakens the apology. Partial apologies are a type of weak apology in which empathy is expressed for the victimized party, but the transgressor does not accept responsibility. They are also less effective—for example, phrases such as "I am sorry you are upset by what I did" or "I am sorry you feel that way." These partial apologies can come across as shifting responsibility onto the victimized party for their negative reaction to the transgressor's action.

In the next section, these differing apology taxonomies will be used to explore a series of case studies. We divide these case studies between apologies that focused on the interests of the apologizer and those that focused on rehumanizing the apologized party.

Partial Apologies

Germany and the Holocaust

No conversation on state apologies would be complete without at least some discussion of German apologies for the Holocaust committed during the Second World War. As Marrus (2007, 88) aptly states, "One can hardly speak of the role of guilt and national obligation, and the consequent collective atonement, compensation, memorization, commemoration, reparation and healing, without thinking of the great impact of Holocaust motifs and reparative programs." Furthermore, this process was not limited to Germany but rather occurred in nearly all territories that had some connection with the decimation of European Jews. It even extends beyond states, with churches and corporations also engaged in the process of atonement for their complicity in the Holocaust. However, qualitatively, the majority of Holocaust apologies—even among nation-states that were complicit in doing little to assist European Jewish refugees, as discussed in Bakan's chapter—exist somewhere between those that are focused on restoring the transgressor to trustworthiness and those intending to rehumanize the apologizer. This is notably evident in examining one of the most famous apologies: Willy Brandt's Kniefall.

On December 7, 1970, West German chancellor Willy Brandt, while visiting Warsaw, fell to his knees in front of the memorial to the Warsaw Ghetto Uprising, remaining completely still on the wet floor for over half a minute (Borneman 2005). This apology—known thereafter in German as Kniefall—was the first time a German leader had so explicitly admitted responsibility and guilt for Jewish and Polish suffering. It is this recognition that Germany now shared social norms with their victims, norms that the Nazis had abhorrently violated, that makes this apology about more than just restoring the state's trustworthiness. Nevertheless, as Borneman (2005, 62) contends, this apology was primarily an act that was necessary as a "symbolic purification ritual" to transform Germany from a "criminal nation to a rehabilitated member of the international community." Put differently, it was a necessary action to restore the state to a position of trust. Brandt's Kniefall provides additional insights into apologies that are important to consider.

One of the unique features of Brandt's apology is that it was entirely unspoken. Therefore, it does not comprise the aforementioned four necessary elements of a complete apology, at least not explicitly. Brandt's apology was effective insofar as it helped restore Germany's relations with the Nazi regime's former victims, particularly Poland and wider Eastern Europe. Here a signalling taxonomy is informative. While Brandt's apology was silent, it did implicitly contain the costly signal of status loss; by its very nature, kneeling reduces an individual's status in the eyes of witnesses. Moreover, the reaction of some German conservatives at home, who questioned his patriotism and whether he should have knelt at all, signalled that Brandt paid a price for his actions. Brandt's apology also provides evidence for the role that the individual representative can have in making an inter-group apology effective. In this case, Brandt's apology carried a particular sense of sincerity and conviction, considering he had spent much of his life actively resisting the Nazi regime, often at substantial risk to his own safety (Borneman 2005). It is entirely possible that such an apology would have been far less effective coming from someone else. Lastly, it must be noted, however, that concerns over the reality that antisemitism is returning to Germany have become widespread, with a number of people within Germany seriously questioning the country's culture of Holocaust remembrance and atonement (Staudenmaier 2019; Weinthal 2014).

Rehumanizing Apologies

South Africa and the Truth and Reconciliation Commission

South Africa represents, perhaps, the most informative case study on the process of rehumanization, apologizing, reconciliation, and peace building in the wake of severe and prolonged injustice during apartheid (1948–94). This policy ensured that South Africa's various ethnic groups would be dominated politically, economically, and socially by a small white population. With the end of apartheid in the early 1990s, one of the most pertinent questions was how to move forward: What was the best way to heal the grievous wounds of the past in a way that allowed for a new democratic, peaceful, multi-ethnic South Africa? The choice was made to embark on an approach of restorative justice in the form of the Truth and Reconciliation Commission (TRC). This process invited victims who were recognized as having undergone gross human rights violations to supply statements about their experiences. The perpetrators of these acts were also able to give testimony and petition for amnesty from both criminal and civil prosecution for politically motivated crimes. It was through this process that the architects of the TRC hoped to heal the deep wounds of the past and rehumanize non-white ethnic groups who had suffered under apartheid (Gobodo-Madikizela 2002; Vora and Vora 2004). Despite these good intentions, the actual successes of the TRC are far more muddled, with examples of both deep failures and some successes.

One of the worst days of the TRC occurred when Frederik Willem de Klerk apologized to the victims of apartheid on behalf of the National Party. Speaking to the TRC (1997), de Klerk, responding to assertions expressing the contrary, insisted that he had previously apologized for apartheid and offered this statement:

> Let me place once and for all a renewed apology on record. Apartheid was wrong. I apologise in my capacity as leader of the National Party to the millions of South Africans who suffered the wrenching disruption of forced removals in respect of their homes, businesses and land. Who over the years suffered the shame of being arrested for pass law offences. Who over the decades and indeed centuries suffered the indignities and humiliation of racial discrimination. Who for a long time were prevented from exercising their full democratic rights in the land of their birth. Who were unable to achieve their full potential because of job reservation. And who in any other way suffered as a result of discriminatory legislation and policies. This renewed apology is offered in a spirit of true repentance, in full knowledge of the tremendous harm that apartheid has done to millions of South Africans.

On the face of it, this apology was profound and sincere, and it should have satisfied even the most exacting of standards. However, during follow-up questioning by TRC staff and commissioners, de Klerk undermined his apology so abominably that the African National Congress issued a statement rejecting it with "contempt" (Govier and Verwoerd 2002). Throughout the entirety of the follow-up, he persistently denied any knowledge of or responsibility for the prevalence of severe mistreatment and torture committed by state agents, especially against anti-apartheid activists. While he claimed to regret the murder, torture, rape, and abduction of anti-apartheid activists, he did not apologize for them, as he believed that he, and by extension the National Party government, was not responsible. He also failed to commit to and was vague in discussing any "practical" or material amends to the victims of apartheid (Govier and Verwoerd 2002). Put another way, de Klerk was unwilling to use costly signals and instead offered a partial apology that did not take responsibility for these heinous transgressions. Additionally, unlike Brandt, whose personal story lent sincerity to his apology, de Klerk had been a member of the National Party since 1972 and had long been a strong proponent of apartheid. These factors made his apology seem insincere at best and very far from a "spirit of true repentance." In reviewing de Klerk's apology, Govier and Verwoerd (2002, 78) contend that "he wanted to take a position of pride (we ended apartheid), not shame (we admit responsibility for gross violations of human rights)." As such, he wanted to rehumanize himself and the National Party but did not attempt to rehumanize the victims of apartheid.

The apology from de Klerk was further undermined because his mandate to speak on behalf of the National Party was extremely dubious. As Govier and Verwoerd (2002, 78) note, "Members of the older (pretransition) party such as former South African President P. W. Botha were not present and had not authorized de Klerk to speak for them. Botha publicly criticized some of de Klerk's statements, immediately revealing that his mandate as a spokesperson was questionable." While serving as a particularly stark example, this reflects a common difficulty in state apologies. That is to say, inter-group apologies are complicated, since groups contain numerous autonomous agents who are capable of acting in distinct ways, even actively opposing the apology or the group receiving the apology. This can, unsurprisingly, serve to compromise the apology in the eyes of the recipient group and raise questions about how committed to reconciliation the perpetrating group truly is.

The TRC itself had noble intentions, and evidence suggests that South Africans, especially the Xhosa, found it was successful in establishing the truth of what happened, an important aspect of rehumanization. Moreover, for some individual members of the TRC, the process proved cathartic and helped provide psychological healing (Avruch 2010). Nonetheless, this was by no means a universal experience; many found that reopening the wounds of the past caused further psychological damage (Vora and Vora 2004). This was especially problematic, as there was a substantial lack of support and mental health resources available to the victims who testified, a common problem in most TRCs (Cilliers, Dube, and Siddiqi 2016). Furthermore, the TRC was not successful at achieving inter-group reconciliation between white and non-white ethnic groups, although interpersonal reconciliation was achieved for some people (see, e.g., Chapman 2007).

Several explanations can be offered to explain this failure. The simplest explanation is that reconciliation is hard and can take generations to occur, and as such, it is no surprise the TRC was unsuccessful at achieving it. Chapman (2007) criticizes the TRC for trying to reduce inter-group reconciliation between white and non-white ethnic groups to the interpersonal and suggests that significantly more attention needed to be paid to the institutions and regimes behind apartheid, such as the police force (eerily similar echoes can be heard in present-day multi-ethnic jurisdictions such as the United States, Canada, and Australia). Critics have also noted that many of the perpetrators, similarly to de Klerk, offered weak apologies, believing they personally had committed no wrong; made excuses for what had occurred; or did not apologize at all (Avruch 2010). Nevertheless, victims were still pressed by the commission to offer forgiveness. Lastly, by embedding amnesty inside the TRC, the cost for perpetrators to apologize was significantly lowered, potentially reducing the efficacy of their apologies.

Costly signalling theory can help illuminate what Tavuchis (1991) classically terms the paradox of apologies. Apologies need to be costly in order to rehumanize the apologizer. However, an apology made with this benefit to the apologizer in mind effectively lowers the cost of the apology, making the apology less credible and thus less effective. While the function of an apology may be to rehumanize the apologizer, an apology that appears to be motivated by restoring the apologizer's status is likely to fail. A good apology has to be focused on the victim. As a consequence, apologies with a focus on rehumanizing the apologized party may be more beneficial for the apologizer as well. We turn to examples of such apologies next.

Canada and Residential Schools

On June 11, 2008, the then Canadian prime minister Stephen Harper apologized to the victims of residential schools. Residential schooling in Canada has a long and tragic history, beginning in the early 1600s with the opening of the first boarding schools. However, it was not until the Indian Act of 1876—which made Indigenous peoples wards of the state and the Canadian federal government responsible for their education—that the system truly took effect. From 1867 to 1983, nearly one-third of all Indigenous children, approximately 150,000 in total, were taken from their families and communities and sent to these schools, which were funded by the state and presided over by the churches (Anderson 2012). These schools were devised to sever the connection of Indigenous children to their cultural identity and traditional practices, which were considered inferior to those of European settlers, and to educate them in "civilized ways." This has become epitomized in Canadian discourse by the phrase "killing the Indian in the child." Beyond the significant damage caused by removing children from their families and denying them access to their languages and cultural practices, students also experienced physical and sexual abuse. Claes and Clifton (1998, 24) note that "brutal and arbitrary punishment was a daily feature of school life; public beatings and humiliations, head shaving, and being kept in locked closets on bread and water for days are described." Many of the students who graduated from these schools had trouble reintegrating into their own communities and yet continued to be victimized by the prevalent prejudicial attitudes in white Canadian society. In effect, they existed in limbo, trapped between two worlds yet fitting into neither.

The impact of this system continues to reverberate throughout Canada's Indigenous communities, with research suggesting that it perpetuates higher rates of alcoholism, drug addiction, domestic violence, mental illness, and suicide among Indigenous people in Canada (see Bombay, Matheson, and Anisman 2014). While complaints and allegations were made, the voices of those who suffered were neither heard nor accepted at the national level until the 1990s Royal Commission on Aboriginal Peoples (RCAP; Anderson 2012). The government of the day, led by Prime Minister Jean Chrétien, responded to RCAP on January 7, 1998, with an announcement of an Indigenous action plan and the reading of a statement of reconciliation by Minister Jane Stewart (Nobles 2008). According to Anderson (2012, 573), many Indigenous Canadians found this response entirely insufficient: "The healing fund did not include all survivors, the statement's language was fairly general, but perhaps most importantly, the symbolism of the event indicated the government was not taking the issue seriously enough." In particular, Chrétien himself was not the one to offer the apology, nor did he attend the lunchtime ceremony where Stewart, a junior minister, read it out. This action can be easily understood as one that is trying to restore the state to trustworthiness rather than rehumanizing the victims. Nearly a decade later, the government of Canada, under Prime Minister Stephen Harper, took a very different approach in addressing the legacy of residential schooling in Canada.

In 2006, the government announced the approval of the Indian Residential Schools Settlement Agreement (IRSSA), which included five components: (1) the Common Experience Payment (CEP), (2) the Independent Assessment Process (IAP), (3) a Truth and Reconciliation Commission, (4) commemoration, and (5) health and healing services. Under the CEP, the IRSSA was to provide CAD 1.9 billion (~USD 1.51 billion) to former living members of recognized residential schools; this was intended to holistically address the experiences of attending residential schooling (Crown–Indigenous Relations and Northern Affairs 2019). The IAP was a claimant-based, out-of-court process that addressed specific claims of sexual abuse, serious physical abuse, and other psychologically damaging acts suffered at Indian residential schools. As of 2017, CAD 3.1 billion (~USD 2.46 billion) has been paid out through the IAP. The IRSSA also included CAD 60 million (~USD 47.57 million) in funds for a five-year-long Truth and Reconciliation Commission and CAD 145 million (~USD 114.96 million) for commemoration and healing events.

The actual apology was offered in the Canadian Parliament. Its tone and substance were directly informed by letters from Indigenous groups such as the Assembly of First Nations and through meetings with survivors of residential schools. This can be understood as an important process in giving voice to the grievances of those who suffered by directly allowing them to have influence in the tenor of the apology. Further, the Harper government "found" a loophole that allowed Indigenous leaders to directly respond to the apology in the Canadian Parliament rather than at a press conference as the government originally planned. Harper's apology was effusive, praising the strength of Indigenous communities and apologizing profoundly for the government's role in the residential school system as well as the damage it caused, and continues to cause, to Indigenous communities. Moreover, he directly referenced how the TRC was an "opportunity to educate all Canadians" on residential schools (Canadian Press 2008). This is important, as misconceptions about residential schools were widespread in Canadian society, and many in Canada, prior to Harper's apology, questioned the need for Canada to apologize at all (Gray 2011). In principle, by shining a bright light on the suffering experienced by survivors of Indian residential schools and giving Indigenous peoples a platform to respond, Harper's apology not only provided greater public awareness of the issue; it also helped build a bridge of greater empathy between Canada and Indigenous people. Put another way, the intentions of Harper's apology and the TRC can be seen as an attempt to rehumanize Indigenous people in the eyes of Canada's general public.

Harper's apology contained all four of the elements Marrus (2007) identified as being necessary for a complete apology. Further, using Ho's (2012) taxonomy, the apology contains costly signals. The tangible cost is evident, as the apology followed on the backdrop of the substantive IRSSA funding. Further, while not expressly promising to not repeat the act, Harper implicitly did so through indicative comments such as this: "There is no place in Canada for the attitudes that inspired the Indian residential schools' system to ever again prevail" (Canadian Press 2008). Furthermore, Harper experienced some status loss through apologizing; foremost, he praised his political rival and ideological opposite Jack Layton, leader of the New Democrat Party, for having spent the last year and a half persuading him to apologize. Praising a rival leader in this manner shocked many in the Canadian media (Anderson 2012).

In theory, the TRC was intended to allow the victims of Indian residential schools to tell their truth and to illuminate to all Canadians the grievances of Indigenous peoples, with the hope that through this process, it would heal the massive traumas they experienced (James 2012). Similar to most TRCs, this was done through interpersonal storytelling, with little focus placed on how the Indian residential school system fit into the broader colonial framework or the public institutions that contributed to Indian residential schools and continue to negatively impact the lives of Indigenous people (Coulthard 2014). The TRC failed to spark meaningful debate because it did not adequately consider that the same systems originally responsible for creating the Indian residential schools continue to impact contemporary Indigenous relationships in almost every respect, including child welfare, criminal justice, health and human services, resource extraction, and sanitation (see; e.g., Coulthard 2014; James 2012).

Finally, while both Harper's apology and the TRC may have had good intentions and may have helped rehumanize some people, both succumbed to one of the biggest pitfalls in apologizing; apologies are not a magic wand that can rectify ongoing transgressions. When going forward, promises to do better only work in the eyes of the apologized party, if, in fact, the apologizer meaningfully improves their conduct. Few Indigenous people in Canada would say this has come to pass in light of continuous and serious injustices perpetrated against them (perceived or real) by the Canadian state, Canadian institutions, and the dominant population.

These include, but are by no means limited to, a failure to fully implement the recommendations of the TRC, disproportionate rates of violence committed against Indigenous women and girls, the overrepresentation of Indigenous people in the criminal justice system, the failure of the treaty process in British Columbia, and pervasive prejudicial attitudes and actions against Indigenous peoples throughout Canada.

Canada and the Chinese Head Tax

In 2006, Prime Minister Stephen Harper apologized on behalf of the Canadian government to all Chinese Canadians for both the Chinese Head Tax, which lasted from 1885 to 1923, and the Chinese Exclusion Act, which was in place from 1923 to 1947. These legislations not only disrupted families and hurt Chinese Canadian immigrants economically; they also conveyed a status of ethnic undesirability (see Winter 2008). The Chinese Canadian community has actively sought an apology and material compensation since the 1980s from the Canadian state. However, a procession of Liberal- and Conservative-led governments refused to supply them. Prior to Harper's apology, previous governments announced their intent to create a memorial fund that would apprise all Canadians of the injustice that had been perpetrated (Li 2008). However, they also stated that they had no plans to apologize. Despite being the first administration to acknowledge the injustice, many members of the Chinese Canadian community were upset by the government's failure to actually apologize. Blatz, Schumann, and Ross (2009) hypothesize that this is a form of reactive devaluation that highlights that during negotiations, if one group offers X but withholds Y, the other group will devalue X and desire Y more. In the context of apologies, this means that if a group demands just an apology and the government provides one, they will likely be satisfied. If, however, the group demands both an apology and financial compensation but the government only offers the apology, the group will devalue the apology, as it fails to fully meet their demands.

Broadly speaking, Harper's apology to the victims of the Head Tax and the Chinese Canadian community was extremely comprehensive and contained nine out of the ten criteria outlined by Blatz, Schumann, and Ross (2009). Furthermore, this apology was arguably about rehumanizing the Chinese Canadian community by highlighting the suffering the community experienced and praising the important role the victims of these policies played in constructing Canada, going so far as to say that the back-breaking labour Chinese immigrants provided in the construction of the Canadian Pacific Railway "helped to ensure the future of Canada" (Deveau 2006). Additionally, Harper stressed the invaluable role Chinese Canadians continue to play in Canada. In effect, this helped shift the narrative concerning Chinese Canadians from that of an undesirable immigrant group to a crucial and valued part of Canadian society. This apology also included a material component, with payments of CAD 20,000 (~USD 15,848) offered to the few remaining survivors of the Head Tax or their spouses and CAD 34 million (~USD 26.94 million) for recognition projects, with CAD 10 million (~USD 7.92 million) earmarked toward educating Canadians about the discrimination and hardship faced by Chinese Canadians due to wartime measures or immigration restrictions. In addition, Harper's apology contained a commitment to improved conduct, stating that the "government will continually strive to ensure that similar unjust practices are never allowed to happen again" (Deveau 2006).

Research conducted following Harper's apology found it was positive overall, but with some caveats. Blatz, Schumann, and Ross (2009), in their survey of both Chinese Canadians and non-Chinese Canadians, found both groups reported significant satisfaction with the apology, although Chinese Canadians evaluated it somewhat less favourably. Both groups assessed the Canadian government and Canadians of European heritage more favourably after the apology, but the apology had little effect on the participants' perceptions of Chinese Canadians. Moreover, Chinese Canadian participants generally possessed greater skepticism toward the motivations behind the apology and were more inclined to view it as a strategy to secure Chinese Canadian votes in the subsequent election (Li 2008). Chinese Canadian participants were also more inclined to believe that negative effects ensuing from the Head Tax on the Chinese Canadian community persisted (Blatz, Schumann, and Ross 2009). Wohl, Hornsey, and Philpot (2011, 86), in their research on inter-group apologies—including the Head Tax—found that "the historically victimized group often waits to see if the apology produces behavioural change after granting forgiveness." In the case of Harper's apology, they found that among Chinese Canadians, the apology increased expectations that it would "lead to conciliatory discourse and behaviours." In a revaluation one year later, they found that "Chinese Canadians who assigned collective guilt were less likely to think that the apology had transpired into actual change."

Discussion and Conclusion

State apologies are typically about signalling trustworthiness; they are generally about restoring the apologizer to full standing within their community. We have argued that a restoration of trustworthiness is demonstrated by an agreement that what happened was a violation, an acceptance of responsibility, an expression of regret or remorse, and an assertion that future actions will be better. Every apology discussed contained these elements to a large extent.

The initial apology from de Klerk signalled trustworthiness but was undermined by his later commentary—in particular, his reluctance to take responsibility or even admit that serious human rights violations toward non-white ethnic groups committed under apartheid were his fault. Those apologies that best signalled trustworthiness were the two provided by Prime Minister Stephen Harper to Indigenous peoples and Chinese Canadian immigrants. Not only did both apologies outline the grievous wrongs that had been committed against victimized groups by the Canadian state, but these apologies also contained promises of a better future. Canada is, of course, not alone in issuing such apologies.

The failure of these apologies can be attributed to the reluctance of the apologizing parties to pay a real cost for their past actions and an insufficient focus on the rehumanization of the victimized party. When considering apologies that are effective, the more effective apologies are those that are costly to fake. Put another way, if the apologizer is sacrificing something to the apologized party, the apologized party is more likely to believe the apologizer is being genuine. This can be further delineated in that an effective rehumanizing apology should

1. clearly identify the violation;
2. promise with clear language ways to make amends for the transgression, that it won't happen again, and an agreement to be held to a higher standard;
3. identify the reason for the failure and admit that it was a failure; and
4. avoid partial apologies that do not take responsibility for what has occurred.

An apology that does not have a guarantee appears to lack sincerity, since the apologizer is leaving open the possibility that they will commit future transgressions.

Applying these criteria to the discussed rehumanizing case studies, a somewhat clear ranking in efficacy appears. The apology from de Klerk, while acknowledging what he perceived to be the main violations, did not acknowledge a number of other violations that the victims of apartheid were seeking an apology for. Moreover, as previously mentioned, throughout his commentary, he refused to accept responsibility for a number of violations that were not included in his original apology. In his answers to questions from the TRC, de Klerk also failed to engage with the idea of reparations, which are an important means of making things better for the victims. He further failed to expressly promise that these types of policies would not occur in the future. While he did acknowledge that the apartheid policy was a failure, he nevertheless did not discuss the prejudicial systems of belief among white South Africans that allowed it to occur. Moreover, in the follow-up questioning, de Klerk frequently engaged in partial apologies, patently demonstrating that he was unwilling to take responsibility for the human rights violations and violence that was committed by the Nationalist Party. Overall, de Klerk's apology largely failed because it contained few of the elements that were necessary for it to succeed.

Harper's apology to Indigenous peoples contained almost all the important elements for a successful state apology. He clearly identified what the violation was and the impact it had on residential school survivors and Indigenous communities more broadly. Moreover, he discussed steps that were being taken to heal what had happened, including the formation of the TRC. He also offered assurances that this would not happen again. However, while he did spend significant time admitting that what had occurred was a moral failure, for some, his explanations of why the policy occurred did not go far enough (see, e.g., Coulthard 2014). Although Harper acknowledged that the Indian residential school system was rooted in prejudicial logic that saw Indigenous peoples and cultures as inferior, he did not discuss how it was only one component of a broader colonial project that sought to dispossess Indigenous peoples of their lands.

The most effective apology was the one offered to the Chinese Canadian community. Harper clearly identified that the Head Tax, the Exclusion Act, and the state's past failure to acknowledge its violations. Moreover, not only did he promise to establish an education fund to help make things better; at the end of his speech, he also stressed that this would not happen again, stating that "our deep sorrow over the racist actions of our past will nourish our unwavering commitment to build a better future for all Canadians" (Deveau 2006). Lastly, he clearly identified that this policy was a moral failure on behalf of the government and that it was rooted in a prejudicial bias against Chinese people, and he did not make excuses for these policies.

Apologizing effectively is a costly process and comes with attendant risks. Apologies can be costly when considering the loss of status for the apologizer, material restitution, and/or a promise to do better in the future. Apologies can be risky, since they can potentially lead to criticisms by other groups in society who are opposed to the offering of apologies, as in the case of Brandt's apology. The apology can fail to achieve full reconciliation or healing, notably if the apologized party continues to suffer transgressions—as is arguably the case with Harper's apology to Canada's Indigenous peoples. The state's promise to do better can also backfire, especially since public officials cannot control the policy of future governments or the attitudes of their citizens, and these groups can transgress again, which will break the trust of the victimized group.

There is also an inherent paradox to apologies. While apologies generally only work if they are costly, an effective apology that restores the transgressor to good standing effectively lowers the cost, making it easier to apologize. Put another way, if the apologizer is more trusted by the apologized party, the necessary costliness for a signal to be effective is lowered.

The lesson here is that the focus ought to be on rehumanizing the apologized refugee, Indigenous, or ethnic minority group(s), not the apologizer. Any apology too focused on the apologizer is seen as self-serving and therefore less costly and less believable. An apology focused on rehumanizing the apologized is therefore, paradoxically, more effective at rehumanizing the apologizer as well.

There is no easy apology; the apologizer will need to experience discomfort. It is by being willing to experience this discomfort that they demonstrate their worthiness and that the apology is more than just "cheap talk." It is through their discomfort that they signal to others that they have changed, that the expectations of behaviour have changed, that the accepted norms have changed, and that the apologized deserves to be treated better and will be treated better in the future. If they are unwilling to pay the price, as it were, and instead offer a weak or partial apology, it signals a lack of sincerity and that nothing has, in fact, changed. If they focus the apology on themselves rather than the apologized refugee, Indigenous, or ethnic minority group(s), then they weaken the signal. For states that are planning to apologize, it is important to be ready to accept the cost, as offering a non-costly apology can be worse than offering no apology at all.

References

Anderson, Willow J. 2012. "'Indian Drum in the House': A Critical Discourse Analysis of an Apology for Canadian Residential Schools and the Public's Response." *International Communication Gazette* 74 (6): 571–85.

Avruch, Kevin. 2010. "Truth and Reconciliation Commissions: Problems in Transitional Justice and the Reconstruction of Identity." *Transcultural Psychiatry* 47 (1): 33–49.

Blatz, Craig W., Karina Schumann, and Michael Ross. 2009. "Government Apologies for Historical Injustices." *Political Psychology* 30 (2): 219–41.

Bombay, Amy, Kimberly Matheson, and Hymie Anisman. 2014. "The Intergenerational Effects of Indian Residential Schools: Implications for the Concept of Historical Trauma." *Transcultural Psychiatry* 51 (3): 320–38.

Borneman, John. 2005. "Public Apologies as Performative Redress." *SAIS Review of International Affairs* 25 (2): 53–66.

Canadian Press. 2008. "Text of Stephen Harper's Residential Schools Apology." CTV News, June 11, 2008. https://www.ctvnews.ca/text-of-stephen-harper-s-residential-schools-apology-1.301820.

Chapman, Audrey R. 2007. "Truth Commissions and Intergroup Forgiveness: The Case of the South African Truth and Reconciliation Commission." *Peace and Conflict: Journal of Peace Psychology* 13 (1): 51–69.

Chaudhry, Shereen J., and George Loewenstein. 2019. "Thanking, Apologizing, Bragging, and Blaming: Responsibility Exchange Theory and the Currency of Communication." *Psychological Review* 126 (3): 313–44.

Cilliers, Jacobus, Oeindrila Dube, and Bilal Siddiqi. 2016. "Reconciling After Civil Conflict Increases Social Capital but Decreases Individual Well-Being." *Science* 352 (6287): 787–94.

Claes, Rhonda, and Deborah Clifton. 1998. "Needs and Expectations for Redress of Victims of Abuse at Residential Schools." Paper prepared for the Law Commission of Canada. https://epe.lac-bac.gc.ca/100/200/301/lcc-cdc/needs_expectations_redres-e/html/claes.html.

Connelly, Brian L., S. Trevis Certo, R. Duane Ireland, and Christopher R. Reutzel. 2011. "Signaling Theory: A Review and Assessment." *Journal of Management* 37 (1): 39–67.

Coulthard, Glen S. 2014. *Red Skin, White Masks: Rejecting the Colonial Politics of Recognition.* Minneapolis: University of Minnesota Press.

Crown–Indigenous Relations and Northern Affairs. 2019. *Indian Residential Schools Settlement Agreement*. Ottawa: Government of Canada. https://www.rcaanc-cirnac.gc.ca/eng/1100100015576/1571581687074.

Deveau, Scott. 2006. "Government Offers Apology, Compensation for Head Tax." *Globe and Mail*, June 22, 2006. https://www.theglobeandmail.com/news/national/government-offers-apology-compensation-for-head-tax/article1104758/.

Diers-Lawson, Audra, and Augustine Pang. 2016. "Did BP Atone for Its Transgressions? Expanding Theory on 'Ethical Apology' in Crisis Communication." *Journal of Contingencies and Crisis Management* 24 (3): 148–61.

Gobodo-Madikizela, Pumla. 2002. "Remorse, Forgiveness, and Rehumanization: Stories from South Africa." *Journal of Humanistic Psychology* 42 (1): 7–32.

Govier, Trudy, and Wilhelm Verwoerd. 2002. "The Promise and Pitfalls of Apology." *Journal of Social Philosophy* 33 (1): 67–82.

Gray, Robin R. R. 2011. "Visualizing Pedagogy and Power with Urban Native Youth: Exposing the Legacy of the Indian Residential School System." *Canadian Journal of Native Education* 34 (1): 9–27.

Halpern, Jodi, and Harvey M. Weinstein. 2004. "Rehumanizing the Other: Empathy and Reconciliation." *Human Rights Quarterly* 26 (3): 561–83.

Ho, Benjamin. 2012. "Apologies as Signals: With Evidence from a Trust Game." *Management Science* 58 (1): 141–58.

James, Matt. 2012. "A Carnival of Truth? Knowledge, Ignorance and the Canadian Truth and Reconciliation Commission." *International Journal of Transitional Justice* 6 (2): 182–204.

Li, Peter. 2008. "Reconciling with History: The Chinese-Canadian Head Tax Redress." *Journal of Chinese Overseas* 4 (1): 127–40.

Marrus, Michael R. 2007. "Official Apologies and the Quest for Historical Justice." *Journal of Human Rights* 6 (1): 75–105.

Mihai, Mihaela. 2013. "When the State Says 'Sorry': State Apologies as Exemplary Political Judgments." *Journal of Political Philosophy* 21 (2): 200–220.

Nobles, Melissa. 2008. *The Politics of Official Apologies*. Cambridge: Cambridge University Press.

Ohtsubo, Yohsuke, Esuka Watanabe, Jiyoon Kim, John T. Kulas, Hamdi Muluk, Gabriela Nazar, Feixu Wang, and Jingyu Zhang. 2012. "Are Costly Apologies Universally Perceived as Being Sincere? A Test of the Costly Apology-Perceived Sincerity Relationship in Seven Countries." *Journal of Evolutionary Psychology* 10 (4): 187–204.

Staudenmaier, Rebecca. 2019. "One in Four Germans Hold Anti-Semitic Beliefs, Study Finds." *DW*, October 24, 2019. https://www.dw.com/en/one-in-four-germans-hold-anti-semitic-beliefs-study-finds/a-50958589.

Tavuchis, Nicholas. 1991. *Mea Culpa: A Sociology of Apology and Reconciliation.* Stanford, CA: Stanford University Press.

TRC (Truth and Reconciliation Commission). 1997. "Transcript of the National Party Political Recall in Cape Town." Department of Justice and Constitutional Development, May 14, 1997. https://www.justice.gov.za/trc/special/party2/np2.htm.

Vora, Jay A., and Erika Vora. 2004. "The Effectiveness of South Africa's Truth and Reconciliation Commission: Perceptions of Xhosa, Afrikaner, and English South Africans." *Journal of Black Studies* 34 (3): 301–22.

Weinthal, Benjamin. 2014. "Germany's Jewish Problem." *Foreign Policy*, September 25, 2014. https://foreignpolicy.com/2014/09/25/germanys-jewish-problem/.

Winter, Stephen. 2008. "The Stakes of Inclusion: Chinese Canadian Head Tax Redress." *Canadian Journal of Political Science* 41 (1): 119–41.

Wohl, Michael J. A., Matthew J. Hornsey, and Catherine R. Philpot. 2011. "A Critical Review of Official Public Apologies: Aims, Pitfalls, and a Staircase Model of Effectiveness: Intergroup Apologies." *Social Issues and Policy Review* 5 (1): 70–100.

Wohl, Michael J. A., Kimberly Matheson, Nyla R. Branscombe, and Hymie Anisman. 2013. "Victim and Perpetrator Groups' Responses to the Canadian Government's Apology for the Head Tax on Chinese Immigrants and the Moderating Influence of Collective Guilt: Apology and Collective Guilt." *Political Psychology* 34 (5): 713–29.

12 Home, Hope, and a Human Approach to Displacement

Jim Gurnett

I was burned out from exhaustion, buried in the hail
Poisoned in the bushes an' blown out on the trail
Hunted like a crocodile, ravaged in the corn
"Come in," she said, "I'll give ya shelter from the storm."

—Bob Dylan 1974

It is not popular to say, but a full, honest look at Canada's record in relation to refugees can be disheartening. The defining words include superficial, simplistic, cosmetic, and self-congratulatory. We need to be more critical as we look at Canada's real role in the global refugee catastrophe. We need to examine both our complicity in why there are so many people who lose the homes they want to have and our self-centeredness in how we act when we do allow a tiny number of those people to come to Canada. Canada's approach to refugees needs to be anchored in human rights and not in public relations and political expediency, but the record shows a different picture. There is no shortage of literature about Canada as a shining beacon in responses to refugee misery, but a wider and deeper perspective is more disappointing. Without such an examination, Canada will miss the potential to be a true global leader, making a long-term difference for a more just and dignified world.

I sometimes lead workshops on political advocacy. As part of this training, I occasionally tell the following story as a reminder of the importance of perspective:

Once upon a time, there was a village located along the banks of a deep flowing river. Life was good there. The rain came when it was needed; the sun shone enough to offer many pleasant days. People had what they needed, lived in comfortable homes, and travelled along smooth streets to pleasant parks or shops where they received a friendly greeting as they stepped inside.

One day, children playing along the banks of the river noticed something in the water flowing past and realized it was a body, a human body. Their cries of alarm brought adults to join them. One brave young person quickly pulled off their boots, dove into the cold water, and struck out with strong strokes to swim toward the body. The swimmer grasped it and, with great effort, drew it back toward the bank, where several others waded out to help pull the body onto the grass. By now, an ambulance had arrived, and skilled EMTs took over. As the man who had been pulled from the water was loaded into the ambulance, he was breathing without assistance.

But he was badly injured and damaged from his time in the water. It was clear he would require a long convalescence in the hospital. Slowly, he began to heal.

As he lay in his bed, attended by able and caring helpers, a few days later, another citizen walking along a riverside path saw another body floating in midstream, and the same selfless courage by villagers saw this person too recovered, revived, and begin to heal.

It was not long before yet another body was seen in the current and rescued. And then another. And another.

Not wanting to see any life lost, the villagers purchased a boat and special equipment. They constructed a launch on the riverbank and set up towers with searchlights so they could keep watch during the hours of darkness. They organized a schedule so there were always some people assigned to keep watch and operate the rescue boat when needed. Everyone was proud to volunteer for their shifts at this important work.

Soon it became a challenge for the hospital to have space for the many survivors now resident there. A special tax was used to build a new facility especially for the recovering rescued people. Additional funds were used to hire specialists to offer a range of care services the survivors needed.

News media came from many other places to document the heartwarming and inspirational story of the commitment of the villagers to the well-being of the rescued people.

Some of the rescued people offered their deep gratitude in effusive words. Some healed enough that they could begin to participate in the life of the village.

But as more bodies kept appearing in the river, the challenge of it all became significant. Some citizens were getting tired of all the tasks related to the rescues and care. Rumours began to circulate about troublesome behaviour by some of them as they began to move about away from their special facility.

Finally, the mayor and council called a special public meeting to discuss the situation. Every seat in the auditorium was filled as the meeting was called to order. Speakers were passionate: some saying things had gone too far and it was time to let other villages downstream start doing more, others urging their neighbours to be even more caring and generous.

After some time, the mayor recognized a young student who had been carefully listening to the speeches. She stood and said, "What I wonder is why all these bodies keep coming down the river."

There was silence in the room as people looked at one another in surprise.

The meeting changed focus in an instant, and soon a group was selected to travel upstream and look for an answer. Equipped with snacks and coffee, they set off.

At first, the road was good, straight, well-paved, and well-signed. But as they travelled farther, the road deteriorated, and after some time, they found themselves on a winding, bumpy track along the very edge of the now steep riverbank. And then disaster nearly struck, as they carefully navigated a sharp curve in the trail, now so near the bank that the outside tires dislodged pebbles that tumbled over the edge to the water far below. They stopped in time, but metres ahead, they could see where vehicle upon vehicle had lost its grip and fallen to the water.

After they had carefully backed away from this hazard and managed to turn their vehicle around, they began to explore the countryside. They came in time to a village and asked about what they had encountered.

"A wealthy man from a far city came here and has bought up most of the best land, and the excellent road we used to use to get our products to market runs through the land he now owns. He will not let anyone else use it, so he has a monopoly to move his own crops easily to the large city markets. Everyone else needs to take the track along the river and go by a long roundabout route. Many who have set off with their wares have never been heard of again," they were told.

I feel privileged to have been able to meet, work with, and learn from people from many parts of the world who have had their homes of origin taken from them and are now in Canada. Some of my involvement has been in my work with immigrant-serving organizations, and some as a community member. I have met special people—friends—who have diverse lived experiences as refugees, and my life is better for their friendship.

Canada has received tremendous value from the hundreds of thousands of people who have come here over the decades, the people we call "refugees."

I have an early memory of a boy in my elementary school class in the 1950s. Older children called him a DP (displaced person), and I needed my parents to explain that meant his parents had come to Canada at the end of the Second World War, a decade before, from Europe because of the damage to his homeland and that I was not to be one of those using those initials to taunt him.

The focus we most often encounter in relation to refugees is on the wonderful charity of Canada, generously giving these struggling people a home. Refugees are the object of the comment, but the subject is *us*, the good folks who offer the asylum, giving ourselves a self-congratulatory pat on the back for using a little of our excess to give them a chance.

There is a need to step back, shake our heads, and look at the issue of refugees with different eyes—eyes that have a human rights lens in place.

The Universal Declaration of Human Rights is clear that a home and citizenship are rights, as is access to asylum. There is no great merit in providing asylum—it is our human duty. Not to ensure our brothers and sisters have a home and citizenship is as much a violation of human rights as slavery. Failure to respond to those who have lost a home or citizenship is criminal, so responding is not something about which we should feel much pride. We are doing our duty as human beings and global citizens.

But, more importantly, it is the complicity of Canadians in the creation of refugees that has most troubled me over the years. This issue is seldom mentioned, but it is key to understanding the horror of the global refugee crisis.

How do any of us sleep undisturbed in our comfortable beds in a world with eighty million people who have been forced from their homes, a third of them officially qualifying as refugees? That scale of suffering should mean none of us can, at a minimum, avoid asking "Why?"

If we honestly and objectively sought an answer to that question, there would be public pressure for changes that would significantly reduce the number of people who lose their homes, and then the need to respond to those without homes would be dramatically decreased.

What displaces people from their homes? Aside from natural disasters like earthquakes or volcanoes, all the major reasons can be traced to human actions—war, poverty, climate change, or persecution due to one's politics, religion, or gender. None of this seems to line up with the Universal Declaration's assertion of "the dignity and worth of the human person and in the equal rights of men and women" (UN General Assembly 1948).

Asking questions to peel back the layers around any war or major violation of the well-being of people leads to the ugly picture of someone else benefiting from what is going on. Sometimes, the path to that answer is long and convoluted, but eventually, the misery of some people is connected with the profits of some others. At the extreme end of this trail is the loss of home.

But, as in the story of the village along the river, most of us never think to ask "But why are the bodies floating down the river?"

We should have been persistent in asking this question long ago and considering the implications of the answers, but it is more urgent now than ever, as the crisis of human-related climate change creates more and more damage and may lead to more people losing their homes than all other causes. A new report from the United Nations Office for Disaster Risk Reduction says the danger is extreme, with the potential to turn much of the planet into an "uninhabitable hell for millions of people" (Yaghmaei 2020, 3), a guarantee of massive increases in the number of those who become refugees.

But facing the reality of how some people become refugees because of the pursuit of an affluent life by others invites a paraphrase of the quote attributed to Brazilian theologian and archbishop Dom Hélder Câmara about poverty. We might say, "When we talk about helping out with refugees coming to Canada, they call us saints. When we ask why there are refugees, they call us communists."

There is no neutral ground in relation to refugees. We are surrounded by comforts and conveniences that connect to the abuse of the human rights of others and treatment that creates refugees. Whether it is a chocolate bar, a smart phone, affordable fashions, cheap gasoline, or good-paying jobs manufacturing equipment or providing services for governments waging war on some of their own people, the dots connect.

Millions of people have become refugees because of wars that can be traced back to the agendas of distant superpowers. Events of the past seventy-five years around the world as nations of the North have pursued their competition make the Great Game of the United Kingdom and Russia in the early nineteenth century seem quaint and modest. It is a moral failing to avoid recognizing this, living with heads buried in the sand about what is happening.

A good starting point for a healthier perspective on refugees (among other issues) would be to admit that we benefit from a global economy built on the abuse of power that depends on the oppression and displacement of other people in the pursuit of profit.

Every time I enjoy the pleasure of meeting someone who is creating a new home in Canada with courage and persistence, often in the face of discrimination and struggle, and listen to their story, I think in the back of my mind, "But why are you having to do this? By what right was the home you knew and loved torn from you?" And research, without fail, leads to a narrative that involves my own guilty exploiting of part of the world.

The choice to not do this honest research is a more dramatic example of the same approach we see regarding the persistence of food banks in our communities. Elected leaders are smiling in news stories as they drop off their bags of peanut butter and macaroni dinners during food drives and urge others to do the same. And we do, happily filling buses and bins with a little extra we have picked up at the supermarket while buying our own food, a good percentage of which we will waste. But year after decade, we fail to demand and leaders fail to enact public policy that will ensure food security— good and appropriate nutrition—for everyone.

So perhaps I should not be surprised that these same citizens and governments in the wealthy North prefer to promote sweet stories of people brought here to new welcoming communities where they are met at the airport with parkas and stuffed toys and to issue press releases bragging of bringing a few thousand, without any mention of the millions still in life-and-death peril and misery, rather than face the significance of why people become refugees and what can be done to stop this.

Setting aside our lack of attention to our complicity in the creation of refugees, Canadian leaders also lie without shame about Canada's proud record in bringing refugees to start new lives here, loving to say we are number one in welcoming refugees per capita. Facts from the United Nations High Commissioner for Refugees (UNHCR) refute that, putting us more around number forty-one (UNHCR 2015). Most refugees are living in countries near where they had their homes, so nations like Lebanon, Jordan, and Chad are, not surprisingly, far ahead of Canada in hosting refugees. But even at a distance, several European countries have higher per capita numbers than Canada.[1]

Most years, refugees barely account for 10 percent of the immigrants who become residents in Canada. We reserve the great majority of our immigration capacity for economic-class immigrants who will make a more immediate contribution to our own economic success.

I had a friend who had been homeless in Canada quite a bit over the years. He was a songwriter, and in one song, he had a line that said all that lies between "home" and "hope" are the letters "N" and "O." M-N-O-P: no home, no hope.

Home is a little four-letter word, but it carries a wealth of meaning. It comes to English with an etymology that means "a place to lie down." The context is ancient, long before hotels. If a traveller found themself at day's end in a community away from home, there was an expectation that hospitality would be offered in some home. But there was also a danger that the hospitality might come from someone who had a connection that would require them to avenge some past deed of the visitor or their family to a member of their family. While the hospitality was good, there was a darker possibility too. And so the traveller would be wise to remain a bit alert as they rested, just in case. Maybe they would just lean against the wall, still holding their walking stick, dozing but ready to wake and react if trouble arose. Only when back in their own place could they let down their guard, lie down, and fully relax.

Greek mythology also captures some of the deep power of home in the role of Hestia, the eldest sister of Zeus. She was the deity associated with the hearth, the home fire, and was of such significance that she received the first offering. Her name derives from the image of a place to stay or dwell. The Greeks were not alone in placing great importance on keeping the sacred hearth fire burning. This priority in the physical world points to the importance at a more profound level of having a place on one's own, where the

---

1 For example, Norway (#19), Switzerland (#22), and Austria (#29). Canada is #41 (UNHCR 2015).

fire is kept burning as the center of the circle of all aspects of human life and meaning.

To be responsible for letting the hearth fire go out carelessly was a serious crime. And only in the most extreme time of danger would there be a deliberate decision by the family or community to extinguish it.

This offers some sense of the deep damage that goes with losing a home. The loss of goods, land, wealth, memories, and relationships, often of health and family too, is not only evident from the outside in the painful journeying without resources, hungry and hurting. It is also deep in the soul and spirit of the refugee. Gone is that place where they can lie down, that place each of us depends on to give context and security to our lives. The mental and spiritual pain that may go with that can be as severe as any of the physical evidence, even if less easily seen. Scars that do not show are scars nonetheless.

During the years I was directly involved with a community organization providing settlement services to refugees, it was a source of anger to me how indifferent Canada was to the mental health realities of many of them. Government-sponsored refugees receive financial support for a bare-bones existence, generally based on the welfare rates of the province where they settle, for a year. Privately sponsored refugees may do better but still often live in poverty. Their finances might be adequate for a basement suite, (day-old) bread on the table, and thrift-shop clothing to maintain physical health. But there is no interest in responding to the deep injuries to their psychological well-being from the loss of their home hearth and the sufferings and abuse they experienced as they fled seeking safety.

This indifference to the mental health challenges has always been an issue but has become more significant in recent years, as many refugees coming to Canada have lived for longer years in conditions of terror and violence we can barely manage to hear described, let alone to have lived. Their sustained and horrifying experiences are triggers to a severity of complex mental health challenges, including post-traumatic stress syndrome. When these circumstances in their lives have been over an extended time and of a more awful manner, the consequences may be more profound than for people who have been able to spend a smaller time displaced before resettlement or who have had the resources to secure better interim shelter conditions.

But there are few sources of specialized mental health services for such people in Canada. Most of the funding for the mental health specialists at my organization a decade ago came from the UNCHR, since no order of government in Canada would consider it. Each year when I would submit our funding application, I would get a letter back from Geneva pointing out that the funding we were seeking was more than the government of Canada was contributing to its fund for refugee mental health and suggesting it was difficult to justify sending funding to Canada when there were huge needs for mental health services for refugees resident in countries that were far poorer than Canada. Fortunately, they did continue to provide some funding, but I shared their concern that the services we were offering in Edmonton reduced the resources available for services in other parts of the world, given the financial capacity of Canada to fund good services for refugees settled in our country.

Without good mental health services provided in a timely way, human and economic costs increase dramatically. Given the brief period refugees are provided with financial support before they are expected to be self-supporting, it is a prescription for trouble to be without the healing benefit of mental health services. For those struggling with significant mental health challenges, the possibility of focusing on successfully learning a new language or gaining skills for the Canadian labour market declines. Threats to family relationships may be increased, and physical health can suffer from not sleeping or eating well. People may deal with their challenges in their own ways, perhaps through self-medicating with alcohol or drugs, to be able to manage. At the extreme, people may be suicidal or aggressive toward others.

Of course, these mental health issues are not a characteristic of all refugees. Adverse circumstances are handled by people in a wide range of ways; many people are glad to finally have safety and freedom, and their settlement takes place smoothly. But Canada's lack of acceptance that the experiences of becoming and being a refugee may lead to significant mental health challenges has meant that some have had a tough time. I think of one woman I watched for more than a year who walked day after day, head down, around and around a block by her downtown home, disconnected from everyone. Once we linked her with a health professional who understood the chronic PTSD of many refugees, she began to heal. But many others never had the opportunity she had to get such services.

One reason we were able to connect this woman with services was that we developed and operated a model of supported housing that was designed by taking time to ask refugees what sort of housing they would like to have, that would be useful to them as they sought to integrate into Canadian society. We did not decide what they needed. We listened to them.

What we heard was their desire for a place that was much like the natural life of many small communities in cultures around the world. They wanted some space that was secure and personal. They wanted the chance to connect with one another in a wide range of ways, offering care to struggling neighbours when that was needed, receiving care from neighbours when that was needed. They wanted a commons where they could come together to celebrate life events. They wanted to share in discussing issues affecting them and to participate in making decisions about them. They wanted children and elders to come together and learn from and encourage one another. They wanted to have access to professional services when they needed them, in a non-judgmental way.

When we were able to renovate a building and provide thirty-five apartments where people could live together in this context, much healing and progress happened in remarkable ways, with the refugee tenants themselves firmly in the driving seat. And the satisfaction that came from feeling in control, not abandoned or paternalized, further nourished that progress.

But this was not seen as fitting in the official definition of settlement and integration services, so finding the funding to sustain such housing was unsuccessful.

Now, a decade later, as I walk the streets and back alleys of Edmonton's urban core, I encounter a new phenomenon—people who came as refugees and are now living rough, unhoused and unwell, struggling with addictions and in some cases dying alone in dark doorways or behind dumpsters.

The failure to address the mental health issues of refugees is just one aspect of what I describe as our public relations approach to refugees. We want good news stories that assure us we are doing wonderful things for these unfortunates. Politicians and the media are looking for those who open their own business a year after arrival or graduate first in their class from college. In Alberta, we celebrated in 2020 when Salma Lakhani, who came in 1977 as a stateless person after her family had its assets seized by Idi Amin in her homeland of Uganda, became the nineteenth lieutenant governor of the province. We have cabinet ministers, business leaders, and school principals in Canada who came as refugees. I am delighted this is the case. We are fortunate, and each of these people is a treasure and deserves sincere appreciation for all they are doing to make our country a great place to live. I am glad they were able to come here. And I am in awe of their ability to build new lives here with courage and persistence despite all the challenges they had to go through before and after getting here.

I know many people who have come to Canada as refugees are very happy to have been able to do this and are grateful to our government policies and investments in supporting refugees. And I am glad for them—and for all of us who become their new neighbours. But that does not mean we can be content.

The troubling issue for me is that when the narrative we have is made up of the stories of the refugees who have done well in Canada and who are thankful to be here, we are ignorant of the rest of the story, of all those who couldn't come or who came but struggled. We fail to share their moments of deepest hurt, when they wish they had not come. We have a mythomania to present Canada and refugees in a feel-good way.

This permits the continuance of policies that are absurd. But few Canadians know about them.

The transportation loan program is one of these policies. These loans for overseas medical expenses and travel can add up to thousands of dollars, especially for a family with several children coming from a more distant part of the world. A moment's consideration of this policy suggests it makes no sense. Here are people with great challenges to begin a new life—including learning a new language and all the complexities of a new culture, addressing all the recovery issues related to physical and mental trauma before arrival, and establishing a source of income to live on—and a day after their first year in Canada ends, they are also expected to begin to repay a loan, with interest, for their travel to come here.

Another is the requirements some need to meet for genetic testing to demonstrate family relationships. I have assisted people needing thousands of dollars for such tests when several children are involved, regardless of how much testimony there might be about the relationships. For refugees who have lost nearly everything meaningful or important in their lives, there is a special cruelty in making family reunifications more difficult. Family is often all a person has that matters.

The treatment of people who make their own refugee claims in Canada through the in-Canada asylum program is another area of policy shame. It often takes immense persistence and bravery to get to Canada as a refugee without having private or government sponsorship. The journey is long, convoluted, and fraught with dangers. Then, having arrived, once a claim for asylum is made, such people are pulled into complex procedural and legal mazes, with limited time or resources to support their claims before a hearing. Not surprisingly, less than half are believed and see their claims accepted. If they come from a country Canada has, in its own ways, decided is "safe," they face even more barriers, and the government also has the power to designate anyone, for its own reasons, as needing mandatory detention.

The Safe Third Country Agreement (STCA) between Canada and the United States is another deliberate obstacle created by the government—which likes to be honored for its concern for refugees—to impair the possibility of a person seeking asylum being successful. It prohibits a person from coming to Canada if they have already been in the United States and made an asylum claim, based on the premise that the person was already safe in the United States and so had no reason to come to Canada. After more than fifteen years in place, in July 2020, Canada's Federal Court ruled the STCA is invalid because it infringes rights guaranteed by the Canadian Charter of Rights and Freedoms. The 2020 Federal Court decision was overturned at the Federal Court of Appeal, and then, in June 2023, the Supreme Court ruled the agreement did not violate section 7 of the Charter but sent it back to review whether it might violate section 15. While these legal challenges move forward, the STCA was updated early in 2023 by the government to make it tougher, especially for asylum seekers and border crossings at irregular locations.

The STCA is part of the formal mechanisms to discourage people from trying to find safety in Canada. The more informal campaign by many politicians and news media to demonize people who seek to enter Canada in irregular ways to make a claim for asylum is another evidence of the darker side of our feelings about refugees. The persistent use of the word *illegal* to describe such efforts is the most evident aspect of this, since it creates an immediate sense such an action is criminal.

The fact is that Canada signed the UN Convention on Refugees (Canadian Council for Refugees 2009). A refugee claimant cannot be punished for the way they enter a country, and the law does not make it illegal to enter using informal border crossings. Yet loud voices demand that such people should be deported immediately without process or that their opportunity to make a claim should be narrower than it is for others.

The purpose of demonizing people who come to Canada to make a claim is to create a fiction of good and bad refugees. The good ones wait patiently in line until Canada brings them, either government-assisted or through a private sponsor. The bad ones come on their own and probably have no real claim. If Canadians can be kept preoccupied and upset by this fiction of fake refugee ne'er-do-wells, they are less likely to ask the more significant question of why we bring so very few refugees at all.

There are more people crossing borders to make refugee claims on a single day in nations near places of conflict and trouble than do so in Canada in a year.

For refugees who look less European, the deep systemic racism finally being discussed more openly in Canada creates another set of challenges and barriers for them.

We like to talk about being a multicultural nation, but we have a long way to go to understand what it means to be an intercultural nation, where we respect, integrate, and benefit from cultural perspectives and practices that are very different from the dominant one. Many of the refugees who do very well have had the benefit of involvement with Euro–North American culture before they came, perhaps from studying in the North or from involvement with people and enterprises from there. They come with some competencies to fit in.

But others, especially from rural areas, may have hardly heard of the world to which they come, let alone have any familiarity with how people think and behave here. Door locks, clocks, thermostats, water taps, ovens, and windows are a few of the things that are entirely foreign to them.

Because I lived there for a few years, I have had a special interest in those who have come over the past four decades from Afghanistan. Many who came in the early 1980s were highly educated, perhaps well-travelled, largely urban people, often from families that were affluent or influential there. In no way do I downplay the hurt and loss they suffered as they escaped for their lives and began to build new ones here, aware they may never see family or home again. But they had some capacity to undertake that huge new challenge. Those who came twenty years later had more often been subsistence farmers or from small villages in central provinces; had never visited Kabul, let alone stepped on an airplane and flown halfway around the world; were members of ethnic groups that experienced discrimination even in Afghanistan; had never been to school; and were without any labour market skills remotely like what would be needed in Canada for decent employment. And they had lived through a generation of war and terror, already deeply traumatized by it.

Our public policy has given little attention to understanding the range of people who are refugees and developing programs or services that are sensitive to that diversity. When it has been politically expedient to act with some generosity in welcoming refugees, we have done it with a dramatic flair. Instead of a generous and consistent commitment to make Canada home to people displaced from their homes in many locations around the world over the decades, we have a series of dramatic vignettes—Hungarians in 1956, Czechs a decade or so later, the Ismaili Muslims from Uganda soon after, the "boat people" as the 1980s arrived, Bosnians and Kosovars in the 1990s, and the most recent welcoming of twenty-five thousand Syrians. These all provide material for stories that generate more positive emotions about our actions than real concern for the full ugly story of refugees' lives.

Perhaps that approach should not surprise us too much. For a century, we participated in the United Kingdom's "home children" program, bringing more than one hundred thousand children who frequently were mistreated or taken advantage of. Yet several years ago, Jason Kenney, recently premier of Alberta but at the time minister of immigration, said that there was nothing to apologize for. And we have persisted in making huge use of temporary work visas to provide Canadian businesses with cheap labour without having to actually increase immigration to the level we should, giving people a real chance to settle and become members of communities in Canada. Why would we want a generous and consistent plan to make a substantial ongoing contribution to the safety and future of refugees?

To approach our own actions and attitudes—or our public policies—with the justice and compassion that express a commitment to human rights requires us to see that we are neither more nor less than siblings in the human family. A line in one of the documents from the Second Vatican Council says, "The joys and the hopes, the griefs and the anxieties, of the people of this age, especially those who are poor or in any way afflicted, those too are the joys and the hopes, the griefs and the anxieties, of [each of us]. Indeed nothing genuinely human fails to raise an echo in their hearts" (Catholic Sensibility 2006).

My disappointment as a Canadian looking at the story of our nation's actions in relation to refugees is that we have not met this standard. For many of us, ignorance of the facts may be the reason. For others, it is greed or political expediency. We could do so much better. Our failure makes the world a poorer place.

I look for the day when Canadians will join to say with open arms to those who have had their homes of origin taken away, "You don't have to earn a place here. You don't have to bargain or beg for it. You are worthy." A home nourishes the hope that gives energy for facing the next day and its challenges. A determination that human rights will be more than a warm sentiment, but will be a guiding reality for daily life, for individuals and governments, is the tool that can make that true for many now denied it.

It's past time for Canadians to look upriver and ask "Why?"

References

Canadian Council for Refugees. 2009. "40th Anniversary of Canada Signing the Refugee Convention." February 5, 2022. https://ccrweb.ca/sites/ccrweb.ca/files/static-files/40thanniversary.htm.
Catholic Sensibility. 2006. "Gaudium et Spes 1." January 2, 2006. https://catholicsensibility.wordpress.com/2006/01/02/113621867384238196/.
Dylan, Bob. 1974. "Shelter from the Storm." Official Bob Dylan Site, February 20, 2023. https://www.bobdylan.com/songs/shelter-storm/.
UN General Assembly. 1948. *The Universal Declaration of Human Rights*. New York: United Nations. https://www.un.org/en/about-us/universal-declaration-of-human-rights.
UNHCR (United Nations High Commissioner for Refugees). 2015. "Figures at a Glance: Refugees." UNHCR, February 5, 2022. http://www.unhcr.org/figures-at-a-glance.html.
Yaghmaei, Nima. 2020. *Human Cost of Disasters: An Overview of the Last 20 Years, 2000–2019*. Geneva: United Nations Office for Disaster Risk Reduction. https://doi.org/10.18356/79b92774-en.

Part IV
Enacting (Re)humanization
Refugee Agency and the Arts

Part IV

13 A Life of Many Homes
Reflections of a Writer in Exile

Jalal Barzanji

I was born in Ashkaftsaqa, an ancient village outside of Erbil, Kurdistan. When I would ask my mother what day I was born, she would answer, "You were born when the grass was turning green, and the flowers were beginning to bloom." No day, no month, just a snapshot of a season. My birthday now is technically July 1, a date assigned by the Iraqi Ba'athist regime to many Kurdish people born in Iraq. My wife, whose mother said she was born when the air was crisp and there was snow on the ground, shares this generic July 1 birthday with me.

Ours was a village without electricity, consisting of about fifty houses made of mud and rocks. About eight hundred years old, it had been ruled by seven clan chiefs, and although the houses were crude, the scenery was beautiful. Very few people were literate, and none were formally educated. Life was simple, and it was there that I learned just how beautiful a simple life could be.

I was seven years old when an old truck entered the village, and two men climbed out. One of them introduced himself as a teacher from the city. "A school will be opening in Ashkaftsaqa," he said to the growing crowd. As a village with little contact with the larger cities that surrounded us, this came as a bit of a surprise. Just two days later, registration started. My father dragged me and my older brother along to put our names down on the class list. My father was a good man and a hard worker. He owned several plots of farmland, some of which he lent to other villagers to use for their crops. Despite a life of hard work, rarely had I ever seen him this determined. "Come, Jalal," he said. "You and your brother *must* go to school so that you won't become blind like us."

I remember on the first day, there were more students than there were chairs. A standing crowd gathered in the back, and Mamosta Mosher (*Mamosta* is the Kurdish word for teacher) told those who were standing to bring containers the next day to sit on. I considered myself one of the lucky kids, as I had secured myself a seat in the middle of the class.

Every morning when dropping their children off at school, parents would stand and linger a while, inquisitively looking at Mamosta Mosher's clothing. Unlike anyone else in the village, he wore Western garb: a white buttoned-up shirt and black dress pants—a rare sight in Ashkaftsaqa. In addition to his clothing, his Elvis Presley hairstyle shone from the hair product as he stood in front of the class, singing the Kurdish anthem none of us had heard before but were made to memorize. He was so well respected he was forced to announce one morning, "Please, thank your parents for the gifts of eggs and yogurt, but tell them not to send them to me anymore! They are piling up under my bed! I don't want any of it to go to waste."

At first, I was not particularly fond of going to school. My mother used to criticize me because I was a serial wanderer. She would grow frustrated because, according to her, every time she would take her eyes off me, I would disappear. After hours of searching, she would find me in a closet or in an empty field staring out into the distance. Although the habit is admittedly a bit peculiar, I catch myself aimlessly staring to this day, letting my mind wander.

Being a wanderer did not fit the strict school rules. The trouble with school was that I was forced to sit in one place for forty minutes at a time. I could not go out and explore, and I was not allowed to let my mind wander. This changed when we shifted from learning the alphabet to using it to learn and read stories. I realized that stories were just little adventures I could go on, letting my mind wander into these new worlds of words. As a bonus, stories became places I could escape to. My home as a child was extremely loud and crowded. Most Kurdish homes had many siblings, married or single, under one roof, sometimes with other relatives. The school became my refuge, a place where even as a young child I was able to escape. I began to think of my school as a second sort of home, one that housed imagination and new adventures every day through the stories and words we learned.

Unfortunately, just as I was beginning this love affair with learning, our lives were shifted. The destruction of what was to me a sacred place would become a common theme in my life, one where the very pieces of my identity that I would try to hold on to would be taken away from me time and time again.

In this case, the Iraqi regime sent two warplanes at dawn, when only the village's shepherds were awake. Two of those shepherds were the first victims of the ensuing firebombing of our simple village. The rest of us woke up, and as quickly as we could, we took cover and ran for the hills. For the first time, I saw genuine fear in the eyes of all the adults who had raised me. They had heard about this regime's tactics when destroying a village like ours. The warplanes would come first. Then missiles would follow, destroying everything that was left. The lack of homes would make it easy to capture any Kurdish fighters they thought may be in the village or those who stayed or were too injured to flee. Every family I knew went in different directions, and none of us ever returned. That school, like my birthday, was taken away from me by a regime I had never provoked. That was the end of my first and second home.

My family was forced to escape to Erbil, one of Kurdistan's biggest cities. When we arrived early one morning, the city was slowly waking up. There were so many cars on the road, and the style of the houses was new to me. I soon saw that each home had its own lights—I had never seen this before.

Slowly, our life began again. This would be another journey: from a familiar life in a village where I knew all my neighbours to a city I knew nothing about.

Although our house was made of mud and rocks in our village, we had a spacious roof where we would often spend our nights. In Erbil, we were confined to a one-bedroom home. My ever-growing frustration with confinement grew, and I once again attempted to take refuge at school. I experienced an ever-growing interest in literature. By the time I was in high school, the home I inhabited grew even more crowded with more siblings, and our small high school was bloated with students. This, combined with an overly eager little brother, made finding a place to be alone more difficult. I knew I would need to go to the library if I ever wanted to get any studying done.

Luckily for me, the Erbil Public Library was a magnificent and peaceful building, and in its quiet shelves, I could escape the crowdedness of reality. The library was built in 1940, before the Ba'ath party came to power. You would enter the grey building through a revolving glass door, the first of its kind in Kurdistan. People would come from all over simply for the amusement of walking through that revolving door. Inside, you were greeted by the quiet of the reading hall that featured the tallest walls I had ever seen. Every wall was covered with shelves of books. At the front of the reading hall, people would sit for hours at beautiful wooden desks, studying or reading or writing. When I did not feel like reading, I would wander through the rows and rows of bookshelves past the reading hall. This library was my most beloved place. There, the reading of literature slowly turned into a love of writing poetry.

Writer in Censorship

Most Kurdish writers began by writing poetry. Usually, it is love poetry in hopes of winning the heart of someone. For me, that came to an end when my initial ambition of attracting girls did not work out. I did not stop writing, and even though I never attended any creative writing classes, I continued to explore my voice. I wrote about other kinds of love—the love of nature, the love of freedom. I wrote about the complexities of human nature.

I remember my mother used to worry about me because I would spend all day surrounded by books. She used to ask me why I wrote and read while other kids my age focused on playing outside with their friends. She did not understand that when I was writing, I felt most free; it was my escape. I was not in a dimly lit room or the corners of a library; I was exploring the world. I was free in the truest sense of the word. That is what writing is for me—untainted, uncensored freedom. Through poetry, I explored the range of human emotions, the nature of the world around me, and my own struggle, as a Kurd, for freedom of expression.

In Iraq, there was no place for writing in the mainstream beyond social realism. Social realism, however, was used not to express things as we saw them but to express things as we were expected to see them—to express what the government wanted us to express: the glorification of Iraqi nationalism under the Ba'athist regime and, more specifically, under Saddam's rule. Iraqis would privately say to one another that there were more photos of Saddam than there were people in Iraq.

During this time, Iraq harboured intense hostility toward the press and media. Any semblance of unbiased reporting was targeted. Articles, newspapers, and journals were co-opted to further Saddam's cause. I remember one such article, front and center in the country's largest paper headed by the journalists' union, that argued voting should be replaced by two choices: "We love Saddam a lot" or "We love Saddam immensely."

As I grew as a writer, I realized that regardless of my talent or the care I put into my writing, it was difficult to publish if it did not push the state's propaganda. Saddam Hussein's Ba'athist party was the only lawful political party in Iraq, and during this era, political criticism of or dissent from the Iraqi government was illegal. In accordance with Saddam's Constitution of 1990, the Ba'athist party would appoint a Revolutionary Command Council. Among other powers, this council had the right to prohibit anything that it felt could harm "national unity," the "objectives of the People," or their "achievements." This vague description meant that censorship was completely subjective, and publishing from outside the regime's mandate could lead to time in prison.

Despite this, I persisted with writing my first collection of poetry, *Dancing in the Evening Snow*. Overcoming this censorship proved itself a more frustrating but slightly artistic endeavour and a process I would have to become familiar with.

I would begin first by writing directly from the heart, looking at the circumstances around me and wildly embracing the need to express myself. The first draft of my poetry felt like the time when my mother would occasionally, on her more overwhelmed days, allow the children to run free in the garden in front of our home. It was an unfiltered and chaotic joy that was perhaps, given the context, childlike in its wonder and naïveté. Like unshackling my weary wrists from the chains of censorship, writing was an almost bodily response to the constant pressure of oversight and restriction.

By the time I had enough work to fill many books and was content I had at least expressed myself to the universe, if no one else, I began stripping away "dangerous" poems. This first phase of editing, or "self-censorship," was extremely important because it was the layer that would prevent me from being arrested, executed, or tortured. Poems that too openly talked about the circumstances of oppressed people—that explored the wonder of liberty, freedom, and self-determination—would all need to be either edited beyond recognition or erased.

Below is an example of such a poem, titled simply "War," removed entirely from *Dancing in the Evening Snow*, to be re-added and published many years later in both English and Kurdish:

War

It was war
that made my first morning sad, it was war
that cast my book to the sea, it was war

that destroyed my evening playground, it was war
that deprived me of flowers, it was war
that drove me to despair, it was war
that made me useless.

War creeps into all aspects. War is my soul flying between being and not being.
War is the record of atrocities.
Between one war and another, barren flowers. Between one ceasefire and another
startled sleep.

Since my beginning
I have been locked inside
a fence with the gate shut behind me.
Since my beginning, I have been embraced by the convexity of the ceasefire.
Since my beginning, I have been like a vanquished army sitting idly behind walls.

I am tired
I am tired of war.
There has never been an evening,
that allowed me to throw down my gun, dust myself, take off my belt.
sleep softly,
without having to be awakened by another morning battle.

I am tired
I am tired of war.
War is without victories and defeats. I am tired.
Since my beginning, I have been wandering from war to war.

After the removal of the blatantly dangerous pieces, which was typically a large portion of the work I had written, I would move on to poetry that may have touched or grazed the embargo of free thought—poems that suggested or subtly referred to forbidden ideology. Many more of these could be edited, but some still had to be removed due to their lack of substance following harsh revision. "Corner," in its original form below, I decided not to publish after realizing it would be unrecognizable following the changes I would need to make:

Corner

There,
in a corner,
light and darkness
had been eager to meet.

For a while,
the sky seemed too narrow for flying;
what we experienced by day seemed unfamiliar by night.

Little by little,
our memories were deserting us.

As exiles,
we didn't even dare to think of home.

There,
where the stars are,
life was returning home, indifferent and morose.

There,
I left shame and sorrow behind. That was a long time ago;
my father's water can flipped;
he never got another chance to water the flowers.

That was the time
when we buried the promises we made to God, when we gave
   imagination a space of its own, when we returned to Sktan by
   moonlight,
when we buried our martyrs.

   Although I considered removing words such as "martyrs" or "exiles," I ultimately decided the poem would lose its meaning, and even behind symbolism, it was unlikely to be included for its tone.
   The last part of the process before submitting for publication involved changing poems that I thought could remain meaningful or enjoyable while posing little risk in halting publication or potentially causing harm to myself or loved ones. These poems were subtly still expressing that which I wanted to express, but under the guise of innocent and perhaps mundane poetry.

"Arrival" describes the first night I was approached by Ba'athist Secrete Police, some of whom were themselves Kurdish:

Arrival

After the moon disappears,
we'll come through the mountains,
I know the rocks will get out of our way.

In this grassy area
noise comes from every side;
the dogs bark non-stop;
they make me dizzy.

Wait, someone's at the door:
"Open the door; we're not strangers."

Only the birds ignore the noises;
they refuse to fly away.

I let them in;
they sit by the fire,
steam rising from their bodies;
under the lantern,
they all look greenish.

In "Arrival," one of the last poems I had written for my debut work, there are subtle and hidden allusions to topics I would have otherwise been reprimanded for writing about. The "noise" represents the violence we are subjected to and the "dogs," or soldiers and officers, that "bark non-stop." The "strangers" are the elements of the regime we must all allow into our lives and homes, into our most intimate moments, while the "birds" that refuse to fly away portray our hope in the face of suppression and adversity. This was the most we could express under the circumstances, a poem that did not entirely tell the story we wished it to but at least held some of the spirit of the writer.

This was a difficult life for a young writer trying to express different feelings and ideas. Despite this pressure, I tried to continue my journey as a writer through such symbolism. I tried to write and express myself through meaning that way. It was exceedingly difficult. Eventually, when I was able to finish *Dancing in the Evening Snow*, despite a process that featured various layers of self-censorship, tedious and meticulous review to shroud meaning with placeholders and symbolism, my book was still rejected three times before publication.

The first time it was rejected, I was not given a clear indication as to why. I simply received word from the censorship office through my publisher that my work would not be permitted to be published. At this point, I was not a well-known poet or author; I simply distributed my pieces by myself to friends and family and perhaps a few work colleagues. Very occasionally, I would present my work at small poetry readings around Erbil. There was no wide audience for me to influence, no awaiting critical acclaim.

Despite this, I persisted, and with no reason given for the rejection, I was forced to comb over my work again and identify what exactly it was that had drawn the ire of the censorship committee. And so the process continued. As an artist writing in a fascist regime, I was forced to continue to strip, continue to rework, until finally given permission to print a work that was so distant from that first heartfelt draft that it was barely recognizable.

A Writer in Prison

Unfortunately, despite my best efforts, in 1986, I returned to my old home in the Erbil Public Library in an unexpected way. The library had been transformed by the Ba'ath regime into a jail, and I was shoved through the revolving door as a prisoner of the regime's secret police.

My sanctuary in that building, where I had enjoyed beautiful books and expanded my world, was now a thirty-five-centimetre-wide space where I was only allowed to sleep on my side in a tight corridor, between a routine of beatings and a life in handcuffs. I was being used as a message to those who would try to think or write about democracy, about freedom of expression or another way of life.

I was being used to tell them that their thoughts and imaginations were under persecution. The physical transformation of the library into a jail—full of not tables and carrels but holding cells and torture chambers—showed the power of the growing Ba'ath regime over our lives. I was being imprisoned in a place that was once my salvation from everyday worries. I had committed no crime but attempting to continue to seek out freedom of expression. For the Iraqi regime, this was enough.

The library cell was built for fifteen people, but forty people were crowded inside it. It was an extremely painful isolation from my family, difficult even for me to reimagine almost forty years later. The daily routine consisted of torture and interrogation. The only time we were able to sleep on our backs was when our cellmates were tortured and interrogated outside of our cells. Very often, those who read my story ask me how I was able to remain peaceful and compassionate in the face of such brutality and humiliation.

There was one guard who was unlike the others: Sergeant Hassan, a Shi'a man from southern Iraq. Hassan's people were also treated terribly by the regime due to their supposed allegiance to the Iranian government. Hassan would show us kindness, routinely buying us small items and smuggling them into our cells. He would let us stay out a little longer when we were afforded opportunities to go outside, and he made sure we got medical attention when we needed it. When family members would come to the doors of the prison to bring us food, he was the only guard who would make sure the food reached us. It occurred to me that in some ways, this place was just as much a prison for Hassan as it was for us.

I had small pieces of paper and a small pencil smuggled in by Sergeant Hassan. On these pieces of paper, I did what I had done my entire life—I wrote and felt free. I expressed myself and continued to live even behind these bars through my poetry. I would pen "Tell Ewar" to my eldest daughter, who lived so much of her childhood with her father imprisoned:

Tell Ewar

Tell Ewar,
If I am released
I would come home running, The next day I'd take her out, I would buy her a doll.

Tell Ewar,
I need to have a small photograph of her, So that every now and then,
I can take it out and kiss her.

Tell Ewar,
Your father sends his apologies
For not being there with her.

> Tell Ewar,
> Your father sends his apologies For not being able to let her in: The keys are with the police.

After two years in this prison, without a trial or lawyer, I was pardoned on Saddam Hussein's birthday, along with hundreds of others, as a sign of his "humanity." The fear of this inhumane treatment never left me. My family, which included a loving wife, two daughters, and a son, and I needed to be free of the Iraqi dictatorship.

In 1996, about five years after my release from prison, a bloody civil war broke out in Kurdistan between two rival Kurdish political parties. Writers, poets, and artists were once again targeted. As before, armed men came to our door in the middle of the night. This time, I was able to sneak into our neighbour's household until we could understand why they were there. When it was confirmed that they had come to take me away, I knew it was time to leave my homeland. In a few short days, I had contacted a smuggler who had been recommended to me, and a few short days after that, I was to meet him to retrieve a fake passport that would allow me to leave the country. When near the border town of Zakho, there was another man who could get me a visa to enter Ankara, Turkey. This man would then give me the address of a third man, who would smuggle me from Turkey to Greece if I were able to make it to Istanbul on my own. From Greece, I would then seek out ways to bring my family to our new home.

I attempted to go to Istanbul by plane, but upon arrival, airport officials were waiting for me at the end of the gate. My heart sank. They apprehended me and told me they knew my passport was forged but were willing to give the passport back should I have any bribe for them. After giving them USD 300, I was able to take my forged documents but would be sent back to Ankara.

I had two options upon my return to Ankara. I could make another attempt to enter Istanbul through a private driver or bus, or I could apply at the UN office in Ankara for refugee status.

I remembered my geography teacher telling me about a distant place called Canada, about the forests that were as big as Kurdistan. I always wondered if someone lost in these forests could find their way out. I was compelled to experience this for myself, and even after being told I would be forced to wait longer as a refugee to get to Canada, I committed to it.

I spent eleven months in Turkey, with seven of them being finally accompanied by my family. We spent those months in a small three-hundred-square-foot rental apartment that we shared with another Kurdish family. There were two bedrooms, each shared by one family. We had no money other than that which we had brought with us and no ability to work. We simply had to sit and endure, and every day, we were expected to check into the refugee office while dodging police who were not particularly fond of Kurdish refugees. Finally, after this long wait, we were sponsored by the Canadian government and able to come to Edmonton in 1998. Our journey in Canada was also not short of adversity. My wife and I found part-time jobs soon after we settled and found some time for ESL classes. It was difficult, though, to start over with three children. Initially, I did not have much time to write, but I still found little opportunities during the day to slip away and work on a few poems.

Then, in the year 2000, two years after we had landed in Canada, a friend of mine from work at a pizza delivery shop suggested I should publish a poem of mine in their community's local newspaper. The poem I chose to publish was "War," the first self-censored omission from *Dancing in the Evening Snow*. It was the first time I had published something freely and the first time I had published anything in Canada.

A Writer in Exile

I have been on this journey as a writer my whole life. In the early days, this path was filled with hazards and stop signs warning me not to explore what I longed to explore. It was not until I came to Canada that these boundaries and borders were removed, and I was able to publish my books. Not only was I given the ability to write what I wanted without censorship; I was also honored for my ability to write.

In 2007, I was named PEN Canada's first Writer in Exile, providing me with one year of exploring ideas with other writers, a year to share in their journeys and to add to mine. I went from being a prisoner for my ideas to being hired to write about them.

I was given an office in the Edmonton Public Library. This library was noisier than the one I fell in love with in Erbil, but this time, I went to the library as a free writer. It also seemed to have more life. But I think this may have had more to do with my feelings than the library.

During this time, I was paid by the University of Alberta Press to write and publish two books. One was a prison memoir, *The Man in Blue Pajamas*, about my life under Saddam Hussein. It was exciting for me to go to my office every day and smell coffee from the cafés on the ground floor. It smelled like freedom.

But it was not always easy. It was a challenge to shape my books from the original language and culture into a new language with entirely new culturally specific ways of expression. I still had the pieces of paper that I had written on and then smuggled out of prison. I carried them with me when I crossed borders. During my fellowship, I kept these on my desk in the Edmonton Public Library, and when I looked at them, I remembered the unspeakably tragic period I had been through. However, I knew that creating art with words and emotions from my dark past was a relief. I was able to freely express what was in my heart and openly share my journey and my story.

Another challenge was discovering myself as a non-fiction writer. Since 1970, I had written poetry, where I used few words to create a blank canvas on which a reader could paint with their own mind. Now I was also writing non-fiction, which meant that every piece of a story had to be told in detail. I found that when I wrote non-fiction, my life did not go from birth to childhood to adulthood; nothing progressed in a straight line. I have been a refugee since childhood, always on the move. My life has been lived in pieces, and turning these pieces into a readable story for Western readers was difficult.

It was also challenging to be a writer in a new country where I could not fully express myself in the spoken language. But by having my story and poems translated into English and published by the University of Alberta Press, I have had the chance to introduce my work to a new audience. The same writing, the same voice, the same spirit that I was punished for in the country where I was born was now giving me the opportunity to continue my journey without restrictions in Canada. I held these stories in my memory for so many years, long before I went on to write about them in my books. I wrote them in my mind while in a library converted into a jail, and then I wrote them on paper in an office in a library in my new home.

And so my story begins and ends with many different homes. To those immigrants and refugees who may wonder, like I did, what home is anymore—who may ask, "Is it the place where you are born and have your first memories?," "Is it the place where your mother is?," or "Is it this new place I am now?"—I offer, maybe home is not just the place where you were born, created your first memories, and began your life journey; perhaps it is also the place that makes you the best version of yourself. In the process of creating new homes, a person does not need to leave their roots, their childhood, their memories, or their culture. We can and should carry our identities with us wherever we go and share them with others in our new homes.

Home in a Suitcase

Thanks to the sea,
the journey from Istanbul to Edmonton
is a seventeen-hour flight. A day earlier,
a thirteen-hour bus ride
brought us to Istanbul's Ataturk Airport. It felt good to say goodbye
   to Sivas—
the city was too conservative for our taste.
The airport was teeming with refugees like us:
some sleeping, some reflecting,
some looking up words
they thought they needed upon arrival in a foreign land, some busy-
   ing themselves with their hats,
some pondering the possibility of failure and disappointment, some
   missing home,
some staring at their new lives in suitcases. months before,
we left Ankara.
where luck turned out to be on my side: I was accepted by the UN as
   a refugee. For six months
in the Ols district,
the hub of refugees from Southern Kurdistan, I was Teza's tenant.
Every morning, Sungul and I
climbed down 122 concrete steps to go to the local bazaar:
Sungul sold ice water,
I reflected on what was to come. I am not a storyteller,
though I do keep a lot in my heart.

In 1961,
at the start of the September Revolution, Iraqi warplanes bombed
   our village.
For several weeks

the nearby caves were our home. Mother missed her vegetable
   garden;
she knew it wouldn't survive under the rubble. Father lost the few
   sheep he cared so much about. And I lost a woollen ball I had
   made myself.

My first time flying
I was unafraid:
I had complete faith in my kite's wings. The second time,
I flew from Ankara to Kiev on a fake visa,
hoping to be smuggled to Sweden. The venture failed;
I was caught
and sent back to Istanbul on a half-empty flight.

My children weren't afraid of flying;
the plane going up and down was like a seesaw for them. For my
   wife,
flying above the rain, the crowds, the city was hard to believe.
In Amsterdam, UN bags in hand,
we stood for six hours near the gate.

Getting lost was our biggest fear. But I did manage to call Hawler.
I don't remember much else from Amsterdam. Crossing the Atlantic
made me realize we were still without an address.

14 Locating Kurdish Cultural Identity in Canada

Louise Harrington and Dana Waissi

The wind is bequeathed from one Kurd to another Kurd in exile, son . . . and the eagles around you and me are many in spacious Anatolia.

—Darwish 2007

Imagining a conversation between himself and his friend, the Kurdish poet Salim Barakat, in the above quote, Mahmoud Darwish ruminates on the Kurdish condition from his position as a Palestinian—all too familiar with the loss of home and the nomadism of exile, particularly as a poet and outspoken critic of the system of occupation. In his ode to Barakat, he raises the complex issue of Kurdish identity in exile and emphasizes the important role that language plays in asserting said identity—and thus the power of words, of poetry. With this principle foregrounded, the current research examines the relationship between cultural production and Kurdish people, a group often referred to as the world's largest stateless nation. We ask how Kurdish cultural production—namely, literature, film, and music—might operate as a site for nurturing Kurdish identity in exile. The hypothesis is that addressing this question will uncover what a Kurdish cultural identity among a widely dispersed community might be founded on. The cartographic absence of a recognized, bordered Kurdistan has fostered the belief that Kurdish cultural identity is not unified but subsumed into or dominated by the four nation-states that exist in the ancestral land of Greater Kurdistan. However, acknowledging that geographical boundaries are not necessary prerequisites for an ethno-cultural identity, this chapter insists that Kurdish cultural identity is cohesive yet located in multiple places, not in a singular site or form. We examine a variety of cultural outputs from 1969 to 2019 to determine the patterns and threads of "Kurdishness" at the heart of some significant cultural forms. A close reading analysis reveals not only how cultural expression renders visible the historical plight of the Kurds and the traumatic reality of their dispossession and exile but also how Kurdish cultural identity is affirmed and celebrated in new homes and places of refuge—for instance, against the backdrop of the refugee resettlement program in Canada.

Historical Context

Composed of more than forty million people, the Kurds are one of the largest nationless ethno-linguistic groups in the world. Features of Kurdish cultural identity include a powerfully rich language stratified according to nuanced dialectical subtleties, a panoply of time-honored faiths like Yarsanism and Yezidism, a diverse culture that bears the ancient signatures of the Mesopotamians and Anatolians, and a deeply rooted history that is as old as civilization itself. For instance, certain practices inherent to Newroz, the Kurdish New Year celebration, such as lighting braziers to usher in new beginnings, were being practiced as far back as the early Bronze Age. The majority of Kurds live in their ancestral homeland, Greater Kurdistan, a continuous and mostly mountainous region in the Middle East that straddles the geopolitically turbulent axis of four contiguous states: Turkey, Iran, Iraq, and Syria. It is therefore unsurprising that while Kurdish identity remains uniquely singular, it is also notably heterogeneous. The national cultures of the four states often impact and dominate Kurdish cultural production. For example, the Kurdish singer Ibrahim Tatlises has replaced the Kurdish lyrics of traditional songs with Turkish ones to appeal more to his audience, while in Iran, the well-known Kurdish singer Shahram Nazeri has long sung in Persian for similar reasons. However, the adoption of a dominant national language perhaps says more about the practical and troubling realities of the endeavour to have a successful artistic career as a Kurd in these places than it does about a willing hybridization or enthusiastic fusion. When it comes to Kurdish culture in the four nation-states, the shadow of oppressive structures maintains an enduring presence.

An independent Kurdistan was a possibility in 1920 under the Treaty of Sèvres but became unattainable as the Kemalist movement gained strength in Northern Kurdistan (Meiselas 1997, 64). Founded on the principles of Mustafa Kemal Atatürk, the founder and first president of the Turkish Republic, Kemalism gained power among the Kurdish tribesmen in Northern Kurdistan by calling for the common action of Muslims against Christians (64). With the help of these Muslim Kurdish tribesmen, the Kemalists were able to control Northern Kurdistan and planned to take Southern Kurdistan from the British, since British Indian troops occupied this land from 1918 to 1926. During this period, the Kurdish movement under the leadership of Sheikh Mahmud Barzinji declared war against the British and began to fight for independence in the south, but in 1922, Barzinji was arrested by the British. In the same year, the French and the British accepted the Kemalists as the only government in Turkey, and Southern Kurdistan remained under British control until it became part of Iraq in 1926 (64).

Ethnic persecution, political oppression, cultural assimilation, forced displacements, and ultimately genocide followed as the Kurds were betrayed and failed by alleged allies and neighbours, as well as enemies. Throughout generations, Kurds have faced mass genocide and sustained discrimination within their own ancestral land. However, in the face of these injustices, there have been many uprisings across Greater Kurdistan. When Saddam Hussein was in power in Iraq (1979–2003), Kurds in Southern Kurdistan held five uprisings against his tyrannical regime. In Iran and Turkey, the Kurds have never stopped fighting their oppressors, while since 2012, the ongoing Rojava revolution in Syria has been well documented. In 2014, the Islamic State (IS) gained control of many Kurdish cities and massacred the Yazidi Kurds, and more than 3,500 women and girls were sold into sex slavery and forced to marry IS members (Tax 2016, 40). Between 2014 and 2019, the Peshmerga in Bashur (Southern Kurdistan)—that is, the military forces of the autonomous region of Kurdistan that is located in Iraq—along with Kurds in Rojava (Western Kurdistan) fought IS, while many Kurds in Bakur (Northern Kurdistan) and Rojhelat (Eastern Kurdistan) also joined these fighters to defeat IS. Additionally, the YPG (People's Protection Unit) and YPJ (Women's Protection Unit) in Western Kurdistan have played central roles in the fight for women's rights and in rescuing women and girls from sexual enslavement. When IS took over major Kurdish cities such as Kobane, Afrin, and Sari Kani between 2014 and 2017, thousands of Kurdish civilians were forced to evacuate. In the ensuing years, YPG defeated IS, recapturing large swathes of territory in Rojava, which enabled the displaced civilians to return home to their burnt cities. This victory was short-lived. Following the US Army withdrawal from Rojava in 2019, the Turkish military began its occupation of these Kurdish-controlled areas, forcing thousands of civilians to evacuate their homes once more.

Kurdish Culture and Canada

The 2016 census states that there are sixteen thousand Kurds living in Canada, but the number of people who identify as Kurdish is estimated as being much higher, in the region of fifty thousand. The reasons for this discrepancy are varied and speculative but might include a lack of education or knowledge about one's own ethno-cultural identity, a fear of persecution, the relentless and historical conditioning that renders Kurdishness invisible, and the desire to "fit in" or be "legitimate" by adopting another dominant national identifier (Iraqi, Iranian, etc.). It is important to note here that there is little scholarly work available to shed light on the Kurdish communities in Canada. Social scientists working in demography, population, and migration studies would do well to investigate the absence of Kurds in the Canadian census results and in society more broadly. Abdurrahman Wahab (2019) highlights the fact that the current academic scholarship that does exist has failed to take into account the heterogeneity of Kurds, who are neither a static cultural group nor a derivative of Iraqi, Turkish, Syrian, or Iranian ethno-cultural identity. Rather, what emerges when we begin to look at Canada is how often other labels and categorizations—ethnic, religious, cultural—supersede or subsume Kurdishness. Frequently, distinct and diverse peoples are conflated in sentences such as "Muslim refugees from the Middle East" or in conversations around "refugees from Syria" that fail to adequately represent the various identities or contexts of these groups. While general categorizations sometimes have their place, the omission of Kurds from various forms of public discourse can denote a lack of awareness ranging from general ignorance to racism. In another context, the annual provincial heritage festivals that celebrate multiculturalism across Canada often require Kurds to self-identify as Iraqi, Syrian, Turkish, or Iranian in order to "fit into" a national category. While this may not pose a problem to some, a person may equally feel very strongly that this other sanctioned national affiliation is not one by which they wish to be defined, particularly in light of the historical context that shapes Kurdish perspectives on these nations. It is unsurprising, then, that Kurds in Canada struggle to find themselves and their ethno-cultural identity recognized or visible. In addition, a lack of education or knowledge within the Kurdish community itself also contributes to an effacement of Kurdishness in Canada. Because Kurdish cultural identity has been oppressed for many generations, the prohibition of language, cultural expression, and history has led to many Kurds having a deficient knowledge of who they are. A consequence of this lack of cultural knowledge is that Kurdish families are less able to preserve their language and culture or pass it on to the next generation. This has become a constant struggle for many Kurds in Canada and around the world. There is an internal endeavour to keep the language and culture alive within the community and resist the supremacy of other national languages and ethno-cultural identities, as well as a fight for recognition and support from external forces.

There has, however, been one conversation in which Kurds appear, one that, despite their presence, also speaks to their absence—that is, the military offensive against IS. The Canadian relationship with Kurdistan goes as deep as the war against Islamic extremism in the Near and Middle East has required. The Peshmerga have been important allies of the American-led coalition, receiving arms and training from the coalition since 2014. While Canada ceased airstrikes in Iraq in 2018, the Canadian military continues to train the Peshmerga, a relationship that is not without complications and certainly one that has attracted considerable concern. For instance, Renad Mansour, a scholar at the Carnegie Middle East Center, states that "helping build the Peshmerga is effectively a form of state-building. These guys are fighting for the Kurdistan Regional Government (KRG), not for Iraq as a country" (quoted in Petrou 2016). His point is that any support for the military forces of the autonomous region of Kurdistan cannot be blind to the nationalist project the KRG is ultimately undertaking, and indeed, such support could be seen as evidence of complicity on the part of the Canadian government or any coalition in a very real way. In recent years, media outlets, foreign policy journalists, and academics in Canada have suggested that caution be exercised with regard to this situation. For example, Walter Dorn, a professor at the Royal Military College of Canada, warns that "[by working with the Peshmerga] there is the danger we are supporting a secessionist movement" (quoted in Pugliese 2016). Such rhetoric in the aftermath of the coalition's success against IS, in which the Peshmerga played an instrumental role, represents an instance of the continued abandonment of Kurds by Western forces.

Beyond the issue of international security and "conflict in the Middle East," the visible presence of Kurdish identity or culture is all but imperceptible in Canadian society. The arrest at gunpoint of the renowned Kurdish musician Şivan Perwer in Toronto in August 2009 made headlines across the Canadian media, which positioned Perwer and his fellow musicians, who were filming a music video on a stretch of highway, as possible armed terrorists. The events began with a tipoff to the Ontario Provincial Police (OPP) that claimed that the men had a weapon in their vehicle (in fact, it was a TV camera), leading to what the OPP term "a high-risk takedown" of Perwer and his crew. The driver, Riza Bildik, recalls the trauma of the affair in an interview with Toronto's CityNews (2009): "Can you imagine more than 15 cops, holding us with guns, they put our face on the road with everyone watching us. I thought they are going to kill us. [. . .] Tomorrow I'm going to meet my lawyer, I have to, because they broke our honour, not just me and him, Kurdish people." When Perwer called for a formal apology, the OPP expressed regret but denied that there was anything excessive about the arrest. The "terrorist" storyline founded on skin colour or facial features is one that Kurds and those of other ethnicities or religious affiliations frequently have to work hard to disprove in Western societies. For all the public professions of diversity and inclusion in Canada, the existence of ignorant, assimilationist, discriminatory, and racist behaviours enacted by state systems (the police force, the education system) as well as on an individual or local level more than calls into question the trumpeted cultural mosaic narrative. Celebratory multiculturalism does not render ignorance and discrimination obsolete (see Hasmath 2011).

As the first country to implement a multiculturalism policy in 1971, Canada made a firm commitment to recognize, foster, and preserve the diverse cultural practices—including languages, customs, and rituals—of its large immigrant population. Bolstered by the position of the minister of diversity and inclusion and youth, the formal collaboration with the Canadian Ethnocultural Council, and the implementation in 1978 of the Refugee and Humanitarian Resettlement Program, supporting all aspects of immigrant culture is part of the Canadian government's mandate. However, research reveals that despite the symbolic recognition of ethno-cultural diversity by the government and the popular support for multiculturalism policy, the dominant preference is for integration into mainstream Canadian society, requiring "them" to become more like "us" (Reitz 2014). Further research exposes the anxiety in English and French white settler communities about the "threat" posed by the languages and cultures of racialized immigrants to official languages and mainstream culture (Haque 2014, 205). Thus, it is imperative to create more spaces for minority cultures to speak in Canada and, echoing the language of the multiculturalism policy, to recognize and appreciate the diverse richness of all languages and cultures, to creatively engage and collaborate across ethnic groups or different origins, and to unreservedly support the sharing of cultural heritage.

So how to approach the complex matter of Kurdish identity in Canada or anywhere? Given the historico-political context, it is often observed that "Kurdish identity is deeply fragmented" in light of both oppressive external states and internal factors relating to territory, culture, language, and politics (Sheyholislami 2011, 55). The conditions of being stateless, exiles, and refugees are all strongly associated with Kurdish people and thus also the attendant condition of disunity or an absence of collective identity. Indeed, exile and forced migration can lead to a separation within the self or in cultural-ethnolinguistic identity, and scholarship is replete with references to dis-location as both a real physical movement and an embodied and psychological dis-order (see Bhabha 1994; Brah 1996; Smith 2004). Edward Said's canonical essay "Reflections on Exile" (1984; Said 2000) situates the condition as one marred by sadness, loss, solitude, and insecurity, wherein the collectivity and community of nationalism are yearned for, encompassed by the desire to belong to the homeland. This is exacerbated when there is no "recourse to a functioning nation-state [...] however distant, that might offer a stable center for identity" (Ghosh 2008, 284). Frequently, this is discussed in relation to Palestinians who might encounter complex identity crises when facing questions about home and national identity, being "defined in terms of the geopolitical transformations in the Middle East" (284). The far-reaching scale of the support for and recognition of the Palestinian national movement is not something that Kurds experience, however, since theirs is a struggle that is less visible, discussed, or circulated in the academic sphere and across mass media. Yet alongside the fracture that Kurdish people in exile and in the diaspora suffer, there is the possibility, some might even say flourishing, of Kurdishness through collective remembering and forgetting, through music, literature, art, and other cultural performances. Sheyholislami argues that "Kurdish diasporas reproduce the fragmentations of Kurdish identity, but they have also become places of convergence, cultural and political revival, and collective identity formation. Diasporas have become pan-Kurdish communicative spaces" (2011, 72). Although multifarious, thousands of Kurds—exiles, refugees, and their descendants—who have made Canada their home engage with and celebrate a cultural identity that deeply connects them to their cultural heritage and homeland as well as a wider, dispersed Kurdish people.

Culture should not be viewed as an objective reality that is static, pure, or singular. It is, rather, a shifting and evolving reality whose impact on group and individual identity formation cannot be ignored. For instance, as noted earlier, Kurds have historically battled the absorption of their cultural identity into other dominant national identities through oppressive systems. Kurds in Canada still struggle to identify themselves as Kurds because of the absence of education on their culture and language within their family structures and communities, in addition to the fear of having to explain "where and what" Kurdistan is. Cultural identity and individual selfhood are intrinsically connected, while culture is also "the publically accessible text of a people," according to Clifford Geertz (in Friedman 1994, 68): a text that is present in society, playing a key role in community building. If we are to consider that a pan-Kurdish cultural identity exists, albeit necessarily nuanced and variable, the matter of which cultural forms are produced, performed, and circulated must be addressed. Kurdish people have a rich cultural history with origin myths (so central to nationalist discourses) rooted in the Median Empire (728–550 BCE), through to pre-modern history, and into the sixteenth century, where oral and written texts and epics detail the existence of a shared but diverse ethnic identity called "Kurd." Moving forward to the twentieth century and against a contemporary backdrop of political upheavals, military interventions, and humanitarian crises, literary and cinematic texts and music are the main venues that reveal the proliferation of Kurdish cultural production.

The scholar Kimberly Wedeven Segall claims that cultural forms exist as places of refuge, especially for those who have experienced war, conflict, and dispossession, but that is not to say that they are passive sites of retreat or inert traditions; instead, they can provide sanctuary while also serving to empower or afford agency. In her book *Performing Democracy*, Segall notes, "Cultural forms have recorded historical events and created communal forums that work toward reconstructing identity after the silencing effect of torture, terror, and ethnic cleansing. In stark contrast to the helplessness of the experience of torture or severe oppression, public commemorations can break through the individual's traumatized alienation; furthermore, a story or song—especially through the acting agent's choice of movement, pace, length, and participation within a community—offers a measure of reassuring control" (2013, 11).

The possibility of community building that is inherent in the circulation of stories and songs elevates the individual endeavour, which nonetheless plays its role in providing a creative outlet for expression and a means to cope with traumatic experiences. For example, the poetry of Şêrko Bêkes, one of the most renowned Kurdish poets, transcends ethnic, religious, and linguistic borders to promote humanity and freedom (Cabi 2019, 8). Further, with respect to the pervasive power of music, Stephen Blum and Amir Hassanpour argue that "singers can dramatise the continuing vitality of Kurdish culture by reviving songs and verses that had almost vanished, by reproducing and adapting rural songs in new performance contexts" (1996, 334). They point to the prolific singer Şivan Perwer as the embodiment of the exilic figure whose repertoire is influenced by a breadth of Kurdish literary and folkloric history from the seventeenth century to the present and who is celebrated across the Kurdish diaspora.

Centering the power of literature, film, and music, then, this research regards such cultural production as a key site of identity formation that thrives even in a scattered or exilic state. But questions remain about how Kurdish ideology, beliefs, or hopes are captured and represented in literature, film, and music. As a dispersed and heterogeneous people, what emerges from their poetry and song, in particular, that might shed light on some essential "Kurdishness" within which a sense of belonging can be found, even as a stateless community in exile? The term *Kurdayetî* is relevant here as a companion to the neologism *Kurdishness* as a way to understand what elemental ideas, beliefs, (hi)stories, traumas, and hopes are at the heart of Kurdish cultural production. Sheyholislami explains that "*Kurdayetî* refers to a movement or action that is carried out on behalf of the Kurds. It can also refer to an ideology or belief system that makes claims about Kurdish identity or Kurdishness" (2011, 202). Much of the poetry and song under discussion in the following section reflects this understanding of *Kurdayetî*. In their meditations on matters of home and homeland, of roots and rootlessness, writers, filmmakers, poets, musicians, and many others capture the realities of Kurdish identity, of the enduring experience of not belonging, and offer the refuge of which Segall speaks by presenting a sense of hope for the future through reclaiming and celebrating the past. The important question is this: In what ways do Kurds, and specifically younger generations who have grown up in communities of exile or in the diaspora in Canada, inherit a sense of belonging to a place, to a land, or to a people in the face of dispossession and oppression? Without a sense of the past, of heritage broadly conceived, it can be difficult to represent the present. For Kurds in Canada, the struggle to maintain their culture and history is real, yet the preservation of these things informs the evolving concept of Kurdishness. Reclaiming the past, when it comes to issues of legitimacy and cultural expression, can be a lifeline for future prosperity. As much as violent histories are inherited through intergenerational trauma, so too are deep and strong cultural connections that are asserted through such media as poetry and song, in which silenced and marginalized voices or stories are recorded, heard, and repeated, where the human spirit resides and where it flourishes.

Oppression, Sacrifice, Resistance, and Hope

One of the most influential contemporary Kurdish poets is Şêrko Bêkes, whose surname, which translates to "alone," aptly represents the Kurdish nation. In his early years, Bêkes joined a liberation movement, a short-lived endeavour, as he was sent into exile by Saddam Hussein's Ba'ath party. He lived in Sweden for many years, where he published several books and where he passed away in 2013. In an evocative poem, "A Letter to God," Bêkes recounts a fanciful tale about his failure to secure God's help following Hussein's genocidal campaign against the Kurds in 1986–89. After writing his letter to God, Bêkes reads it to a tree, and the tree breaks down into tears as a result. A nearby bird who witnesses the recital promptly refuses to act as a courier to God, saying, "There's no way I can reach Him" (Bekas and Sinjari 1988, line 9). Thankfully, the living embodiment of the poem appears in the form of a black crow and promises Bêkes to take his missive to God. The following day, the crow returns with the letter, dejected because written on the letter is an Arabic message from one of God's secretaries that reads "You fool! Write in Arabic. No one here speaks Kurdish" (lines 28–29). This final verse powerfully encapsulates the thematic essence of Bêkes's poem by indicating that not even divine intervention can remedy the abject loneliness of the Kurdish experience. Indeed, most of Bêkes's poetry focuses on how Kurdish identity has been shaped by some form of adversity. Faced with the injustices of Hussein's regime, Bêkes's "main theme is the defense of human dignity and freedom" (Bekas and Sinjari 1988,

17), and this theme "[is reflected by] his close association with the Kurdish National Liberation Movement (KNLM) which he joined in 1965, working in the Movement's radio station—the Voice of Kurdistan" (17). Bêkes wrote "A Letter to God" following the Halabja massacre of 1988, when the world had turned a blind eye to the suffering of the Kurds as thousands of civilians died in a matter of a few hours when chemical bombs rained down upon them. Kurds were alone, suffering, and rejected by the international community, a reality that is echoed throughout Bêkes's poem, as the dismissal of his letter to God represents a rejection of the Kurdish identity, language, and homeland.

Like Bêkes's poetry, the films of Behmen Qubadî, a Kurdish film director, producer, and writer, emphasize the sociopolitical implications of Kurdish culture, the tragedies and discrimination Kurds have faced, and how these realities have shaped their identity. Qubadî is also a Kurdish activist interested in freedom of expression and Kurdish self-consciousness. His narrative archetypes often involve border crossings and being an outsider in one's own homeland. For instance, in his first feature film, *A Time for Drunken Horses*, the first Kurdish film produced in Iran, Qubadî (2000) portrays the difficulties Kurds face across the borders of Iran, Iraq, Turkey, and Syria. In addition to depicting the logistical struggles Kurdish people must overcome when traversing these borders in harsh conditions, *A Time for Drunken Horses* also explores the cultural oppression that Kurds face at the hands of border guards. The film tells the story of recently orphaned Kurdish children struggling to survive in the in-between spaces of the Iranian and Iraqi borders. Qubadî emphasizes the unforgiving mountainous environment through a succession of wide shots that capture the harshness of the wintery landscape, which dramatically contextualizes the difficult living conditions these orphans experience daily. In one important scene, the children illegally cross through the hills from Southern Kurdistan, located in northern Iraq, to Eastern Kurdistan, located in western Iran, while trying to avoid detection by Iranian border patrols who are authorized to use deadly force. This depicts the sad reality that Kurds are bound by hostile borders within their own homeland of Kurdistan. In the following scene, Iranian guards seize the books that the orphans are smuggling (see figure 14.1), which speaks to the importance of the freedom of education. The Iranian government is fearful of Kurdish-led education because it recognizes it as an existential threat to state authority. Thus, by confiscating the books, the authorities are seizing the very instrument of Kurdish emancipation.

Figure 14.1. *A Time for Drunken Horses* (Qubadî 2000). Reprinted with permission from Kino Lorber EDU.

Following up on the success of his first film, Qubadî's (2006) *Half Moon* centers on a group of Kurdish musicians from Eastern Kurdistan having difficulty crossing the border into Southern Kurdistan, where they are planning to perform a concert. Kurdish music is the cultural expression that the film is set against. In one scene, the group's minibus is stopped by Iranian border guards who proceed to throw the musical instruments out on the road as the powerless and dismayed Kurdish musicians look on; as the soldiers "trash their instruments, the musicians come to the realization that the Iranian authorities have no intention of ever letting them travel into Iraq [Southern Kurdistan]" (Film Sufi 2008). As a result of this portrayal, the film was banned in Iran, and Qubadî was warned by authorities not to make cinematic productions that are critical of the Iranian government. In a 2007 interview in *Tribeca News* magazine, he claims that he is "a second-class citizen as a Kurd" and makes it evident that language is very important to him, as he states that "Kurds do not have the same rights as the Farsi-speakers and [he is] trying to discuss this with the camera, to use the camera to bring this issue to the fore" (*Tribeca News*, n.d.). Highlighting the language politics of the Kurdish situation, Qubadî believes that "people should make films in which they tell people their stories in their own language." He further states, "Of course, I have respect for Turkish and Persian languages. Yet I demand the same respect from others. I am a refugee right now. I am here as a Kurdish man who is forced to shoot his film in Persian and Turkish" (Kocar 2013). Being bound by constant restrictions, Qubadî cannot fully represent Kurdish identity, which is instead filtered through the limits and checks of oppressive state systems. However, in spite of this, Qubadî's carefully conceived films ultimately characterize Kurdish identity, connect with Kurds wherever they may be, and further, remind the world that they are still here.

Since the division of Kurdistan under the Treaty of Sèvres, in each part of Kurdistan, the Kurds have been fighting for the same cause: their homeland. In 1991, a Kurdish politician and activist, Layla Zana, joined the Turkish parliament; she took an oath in Turkish, but the closing sentence of her oath was in Kurdish. At this time, the Kurdish language was illegal in public and private places, and thus, in 1994, Zana was charged with treason and sentenced to fifteen years in prison for speaking in Kurdish and for wearing the colours of the Kurdish flag: red, green, and yellow. Zana's experience also "testifies to the double burden of being a Kurdish woman in Turkish society," which Zana refers to as a "martyrdom" (Karlsson 2003, 159). She is seen as a "political subject" because her book *Writings from Prison* contributes greatly to not only the "genre of female prison literature but also [...] a literature of the Kurdish diaspora," which then "educates the western reader on the Kurdish question in Turkey and the devastating effects that state-induced hatred has had on Kurdish communities" (159). Similarly, in 1945–46 in Iran, a Kurdish leader and politician, Qazi Muhammad, made a deal with the Iranian government that he would stop fighting for Kurdish independence if Kurds were given the right to study and learn their own language in school. The Mahabad Republic, which Qazi Muhammed founded in 1946, had created a universal education system to teach in Kurdish, but his presidency was short-lived because the "Iranian forces entered Mahabad, closed Kurdish printing presses, banned the teaching of Kurdish, and burned Kurdish books" (Arizanti 2020). Qazi Muhammed was executed in 1947.

Kurds across Turkey, Iran, Iraq, and Syria are continuously creating cultural and artistic works that represent Kurdish identity, but there is no reliable data, scholarly or otherwise, on this, as creative projects often face censorship or restrictions on circulation. The successful artist Zehra Doğan's experience in Turkey is a case in point. After being jailed for her painting of a Kurdish town in the majority-Kurdish southeast of Turkey, Doğan used her three years in prison to create art out of the materials she had around her, which she then smuggled out as dirty laundry. Now in exile, and in the face of the shutdown of Kurdish cultural projects in Turkey, Doğan's art has recently been exhibited in Istanbul and receives much international attention. Yet she cannot return to Turkey. Doğan has found fame in exile, but many other artists and creators do not, and their work may never come to light if it is not published, released, circulated, or marketed under restrictive systems of control.

These few examples of injustice and discrimination against the Kurdish linguistic or cultural identity have led activists, politicians, journalists, writers, and artists to make great sacrifices in an effort to change systems that try to eliminate the existence of Kurds. Many musicians, such as Ahmet Kaya, have reflected on the betrayal and sacrifices of historical Kurdish figures. Kaya was a folksinger born in Northern Kurdistan (southern Turkey) with mixed Kurdish-Turkish origin but identified as a Kurd. He was one of the most influential and controversial artists in Turkey because he claimed his Kurdish identity and had a desire to sing in Kurdish after many years. As a result, he had to flee Turkey and live in France, where he died in exile in November 2000. In his music, Kaya tells his story of suffering and longing for the people of his homeland, Kurdistan, which he was torn away from. In the song "How Can You Know?" (1998), Kaya expresses his frustration at the oppression he faced in Turkey. He articulates questions that only the oppressed can answer, such as, "How can you know how I have been burning?" (Subtitled Turkish Songs 2017, 0:49). Kaya reveals how he was burning with rage and became a "storm" (1:28) as a result of not being treated with dignity and respect. Later in the song, though, after being broken and betrayed by the Turkish state, he sings of how he has "settled" and is "tired, quite tired" (1:28–1:35) because he had been trying to peacefully represent Kurds for so long.

In his 1999 acceptance speech during a televised music awards ceremony in Turkey, Kaya openly expressed his wish to produce Kurdish music videos, stating, "I accept this prize on behalf of all of Turkey. This said, I wish to add something. Let no one come and tell me, 'but who gave you such a mission?'! History gave it to me. In my upcoming album, my next album, because of the fact I am of Kurdish origin, I will include a title in Kurdish and have a video clip of it. I know that some people will have the courage to distribute this clip" (Aktan 2017). Immediately after this, the audience started to shout, "Such a thing as a Kurd doesn't exist!" (Aktan 2017). He was declared a threat by Turkish authorities and was called a "traitor" in Turkey. In his song "How Can You Know?," he sings that he has "come to these days by sacrificing [his] life" (Subtitled Turkish Songs 2017, 2:25)—that is, by sacrificing his own

Kurdish language to sing in Turkish, which makes him feel like a fountain that has now been "soaked in blood" (4:12). He then feels ashamed and that he has "gone to waste" (4:22) for singing in Turkish. Today, many Kurdish artists, politicians, and citizens borrow from his most famous song to question their oppressors and ask "How can you know?," "How can you know why I have been in silence?" (4:26) when confronted with injustices because of their ethno-cultural identity. The power of these lyrics endures as they resonate with the silencing of the Kurdish nation, echoing the axiom "Kurds have no friends but the mountains."

The political environment experienced by Kaya was very much the same for Kurdish artists in Eastern Kurdistan. Nasir Rezazî, a Kurdish singer who has mainly lived in exile, performs traditional Kurdish folk songs in four major Kurdish dialects: Sorani, Kurmanji, Hewrami, and Kalhori. His songs combine many different Kurdish genres, dialects, and musical styles and thereby speak to the diversity of Kurdish people. In a picturesque music video titled "Şarekem," meaning "my city," which he produced himself, Rezazî movingly sings about his experiences away from his homeland and his joy upon returning to Southern Kurdistan. He engages with nature—the trees, rivers, mountains—to emphasize that this is where he belongs. Although life may be difficult as a Kurdish exile, Rezazî nonetheless praises his identity. Preserving culture, tradition, history, and one's ethnicity are recurring themes of Kurdish artistic expression. He cries out in despair, "[I have been] separated from my homeland" (Hely Deng 2020, 2:01), and believes that no matter where he is, "[his] thoughts will always be with Kurdistan" (2:37), and his longing for home "is the reason why [his] heart is always full of sorrow" (2:41).

In stark opposition to the international boundaries that divide the Kurdish nation, many artists celebrate Kurdish identity in their creative works to keep a national spirit alive. Thus, disputing the legitimacy of borders, Kurdish artists aspire to promote a cohesive sense of identity in the collective psyche of the Kurdish people in order to counteract the divisive forces that partition Kurdistan along geographical, historical, and cultural lines. Rezazî still cannot return to Eastern Kurdistan for fear of persecution by Iran, so he dedicates his songs to the movement for an independent Kurdistan. This claim to Kurdish unity echoes another well-known song, Ayub Ali and Gare Sazkar's "Kurdim"—"I Am Kurd"—in which they proudly assert, "My language is Kurdish, and I am from Kurdistan" (Ayub Ali 2015, 0:13). Like many other Kurdish artists, they challenge preconceived notions of a divided Kurdistan.

Ali and Sazkar emphatically call upon all Kurds to come together and take pride in their Kurdishness. By stating "I am Kurd, from Kurdistan and my language is Kurdish" (0:45), Kurds can reaffirm their unity in the face of conflict and oppression.

Much like Rezazî, in her song "Welat," meaning "Homeland," Melek Rojhat, one of the many celebrated female Kurdish singers, depicts a journey in Kurdistan. Her poetic verses nullify any pre-existing boundary by claiming that one's homeland is where "life, being [and] love come into existence" (Bilal 2018, 0:15). Rojhat's song reveals the people's love of their land, whether from North, South, East, or West; the current cartographic borders do not exist within the collective psyche, as they are willing to "sacrifice [their lives] for" their homeland (4:13). With her lyrics, Rojhat takes us on a journey through history, one of tranquility and hope, for as long as the "Hewler and Dimdim castle" remain "symbols of [. . .] resistance," there will always be "proof of [Kurdistan's] civilization" (4:50–5:00). Many Kurdish artists uphold this sentiment of hope by resisting the influence of those who misrepresent and silence the voice of the Kurdish people within their homeland. Through its composition and powerful lyrics, Rojhat's music becomes crucial in protecting and reaffirming Kurdish identity because it advocates for being able to identify as a Kurd from the land of Kurdistan.

The hope for a unified Kurdistan ultimately takes center stage in the music of the Kamkars, a family of musicians with seven brothers and one sister who have performed numerous concerts worldwide and are widely recognized as one of the leading musical ensembles in Kurdistan. The music of the Kamkars is founded on Kurdish folklore and tradition, instantiating a panoply of emotional and spiritual dimensions inherent to the Kurdish experience throughout history. Thanks to their mastery and harmonious implementation of various traditional Kurdish instruments (e.g., Tembur, Santoor, Kamanche, and Daff) invigorated by delicately balanced vocals, the Kamkars vividly capture Kurdish identity in epic melodies. Their distinct aptitude for integrating virtuoso musical performance with complex compositions and arrangements enables them to revitalize the Kurdish culture and traditions and thereby resist some of the barriers Kurds face in Iran to maintain their Kurdish identity. Their music is conscientiously composed to revolt against Iranian restrictions by drawing on ancient Kurdish history and the folk customs of each region of Kurdistan to undo established political, linguistic, cultural, and geographical schisms.

In addition, many musicians combat oppressive regimes through their lyrics and through a formidable tone that influences revolutionary ideas. Şivan Perwer is one the most famous Kurdish singer-songwriters whose epic songs have galvanized entire Kurdish generations into action by denouncing occupiers and oppressors alike. Forced into exile as a result of his revolutionary songs about Kurdish identity, Perwer, who has been living in Germany for the better part of four decades, continues to remind the Kurds to be brave and unyielding in the face of opposition. In his most popular song "Kîne Em?" (1991; United Kurdish Forces 2008), which literally translates to "Who are we?"—based on the Kurdish poet Cigerxwîn's "Kîme Ez?" (1973), meaning "Who am I?"—Perwer recounts the history of the Kurdish nation and how, over time, the Kurds started to forget their identity only to rediscover it with a sense of renewed hope for the future of Kurdistan. In this song, Perwer directly calls on the Kurds to remember who they are and reminds them that their sense of unity is what will keep their nation alive. Perwer's original compositions about celebrated historical Kurdish figures who have been assassinated by oppressors inspire countless Kurdish men and women to take up arms against the ruthless autocratic regimes that tyrannize the Kurdish people. Like Şêrko Bêkes and Abdullah Peşêw, Perwer believes that Kurds are alone in their fight for recognition and autonomy, necessitating unity to protect their identity and culture.

Just as Perwer has galvanized the Kurdish nation through powerful songs and messages, Abdullah Peşêw has been regarded as one of the most influential contemporary political satirists in Kurdistan. Through his many literary works, Peşêw vehemently criticizes world leaders for closing their eyes to Kurdish suffering. His criticism does not stop at foreign leaders, however; far from it, Peşêw is perhaps best known for his condemnation of current Kurdish politicians who he believes have done little to unite the Kurdish nation. In "The Dagger," a short yet striking poem, Peşêw shatters preconceived notions about Kurds as bloodthirsty marauders, writing,

> I am a bare dagger!
> My Motherland is a stolen sheath.
> Don't think I am bloodthirsty!
> Go; find fault with the one,
> Who unsheathed me! (Kurdish Academy, n.d.)

Peşêw also portrays Kurdish identity in his poems, but from a different angle to Bêkes's perspective. While both focus on the same general theme,

Peşêw's message is much more politicized. Where Bêkes invokes a letter in "A Letter to God," Peşêw gives us a "dagger," and while the former laments his nation's loneliness, the latter denounces its usurpers. Peşêw's motherland is depicted as a "stolen sheath," and this eradicates doubts of Kurdistan being a stolen land. Thus, it is not Peşêw who is "bloodthirsty"; rather, it is the oppressor and the enemy who "unsheathed [him]." Peşêw's political and charismatic words have, in fact, awakened the Kurdish masses by fomenting in the collective Kurdish psyche a sense of national awareness.

The many calls for unity from the writers, musicians, and creators explored above are undoubtedly thwarted by divisions among the Kurds themselves. It is not easy to keep the hope alive that one day the people of Kurdistan will unite and be able to form an independent country when rifts between political parties and schisms pertaining to language and religion abound. However, hope does endure and proliferates in cultural production. For instance, despite the restrictions set upon them, the Kamkars perform traditional Kurdish music that travels across the world to awaken Kurdish cultural identity. The Kamkars often begin their concerts cautiously, since they are sometimes forced to introduce their performances with Persian songs, with the female performers wearing headscarves, and with the performers looking restricted. This is the only way they are able to perform as Kurds in Iran; their cultural self-expression is stymied. Then, for the second part of their concerts, they re-emerge in traditional clothes, full of energy, and ready to assert their real identity as Kurds, proudly expressing each and every note of the traditional melodies. In doing so, they adhere to Iranian regulations while also maintaining their Kurdishness.

Cultural figures and creators of all kinds have found ways to navigate what it is to be Kurdish in "other" lands, not without suffering or difficulty, but nonetheless with a passion for their culture and language and hope for the future. Mahmoud Darwish, whose words from "The Kurd Has Only the Wind (for Saleem Barakat)" opened this chapter, states that language has been the most powerful tool or form of activism employed by Kurds. He claims that "with language [Kurds] took revenge on absence" (Darwish 2007, 319), suggesting that through poetry, song, writing, and expressing their presence, their right to land, and their unique cultural identity, Kurds have been able to challenge the various mechanisms that render invisible entire groups of people.

Dana Waissi: A Personal Reflection on a Poem by Hama Aziz Waissi

My father—Hama Aziz Waissi, a Kurd living in exile in Canada—embodies the fire of Kurdish identity that still burns in many. My father has always devoted his life to maintaining a sense of hope for the Kurds and Kurdistan. Therefore, I have always dreamt of an independent Kurdistan because my father has instilled in me a sense of Kurdishness and what it means to be Kurdish while also respecting and appreciating other cultures. He was exiled from Eastern Kurdistan at the start of the Iran-Iraq War in 1980 and lived in a refugee camp in Iraq for twenty-one years, where I was also born, before resettling with the family in Canada in 2001. Given this experience, he has always sought to understand why the Kurds have been displaced and oppressed. He educated me and my siblings in this manner, endowing the next generation with a strong understanding of the importance of one's identity and the significance of the preservation of one's culture and history. Since living in Canada, my father has produced many writings, specifically poems, in order to make sense of, document, and honor the very substance of being Kurdish and the Kurdish experience.

In one of his most compelling poems, "I Am Kurdistan," originally written in Kurdish in 2015, my father not only expresses his roots but also uniquely documents the origins of Kurdistan by connecting Kurdish cities, language, culture, and history as well as the genocide and loss of life in order to manifest the Kurdish experience. The title of the poem is an instance of claiming his roots, as it indicates that he is Kurdistan himself, and although Kurdistan might not be on a map, it is inherent to his identity. Meanwhile, the words "I am" from the title are continuously repeated throughout the poem as a means to reclaim every aspect of Kurdistan; all the historical events, including genocide and oppression, are related to one Kurdish identity. The poem echoes many themes that have previously been explored in this chapter, such as the importance of language and the memory of the suffering that Kurds have faced. The commemoration of the past is also central for the Kurds, and when my father states "I am the age-old citadels of Ûrbîl and Kerkûk" (Waissi 2015, 13), the significance here is that the citadels (standing within the borders of Kurdistan) are living reminders of Kurdistan's civilization and represent the existence of Kurds in this land. As my father catalogues the names of cities, he calls attention to what has been lost or forgotten in all four parts of Kurdistan:

> [...] I am the lives that Anfal took.
> [...] I am the scars of Helebce, the mass graves of Germîyan.
>
> I am the tragedy of the Êzîdî, I am woe; [...]
> I am the peerless Revolutionary, the girls and boys of Kobanî. (Waissi 2015, lines 14–19)

His endless record of the shared experience of the many Kurdish cities conveys the essential message for Kurds to unite. This idea and dream of unity has resonated across many forms of Kurdish cultural production because in unity, there is the power to create and hope for a recognized Kurdistan, hence the title, "I Am Kurdistan." To achieve statehood and to become Kurdistan, one has to embody the very nature of the culture, and the preservation of the Kurdish cultural identity is what allows my father to state the following:

> I am the ancient and uncompromising wall of Amêd.
> I am the mighty Ararat and the flames of Newroz;
> I am the fire that burns strong and casts away the Undead. (Waissi 2015, lines 22–24)

The flames of Newroz, which is a celebration of unity summoning a new day, have made the Kurds a strong nation that preserves their culture and history. Although many have tried to contradict the fact that Newroz is the Kurdish New Year, the event has been able to revitalize the very existence of Kurds because through its existence, many Kurdish artists, similar to my father, have been able to galvanize a cultural revolution by honoring and bringing to light Kurdish identity. Newroz has not only been a celebration of unity; it has also strengthened the hope of independence and freedom by peacefully bringing millions of Kurds together worldwide through culture, music, and history. Thus, for instance, the "fire" quoted above gives life, meaning, and strength to the existence of the Peshmerga, as my father writes, "I am the Pêşmerge and the Gêrîla who fights the Misanthrope. I am undying Will, I am Courage, I am Hope" (Waissi 2015, lines 25–26). The courageous freedom fighters of Kurdistan are the "undying Will" of the nation and are the foundation for hope because to call yourself Kurdistan, you must assert that "I am Hope." Therefore, in calling out to every part of Kurdistan, referencing the speakers of different Kurdish dialects, my father draws attention to the crucial role of hope and commits to a sense of unity at the close of the poem by stating "I am Kełhor, Kurmanc, and Soran; I am united, I am Kurdistan" (line 28).

Many examples of Kurdish cultural production repeat this sentiment of the undying will of Kurdistan and the undeniable existence of Kurdish identity to combat the loss and oppose any hopelessness. In his poetry, my father aims to emphasize and resist oppression and discrimination from the four states: Turkey, Iran, Iraq, and Syria. He further endeavours to unite the Kurds through their origin and their shared losses to disseminate hope and unity and to celebrate the unique cultural diversity that makes Kurdistan, as the Kurdish saying goes, "the Bride of the world."

I Am Kurdistan

I am Lek, Lor, Goran;
I am Îlam, I am Kirmaşan.

I am the lost history of Hemedan;
I am the standing peak of Dałeho in Yarsan.

I am Sine, the Heroic,
And the mystifying cries of Bokan. I am Mehabad, the Stoic,
And the remote past of Serdeşt and Mukrîyan.

I am Ûrmê, the betrayed city of Simko Xan; I am the Twelve Horsemen hailing from Merîwan.

I am the sweet and seductive prose of Avestan,
I am the Avestan of Zarathustra and Hewraman.

I am the age-old citadels of Ûrbîl and Kerkûk, I am the lives that Anfal took.
I am the fire-breathing mountains of Badînan. I am the scars of Helebce, the mass graves of
Germîyan.

I am the tragedy of the Êzîdî, I am woe; I am that which I am for I am Qamîşlo.

I am the peerless Revolutionary, the girls and boys of Kobanî;
I am that which I am for I am Silêmanî.

I am the life-giving sweet source that Wan's perennials chose;
I am the ancient and uncompromising wall of Amêd.
I am the mighty Ararat and the flames of Newroz;
I am the fire that burns strong and casts away the Undead.

I am the Pêşmerge and the Gêrîla who fights the Misanthrope.
I am undying Will, I am Courage, I am Hope.

I am Kełhor, Kurmanc, and Soran;
I am united, I am Kurdistan.

By: Hama Aziz Waissi
Translated by: Shahin Tavakol

من کوردستانم

من لەکم، لورم، گۆرانم،
من ئێلام و کرماشانم.
من مێژووە ونبوەکەی ھەمەدانم.
من چیای خۆراگری دالەھۆی یارسانم.
من سنەی قارەمان و،
چریکە ئەفسوونناویبەکەی بۆکانم.
من مەھابادی خۆراگرو،
مێژووە دێرینەکەی سەردەشت و موکریانم.
من ورمێی خەیانەت لێکراوی سمکۆ خانم.
من دوانزە سوارەی مەریوانم.
من زمانە شیرین و ئەفسوونناویبەکەی ئاقێستای زەردەشت و ھەورامانم.
من قڵای دێرینی ھەولێرو کەرکووک و، گرکانی چیاکانی بەھدینانم.

من قەتماغەی برینی قوڵی هەڵبجەو،
گۆڕی بە کۆمەڵی ئەنفال کراوی گەرمیانم.
من تراژیدیای دنیا هەژینی ئێزیدیانم.
من بەرخۆدانی بێ وێنەی کچان و کۆڕانی کۆبانم.
من سلێمانی و قامیشلۆو ئاوی شیرین و،
پاراوی گۆڵی وانم.
من دیواری دێرین و ئەستووری ئامێدو،
کێوی سەر بەرزی ئارارات و نەورۆزی ئەهریمەن
سووتێنی کوردستانم.
من کەڵهورو سۆران و بەهدینانم.
من پێشمەرگەم، من شەرڤانم.
من هیوام،
هیوای دوا رۆژی گشت کوردستانم.

References

Aktan, Irfan. 2017. "Kurd, Kurdistan, None of That Exists." *Kedistan*, December 18, 2017. http://www.kedistan.net/2017/12/26/kurd-kurdistan-none-of-that-exists/.

Arizanti, Michael. 2020. "Today We Remember the Martyrdom of Qazi Muhammad." *Times of Israel*, March 31, 2020. https://web.archive.org/web/20200629112220/https://blogs.timesofisrael.com/today-we-remember-the-martyrdom-of-qazi-muhammad/.

Ayub Ali. 2015. "Ayub Ali & Gare Sazkar—Kurdim." YouTube, July 27, 2015, 5:38. https://www.youtube.com/watch?v=6YGWkFWHaSM.

Bekas, Sherko, and Hussain Sinjari. 1988. "Poems." *Index on Censorship* 17, no. 6 (June): 17–17.

Bhabha, Homi. 1994. *The Location of Culture*. London and New York: Routledge.

Bilal, Rojava. 2018. "Welat." YouTube, January 25, 2018, 5:46. https://www.youtube.com/watch?v=o-XIX0PN2go\.

Blum, Stephen, and Amir Hassanpour. 1996. "'The Morning of Freedom Rose Up': Kurdish Popular Song and the Exigencies of Cultural Survival." *Popular Music* 15, no. 3 (October): 325–43.

Brah, Avtar. 1996. *Cartographies of Diaspora: Contesting Identities*. New York and London: Routledge.

Cabi, Marouf. 2019. "Now a Girl Is My Homeland: Sherko Bekas and the Emergence of a Post-national Literature." Paper presented at the Contemporary Kurdish Literature Conference, University of St. Andrews, Scotland, April 2019.

CityNews. 2009. "Famous Kurdish Singer Claims OPP Used Excessive Force During Highway Takedown." August 18, 2009. https://toronto.citynews.ca/2009/08/18/famous-kurdish-singer-claims-opp-used-excessive-force-during-highway-takedown/.

Darwish, Mahmoud. 2007. "The Kurd Has Only the Wind (for Saleem Barakat)." In *The Butterfly's Burden*, 313–19. Port Townsend, Washington: Copper Canyon Press.

Film Sufi. 2008. "'Half Moon'—Bahman Ghobadi (2006)." November 2, 2008. http://www.filmsufi.com/2008/11/half-moon-bahman-ghobadi-2006.html.

Friedman, Jonathan. 1994. *Cultural Identity and Global Processes*. London: SAGE.

Ghosh, Devleena. 2008. "Coda: Eleven Stars over the Last Moments of Andalusia." In *Exile Cultures, Misplaced Identities*, edited by Paul Allatson and Jo McCormack, 277–87. Amsterdam: Rodopi.

Haque, Eve. 2014. "Multiculturalism, Language, and Immigrant Integration." In *The Multiculturalism Question: Debating Identity in 21st Century Canada*, edited by Jack Jedwab, 203–23. Montréal: McGill-Queen's University Press.

Hasmath, Reza, ed. 2011. *Managing Ethnic Diversity: Meanings and Practices from an International Perspective*. Burlington, VT, and Surrey, UK: Ashgate.

Hely Deng. 2020. "Sharakam." YouTube, January 17, 2020, 5:55. https://www.youtube.com/watch?v=0owFaIUj814.

Karlsson, Helena. 2003. "Politics, Gender, and Genre-the Kurds and 'the West': Writings from Prison by Leyla Zana." *Journal of Women's History* 15, no. 3 (Autumn): 158–60.

Kocar, Suncem. 2013. "'Rhino Season Is in Exile, Just like Me' an Interview with Bahman Ghobadi." *Anthropology of the Contemporary Middle East and Central Eurasia* 1 (1): 74–79.

Kurdish Academy. n.d. "Abdulla Pashew." Accessed December 29, 2023. http://kurdishacademy.org/wp/abdulla-pashew/.

Meiselas, Susan. 1997. *Kurdistan: In the Shadow of History*. New York: Random House.

Petrou, Michael. 2016. "Out of Iraq's Ashes, Kurdistan Grows." *Open Canada*, June 22, 2016. https://www.opencanada.org/features/out-iraqs-ashes-kurdistan-grows/.

Pugliese, David. 2016. "The 'Ripple Effect': Canada's Support for the Kurds Brings Unintended Consequences." *Ottawa Citizen*, February 5, 2016. https://ottawacitizen.com/news/politics/the-ripple-effect-canadas-support-for-the-kurds-brings-unintended-consequences.

Qubadî, Behmen, dir. 2000. *A Time for Drunken Horses*. New York: Kino Lorber.

Qubadî, Behmen, dir. 2006. *Half Moon*. Culver City, CA: Strand Home Video.

Reitz, Jeffery G. 2014. "Multiculturalism Policies and Popular Multiculturalism in the Development of Canadian Immigration." In *The Multiculturalism Question: Debating Identity in 21st Century Canada*, edited by Jack Jedwab, 107–26. Montréal: McGill-Queen's University Press.

Said, Edward. 2000. "Reflections on Exile." In *Reflections on Exile and Other Essays*, by Edward Said, 173–86. Cambridge, MA: Harvard University Press.

Segall, Kimberly Wedeven. 2013. "Radio Songs, Kurdish Stories, Videos: Politics of Healing After Ethnic Cleansing." In *Performing Democracy in Iraq and South Africa: Gender, Media and Resistance*, by Kimberly Wedeven Segall, 1–29. New York: Syracuse University Press.

Sheyholislami, Jaffer. 2011. *Kurdish Identity, Discourse, and New Media*. New York: Palgrave.

Smith, Andrew. 2004. "Migrancy, Hybridity, and Postcolonial Literary Studies." In *The Cambridge Companion to Postcolonial Literary Studies*, edited by Neil Lazarus, 241–61. Cambridge: Cambridge University Press.

Subtitled Turkish Songs. 2017. "How Can You Know?" YouTube, April 14, 2017, 5:57. https://www.youtube.com/watch?v=soXj85HzhBk.

Tax, Meredith. 2016. *A Road Unforeseen: Women Fight the Islamic State*. New York: Bellevue Literary Press.

Tribeca News. n.d. "Tribeca Tribute: Bahman Ghobadi." Last modified December 19, 2007. https://www.tribecafilm.com/news/512c0dd81c7d76d9a90005f8-tribeca-tribute-bahman-gh.

United Kurdish Forces. 2008. "Sivan Perwer—Kine Em—with Translation, Mit Übersetzung." YouTube, September 12, 2008, 7:25. https://www.youtube.com/watch?v=M5wtlIaMseQ.

Wahab, Abdurrahman. 2019. "Kurdish-Canadian Identity and the Intricacies of Acculturation." *Journal of Ethnic & Cultural Studies* 6, no. 2 (August): 94–104.

Waissi, Hama Aziz. 2015. "I Am Kurdistan." Unpublished poem.

15 How Can Music Ameliorate Displacement, Disconnection, and Dehumanization?

Michael Frishkopf

How can music ameliorate refugee crises of displacement, disconnection, and dehumanization? What can ethnomusicology—the study of music in its socio-cultural context—contribute toward formulating effective musical interventions? Certainly, neither music nor ethnomusicology springs to mind as a first response to such crises. Essential needs for security, shelter, nutrition, and sanitation demand precedence, whether refugees are in transit, in refugee camps, or in more stable host societies. But neither is music a pure luxury, to be deferred to some distant future moment when physiological needs have been met, or to be enjoyed only by those who have clambered to the summit of Maslow's famous pyramid (1943).

Rather, evidence from refugee experiences suggests that once essential needs have been even partially satisfied, music and related performance arts (dance, theatre, storytelling, oral poetry[1]) spontaneously emerge as a powerful

---

1 Taxonomies (even in science) are always cultural constructions, and the performing arts are no exception. The definition of "music" as an independent "art of sound" is not present in many cultures; for instance, in most West African ethnolinguistic groups, music, poetry, and dance are traditionally inseparable ("music" per se being a colonial imposition). Therefore, in this chapter, I interpret "music" broadly to include all allied expressive arts and "musical participation" to include all roles, from playing or singing to toe tapping, akin to Christopher Small's generalized idea of "musicking" (Small 1998).

social technology for rehumanization, solidarity, and meaningful intersubjective connection (Frishkopf 2018; Frishkopf, Morgan, and Knight 2010; La Rue 1993; Reyes 1999; Schmidt et al. 2018; A. R. Schramm 1986, 1989, 1990; K. Schramm 2000; Arts Research Network, n.d.; Gonzales 2017).

As Dwight Conquergood writes in an article about Hmong refugees in Thailand's Ban Vinai refugee camp,

> Camp Ban Vinai may lack many things—water, housing, sewage disposal system—but not performance. The Camp is an embarrassment of riches in terms of cultural performance. No matter where you go in the camp, at almost any hour of the day or night, you can simultaneously hear two or three performances, from simple storytelling and folksinging to the elaborate collective ritual performances for the dead that orchestrate multiple media, including drumming, stylized lamentation, ritual chanting. [. . .] Performance permeates the fabric of everyday life in Ban Vinai. (1988, 176)

He goes on to remark,

> A high level of cultural performance is characteristic of refugee camps in general. Since my work in Ban Vinai I have visited or lived for short periods of time in 11 refugee camps in Southeast Asia and the Middle East, not counting a shantytown for displaced people in Nigeria.
> In every one of them I was struck by the richness and frequency of performative expression. One explanation for this is that refugees have a lot of time on their hands to cultivate expressive traditions. But I think there are deeper psychological and cultural reasons for the high incidence of performance in the camps. Refugee camps are liminal zones where people displaced by trauma and crisis—usually war or famine—must try to regroup and salvage what is left of their lives. (1988, 176, 180)

Regrouping is key and a primary function for arts-based socialization; refugee communities typically comprise a heterogeneous mix of social classes and ethnic groups who would not ordinarily interact. Music and performing arts indeed have the capacity to link refugees not only to one another but also to their host societies and to their homelands, respectively empowering the refugee community, catalyzing social integration with a host community, and maintaining personal identity, spinning intersubjective threads to weave a new social fabric, comprising resonant, resilient, affective connections across these cultural boundaries (Frishkopf 2022, 79).

By enhancing empathetic, affective communication, music provides a development function toward well-being, not simply for refugees, but for everyone: music for global human development, toward the development of the global human (Frishkopf 2022, 84). As Paulo Freire emphasizes, *everyone* is dehumanized by oppression, oppressor and oppressed alike—though he believes it is up to the oppressed to "wage for both the struggle for a fuller humanity" (2000, 47, 56). Through *transcultural music*—deliberately crossing and thereby critiquing and undermining artificial cultural divisions (putatively symbolic but actually ideological)[2]—refugees and hosts alike develop their humanity, individually and dialectically, across the artificial system-induced boundaries masking our humanity from one another.

Music naturally supports regrouping, emerging bottom-up to heal disconnections, though not necessarily quickly or even for the better, since enhancing empathy in one group can trigger (or even depend on) dehumanizing another. Carefully planned musical interventions help avoid such social pathologies. Here, ethnomusicology—the study of music in its socio-cultural context—provides valuable guidance, particularly in its applied, activist forms (Rice 2014; Pettan and Titon 2016; Harrison, Mackinlay, and Pettan 2010; Diamond and Castelo-Branco 2021).

In a method I call "Music for Global Human Development" (M4GHD), applied ethnomusicology can purposefully guide this "aesthetic technology" toward effective, sustainable, rehumanizing interventions (Frishkopf 2021, 2022).

---

2 The concept of "transcultural music" is inspired by the ideas of Fernando Ortiz, which underlie my conclusion that cultural "boundaries" (and the very idea of "culture" as a countable noun) are contemporary constructions, invariably artificial, perspectival, situational, and ultimately ideological in nature. They are liable to freighting with differential values—generating competition and conflict, which is often dehumanizing—and always distort humanity's underlying unity (Cuccioletta 2001; Ortiz 1947).

Humanization, Rehumanization, and Social Transitions

Humanization is the process of recognizing the other as a human being in an intersubjective space, a "transcultural" endeavour of recognizing the self in the other, a subject like oneself, constructing a collective "we," transcending putative boundaries (whether of race, ethnicity, religion, nation-state, or other markers) underpinning the pernicious tribalism mutilating humanity's underlying unity. Within a suitable environment, given sufficient cognitive and emotional communication, we quite naturally come to recognize one another as humans like ourselves and act accordingly, treating one another as subjects, not objects, ends rather than means, in a principle both philosophy (Kant's categorical imperative) and theology (the Golden Rule) have theorized as the basis for all ethical behaviour.

Crucial to this communicative process is a phenomenon I term *resonance*, requiring flexible communication proceeding in both directions, thereby enabling mutual adaptation, by which communicating individuals—whether in dyads or larger groups—converge in a connected emotional, affective space, becoming aware of their collective participation and the commonalities generated or revealed by such communicative processes. While cognitive communication is not unimportant, it is the more ineffable process of affective communication, toward what I call "common feeling" (Frishkopf 2010, 22; 2022, 78), that is of overriding significance in the generation of resonance. Such collective performance presents a form of "plural reflexivity, the ways in which a group or community seeks to portray, understand, and then act on itself" (Turner 1979, 465).

What impedes this process, particularly in the case of forced migration, is attenuated affective communication, an absence that may be exacerbated by linguistic difference, socio-cultural difference, visible difference, or sheer distance. For refugee populations cohabiting with a host population, physical distance may evaporate, but other differences persist. Here is where the resonant "common feeling" of shared musical experience can make its mark.

But let us begin by considering (re)humanization in the context of more "ordinary" life processes in a cultural steady state. Humanization unfolds first of all, and most unremarkably, following the birth of a human being into a stable social context. The unborn is not yet an independent human being—and in many cultures, neither is the newborn—until humanity is formally recognized, often conferred through a naming ceremony (Alford 1988).

The infant then enters a coherent, stable web of connections (relationships with family, friends, community), linking to others who recognize her or him as a subject, increasingly so as the baby grows and communicates, affectively and with the acquisition of language.

This infantile process of humanization repeats as what might be called "rehumanization" during life cycle transitions from one social category to another, when old connections are broken and new ones created, via formal "rites de passage" (Gennep 1960), rituals entailing a process of separation, liminal transition, and reincorporation. Each such ritual (e.g., marriage) precipitates a shift into a new, culturally recognized social status accompanied by social and often spatial movement (e.g., the bride's transfer to the husband's home in cases of patrilocality). Such movements may transform or sever old relationships, and call for new ones, in a process of rehumanization, through the spinning of new threads: resonant connections.

Sometimes, multiple relations are jeopardized all at once: the crisis of the "social drama" and its four phases of separation (breach, crisis) and resolution (redress and integration or schism), as theorized by Victor Turner (1980, 149). Both ritual transition and social drama can be viewed as forms of movement in physical, social, or cultural space, straining human connections, sometimes to the breaking point, and spinning new ones, ensuring that the individual remains safely ensconced in a humanizing web of intersubjective relationships. What is the place of music in fostering such (re)humanization? While most cultural anthropologists attending to the intensive interactions of ritual and social drama do not dwell on music, music nearly always appears in their ethnographic accounts. Ethnomusicologists fill this gap, focusing on music's many roles in expressing or catalyzing socio-cultural transformations.

But beyond these theatrical moments of transformation, at the individual or social level, rehumanization is also required in more prosaic processes of resocialization following the migrations that increasingly characterize the modern world, whether intranational economic displacements from a rural to an urban environment, or overseas to another country. Music takes its functional place in such instances as well, solidifying the new collectivities that form in order to effect smooth transitions, performed in church, school, or community groups (Avorgbedor 1992; Manuel 1995). Music is performed by funeral associations in Greater Accra, serving to bind and integrate a diverse group of rural immigrants (Frishkopf 1989), and by nation-based but heterogeneous community associations in Edmonton during their annual celebration of Canadian multiculturalism in a secular rite called the Edmonton Heritage Festival (Heritagefest, n.d.).

In each case, social connections are strained, even broken, as a result of movement in physical and social space—but, subsequently, new ones form, catalyzed by the mass-emotional power of participatory performing arts, centered on music and dance, which also help maintain cultural connections to the homeland (and thus to one's past and social identity), as well as weaving interstitial connections to the host society. The social bonds of intersubjectivity are constantly being reformulated alongside such transformations, whether individual or collective, and while each case is unique, music always provides the same generalized functions: to bind the displaced together, to integrate them with their new environments, and to tether them to their individual pasts.

Music: Transcultural Meaningfulness, Connection, and Resonance

From the Romantic period came an oft-heard refrain: "Music is the true universal language," as Schopenhauer announced in 1851, and many others preceded or followed him in a claim that has echoed to the present day (Longfellow 1861, 357; Clarke 1855, 322; Schopenhauer 1851, 162; Gottlieb 2019; Mehr et al. 2019). According to this view, while no language is universally understood, everyone understands music, the language of feeling.

Even before the field was formalized in the 1950s, ethnomusicology was quick to negate such a broad claim based on ethnographic studies of music cultures around the world (Seeger 1941), as anticipated by a few earlier writers (Jacques 1888); more recently, such a view has been reinforced by big data analysis (Daley 2018; Panteli, Benetos, and Dixon 2017). "Musical sound and meaning are cultural," declares a primary ethnomusicological postulate, and as culture is diverse, so are sound and meaning. Following anthropological colleagues in conceiving "culture" as a countable noun, a separable world of meaning, and a discrete, well-bounded "object" that can be classified (Human Relations Area Files, n.d.; Lomax, Erickson, and American Association for the Advancement of Science 1968), musical meaning is, likewise, held to be highly variable. Further, only ethnographic fieldwork can reveal music's particular meaning for its users in each "world of music" (Titon 2009). Universalism was out; relativism in.

Yet there is a sense in which the Romantics were right. Music is a universal language, even if its sounds are diverse and its meaning is highly variable. Music is a language—but one that does not "communicate meaning," at least in the ordinary sense of "communicate" as error-free transmission and "meaning" as reference (Cherry 1966). Meanwhile, "culture" was never a countable noun, compartmentalized into closed, mutually incomprehensible worlds—and certainly not in the contemporary reality of globalized flows (Appadurai 1996). Increasingly, culture is borderless, an uncountable noun like water—a global landscape rather than a discrete set of closed worlds. Unlike language, "culture," considered broadly to include all systems of non-referential signs, presents no impassable boundaries of comprehensibility, only gradients of change, steeper or shallower, but never absolute—though to affirm borderlessness is not to unreservedly affirm universality either.

Rather, what is universal about an utterance in a non-referential "language" like music (and the same would hold of other non-referential systems such as clothing, food, or kinship relations) is not meaning but *meaningfulness*; what is expressed, transmitted, and ultimately communicated is not a fixed meaning as reference but a fluid semantic potential, imprinted as a mental state, along with an awareness of meaningful communicative intent, and a feeling (short of provable certainty) that one is sensing what the "sender" intended, even if that is not the case.

For sound, such meaningfulness is particularly intimate, since music—according to composer and sound theorist Murray Schafer—constitutes a form of "remote touching," passing from the tactile to the acoustic at around 20 hertz (Schafer 1994, 11). Music also represents an acoustic and auditory extrusion of the self, the projection of a personal voice carried far beyond the body's physical boundaries. While each voice remains deeply anchored in a human performer, multiple voices interpenetrate and fuse in a resultant soundscape.

Such collective communication of meaningfulness is not the mere perception of possible meaning (as when we hear someone speaking in a language we do not understand, knowing meaning must be present but not receiving it) but actual meaning, formulated first in the sender and subsequently in the hearer. The problem with the linguistic analogy is that such meaning is not necessarily the same on both sides; this is not a communicative process in the ordinary technical sense. Indeed, with music, what we receive is always other than what was sent, even when sender and receiver (assuming boundaries could be drawn) belong to the "same culture." Yet a bond is nevertheless established in the process, via individual meaning coupled with an affective awareness of mutual meaningfulness, the analogue to Michael Chwe's "common knowledge" (2001) that I call "common feeling."

Indeed, this individualization of musical meaning, while retaining a sense of connection, is an important source of music's social power. Music needn't mean the same thing to all participants in its processes; it is connective because it is universally meaningful.

Musical behaviour, in its generalized sense, includes sound, movement, gesture, facial expression, and poetic verbalization, whether produced by "musician," "singer," "dancer," or "listener" (and the distinction is not always clear). Defined in this way, the space of musical participation is broad. Thus construed, music is naturally a mass medium, from the perspectives of both sender and receiver, "broadcast" (whether live or through synchronous or asynchronous media channels—radio, CDs) from and to the many in an act of collective participation (unlike speech, which, with the exception of ritual chant—which is actually closer to music—flows from one to one or one to many).

From the standpoint of the group, musical connection fosters resilience because it tends to link all participants, everyone to everyone—what the social network analyst calls a "clique" (Wasserman and Faust 1994, 254)—at least in principle. The resulting network is "robust": its overall connectedness is maintained, even if a few links do not form or are lost. From the standpoint of the individual, affective links are resilient because they cannot be weakened or even contradicted by the introduction of new information—they are pliable, unlike the brittle connections resting upon cognitive consensus (political or religious views, say), which are vulnerable to disagreement. By contrast, music is not subject to argumentation; as Maurice Bloch quips, "You cannot argue with a song" (1974, 71). Music thus weaves an extensive resilient web of participation, flexibly linking the participating group, yet without requiring semantic unanimity, unlike ordinary speech (but analogous to poetry, which thus stands as metaphor of, as well as being embedded in, music per se).

Such music-induced bonds drawing people together through meaningfulness intensify when music circulates among a group of active participants, creating feedback loops shaped by but also shaping participants' internal mental states, moving them (though not in the same way) and moving them together.

If the patterns of such generalized musical communication are furthermore flexible enough to adapt to such exchanges, intensifying its effects through continuous and dynamic adjustments on the part of each participant, a state I call "resonance"—by analogy to the resonant frequencies of acoustical cavities—may emerge, capable of catalyzing new social bonds or reinvigorating extant ones. Such a process, and its resulting state, is approximately equivalent to what Durkheim calls "collective effervescence," as in his famous description of a "corroboree" performed by Australian "Aborigines":

> The very act of congregating is an exceptionally powerful stimulant. Once the individuals are gathered together, a sort of electricity is generated from their closeness and quickly launches them to an extraordinary height of exaltation. Every emotion expressed resonates without interference in consciousnesses that are wide open to external impressions, each one echoing the others. The initial impulse is thereby amplified each time it is echoed, like an avalanche that grows as it goes along. (1976, 217–18)

To what extent is non-referential meaning actually shared? It varies. In traditional settings, such as this Indigenous one, perhaps to a greater degree, carried perhaps most overtly through lyrics and contextual references, as well as sedimentation of indexical meaning (Turino 1999) accruing from past performances, though even here the idiosyncrasies of music as a non-referential art form enable a great deal of individual interpretation, particularly due to sedimented memories. Thus, a young participant can hardly experience the same emotions as an aged one, who has attended the corroboree many times in the past, associating it with long-gone eras and people.

But the same process works when music is performed transculturally: meaning is projected from the performer, even as it changes in transit, arriving in a new form. Everyone wrings meaning from music, though each in their own way; all understand that some musical meaning has been sent and received, alongside a rational awareness that these may not be the same and an affective sense that they are. Again, there is no universal meaning but rather universal meaningfulness and an understanding of that shared meaningfulness resulting in a sense of empathetic connection enabling a diverse and far-flung connective tissue to form. When music is distributed through a network (whether in a public performance or via the media), this network extends through a potentially heterogeneous assortment of participants, who are thereby linked together in intersubjective relationships of common feeling.

This power of music to induce "common feeling" even across putative linguistic and cultural boundaries is amplified by basic properties of sonic (unlike visual) performance: rapid mass diffusion of sound waves outward in three dimensions, audio diffraction (passing around obstacles), masking (blocking competing dyadic communications), and carrying of paralinguistic information conveying expressive affect.

To summarize: I propose that music (re)humanizes by establishing and maintaining intersubjective connections among participants in a process of musical semiosis generating common feeling; this process is intensified through fuller participation, the formation of feedback loops, and flexibility in the musical system itself, conditions leading to a state of socio-affective "resonance," the ephemeral dissolution of interpersonal boundaries, and an intensive shared feeling underlying the construction of a collective "we."

When these intersubjective connections can be sustained also by durable social bonds lying beyond the boundaries of musical performance (resulting, for instance, from shared membership in a church or community group), the sense of a humanized collectivity can likewise endure, recharged by each subsequent performance, when existing bonds are reinfused with sustaining affective energies, and new ones are created. Resonance may occur to varying degrees and with variable impact, but the process is the same: moving participants (individually) and moving them together (socially).

Transcultural Music for Global Human Development: (Re)humanization After Displacement

In all societies, music's resonant power to catalyze and maintain human connections emerges naturally, requiring neither plan nor planner, adapting to social, cultural, and natural environments. Such music functions alongside the more prosaic, universal communicative form of language throughout human societies, becoming more essential during moments of individual or collective transition, when intersubjective connections require protection, maintenance, or reformulation, whether in life cycle rituals, social dramas, or other social movements, as outlined earlier in this chapter. Music and musical resonance play prominent roles in restoring equilibrium, maintaining homeostasis by mending and spinning social threads. At times of transition, music appears to revitalize solidarity or reweave the social fabric.

These musical roles transpire within the lifeworld of lived experience and meaning, traditionally in balance with the abstract structures of the system, lying beyond direct experience, but instantiated in a set of political and economic positions, connections, and institutions that help coordinate the lifeworld and provide continuity from one generation to the next. In such a mutualistic relation, the system serves the lifeworld, opening the possibility for larger collectivities, typified by an interdependent division of labour and what Durkheim calls "organic" solidarity.

But in keeping with Durkheim's structural functionalism, it could be argued that in modern times, social pathologies have begun to proliferate, signals that the lifeworld and system are wildly out of balance, indeed tending toward a parasitic relationship, whereby the system "colonizes" the lifeworld, as Habermas describes it, increasingly coming to mediate all human relationships in an inexorable quest to accumulate money and power, ultimately destroying the lifeworld (and hence itself) as the outcome of this unsustainable process (Habermas 1984, 2:325).

The system's positions are intrinsically dehumanized and therefore impose dehumanization on the subjects inhabiting them, as well as dehumanizing induced connections mediated by the system. Within the system context, they become merely interconnected objects, communicating to support the system's maximization of its steering values: money and power. In conditions of system-lifeworld balance, such dehumanized relationships exist in parallel with richer intersubjective ones, placing a moderating brake on system tendencies. But when the system comes to thoroughly colonize the lifeworld, it induces a pervasive dehumanization there as well, leading to the negation of basic human rights, socio-economic injustice, and massive inequality, all completely incompatible with humanized intersubjective relationships.

What I call "big problems" are those resulting from these large-scale social pathologies, triggered by an increasingly rapacious, violent global system, dehumanizing all and everything in its path toward the accumulation of money and power. Such problems are today occurring on an unprecedented scale, with unprecedented frequency, requiring explicitly targeted and carefully calibrated interventions.

For instance, so long as relations between rich and poor countries are mediated by the current system of politics unmitigated by any intersubjective fabric, the majority of citizens of the former will feel little compassion for those of the latter, who—in the absence of other humanizing factors—remain as faceless objects, dehumanized citizens of a foreign nation-state. The same considerations apply to the corporate elite's exploitation of the working classes, their illegal dumping of toxic waste on poorer nations' shores, or their pursuit of corporate profit even at the cost of irreversible, catastrophic environmental damage. Political oppression (surveillance, incarceration, even torture and executions), economic exploitation (even slavery), environmental plunder, war, famine, economic collapse, xenophobia and racism, and even genocide are the tragic results. All these eventualities induce forced migration, displacing people who become refugees, travelling, even at great risk, in search of safety and a better life elsewhere.

Indeed, "big problems" are doubly intertwined with refugees: first, as triggers of forced migrations, and, second, as consequences of social and cultural dislocations that trigger personal, economic, and food insecurities alongside xenophobia—often outright racism—as well as a denial of life's essentials as a consequence of dehumanization, rather than actual scarcity.

The rapid displacements triggered by such social upheavals leave little time for emergent music making of the sort that might mend rifts in the social fabric under more ordinary conditions. Thus, in such cases, a more deliberate, intentional musical intervention is required—the type that can be prepared by a suitably trained, experienced applied ethnomusicologist, who helps guide, focus, and accelerate an inclusive and sustainable process of music-induced healing by introducing and nurturing socio-musical resonance toward rehumanization.

For this purpose, the ideal methodology is participatory action research (PAR; Fals-Borda 2005; Kemmis and McTaggart 2005), promoting full participation by members of the displaced group, who are best positioned to design and guide a successful, sustainable intervention. Such participation renders musical action both more effective and more ethical. In PAR, the intervention process is itself humanized, since the relationships comprising the intervention are themselves instances of the kinds of intersubjectivities such an approach aims to foster. Successful PAR projects spiral upward, from planning to acting, observing, and reflecting, then back to planning, each new round a refinement of the previous, informed by past results, which are the subject of research.

I call such PAR-powered musical interventions "Music for Global Human Development" (Frishkopf 2015, 2021, 2022), defined as a form of participatory applied ethnomusicology in which a diverse, global project team, well-knit through humanized relationships, deploys transcultural music, capable of interconnecting across vast cultural and social divides, both to promote a humanized response to "big problems" of development and to foster the development of the "global human."

Once again, the threat of dehumanization may appear in three contexts of forced migration: among refugees (often diverse in ethnicity and class; sometimes in conflict due to civil war or scarce resources), between refugees and host societies along the migration path, and between refugees and their homelands, receding into the distance (particularly for those born in diaspora) and jeopardizing an existential prerequisite—continuity of the self.

In each context, performing arts–based modalities can serve to effectively weave or repair the social fabric.[3] In particular, musical interventions—fostering resonant connections—operate in each context, assuming three essentially different directions and modalities, fostering three forms of transcultural rehumanization. First, resonance connects refugees to one another, creating social solidarity—whether in an ephemeral camp, in transit, or in a safe haven host society—despite cultural differences, and generating the empowerment required for collective action necessary to (re)gain human rights in new social contexts. Second, resonance connects refugees to the host society, weaving a new transcultural social fabric, toward a social integration avoiding the extremes of both assimilation and balkanized "multiculturalism." Rather, this fabric undergirds intersubjective understanding, across putative "cultural boundaries," a humanized recognition of the "other" as "self" and "self" as "other," toward a fuller humanity for both the newcomer and the host, as per Freire. Third, resonance within the self, between its own present and perceived past, helps maintain a felt connection to the culture of the homeland, extending a lifeline of belonging to a place of origin (Walker 2003), thus maintaining identity and self-worth—and the existentially critical continuity of the self (M. Freire 1989, 57).

At the same time, it must be stressed that the arts are not a panacea or even an unmitigated good when it comes to countering social differentiation and dehumanization. Tracing the boundaries of conflict, resonance can exacerbate division and even promote dehumanization. For instance,

---

3 Alternatives to performing arts exist in the literature—for example, Camia and Zafar's (2021) research on autobiographical life narratives. See Barzanji in this volume.

in 2022, Russian president Vladimir Putin organized a musical concert featuring the Russian band Lyube performing patriotic songs, as the nucleus for a massive pro-war rally, mustering support for war crimes in Ukraine (Pavlova, John, and Graham-Yooll 2022). While reports suggest that many participants were coerced into attendance, here musical resonance is arguably responsible—albeit indirectly—for the forced migration of millions of Ukrainian refugees. Nationalistic music has often been deployed in this way to promote violence, aggression, and hate.

Resonance is thus revealed as a neutral force. Left to its "natural" emergent forms in times of social drama, musical humanization may serve to bolster in-group solidarity at the cost of dehumanizing outsiders. However, carefully formulated as an ethical ethnomusicological intervention, the musical arts can help restore humanity and reweave the social fabric across boundaries.

* * *

Finally, I illustrate the above arguments with three relevant examples of humanizing ethnomusicological interventions in the M4GHD mould. I conclude this chapter with a brief description of "Giving Voice to Hope," a PAR collaboration between the University of Alberta and Liberian refugees, then living in the Buduburam camp, near Accra, Ghana. The following chapter centers on the role of music for an African artist in exile the legendary Zimbabwean musician and political activist Dr. Thomas Mapfumo. A third chapter introduces a concert featuring refugee musicians from Iraq and Syria, who performed with professors from the University of Alberta's Department of Music, in the public event—also featuring Dr. Mapfumo—inaugurating the conference that led to this book, thus closing the circle.

Liberian Refugees in Ghana

The Buduburam Liberian refugee camp, designed to accommodate eight thousand refugees from Liberia's civil conflict, was packed with some forty thousand people when I first visited in 2007. I was in Ghana on an inaugural study abroad program of my own design, centered on the ethnomusicology of West Africa (Frishkopf 2012). One of my students, Eilis Pourbaix, had previously volunteered at a camp NGO (the Center for Youth Empowerment, CYE) and linked me to its director, Slabe Sennay, himself a refugee. Together, we began thinking about ways we could formulate a PAR ethnomusicological intervention involving musicians and students to help support refugees. Slabe introduced us to the camp's extraordinarily vibrant musical life.

Despite a minimal standard of living—overcrowded, insect-infested dwellings, frequent electrical outages, and lack of basic sanitation—music scenes miraculously flourished, both live (especially in church) and mediated. A few popular musicians even produced music in their own camp studios. Many songs expressed war's horrific impact and hopes for peace while critiquing power and corruption. The camp's musical life appeared to help generate solidarity, bringing residents together, uplifting the refugees, and ameliorating despair.

Once we discovered the popular music scene and met a few musicians, a path forward appeared. Musicians and CYE, along with University of Alberta students, staff, and faculty, joined together in a PAR network to produce an album, *Giving Voice to Hope*, featuring sixteen musical groups in the camp. We added extensive liner notes, telescoping from historical context to camp life and including biographies of the musicians based on interviews (GVTH 2009). Together, we aimed to support musicians both symbolically—by raising their international profiles—and financially, generating needed royalty income just around the time they were beginning to return to Liberia. The project also helped "musicify" and hence humanize camp life, generating hope for refugees and awareness of their predicament in North America, where so many Liberians ultimately settled. Following the PAR methodology, the project subsequently spiralled forward into several subsequent initiatives in Ghana and Liberia that have continued, in different ways, to the present (Morgan and Frishkopf 2011; Frishkopf and Morgan 2013b, 2013a; Frishkopf 2017; 2022, 88).

References

Alford, Richard D. 1988. *Naming and Identity: A Cross-Cultural Study of Personal Naming Practices.* New Haven, CT: HRAF Press.
Appadurai, Arjun. 1996. *Modernity at Large: Cultural Dimensions of Globalization.* Minneapolis: University of Minnesota Press.
Arts Research Network. n.d. "Giving Voice to Hope: Music of Liberian Refugees." University of Alberta, Wiki. Accessed August 14, 2016. https://www.artsrn

.ualberta.ca/fwa_mediawiki/index.php?title=Giving_Voice_to_Hope:_Music_of _Liberian_Refugees.

Avorgbedor, Daniel K. 1992. "The Impact of Rural-Urban Migration on a Village Music Culture: Some Implications for Applied Ethnomusicology." *African Music* 7 (2): 45–57.

Bloch, Maurice. 1974. "Symbols, Song, Dance and Features of Articulation: Is Religion an Extreme Form of Traditional Authority?" *European Journal of Sociology* 15 (01): 54–81.

Camia, Christin, and Rida Zafar. 2021. "Autobiographical Meaning Making Protects the Sense of Self-Continuity past Forced Migration." *Frontiers in Psychology* 12 (February): 618343. https://doi.org/10.3389/fpsyg.2021.618343.

Cherry, Colin. 1966. *On Human Communication: A Review, a Survey, and a Criticism*. Cambridge: MIT Press.

Chwe, Michael Suk-Young. 2001. *Rational Ritual Culture, Coordination, and Common Knowledge*. Princeton, NJ: Princeton University Press.

Clarke, Mary Cowden. 1855. "Music Among the Poets and Poetical Writers (Continued)." *Musical Times and Singing Class Circular* 6 (140): 322. https://doi.org/10.2307/3370895.

Conquergood, Dwight. 1988. "Health Theatre in a Hmong Refugee Camp: Performance, Communication, and Culture." *TDR (1988–)* 32 (3): 174–208.

Cuccioletta, Donald. 2001. "Multiculturalism or Transculturalism: Towards a Cosmopolitan Citizenship." *London Journal of Canadian Studies* 17:1–11.

Daley, Jason. 2018. "Big Data Traces the World's Most Distinctive Musical Traditions." *Smithsonian Magazine*, January 4, 2018. https://www.smithsonianmag.com/smart-news/big-data-reveals-worlds-most-distinctive-musical-traditions-180967685/.

Diamond, Beverley, and Salwa El-Shawan Castelo-Branco. 2021. *Transforming Ethnomusicology*. Vols. 1 and 2. New York: Oxford University Press.

Durkheim, Émile. 1976. *The Elementary Forms of the Religious Life*. New York: Free Press.

Fals-Borda, Orlando. 2005. "Participatory Action Research." In *Fundamentals of Action Research*, edited by Bill Cooke and Julie Wolfram Cox, 3–9. Vol. 2. London: SAGE.

Freire, Marlinda. 1989. "Latin American Refugees: Adjustment and Adaptation." *Canadian Woman Studies*, April 1, 1989. http://cws.journals.yorku.ca/index.php/cws/article/view/11313.

Freire, Paulo. 2000. *Pedagogy of the Oppressed*. New York: Continuum.

Frishkopf, Michael. 1989. "The Character of Eve Performance." Master's thesis, Tufts University. Department of Music.

Frishkopf, Michael. 2010. "Music and Media in the Arab World and 'Music and Media in the Arab World' as Music and Media in the Arab World: A Metadiscourse." In *Music and Media in the Arab World*, edited by Michael Frishkopf, 1–66. Cairo and New York: American University in Cairo Press.

Frishkopf, Michael. 2012. "Study African Arts and Culture in Ghana." Arts Research Network, University of Alberta, Wiki, 2012. http://bit.ly/ghanamusic.

Frishkopf, Michael. 2015. "Music for Global Human Development." Arts Research Network, University of Alberta, Wiki, 2015. http://m4ghd.org.

Frishkopf, Michael. 2017. "Popular Music as Public Health Technology: Music for Global Human Development and 'Giving Voice to Health' in Liberia." *Journal of Folklore Research* 54 (1–2): 41–86.

Frishkopf, Michael. 2018. "Music for Global Human Development, and Refugees." *Ethnomusicology* 63 (2): 279–314.

Frishkopf, Michael. 2021. "Music for Global Human Development." In *Transforming Ethnomusicology*, edited by Beverley Diamond and Salwa El-Shawan Castelo-Branco, 2:47–66. New York: Oxford University Press.

Frishkopf, Michael. 2022. "Music for Global Human Development: Participatory Action Research for Health and Wellbeing." *MUSICultures* 49:71–109.

Frishkopf, Michael, and Samuel Morgan. 2013a. "Giving Voice to Health: Sanitation and Safe Water—Music for Social Justice in Liberia." Playful Porpoise. YouTube, June 8, 2013, 4:55. http://www.youtube.com/watch?v=AmCk4WHPfSU&feature=youtube_gdata_player.

Frishkopf, Michael, and Samuel Morgan. 2013b. "Giving Voice to Health: Sanitation and Safe Water in Liberia Documentary." Playful Porpoise. YouTube, November 14, 2013, 10:58. http://www.youtube.com/watch?v=5eDal4NaYbw&feature=youtube_gdata_player.

Frishkopf, Michael, Samuel Morgan, and W. Andy Knight. 2010. "Sustainable Peacebuilding Through Popular Music in the Buduburam Refugee Camp: Interdisciplinary Perspectives on R2P from Political Science, Ethnomusicology, and Music." Presented at Pop Culture and World Politics 3, York University, Toronto. http://yciss.info.yorku.ca/files/2012/06/PCWP3_program_oct291.pdf.

Gennep, Arnold van. 1960. *The Rites of Passage*. Translated by Monika B. Vizedom and Gabrielle L. Caffee. Chicago: University of Chicago Press.

Gonzales, Giulia. 2017. "Displacement and Belonging: Musical Consumption and Production Among Malian Kel Tamasheq Refugees in Burkina Faso." *St Antony's International Review* 12 (2): 89–113.

Gottlieb, Jed. 2019. "New Harvard Study Says Music Is Universal Language." *Harvard Gazette* (blog). November 21, 2019. https://news.harvard.edu/gazette/story/2019/11/new-harvard-study-establishes-music-is-universal/.

GVTH. 2009. *Giving Voice to Hope*. Edmonton: University of Alberta. http://bit.ly/buducd.
Habermas, Jürgen. 1984. *The Theory of Communicative Action*. Vol. 2. Boston: Beacon.
Harrison, Klisala, Elizabeth Mackinlay, and Svanibor Pettan. 2010. *Applied Ethnomusicology: Historical and Contemporary Approaches*. Newcastle upon Tyne: Cambridge Scholars.
Heritagefest. n.d. "Edmonton Heritage Festival." Accessed March 20, 2022. https://www.heritagefest.ca.
Human Relations Area Files. n.d. Human Relations Area Files: Cultural Information for Education and Research (website). Accessed January 14, 2019. http://hraf.yale.edu/.
Jacques, Edgar F. 1888. "The Laws of Progress in Music." *Proceedings of the Musical Association* 15:109–31.
Kemmis, Stephen, and Robin McTaggart. 2005. "Participatory Action Research." In *The SAGE Handbook of Qualitative Research*, edited by Norman K Denzin and Yvonna S Lincoln, 559–603. Thousand Oaks, CA: SAGE.
La Rue, H. 1993. "Music and Forced Migration Vol. 32(3) of the World of Music (Guest Editor Adelaida Reyes Schramm)." *Journal of Refugee Studies* 6 (1): 81.
Lomax, Alan, Edwin E. Erickson, and American Association for the Advancement of Science. 1968. *Folk Song Style and Culture*. Washington, DC: American Association for the Advancement of Science.
Longfellow, Henry Wadsworth. 1861. *The Prose Works of Henry Wadsworth Longfellow*. London: W. Kent.
Manuel, Peter. 1995. "Music as Symbol, Music as Simulacrum: Postmodern, Pre-Modern, and Modern Aesthetics in Subcultural Popular Musics." *Popular Music* 14 (2): 227–39.
Maslow, A. H. 1943. "A Theory of Human Motivation." *Psychological Review* 50 (4): 370–96.
Mehr, Samuel A., Manvir Singh, Dean Knox, Daniel M. Ketter, Daniel Pickens-Jones, S. Atwood, Christopher Lucas, et al. 2019. "Universality and Diversity in Human Song." *Science* 366 (6468): eaax0868. https://doi.org/10.1126/science.aax0868.
Morgan, Samuel, and Michael Frishkopf. 2011. "Shadow and Music in the Buduburam Liberian Refugee Camp of Ghana." Michael Frishkopf. Vimeo, February 16, 2011. http://vimeo.com/20009721.
Ortiz, Fernando. 1947. *Cuban Counterpoint: Tobacco and Sugar*. Translated from the Spanish by Harriet de Onís. Introduction by Bronislaw Malinowski. Prologue by Herminio Portell Vilá. New York: A. A. Knopf.

Panteli, Maria, Emmanouil Benetos, and Simon Dixon. 2017. "A Computational Study on Outliers in World Music." *PLoS ONE* 12 (12): e0189399. https://doi.org/10.1371/journal.pone.0189399.

Pavlova, Uliana, Tara John, and Anastasia Graham-Yooll. 2022. "Putin Celebrates Crimea Annexation at Stadium Rally amid Russia's Onslaught of Ukraine." CNN, March 18, 2022. https://www.cnn.com/2022/03/18/europe/russia-putin-ukraine-invasion-rally-intl/index.html.

Pettan, Svanibor, and Jeff Todd Titon. 2016. *The Oxford Handbook of Applied Ethnomusicology*. Oxford: Oxford University Press. http://dx.doi.org/10.1093/oxfordhb/9780199351701.001.0001.

Reyes, Adelaida. 1999. *Songs of the Caged, Songs of the Free: Music and the Vietnamese Refugee Experience*. Philadelphia: Temple University Press.

Rice, Timothy. 2014. *Ethnomusicology: A Very Short Introduction*. New York: Oxford University Press.

Schafer, R. Murray. 1994. *The Soundscape: Our Sonic Environment and the Tuning of the World*. Rochester, VT: Destiny Books.

Schmidt, Cynthia Meersohn, Paulina Osorio-Parraguez, Adriana Espinoza, and Pamela Reyes. 2018. "After the Earthquake: Narratives of Resilience, Re-signification of Fear and Revitalisation of Local Identities in Rural Communities of Paredones, Chile." In *Resilience and Ageing*, edited by Anna Goulding, Bruce Davenport, and Andrew Newman, 111–28. 1st ed. Creativity, Culture and Community. Bristol: Bristol University Press. http://www.jstor.org/stable/j.ctv8xnhxv.11.

Schopenhauer, Arthur. 1851. *Essays and Aphorisms*. Translated by R. J. Hollingdale. Harmondsworth: Penguin. http://archive.org/details/essaysaphorismsooscho.

Schramm, Adelaida Reyes. 1986. "Tradition in the Guise of Innovation: Music Among a Refugee Population." *Yearbook for Traditional Music* 18:91–101.

Schramm, Adelaida Reyes. 1989. "Music and Tradition: From Native to Adopted Land Through the Refugee Experience." *Yearbook for Traditional Music* 21:25–35. https://doi.org/10.2307/767766.

Schramm, Adelaida Reyes. 1990. "Music and the Refugee Experience." *World of Music* 32 (3): 3–21.

Schramm, Katharina. 2000. "The Politics of Dance: Changing Representations of the Nation in Ghana." *Afrika Spectrum: Deutsche Zeitschrift Für Moderne Afrikaforschung* 35 (3): 339–58.

Seeger, Charles. 1941. "Inter-American Relations in the Field of Music." *Music Educators Journal* 27 (5): 17–65. https://doi.org/10.2307/3385965.

Small, Christopher. 1998. *Musicking: The Meanings of Performing and Listening*. Hanover: University Press of New England.

Titon, Jeff. 2009. *Worlds of Music: An Introduction to the Music of the World's Peoples*. 5th ed. Belmont, CA: Schirmer Cengage Learning.

Turino, Thomas. 1999. "Signs of Imagination, Identity, and Experience: A Peircian Semiotic Theory for Music." *Ethnomusicology* 43 (2): 221–55. https://doi.org/10.2307/852734.

Turner, Victor. 1979. "Frame, Flow and Reflection: Ritual and Drama as Public Liminality." *Japanese Journal of Religious Studies* 6 (4): 465–99.

Turner, Victor. 1980. "Social Dramas and Stories About Them." *Critical Inquiry* 7 (1): 141–68.

Walker, Denis B. 2003. "The Displaced Self: The Experience of Atopia and the Recollection of Place." *Mosaic: An Interdisciplinary Critical Journal* 36 (1): 21–33.

Wasserman, Stanley, and Katherine Faust. 1994. *Social Network Analysis: Methods and Applications*. 1st ed. Cambridge: Cambridge University Press.

16 Music, Weapon of Change, Weapon of Peace

Thomas Mapfumo, Chimurenga, and the Power of Music in Exile

Thomas Mapfumo, Chiedza Chikawa, and Michael Frishkopf

Introduction by Michael Frishkopf

Artists who embody local music—popular or traditional—are more deeply rooted in their homelands than nearly anyone else. Particularly when they achieve renown, they are richly connected to and sustained by the local. They are culturally connected and sustained through music; they are socially connected and sustained through fans and musical colleagues. They depend on these connections, this complexly woven web, not only for their livelihoods but for their core identities. They cannot uproot and emigrate the way engineers and doctors do, seeking greater prosperity abroad in nearly identical positions. No such alternatives exist for the localized artist. Social and cultural connections, as well as economic interests, restrain them. Abroad, they may find a diasporic audience, but it is not the same. Similar constraints apply to social activists engaged in grassroots struggles for liberation or social justice, whose lives are enmeshed with a local context, with momentous contemporary events and social movements. Dr. Thomas Mapfumo, renowned artist and activist, is thus doubly rooted in his homeland of Zimbabwe.[1]

---

1 In 2001, Mapfumo was awarded an honorary doctor of music degree in recognition of his songs of liberation (Ohio University 2001; Eyre 2015, ch. 14).

Yet music also enables the spinning of new social threads, the weaving of a new socio-cultural fabric, one that can sustain the artist-activist, even far from home. This is particularly true for African music, already deeply woven into popular musics around the world, especially in the Americas. Nearly all North American, Caribbean, and Latin American popular music has roots in African music: blues, rock, jazz, R & B, soul, reggae, hip hop, and salsa. Furthermore, African music's North American transformations returned to Africa via artists as diverse as Dizzy Gillespie, Bob Marley, Elvis Presley, and James Brown through tours, recordings, and radio in the past—and internet in the present. For African immigrants to North America, in particular, a firm musical basis for the weaving and reweaving of social fabrics—connecting to one another, to the wider host society, and to the homeland—is already in place.

I fell for Chimurenga, Dr. Mapfumo's revolutionary Zimbabwean music, as soon as I heard it, in a graduate school course surveying popular music of Africa. Love at first listen. Like many ethnomusicologists, I had been drawn to African lamellophone traditions, with their intricate interlocking melodies, cyclic polyrhythms, and dulcet metallic tones, particularly the large *mbira dzavadzimu* (*mbira* of the ancestors) of Zimbabwe, used in Shona spirit ceremonies, accompanied by the steady swing of the *hosho* rattle, both instruments supporting a captivating yodelling vocal style. I eagerly read Paul Berliner's ([1978] 2007) famous book, *The Soul of Mbira*, about Shona musical traditions and purchased an *mbira dzavadzimu* from the celebrated performer Ephat Mujuru. I was equally fascinated by the amazingly polyphonic guitar styles of urban Africa, particularly Soukous and Congolese rumba.

Mapfumo's songs drew on both. His soft, deep voice flowed over cyclic forms, buoyed by guitar lines drawing upon the extraordinary polyphonies, polyrhythms, and inherent melodies of traditional Shona *mbira* music, as well as popular guitar styles of southern Africa. On some tunes, the band even incorporated the traditional instruments—*mbira* and *hosho*—or compositions, such as Nhemamusasa, adapted as "Chitima Nditakure (Train Carry Me)" (Brown 1994; Eyre 2015; Nonesuch Explorer Series 1973). And yet these were contemporary songs addressing social issues, inducing connections in this world, not in the world of spirits.

Our paths crossed again when I attended a live performance of his celebrated band, the Blacks Unlimited, at the Middle East Restaurant in Cambridge, Massachusetts, around 1994—though, of course, I did not meet him. Many years later, when I was co-producing the *Giving Voice to Hope* CD (GVTH 2009; see chapter 15), I mulled over which international musician I might approach to provide an endorsement. I knew I'd never reach Western superstar philanthropists like Sting and Bono of Live Aid fame. Then I remembered Mapfumo and reached out through his agent. Thomas kindly responded with a pithy phrase highlighting the power of music for social change: "Music is the best weapon to bring change and also bring peace to the world. I and the Blacks Unlimited wish these musicians in Buduburam refugee camp all the best in their endeavours." We proudly featured his inspiring words on the CD's back cover.

Thomas Mapfumo, also known as Mukanya and the Lion of Zimbabwe, is a living legend: for nearly fifty years, one of that country's most celebrated popular singers and activists, unwaveringly committed to uplifting his people. His music—sung in Shona and sometimes English, a musical blend of local Shona musical rhythms, melodies, and instruments and African and international guitar-band styles (themselves inspired in part by African American musics, infused in turn by African music)—is "the music that made Zimbabwe," as writer Banning Eyre (2015) subtitles his authorized biography. Mapfumo's incendiary songs inspired the fighters who ultimately overthrew the white regime of Rhodesia in 1980, and he was jailed for a time. Undeterred, he continued his musical struggle for freedom and good governance. Despite initial optimism following independence in 1980, many Zimbabweans left their country, as it fell prey to tyrannical rule and a collapsing economy. Mapfumo stayed on, dedicated to his art, his cause, and his people. Despite threats and harassment, his music continued to critique power, this time the increasingly corrupt, partisan regime led by Robert Mugabe.

Mapfumo called this music "Chimurenga" ("struggle"), referring first to the 1890s Shona uprisings, then to the 1970s liberation struggle (Eyre 2015, 5). It is a music expressing the thread of his personal lifeworld. Born and raised in rural Zimbabwe, immersed in Shona traditions, he moved to a Harare suburb, Mbare, where he attended school. Later, he travelled abroad—to southern Africa, then (through musical tours) around the world. Throughout his varied musical career, he has struggled mightily for his people, for the poor and oppressed. Rooted in the popular guitar styles of southern Africa, moulded by the traditional musical elements of the indigenous Shona, his music, fuelled at its core by compassion, helped humanize the downtrodden people of his country; give voice to their suffering; liberate them from oppressive governments, white and Black alike, locally, regionally, and globally; and galvanize solidarity.

Thomas Mapfumo is thus deeply connected to his homeland both as a locally rooted musician and as a social activist—a musical icon, a legend, an inspiration, a political force—uncompromisingly, unremittingly committed to his people. And yet, following increasing harassment from the Mugabe regime, he too finally chose exile. For the sake of his family's well-being, he left his beloved country in 2000, settling them in the leafy, artsy college town of Eugene, Oregon, where he has remained.[2] Perhaps no two places on earth could be more different.

How did he cope with this transition, far from the socio-musical connections that had supported him? Music continued to sustain him, albeit in new ways, through new connections. His musical and political stature provided recognition and official asylum. He brought family and many band members along and connected to musicians in the United States while maintaining his connections to Zimbabwe through new musical releases and media. His fame (including prior tours) allowed him to quickly establish himself in the North American scene, playing African, fusion, and world music festivals and catalyzing a new set of socio-musical connections around himself. He performed for the local Eugene community (e.g., Mapfumo 2011) while connecting to the wider North American musical scenes, which he'd long admired, through festivals and collaborations (Piotrowski 2019; Toombs 2008; Music Sumo 2002). As someone who grew up playing rock 'n' roll covers, he was intimately familiar with American music and could adapt, blending languages and styles, while his Chimurenga style became immensely popular among non-Zimbabweans.

His music helped interconnect the Zimbabwean diaspora through performances and collaborations with artists such as dancer and choreographer Nora Chipaumire (Chipaumire, Mapfumo, and the Blacks Unlimited 2009). He also wove new connections to American artists like avant-garde trumpeter Wadada Leo Smith, with whom he recorded an album in Eugene (Piotrowski 2019; Leo Smith and Mapfumo 2020; *Dreams and Secrets* 2001).

During Mugabe's waning days, Mapfumo toured North America, galvanizing the diaspora with a speaking and performing tour. Encouraging political action, he undoubtedly hastened (albeit indirectly) Mugabe's fall in

---

2 The University of Oregon is located in Eugene.

2017. Mapfumo's power inheres not merely in his songs, whether their lyrics are overtly political or have simply accrued political meaning through the uptake of Shona traditional musical symbols (Turino 1999, 246), but also more directly in his personal charisma and social influence as a revered cultural figure, so closely intertwined with his music.

Despite all the years of listening to that music, I only had the opportunity to witness his leadership—as a revolutionary musician and champion of his people—first-hand when he visited Edmonton in 2016, one stop on that tour. At last, I had the opportunity to meet him face to face, at the Massawa Café in downtown Edmonton. A small group had gathered there, mainly Zimbabweans. We were treated to a performance by a local Zimbabwean band called Mbira Renaissance, after which Mapfumo gave a lengthy but impromptu speech in Shona. Of course, I could not understand his words, but I got his message anyway; his passion shone through his resonant vocal rumble. I knew that he was visiting not to sing but to gather support for political change in Zimbabwe. He appeared at two other events in town during that weekend trip. Two months later, he returned to Edmonton to play a sold-out concert to a largely Zimbabwean expatriate audience. Through music and speech, as a performer and political activist, Mapfumo not only called for a "new Zimbabwe"; he called it into being. Less than a year later, on November 21, 2017, Mugabe finally resigned, ending a thirty-seven-year tyrannical rule.

No musician could be more deeply wound into his country's modern history. Mapfumo was forced to leave his beloved people of Zimbabwe because of his music. But equally, it was his music that sustained him in exile. Indeed, Mapfumo's music is all about weaving social connections. Once asked in a TV interview about whether he sings love songs, he replied,

> It is good to sing about love [. . .] but sing about the important love. [. . .] We have had enough conflict in this world. There's no use in trying to sing about love between two people. [. . .] The love that I am talking about is the love amongst the people. [. . .] We have to love each other. [. . .] Let's sing about the love between the people of different races [. . .] that is a very important issue. Because there is no love amongst the people. (Mega Video Zimbabwe 2020)

Through the dense weave of his music, his bands, and his audiences, crisscrossing all manner of socio-cultural boundaries, Dr. Thomas Mapfumo has indeed created "love amongst the people."

In the following sections, we present Mapfumo in his own words in three parts:[3] first, his life story as he recounted it during our 2020 conference event, "Transpositions"; next, a follow-up interview by myself; and, third, an interview conducted by his daughter Chiedza Chikawa (which she kindly translated from Shona to English). Both interviews were recorded and transcribed. I conclude with an important moment in my conversations with Chiedza and a poignant song of exile. Links to audio and video examples are provided in the references section, and my explanatory comments are in footnote annotations.

Thomas Mapfumo's Conference Address, February 6, 2020

Hello, everybody. My name is Thomas Mapfumo. My friends call me Mukanya.[4] Mukanya is my totem. I was born in the rural areas of Zimbabwe. I was a herd boy, herding cattle, goats, and donkeys. I spent seven years in the rural areas, where I grew up with my granddad and my grandma.[5] Those are the people who actually looked after me when I was a boy. I learned a lot of things when I was living in the country. The music that I am playing today is the music that I learned in the country. As a herd boy, I had instruments that we used to communicate as herd boys. When we would go out there to herd cattle and goats, we used to play traditional instruments to communicate with the other herd boys.

I started going to school in 1954, in the rural area, where I did my Sub A. After seven years in the rural areas, my parents called me to come and join them in the city, where I did my Sub B.[6] I was at John Brooke school for Sub B, Standard One, Standard Two, Three, Four, and Five. Then I moved on to Mbare; they used to call that place "National." I went to Chitsere School for Standard Six.

Then I went to Zambia to join my friend Naboth, who was also a musician. I lived with my friend, and we were playing a lot of music together. I wasn't a star at that time. After some time, I left Zambia and went back to

---

3 The oral texts are condensed and lightly edited for readability.
4 The praise name of his Shona clan.
5 According to biographers, he lived in the town of Marondera.
6 Rhodesia's education system began with Sub A and Sub B, followed by Standards 1–5, corresponding to what were later considered grades 1–7, respectively.

Zimbabwe—Rhodesia at that time. I joined a band called the Springfields. The Springfields were a rock 'n' roll outfit. They used to play music by Elvis Presley, Cliff Richard—music from all the rock 'n' roll stars of that time. I used to sing rock 'n' roll music too. I enjoyed Elvis Presley; he was my idol. I loved everything that he used to do on the stage. I was into rock 'n' roll music.

As time went on, I was into a lot of different types of music. I did rumba music from the Congo by Franco.[7] I thought he was a great artist, and I liked his style of rumba. He was really good.

That time was during the colonial era. We were living under bondage; our people were not free. Our people decided to fight for their freedom, and they went out to get trained. A lot of youngsters left the country to go and get friends, and they came back fighting the white regime. They were living in the bush.

That's the time that I started thinking about my own identity. I started thinking, Where do I come from, who am I, what am I supposed to be? That alone made me change. I started thinking of my own identity, thinking of my own people. They were suffering. Well, that brought something to my mind. I had to change—I had to look for my identity. And the only thing that I had to do like a musician was to actually play the music of my own people—the music that I grew up with in the country.

When I started doing this music, that's when the Chimurenga war broke out,[8] and I decided to name my music Chimurenga music.

I recorded a lot of songs opposing the white regime, and that got me arrested by the regime. I was arrested, and I was sent to detention for three months. I was there for three months. They kept sending a plainclothes policeman to interrogate me. Sometimes, they would come with a lot of singles, and some of these singles were not even mine. They said, "You are singing about politics." I said, "No! My music is not political. This is the music of my people, the music of my ancestors."

---

7 François Luambo Luanzo Makiadi (1938–89), one of southern Africa's most influential popular musicians.

8 The Second Chimurenga (revolutionary struggle) was a civil conflict from July 1964 to December 1979 in Rhodesia involving three forces: the Rhodesian white minority government; the Zimbabwe African National Liberation Army, led by Robert Mugabe's Zimbabwe African National Union (ZANU); and the Zimbabwe People's Revolutionary Army.

So I stayed in detention for three months. After three months, they decided to let me go on condition that I had to go to Bulawayo to go and play for Bishop Muzorewa, where there was a rally.[9] When I got out, I went straight home, and I contacted the other band members. They came to my place. We sat down and talked about this show for the Muzorewa rally, which was going to happen in Bulawayo. Some of my band members didn't want to go there, but I told them, "Look, we are just musicians; we don't have guns to defend ourselves, so we have to go to Bulawayo and play our music."

When we went to Bulawayo, we were still playing the same songs, the revolutionary songs that I had been arrested for. People were asking questions—why we were still playing the same songs. I said I didn't have time to compose songs for this occasion. They understood what I said to them. After that, we were the only band that was supporting the liberation struggle in the country, and when these guys in from the bush heard that Thomas Mapfumo had played at Bishop Muzorewa's rally, they thought I had sold out. But no, I hadn't sold out! My songs were still the same. The messages within my songs were still the same. I was still singing about the freedom of my people.

So a lot of people didn't want to come to our shows. We sometimes had big flops. People didn't want to come. But we never changed; we kept singing the same songs. We just wanted to show them that we were still freedom fighters. In the end, they started coming back to our shows. They realized that they had actually made a very big mistake.

When Mugabe became president, we all went wild.[10] We thought, "Oh, the country was free, and our people were free now." Everybody was rejoicing. We thought everything was going to be rosy. We had won the war, and the Black people were now in power.

---

9 For several months in 1979, Bishop Abel Tendekayi Muzorewa (1925–2010) served as the prime minister of what was then called Zimbabwe Rhodesia. He opposed armed revolutionary struggle and was viewed by some Blacks as a collaborator of the white regime.

10 In 1980, Robert Mugabe, the leader of ZANU, became the prime minister of independent Zimbabwe. Subsequently, he served as the president from 1987 to 2017 and as the leader of the ZANU–Patriotic Front (ZANU–PF), a merger of ZANU with the Zimbabwe African People's Union.

Well, we were wrong, because after eight years of independence, we started noticing corruption, and that made me compose a song, "Corruption."[11] From there, some of them were asking me a lot of questions: Why am I singing about corruption? I said, "Well, the government has got a lot of corrupt people." Some of the ministers were corrupt; the president was also very corrupt.

Yesterday, I sang against oppression by the white people, and today, the man who is in the forefront is our man, a Black man like me, and he is also corrupt. I can't take that! I can never take that, and I won't even look at the colour of your skin. What you do to the people, how you treat your people, how you see them—you understand? If you are a leader, you are not a leader of a certain political party. You are a leader of the people, even those who don't like you; you are still their leader. So you must show the qualities of good leadership.

This is what is lacking in Zimbabwe today. Today, people are still crying, and it's almost forty years. I don't know where we are because our people are suffering. They are suffering. I was there for the last four months; after I was there, I could see a lot of youngsters. They've been turned into beggars, moving up and down the streets looking, begging for money, begging for food. That's not the way our people should live. We need good leadership; we don't need a corrupt government, people who are stealing from their own people. That's a disgrace; it is a disgrace, and the world should be talking about this.

We always listen; we always watch the news. On CNN, they don't talk about Zimbabwe. BBC doesn't talk about Zimbabwe. You forget there are people there, who are supposed to be human. The world is not doing anything for the Zimbabwean people. They are suffering; the people of Zimbabwe are suffering. They need your help. They need your help. There is no democracy in Zimbabwe, no freedom of speech in Zimbabwe, no freedom of movement in Zimbabwe. If you criticize the president, you are going to be arrested in Zimbabwe.

I don't know whether you know about that. Most of you don't know about that because you don't hear any news from Zimbabwe.

---

11 "I'll give you something / That is if you give me something in return / That is the slogan of today / Meaning corruption in the society" (Mapfumo 1988).

Michael Frishkopf's Interview with Thomas Mapfumo, July 24, 2020

MF: Can you tell me about your experience leaving Zimbabwe, coming to live in the USA with your family?[12] Why did you leave? What was the role of music in that move for you?

TM: I think music played a very big role for me when I left Zimbabwe with the rest of my family. My brothers are also here with their families. I didn't want to leave Zimbabwe. Even my wife always talks about that. I didn't want to come to live here, but then when we talked about our future and our children . . . when we look back at the situation in Zimbabwe, we thought it was the right thing to be here. We just wanted our children to finish their education where they have freedom, so we thought the United States was a good place.

I was known all over the world. The US government actually knew who I was. They read about me and my biography; they knew exactly what I stood for. I didn't want to be involved with the government that is there today in Zimbabwe. I fought in my music, played a very big role during the liberation struggle, and we supported these people. My music inspired a lot of young people to get out of the country, be trained, and come back. A lot of youngsters were inspired by my music.

When they took over, we started noticing that after eight years, there was corruption within the people who were working with the government, and that's what made me compose the song "Corruption." Some government officials didn't like this song because they knew what I was talking about, and a lot of people never realized what I was trying to tell them, but at last, they realized.

They thought I was a supporter of Robert Mugabe. I wasn't a supporter of Robert Mugabe; I was a supporter of the people. I stood by the people, and that's where I am today. I'm not going to abandon the people. My freedom and the freedom of my

---

12 In 2000, Mapfumo moved with his family to Eugene, Oregon, returning to Zimbabwe for concerts until 2004 (Eyre 2015).

people cannot be separated. I don't care whether I have money or I don't have money.

MF: So through music, you were able to keep that connection to your people, even though you were in Oregon?

TM: Yeah, that's very true.

MF: How did that work? You weren't able to visit, but you were able to send your music or . . .

TM: I went back sometimes.

MF: I think a year ago?

TM: Yes, I actually played a very big concert in the stadium.[13]

MF: But that was after Mugabe stepped down?

TM: Yeah, after Mugabe stepped down. A lot of people came—it was filled to capacity.

MF: So, obviously, you were able to maintain your audience throughout the period you were away. How were people getting your music? Were they getting new music, or were they listening to the old music?

TM: You know, my music is sold online, and whoever wants to buy my music can get my music online.

MF: So you were continuing to address your people even though you were far, far away?

TM: That's what I do always. Sometimes, I had interviews with radio stations in the UK and also Zimbabwe News.[14] I'm always telling people to keep focusing; they have to fight for their freedom because freedom doesn't come on a silver plate. If you don't stand up for your rights, no one will ever do that for you. At the end of the day, it's the people who actually have the power.

MF: What about Zimbabweans in the USA? When you moved, did you start to connect with the community there, either in Oregon or somewhere else?

---

13 Saturday, April 28, 2018, at Glamis Stadium in Harare, with some twenty thousand fans of three generations in attendance (Eyre 2018; BBC News 2018).

14 Mapfumo has been interviewed many times since taking up residence in the United States, both in mainstream Western media and specifically for Zimbabwean audiences (NPR 2015; Mega Video Zimbabwe 2020; Nehanda TV 2016).

TM: Well, I speak to a lot of people here because I always talk to a lot of people. Right now, I've been on the phone with someone in Ohio who represents the MDC Alliance,[15] and we have been discussing the problems that the people are facing at home. They are supposed to demonstrate on the thirty-first of this month, so we are encouraging people to get out in big numbers—get out there and protest. If they want to be free, this is the only way to do it.

MF: What about in the States? Are people there also demonstrating in support?

TM: That's right. I've been on the phone with a member of the MDC Alliance and with a lady activist; they are organizing that.

MF: In Oregon or across the country?

TM: Across the country.

MF: And would music play a role in those demonstrations? Your songs or some other kinds of songs?

TM: Of course; we have a Twitter account, so every song that I wrote during the liberation struggle and some songs that are my latest music, we are actually posting them on my Twitter.

MF: Oh great.

TM: Yes.

MF: So in the actual demonstration, do you ever perform a concert in the US that gathers people together?

TM: Yeah. We can always do one online,[16] so that's the one we want to arrange right now.

MF: Do you have a large following among non-Zimbabweans?

TM: Yes, I do.

MF: I heard you back in the early nineties in a club in Cambridge, Massachusetts, called the Middle East Restaurant. I don't know if you remember. That was probably twenty-five years ago.

TM: I know!

---

15 Movement for Democratic Change Alliance, a coalition of political parties united with the Movement for Democratic Change, formed in 1999 to oppose the ZANU-PF.

16 Due to COVID restrictions, a live concert was not possible at this time.

MF: So who are the musicians you have worked with since coming to the US? Did you work with some musicians who are not from Zimbabwe?

TM: Yeah, I've worked with a lot of different people here; there's a young lady, Stormy—I did a song ("Music") with her. She's an African American. Another white girl—I did a song, "Shabeen," with her. She has a very good voice.[17]

MF: Who's been in the band over the years since you moved to the US?

TM: Gilbert Christopher, myself, and Chaka, and we have a drummer, he's white, from Arizona: Eddie.

MF: And the others are Zimbabweans?

TM: The rest are Zimbabweans.

MF: In the songs that you did with the African American and the white lady, were you crossing into different styles with those?

TM: You know, I just love to write any kind of music. Yeah, this was a different style, but you know, that was me, and that's what I do. I'm not specializing in Zimbabwean music only. When I started music, I played a lot of other people's music, like I was into the Beatles, the Rolling Stones . . .

MF: So since you came to the US, did you develop some new musical directions or styles?

TM: No, but I always listen. If I happen to come up with a different tune, I just have to write it down, yes.

MF: Did you ever do anything, for example, with jazz or R & B?

TM: I love Frank Sinatra and also Sam Cooke. I used to follow all those guys; I was into every type of music. I just love good music. I listen to everything, even dancehall, that is all new styles from Jamaica. Bob Marley was my idol.

---

17 In 2012, Mapfumo worked with an LA-based DJ, Charlie B. Wilder, to add new beats to his sound and subsequently released *Danger Zone*, containing several English-language songs directed to a Western audience, most of them produced by keyboard player Fernando Bispo, from Track Town Records in Eugene, where Mapfumo recorded (see Drop in Films 2015). Both the new song "Music" (featuring singer Stormy) and a remix of his older "Shabeen" (featuring singer Natalia Rollins, a.k.a. Moxie, with his daughter Chiedza on backup vocals) appear on this album (*Herald* 2014).

MF: Were there other Zimbabweans who felt they had to leave the country because of political persecution and came to the USA?

TM: A lot of them. We cannot name them by their names, but a lot of them are here.

MF: I imagine that your music would be an inspiration and a hope for them to keep in touch with their culture and their identity.

TM: That's really true, yeah.[18]

MF: So where did your tours take you? I'm sure you've had a lot of tours across the US since moving here.

TM: Yeah, yeah! I know every part of the United States [*laughs*]. I started coming here in 1994, before I moved.

MF: And then since you moved here, you've been touring also?

TM: Yeah, every year. Right now, we were supposed to go to Australia, but because of COVID-19, we're just waiting.

MF: Where would you normally play on your US tours? What sorts of venues?

TM: Most of the time, we used to come here for festivals. And we played a lot of universities, yes.

MF: Which festivals did you play?

TM: I played the Grassroots Festival; also the Reggae on the River; the Chicago Festival, I played there several times; and also Yoshi in California, Triple Door in Seattle, House of Blues—we played that. I've lost count of them.[19]

---

18 Mapfumo collaborated with another Zimbabwean exile, the acclaimed contemporary dancer and choreographer Nora Chipaumire, in a live performance program at Chicago's Museum of Contemporary Art: "Living as exiles in an increasingly globalized world, Nora and Thomas unpack the experience of the migrant, using their impassioned voices to speak about living as Africans in an increasingly borderless world" (Chipaumire, Mapfumo, and the Blacks Unlimited 2009). Chipaumire herself spoke movingly about this collaboration: "I empathize with other Zimbabweans who are dislocated, and who are dislocated not out of personal choice, and the sort of situation, the trauma, that condition of being the other in a hostile environment redefines, makes you understand again who you are" (651 ARTS 2010). Mapfumo also provided music for the film about Chipaumire's life (Hinton and Kovgan 2008).

19 I located the following festivals and club dates for Thomas Mapfumo based on this interview: Yoshi's (2007), House of Blues (2002), Chicago Festival (?), Reggae on the

MF: And what sort of audience did you get? I mean, who would come?

TM: A lot of white people. They really support us; they give us that inspiration. They give us the support we've been looking for, and we thank them very, very much because, I mean, that's our culture, so if they can appreciate our culture, that's a good thing for us.[20]

MF: Do they tend to be younger?

TM: Young and old.

MF: And for many of them, do you think that was the first exposure they had to music from Zimbabwe?

TM: Some of them have been listening to South African music, and Zimbabwean music is almost the same, so it's not a new thing to them.

MF: I know also in Seattle, there was a very big traditional music scene with the *mbira*.

TM: Yes.

MF: There was an *mbira* player who was invited there; he had a lot of students: Dumisani Maraire.

TM: Oh, Dumisani Maraire? I just did something with his son. His son is a rapper.[21] I edited something on his music.

MF: You're in Eugene. Is there a lot of interest there too?

TM: There's a lot of interest. Yeah, there are even a lot of white people who are trying to play the *mbira* instrument.

MF: Yeah, like me! I love it, but I'm a beginner.

TM: All right, keep playing!

MF: Thank you, thank you so much. Take care.

TM: Bye-bye.

MF: Bye-bye.

River (1992), Grassroots (2012), Live 8 (2005), Triple Door (2008), Ashkenaz (2017), Central Park Summerstage (2004), Black Arts Fest (2020), and Summer Soulstice (2013).

20 Chiedza later confirmed that the festival audiences she saw were largely white.

21 His son goes by the stage name Draze (https://thedrazeexperience.com/).

Chiedza Chikawa's Interview with Her Father, Thomas Mapfumo

Part 1—December 2020

CC: When you relocated to America, how did you connect with American society, specifically Eugene, through your music?[22]

TM: We always came here on tour, so for us to get to Eugene, it was due to the touring we did. We toured around the United States; that is how we got to Eugene and met people like Mr. Green.[23]

CC: When you started living in Eugene, did you connect to the Eugene community—you know, connecting with the people of Eugene?

TM: Yes, a lot of them.

CC: How did you connect with them?

TM: We were well known, so the moment they knew that we had settled in Eugene, they wrote about it in the local papers.

CC: Usually, you were with the band; you were always with the band, so you didn't socialize too much with the local Eugene community unless you were playing locally at places like the WOW Hall.[24]

TM: That is right.

CC: Was the Eugene community supportive of you?

TM: Yes, very much. They were really supportive.

CC: When you moved to America, how did you stay connected to the community of Zimbabwe? Now that you lived in America, how did you connect?

---

22 The recorded phone interview was conducted in Shona in December 2020, with a follow-up in January 2021. Chiedza Chikawa kindly transcribed the interview and translated it from Shona.

23 Al Green was an American musician who lived in Eugene and became Mapfumo's manager (Eyre 2015, ch. 13).

24 WOW Hall is a prominent and historic music venue in Eugene where Mapfumo has performed (Mapfumo 2011).

TM: These are modern times; we connected with phones and through music. We connect through music, internet, and social media.

CC: But you are very involved with the things that happen at home (Zimbabwe)—politics and, you know, social awareness on issues at home. Now that you were here, how did you stay connected? Plus, how did you stay connected with your fans who were in Zimbabwe after moving to Eugene?

TM: We spoke on the phone.

CC: Who told you about the things that were happening at home?

TM: We saw some stuff on the news; we have modern phones, so we were able to google on our phones to see what was happening.[25]

CC: Did you feel any type of disconnection when you started living in Eugene?

TM: Of course. When you are coming from your homeland, where you are used to, and going to live in another country, it is so different. The feelings are different because now we are far from family, so it's not . . . yes, it's nice that we are living a better life, but at the same time, it is not pleasant because we are so far from our family. That's another thing that pains me a lot.

CC: Did it affect you a lot in the first years after relocating? Especially because you had a large fan base at home—you were like the most popular artist—so for you to leave your fan base at home, you know, coming to live here, I can only imagine how you must have felt in those first few years.

TM: Yes, it is very painful to come into what you call a strange land you don't know much about. Where you are coming from is where your family is, where your everything is. If we were home, we would not be where we are today. We would be well developed if the country were functioning properly. But it set us behind.

CC: Yes.

TM: Yes.

---

25 Chiedza notes that this was not possible in the early 2000s.

CC: Even for you personally, your businesses and everything.

TM: It killed us, even the issues with our money. Nothing went well after that. Money that we had at the Building Society[26]—we just woke up one morning to be told that we had lost our money to inflation.

CC: Yeah, really.

TM: So all the money that we put there, all the money we got from our record sales, that's where we put it. We had a lot of money there, and then you wake up to be told one day that you have lost all your money due to inflation. So who has the problem here? Give us our money back; you are the government.

CC: I don't know.

TM: It's so painful; it really set us back to the point that our lives never recovered.

CC: What kept you hopeful or kept you going afterward? It's depressing, to be honest, to see what happened. But what kept you fighting and moving forward even though, at this point, you had left your home, had left your fan base, and were here in a strange land? What keeps you going and fighting?

TM: I am the type of person who does not give up hope. I keep hoping that it will get better at some point. I trust in my God and my ancestors. It's not my own doing that has gotten me this far, and it's not my cleverness that has gotten me to live this long; it is my God and my ancestors. So those are the two that I put forward in my life. I don't have any power/strength; I cannot say "Tomorrow I will do this and that." Uh-uh. I have to ask my God and my ancestors to guide me so that I may get to see tomorrow.

CC: When you moved, the band—your band—was a big band, and you had a lot of members. Did you ever think that you would keep all the members, or, you know, you ended up finding some local musicians here [in Oregon]. Can you please talk a bit about the changes that have taken place in your band since you moved?

---

26 A Zimbabwean bank-like institution (see Roux and Abel 2017).

TM: Yes, you know, at home, we had enough people. Though a lot of our people left us (passed on and left), we kept on adding people when anyone left in order to replace those who had left. In Zimbabwe, we had a full band, so we felt the burden of leaving and then had to find other people, like Brooks.[27] We were used to having a big band, and we always had a brass section, so we brought people like Brooks who play brass into the band and taught them our music. They didn't even know our music, and now they know Zimbabwean music well.

CC: Where did you find people like Brooks?[28]

TM: We found Brooks in Eugene. I don't remember how . . . Oh, wait—he hung out with that guy who owned Tsunami Books, who also played the saxophone.[29] He now lives in Hawaii.

CC: Oh, okay!

TM: Yes, so he and Brooks used to play together; we met Brooks through him.

CC: And how did you find him?

TM: We were looking for people who would play, and someone introduced him to us. I don't remember who introduced him to us.

CC: So how was it playing with people who were pretty foreign to your type of music—to have to teach them your music and also them not knowing the Zimbabwean culture and not necessarily understanding it?

TM: That is why we say we are one people. Music is music and how you hear it. We also play their type of music too! So music is music. If someone listens to it, they can tell that it's not the

---

27 Jazz trumpeter Brooks Barnett—a University of Oregon graduate, "blond, blue-eyed, and one day shy of his twenty-third birthday" when he played his first gig with the Blacks Unlimited at the House of Blues in Cambridge, Massachusetts (Eyre 2015).

28 From here, Chiedza's interview clearly illuminates the local network enabling Thomas to link to the Eugene environment through music despite radical differences.

29 http://www.tsunamibooks.org/.

same as their type of music, but if you are a musician, you can tell what's good music.[30]

CC: So they really understood your music?

TM: Yes, they understood it.

CC: And then you have people like Paul Prince.[31] Those were the people who were part of your community in Eugene, right?

TM: Yes, that's right.

CC: How did you meet Paul?

TM: We met him here in Eugene.

CC: Did you first meet him on your tours?

TM: Through touring. We met him here while on tour.

CC: So coming here while on tour before moving to settle here helped you settle better because you were a bit familiar with Eugene?

TM: That's right.

CC: After moving to America, you released some albums from here. Did you feel like you were still connecting with the Zimbabweans living in Zimbabwe? Did they connect with your music, or did you feel like it would be better if you were releasing your music from home?

TM: It was much better releasing from home. That's where the majority of our fan base is. Now from here, you release the music and hope it will be sold in Zimbabwe, but then they sell it in the streets. No one is really buying genuine CDs. They now buy the piracy copies, so it doesn't work. Things died, especially music—it's dead in Zimbabwe. There are a lot of little studios where individuals just make their own CDs. All those Zimdancehall artists just make their own studios and make their own CDs.[32]

---

30 This statement is a wonderful encapsulation of Frishkopf's theory of music's universality: not in meaning, but in *meaningfulness*. Understanding entails sensing this capacity for meaning inherent in "good music."

31 Paul Prince is a guitarist and woodworker based in Eugene. He performed a concert at Tsunami Books in 2014 (see Tsunami Books 2014).

32 A popular genre in Zimbabwe combining local music with Jamaican dancehall.

CC: Plus, do you think the issue with your music being banned on the radio affected your connection with people in Zimbabwe, since your music wasn't being played on the radio?

TM: Yes, even today, they don't play it. It affects us a lot. It hurts our livelihood. It's thoughtless because you are hurting my family. That is my farm (where I harvest), so if you are closing doors on me, you are not thinking. Just because I am speaking against you, it does not mean you should shut my resources down. It is not right.

CC: So how do you think people heard your music, with it being banned on the radio?

TM: They would just buy it wherever they could find it. Some of it ended up on the streets, with individual people making their own versions and selling them on the streets for less. That killed the music industry. I asked Mr. Sibindi for money from my royalties, as he has not paid me in years. I said give me even $250, and he laughed. He said he doesn't get that much due to piracy.

CC: The story of Zimbabwe is a tough one.

TM: It is very tough. It's very tough. It's not something to play with. Whoever takes power next must correct all these things.

CC: Yes, that's true. So how did you connect with the Zimbabweans who are living in diaspora like you? How did you connect with them through your music?

TM: Since we toured a lot, we would go to some places where there were Zimbabweans. So when they heard that we were living here, they would look for our numbers and call us, and we would see them when we toured.

CC: And how did it make you feel to meet with other Zimbabweans who were in a similar situation as you, knowing that you were all in exile or came to look for a better life?

TM: It hurts a lot. It is not fun. One day, we were playing in England for Zimbabweans. There were so many of them; it was a packed show. We played the song that goes [*singing*] "*kuchema chete nguva dzose, hapana kufara mwana wamai*" (we are crying all the time, there is no happiness).³³ We cried real tears, seeing that all these people fled from poverty, and you know how this life of living in other people's countries is. Their home is their home, and the one that you are used to is yours. It is very sad to see all these people running from Zimbabwe and having to stay in foreign lands.

CC: Yeah, it is sad, and it hurts.

TM: It hurts a lot.

CC: I do not know when it will get better.

TM: I don't know.

CC: Yeah, I don't know either. But how do you feel now knowing that there are a few more Zimbabweans in Eugene because for the longest time, it was just us?

TM: That's family now. The more of us, the better. We get to socialize with one another.

CC: It also helped that you had your brothers with you when you moved, right?

TM: That's right.

CC: And other band members like Uncle Chris and Uncle Gilbert.

TM: Yes.

CC: Okay, I think that's all I got for now. If I come up with any more questions, I will ask you, Dad.

TM: Okay, that sounds good.

Part 2—January 2021

CC: Today, I wanted to talk about culture and how you were able to preserve your culture in a different country that holds a different culture and lifestyle. You have been living in the States for twenty years. How do you manage to preserve your Zimbabwean culture, since it is different from the American culture and you are not around many Zimbabweans?

---

33 Lyrics from the song "Manhungetunge," on the album of the same name (Mapfumo 2002).

TM: Wherever a person is, they don't forget where they came from and their values and lifestyle. Those are things that one preserves, even food—you see that we cook at home because that is part of our culture; we don't go out and buy takeout food a lot. We cook at home. Those are some of the things we value.

CC: How about your children, like me, Tai, and Mati? Well, Mati was so young (three) when we moved here; Tai and I grew up in Zimbabwe and moved here in our teens. What do you think allows us to keep our culture, if you think we have kept the Zimbabwean culture? What do you think has allowed your family to hold on to Zimbabwean culture after all this time? Do you think it's you or something else?

TM: Children see how their parents behave, so that is usually what they follow. They follow what their parents teach them in terms of their values and lifestyle.[34]

CC: Tai and I know the Zimbabwean culture pretty well, but Mati pretty much grew up in the States. Do you think she understands the Zimbabwean culture possibly because she lived with us and heard us speak Shona? Do you think that helps her understand our values and makes her who she is, even though she may be more Americanized, when she is out in the world?

TM: That is true. That is what helps her. She sees through you guys and how you carry yourselves and knows that those are part of her values as well, and she takes that and uses that.

CC: Of all the things you left behind in Zimbabwe, what is that one thing from your culture that you can never let go or that you hold on to so tightly?

---

34 Although Mapfumo doesn't mention music explicitly here, it is clear that his music was always present in his family. It is an ethnomusicological truism to say that music carries its culture, but this statement is singularly true for Mapfumo's music, being intimately connected to traditional Shona culture, to popular Zimbabwean culture, and to the country's entire modern political and social history. By following what their father taught them implicitly through song, Mapfumo's children would have been closely linked to Zimbabwe.

TM: Talking to our ancestors. That is something we always think of. As you can see right now, we are lamenting the issue of your grandfather's [TM's biological father] resting place and how it needs to be fixed so that we make sure that we sort out our stuff. Those are the kinds of things we worry about.

CC: So your ancestors are one of your biggest priorities?

TM: Yes, our ancestors and God. God comes first, then the ancestors come after God.

CC: Last time we spoke, I asked you about how you were able to know what was happening in Zimbabwe after you first left, and you spoke of smart phones. I just wanted to clarify because at that time, there were no smart phones, remember? We still had old phones that were not iPhones. So I wanted to go back to that question and ask about how you were able to get the scoop on what was happening in Zimbabwe.

TM: There were people who called us from home, and they would tell us what was going on. Some stuff we would see on television, like BBC.

CC: So back to the culture and coming to America, I know you left Zimbabwe while Gogo [grandmother] was still alive. Did you talk to her and keep in touch with her when you moved to America? And what did she say about you leaving and not coming back, and how did that make you feel?

TM: She didn't say much about us leaving the country. She knew the issues we faced with the government of Zimbabwe.

CC: But didn't she worry too much that all three of her sons had fled the country?

TM: Of course, it worried her, but there was nothing she could really do because she knew we were trying to survive.

CC: How about your two sisters—how did they feel about you guys leaving?

TM: They were worried, just like our mother was worried.

CC: And then when she (grandma) passed away, I'm sure it pains you that you weren't able to go home and attend her funeral, but how did you deal with it, knowing that you couldn't go home to be there?

TM: It was a very hard day; we lost our mother. We were supposed to be there, but because of the state of things with the country, we couldn't go. We ended up going recently when things got better. But we should have been there at the time, and that pains us a lot.

CC: I know our family in the States got together on that day, but how did you process it all? In Zimbabwe, the community gathers when someone dies, and they cry together. You had your brothers and their families and managed to get together to do something similar. Did that help you a little? Did it help knowing that you had some of your family with you during that difficult time?

TM: Yes, we got together, and we also spoke to the people in Zimbabwe.

CC: Is there anything you regret about coming to America?

TM: The thing that I regret about moving to America is losing everything I worked for in my lifetime. I left everything in Zimbabwe, and I ended up losing it. It was my children's wealth that I had built. We had done a lot, bought properties, and so on, and we lost all that due to the way the country was run. That is not something that pleases me.

CC: Is there anything you hope for in the future, or something you look forward to, or something positive that you would like to see happen?

TM: I would like to see the people of Zimbabwe be free. If those people start living a better life, then we can all be happy. That is the biggest thing. A lot of people are struggling back home. They have been lied to for forty years, being told that they are independent when there is no freedom. It hurts a lot.

CC: What would you say you appreciate about your life in America?

TM: I appreciate the way America is governed because people have a say. People have a voice here in America. You saw what recently happened with Donald Trump. It shows that the people have power.

CC: Okay, well, I think that was my last question, Dad.

TM: Okay, thank you.

CC: Thanks!

Michael Frishkopf's Interview with Chiedza Chikawa, January 2021

After both of us had interviewed her father, I conducted a follow-up interview with Chiedza in order to learn more about her life in Zimbabwe and the United States, as well as to clarify a few points and check names.

We were just about winding up when she told me she wanted to add something very important about cultural preservation that had not arisen throughout our interviews: the role of *music*.

She told me that her father's music played a very important role in maintaining Zimbabwean culture for his children. He writes his own lyrics and expresses the culture in them, she said. His music was always present in their lives. Personally, she loves his music, and her brother, sister, and mother feel the same. "Of course, we're biased," she said, laughing.

Mapfumo grew up in a traditional Shona family, very aware of his musical and cultural roots. His songs carry that feeling because they draw on Shona cultural traditions associated with *mbira* music and carried through the poetry as well. The language of his songs is not ordinary conversational Shona but rather deep Shona, like Shakespearean English. Often, she would have to ask her father what they meant.

This music, then, is what kept them all close to Zimbabwean culture, even in exile. When she got married, her father insisted that she had to perform the traditional Shona rituals. She listens to his music a lot now. Perhaps she didn't appreciate it as much when she was younger, she says, but it was part of everyday life at home in Eugene. Now she's living far away, in Canada. She regularly listens to a playlist of her father's songs, bringing her closer to home. His music is not like that of other artists, she says; it's more spiritual. It contains something that connects her.

Chiedza used to braid her own hair—a process that takes many hours—continuing late into the night. Sometimes at 3 a.m., she would still be braiding, listening to her father's music. Her mother would awaken, join her, and sing along.

Perhaps Chimurenga music itself is a braid—weaving sounds, people, and places.

Song of Exile: "Ndangariro" (Mapfumo 2010)

I conclude with a beautiful, wistful song from Mapfumo's 2010 album *Exile*, encapsulating music's power to weave connections, especially people and places of one's homeland, to evoke their memory for everyone living in exile:

> Sleepless nights thinking about you, Zimbabwe; I lie thinking about the Zimbabwean family; Thoughts trouble me, far away as I am; Family don't mourn me, I'm coming; I am always thinking about family back home; I am always shedding tears father,

> When I remember Zimbabwe
> When I think of Harare
> When I remember Bulawayo
> When I think of Gweru
> When I remember Kwekwe
> When I think of Kadoma
> When I think of my mother back home

> I left her a long time ago; She cries for me; Chimurenga fans, I trust in you; Wherever I go, I go with you; It just takes strength, we will prosper; Dreams and thoughts trouble me,

> When I remember Chegutu
> When I think of Chinhoyi
> When I remember Marondera
> When I think of Rusape
> When I remember Mutare
> When I think of Masvingo

> We greet you all, Zimbabwean family; We say how are you doing; We are coming; I am a child of the ghetto; You know that; My family and friends think about me; Honestly I miss them; I left them a long time ago; Even though I am far away; I don't forget my home; By God's grace, we'll see each other; The thing that pains me are my thoughts,

> When I remember the ghettos
> When I think of Mbare
> When I remember Fiyo

When I think of Mabvuku
When I remember Mufakose
When I think of Chitungwiza

We greet you all, Zimbabwean family
We say how are you doing
We are coming.[35]

Acknowledgements

My heartfelt thanks to Dr. Thomas Mapfumo, his daughter Chiedza Chikawa, and his biographer Banning Eyre for their generous cooperation in the preparation of this chapter.

References

651 ARTS. 2010. "Nora Chipaumire at 651 ARTS." YouTube, May 14, 2010, 6:14. https://youtu.be/yzJg53E2YDI?t=102.
BBC News. 2018. "Letter from Africa: Thomas Mapfumo, Zimbabwe's Lion, Roars for His Fans." May 1, 2018, Africa. https://www.bbc.com/news/world-africa-43963049.
Berliner, Paul F. (1978) 2007. *The Soul of Mbira: Music and Traditions of the Shona People of Zimbabwe: With an Appendix Building and Playing a Shona Karimba.* Chicago: University of Chicago Press.
Brown, Ernest D. 1994. "The Guitar and the 'Mbira': Resilience, Assimilation, and Pan-Africanism in Zimbabwean Music." *World of Music* 36 (2): 73–117.
Chipaumire, Nora, Thomas Mapfumo, and the Blacks Unlimited. 2009. "Lions Will Roar, Swans Will Fly, Angels Will Wrestle Heaven, Rains Will Break: Gukurahundi." MCA, October 4, 2009. https://mcachicago.org/Calendar/2009/10/Nora-Chipaumire-With-Thomas-Mapfumo-The-Blacks-Unlimited.
Dreams and Secrets. 2001. Eugene, OR: ANOnym ReCOrds.
Drop in Films. 2015. "Thomas Mapfumo 'Chikonzero.'" YouTube, March 13, 2015, 9:09. https://www.youtube.com/watch?v=AO627BzBG6U.
Eyre, Banning. 2015. *Lion Songs: Thomas Mapfumo and the Music That Made Zimbabwe.* Durham, NC: Duke University Press.

---

35 Translated from Shona by Chiedza Chikawa.

Eyre, Banning. 2018. "Thomas Mapfumo, 'Lion of Zimbabwe,' Returns from Exile with Triumphant Homecoming." *The Record* (blog), May 7, 2018. https://www.npr.org/sections/therecord/2018/05/07/609046651/thomas-mapfumo-lion-of-zimbabwe-returns-from-exile-with-triumphant-homecoming.

GVTH. 2009. *Giving Voice to Hope*. Edmonton: University of Alberta. http://bit.ly/buducd.

Herald. 2014. "Mukanya Readies 'Shabeen' Ahead of Mzansi Gig." March 10, 2014. https://www.herald.co.zw/mukanya-readies-shabeen-ahead-of-mzansi-gig/.

Hinton, David, and Alla Kovgan, dirs. 2008. *Nora*. Movement Revolution Productions.

Leo Smith, Wadada, and Thomas Mapfumo. 2020. "Wadada Leo Smith and Thomas Mapfumo—South Central LA (Jazz) (2000)." Foreal. YouTube, February 16, 2020, 5:50. https://www.youtube.com/watch?v=2aMk5CpXqX4.

Mapfumo, Thomas. 1988. "Corruption." Track 14 on *Lion Songs: Essential Tracks in the Making of Zimbabwe*, compiled by Banning Eyre. https://open.spotify.com/track/0sajM7lNMOPnBZnWChfg7X?si=bcb7edcb59104d9c.

Mapfumo, Thomas. 2002. "Manhungetunge." Track 15 on *Chimurenga Rebel/Manhungetunge*, by Thomas Mapfumo and the Blacks Unlimited. https://open.spotify.com/track/30BHaXX2AL6ez4Jz5EPJNu?si=dc51a441c85d45f3.

Mapfumo, Thomas. 2010. "Ndangariro." Track 1 on *Exile*, by Thomas Mapfumo and the Blacks Unlimited. https://open.spotify.com/track/3kZ0Qo4YIl1TxrdzNS6SPZ?si=c4141422bf7a428d.

Mapfumo, Thomas. 2011. "Thomas Mapfumo & the Blacks Unlimited at the Wow Hall Evan Belize on Trap Set.Dv." Evan Belize. YouTube, September 16, 2011, 32:39. https://www.youtube.com/watch?v=00cN9qWTVs4.

Mega Video Zimbabwe. 2020. "Thomas Mapfumo Interview 2000." YouTube, March 2, 2020, 22:41. https://www.youtube.com/watch?v=ykLgAFn4vcE.

Music Sumo. 2002. "Thomas Mapfumo & the Black Unlimited @ House of Blues." Pinterest, 2002. https://www.pinterest.com/pin/37576978111161619/.

Nehanda TV. 2016. "Thomas Mapfumo on Nehanda TV (April 2016)." YouTube, April 20, 2016, 23:17. https://www.youtube.com/watch?v=aGU6147M4ZU.

Nonesuch Explorer Series. 1973. "Nhemamusasa." Track 1 on *Zimbabwe: The Soul of Mbira / Traditions of the Shona People*. https://open.spotify.com/track/4LbpmU17fTS5jUfalOjo73?si=1596bbfec078490c.

NPR. 2015. "Thomas Mapfumo, Zimbabwe's Cultural Advocate in Exile." May 28, 2015. https://www.npr.org/2015/05/28/410251736/thomas-mapfumo-zimbabwes-cultural-advocate-in-exile.

Ohio University. 2001. "Honorary Doctorate Recipients." 2001. https://www.ohio.edu/president/honorary-degree-recipients.

Piotrowski, Daniel. 2019. "Wadada Leo Smith / Thomas Mapfumo: Dreams and Secrets." *JazzTimes*, 2019. https://jazztimes.com/archives/wadada-leo-smiththomas-mapfumo-dreams-and-secrets/.

Roux, Pierre le, and Sanderson Abel. 2017. "An Evaluation of the Efficiency of the Banking Sector in Zimbabwe." *African Review of Economics and Finance* 9 (2): 285–307.

Toombs, Mikel. 2008. "Mapfumo Wows the Crowd at the Triple Door." *Seattle Post-Intelligencer*, January 14, 2008. https://www.seattlepi.com/ae/music/article/Mapfumo-wows-the-crowd-at-The-Triple-Door-1261558.php.

Tsunami Books. 2014. "Paul Prince: Solo Acoustic Guitar." Facebook, 2014. https://www.facebook.com/events/1463805020515468/.

Turino, Thomas. 1999. "Signs of Imagination, Identity, and Experience: A Peircian Semiotic Theory for Music." *Ethnomusicology* 43 (2): 221–55. https://doi.org/10.2307/852734.

17 Music Enacting (Re)humanization
Concert Introduction, Program, and Link

Michael Frishkopf

The following text is a revised version of Michael Frishkopf's introduction to a special concert held on February 6, 2020, featuring two refugee musicians from the Middle East, Roy Abdalnour and Ahmed al-Auqaily, entitled "Transpositions: Music for Resilient Communities." This concert formed part of the University of Alberta's International Week and, together with a Zoom presentation from Dr. Thomas Mapfumo, served as the opening event for our workshop "Ethics, Rights, Culture and the Humanization of Refugees," the basis for this book. A link to the concert video follows.

Musical Connection and Reconnection

I'd like to start with a few words about the power of music. What does music do? Mostly, we consider music as mere entertainment. But what does it actually *do* for people? Philosophers and ethnomusicologists have provided many answers to this question in the past. My position is that *music is a powerful social technology* like no other, a technology *forging and maintaining intersubjective connections* (Frishkopf 2018, 2021). In particular, music offers powerful potential for resisting the dehumanization of refugees.

Our concert is entitled "Transpositions." In a musical context, the word *transposition* carries the sense of "transfer": to transpose a song is to change its key by moving all its pitches by a fixed tonal distance in a single direction, up or down. A transposition thus preserves the relationships between tones, even if their absolute locations change.

There are also social transpositions—movements of people through space and time. People, like tones, are related through social connections. But, unlike music, social transpositions do not move all people a fixed distance in a fixed direction. Some groups of people may move together. Others move independently or not at all. Social transpositions thus strain relationships—social connections—stretching, and even breaking them. Many connections are resilient. But sometimes they are stretched beyond their capacity. Social strains are more intense when transposition is forced and sudden, resulting from unpredictable disasters, natural or (more often) human-made, scattering people in different directions as refugees, seeking safe havens elsewhere.

We are social creatures. Connections are not accessory but integral to our humanity, which is essentially interpersonal. We live intersubjectively through our myriad connections to others. Our existence through time also depends on the continuity of the self, on an identity that changes only incrementally, continuously. This continuity of the self can also be interpreted as a set of connections of the self to its own past, producing a series of selves, linked together over time. These self-connections too are resilient, but social transpositions can strain them as well, sometimes to the breaking point.

Music can ease the pain of social transposition and the attendant loss of human connection in a specific space and time by strengthening intersubjective connections, enhancing their resilience, and creating new ones. Music supports social resilience by fostering sustainable, robust human connection. This is among the most important answers to this question: "What does music actually do?"

I argue that the most socially powerful such music possesses three key attributes, leading to an emergent dialogic process and intensive affective state I call social "resonance." First, it is fully participatory. Anyone can join as an active participant, though this participation can take many forms: performing an instrument or singing, certainly, but also dancing, clapping, tapping, exclaiming, singing along, or simply swaying—any social projection of inner feeling. Second, it is flexible, containing parameters (sonic or social) that adapt dynamically to its environment. Third, it enables communicative feedback loops among participants, and that feedback in turn enables an adjustment of music's dynamic parameters to maximize musical emotion. Musicians react to feedback by fine-tuning their performances, seeking an ineffable resonant frequency, as this emotion, projected outward to active listeners and returned through various forms of expression (sonic, verbal, gestural, postural, kinetic), spirals upward. Through this process, everyone is brought together into a shared musical alignment, a collective, empathic "mutual tuning in" (Schutz 1951) and thus an implicit recognition of our common humanity. Intersubjective bonds arise, and individuation fades, as all "tune in" and recognize that such "tuning in" is shared.

This "common feeling" is analogous to what has been called "common knowledge" (Chwe 2001): during collective musical experience, we deeply feel that we feel one another's feeling. Extrusions of each participant's self—diffusing, diffracting, and interpenetrating through highly charged expressive media—congeal in an intersubjective space, producing a powerful, even if ephemeral, sense of a unified collective body, permeated and supercharged with an intensively human sense of empathetic connection. This is the state of intensive shared emotion that I call social resonance. At this point, boundaries of self dissolve away, and the Golden Rule of humanization—treating the other as one would treat oneself—becomes a mere tautology as I-it relations (to a dehumanized other) shift first to I-you (recognition of the other as a person), then to I-thou (full recognition of the other as a spiritual being; Buber 1958). Finally, at its ecstatic emotional pitch, interpersonal differences may be entirely erased, dissolving into a collective "we."

Of course, not all musical styles and performances produce such a dramatic outcome, and there is a continuum from the most distanced to the most intimacy-generating forms. The more participants are separated—in space or in time (e.g., through mediated forms such as radio)—the weaker the feedback cycle, the lesser the resonance. Perhaps the ideal type occurs most often in ecstatic ritual—when music nearly always plays a central role. But even if the ideal type is seldom encountered, many partial resonances illustrate the same principle.

Beyond binding participants to one another, resonance-inducing music is tightly bound to memories of past resonances, which each resonance evokes, thus sustaining connections to people who were formerly present, in other times and places, including our former selves, in an imagined interaction. Intersubjective connections, depending on empathy, are thereby recharged.

Resonance itself may be ephemeral, but its connective residue can be enduring, particularly when other factors—proximity, a common social group, or shared beliefs—are available to sustain connections afterward. These factors help ensure continuity of connections, imbued with the emotions of performance and periodically recharged by them. This is the phenomenon Durkheim (1976, 217–18) analyzed as "effervescence" in stabler small-scale communities, but the same process applies to any collectivity, even those connected by mediated (i.e., via virtual, broadcast or product media) rather than face-to-face links.

Refugees, whether fleeing political persecution, war, or environmental disasters, are in particularly dire need of intersubjective reconnection, by which "self" and "other" are mutually perceived as fully human. They have escaped acutely difficult and dehumanizing circumstances. This experience, as well as rapid flight to a safer place, leaves them disconnected. They may remain in a liminal state, whether in transit, or living in shelters, guest rooms (hotels or homes of friends and family), or temporary camps ("temporary," for such camps can persist for years, even decades), excluded from the wider society and often suffering deprivation, and lacking basic needs, including security. Or they may have found refuge in a stable, secure destination, even a welcoming one.

Whatever the situation, for a refugee community, social well-being requires new intersubjective connections of three basic types: connections to one another, generating social empowerment; connections to the host society (whether in transit or as a destination), fostering social integration; and connections to the homeland, preserving continuity of the self. Each will be considered in turn.

First, forced migration gathers refugees, hailing from all walks of life, in a disconnected jumble and in a new place. Beyond close family, they do not necessarily know one another; indeed, many would never have known one another in the home society had fate not collected them through some tragic dispersive event. But here, in a new place, they meet and begin to connect collectively, whether via intensive musical resonance or in more pedestrian forms of social interaction. Newly wrought intersubjective connections weave a supportive and empowering network, enabling them to help one another, producing a new sense of community (potentially crossing lines of class, gender, religion, and ethnicity in the home society), whereby they can begin to advocate for one another, to seek and secure basic human rights. The prominent role of music in refugees' voluntary associations, including church congregations and other ethnically based community groups, illustrates the importance of social resonance as a technology weaving this new social fabric.[1]

Second, there is also an acute need for social integration with the host society through the formation of adaptive connections. It is not only refugees who must adapt, as per an imbalanced and outdated assimilative model, for the host society must also adapt to the refugees, in a dialogic process of integration, through which members of both refugee and host communities change, humanizing one another. This process transpires through the weaving of an intercultural connective fabric, comprising connective threads of intersubjective recognition.

Once again, musical resonance—in different contexts (perhaps at a church congregation, school assembly, civic event, or neighbourhood association meeting)—plays a key role in fostering this recognition, this transformation from "I-it" (the dehumanized refugee, as constructed by xenophobia) to a recognition of personhood as "I-you" and finally "I-thou" and "we," through a deep affective understanding that "self" and "other" are one—mere variants of the same underlying humanity. Integration is a fundamentally intersubjective and dialogic process, leading to empathy, acceptance, and friendship instead of mistrust, demonization, or fear: a process of humanizing the other.

Finally, it is of utmost importance that refugees retain connections to their home societies, not merely because family and friends may continue to reside there, but because their past selves will always reside there. The continuity of the self is tantamount to a slowly changing identity transmitted from past to present. Music unlocks memory and thus supports continuity. It powerfully adheres to all the contexts of its past production, particularly moments of resonance, evoking them with visual, auditory, and affective vividness. Musical resonance not only imbues contemporary relationships with humanizing emotion but also brings the past to life, enabling the individual to reconnect with past selves, to root the new life in a prior life, stabilizing the self like the roots of a tree. While that old life may be gone, it grounds the present. And sometimes it returns, at least in part, when the refugee returns home once again.

---

[1] For instance, music plays a prominent role in the Edmonton South Sudanese Mennonite Church on Edmonton's north side (https://sites.google.com/site/sudanesemennonite/).

Tarab in Arabic Music

Social resonance is never more apparent than in the Arabic music known as *tarab* (Racy 1991). Such music is highly participatory. Singers sing and musicians play, but the audience too is free to exclaim, to gesticulate, to emote, to dance—to play. *Tarab* enables a high degree of flexibility through melodic ornamentation as well as reinterpretation and full-blown improvisation. And it offers many opportunities for feedback among participants, including singers, musicians, and listeners. All this enables resonance. In Arabic, such resonance is also called *tarab*, sometimes translated as "ecstasy."

Arabic music provides a rich palette of musical resources for ornamentation and improvisation, including several dozen scales called *maqamat*, many featuring subtle microtonal intervals as well as distinctive ornaments, improvisations called *taqasim*, and a set of rhythmic cycles known as *iqaʿat* (Farraj and Shumays 2019).

Traditionally, the music is performed by ear, but even when a score exists, musicians rarely feel enslaved to it. Rather, they typically enjoy flexibility, including great freedom to respond to listeners. Arab audiences are very expressive. They react to beautiful music through gestures, claps, cries, or expressions, such as *ya salam* (oh wow!), sometimes directly requesting a repetition, as in *marra tanya* (repeat!).

This concert is a participatory demonstration of music's power to reinforce, create, and recreate connection, one I hope you will not only witness but also feel. Allow yourself to be moved, to react to the sounds you hear, as our live audience did. Music breaks down barriers, as it reminds us of our shared humanity, allowing new, more humanized, connections to form.

The Musicians

Now it is my pleasure to introduce two virtuoso musicians whom I have the honor of calling my musical companions and friends, with whom I've had the privilege of performing, and from whom I've learned immeasurably.

Both were highly successful musicians in their home countries of Syria and Iraq. Both are refugees of tragic wars. Arriving in Canada, they connected to the local Arab community and to the wider Canadian communities, including non-Arab musicians like myself, while maintaining a connection to their homelands. And they have done so through the power of music. Everyone who has had the opportunity to hear them has been greatly enriched by their extraordinary musicality.

Roy Abdalnour, virtuoso violinist, hails from Syria, where he studied at the music conservatory. He has performed with several of the greatest singers of the Arab world, such as Elias Karam, Sabah Fakhri, Nancy Ajram, Dominique Horany, George Wassouf, and many others. He participated in the Fourth Arab Music Festival and Conference in Cairo. A member of the Syrian Artists Association, he ran a musical institute to teach children and adults in his native land. In Canada, he continues to perform with touring Arab singers, such as Mohammed Eskander, Hadi Khalil, and Ziad Burgi, as well as with many local musicians.

Ahmed al-Auqaily, virtuoso percussionist on the *riqq* (frame drum) and *tabla* (goblet-shaped drum, also known as *darabuka* or *dumbek*), hails from Baghdad, Iraq, where he began playing music at age thirteen. He studied in music school for three years, then launched a professional career. Displaced by the first Gulf War, he arrived in Canada in 1997. Here he has continued to play with many bands, including the University of Alberta's MENAME, our own Middle Eastern and North African Music Ensemble, and also to teach, and he is constantly in demand for community events.

We are delighted to have this opportunity to present a program of Arabic music for you.

I should add that in Arabic music, the ultimate creator of *tarab* is the *mutrib* (literally "generator of tarab"): the singer, for the voice is the ultimate expressive instrument. Our concert lacks a singer. Since most of our listeners don't understand Arabic, it is perhaps suitable that we are performing *tarab* music instrumentally. But in the expressive tone of Roy's violin, you will hear him singing, as you'll hear Ahmed singing through his *riqq* and *tabla*. The *mutrib*, generator of *tarab*, is our instrumental group.

Toward the end of our program, we introduce a surprise: a Canadian-born guest artist, Professor Guillaume Tardif, bringing a song from Québec about the pain of exile, further demonstrating music's power of connection.

Program Notes

We begin with a traditional introductory prelude called *dulab* in the *maqam* Shadd Araban, followed by a *taqsim* (improvisation) by Roy on the violin, leading into a traditional Turkish form, *sama'i*, in a related maqam called Nawa Athar:

1. "Dulab Shadd Araban," traditional.
2. Taqsim (violin), improvised.
3. "Sama'i Nawa Athar," composed by Jamil 'Uwis (1890–1955), a Syrian composer from Aleppo.

Next, we perform a famous song, "Ana Fintizarak" (I'm waiting for you), composed by Zakaria Ahmed (1896–1961) in 1943, with lyrics by Bayram al-Tunisi (1893–1961), and performed by Egypt's greatest singer, the incomparable Umm Kulthum (1898–1975). Here, the violin becomes her singing voice. This is followed by another taqsim, this time on the *nay* (reed flute), and a song originally performed by Lebanon's legendary icon Fairouz, composed by her son Ziyad, with lyrics by her husband, Assi, and his brother Mansour. We conclude this section with two instrumental pieces, a *longa* (fast, virtuosic instrumental piece from the Ottoman tradition) and the introduction to another Umm Kulthum song, "Laylat Hubb" (Night of love):

4. "Ana Fintizarak" (I'm waiting for you), 1943, Zakaria Ahmed and Bayram al-Tunisi, in maqam Hijaz.
5. Taqsim Bayati, improvisation in maqam Bayati, nay.
6. "Sa'aluni al-nas" (People asked me), 1973, melody composed by Ziyad Rahbani, lyrics by Assi and Mansour Rahbani, in maqam Bayati.
7. "Longa Sabukh," nineteenth century, by Sabukh Effendi.
8. Instrumental introduction to "Laylat Hubb" (Night of love), 1973, composed by Mohamed Abdel Wahab for Umm Kulthum, in maqam Nahawand.

To further demonstrate the connective power of music, we conclude by featuring special guest artist and violinist Professor Guillaume Tardif in a duet with Roy Abdalnour, demonstrating how musical connections—from Arabic to Canadian music—foster social ones.

Two songs—one Arabic and one Canadian—each express, in similar musical ways, the longing induced by separation from the beloved, whether person or homeland. We then close with a famous Turkish longa:

9. "Zuruni kulli sana marra" (Visit me yearly), Sayyid Darwish (1892–1923) and Muhammad Yunis al-Qadi, in maqam 'Ajam.

10. "Un Canadien Errant" (A wandering Canadian, i.e., exiled from his home), a Québécois folk song, presents a similar theme.
11. "Zuruni," reprise.
12. Longa Nahawand, Jamil bek, Turkish, nineteenth century.

Thank you very much for joining us in this program full of musical connections. *Our sincere thanks to Russ Baker and Pat Strain for the beautiful sound, to the Department of Music for the hall, and to Nancy Hannemann and Yasmeen Abu-Laban and their teams, sponsors of International Week and the workshop on refugees, respectively.*

Concert link. Please point your browser here to watch and hear "Transpositions: Music for Resilient Communities": https://www.youtube.com/watch?v=w8QP45UFIWA.

References

Buber, Martin. 1958. *I and Thou.* New York: Scribner.
Chwe, Michael Suk-Young. 2001. *Rational Ritual Culture, Coordination, and Common Knowledge.* Princeton, NJ: Princeton University Press.
Durkheim, Émile. 1976. *The Elementary Forms of the Religious Life.* New York: Free Press.
Farraj, Johnny, and Sami Abu Shumays. 2019. *Inside Arabic Music: Arabic Maqam Performance and Theory in the 20th Century.* Oxford: Oxford University Press. https://public.ebookcentral.proquest.com/choice/publicfullrecord.aspx?p=5825015.
Frishkopf, Michael. 2018. "Music for Global Human Development, and Refugees." *Ethnomusicology* 63 (2): 279–314.
Frishkopf, Michael. 2021. "Music for Global Human Development." In *Transforming Ethnomusicology: Political, Social & Ecological Issues*, edited by Beverley Diamond and Salwa El-Shawan Castelo-Branco, 47–66. New York: Oxford University Press.
Racy, Ali Jihad. 1991. "Creativity and Ambience: An Ecstatic Feedback Model from Arab Music." *World of Music* 33 (2): 7–26.
Schutz, Alfred. 1951. "Making Music Together: A Study in Social Relationship." *Social Research* 18 (1): 76–97.

Contributors

Yasmeen Abu-Laban is a professor and Canada Research Chair in the Politics of Citizenship and Human Rights in the Department of Political Science at the University of Alberta. Her published research comparatively addresses subjects relating to ethnic and gender politics; nationalism, globalization, and processes of racialization; immigration policies and politics; surveillance and border control; and multiculturalism and anti-racism. Cutting across this work is a concern with how people are differentially accorded citizenship and human rights. She is co-author (with Ethel Tungohan and Christina Gabriel) of *Containing Diversity: Canada and the Politics of Immigration in the 21st Century* (University of Toronto Press, 2023) and co-editor (with Alain-G. Gagnon and Arjun Tremblay) of *Assessing Multiculturalism in Global Comparative Perspective: A New Politics of Diversity in the Twenty-First Century?* (Routledge, 2023).

Jeffrey M. Ayres is a professor and Chair of the Department of Political Science and International Relations at Saint Michael's College in Colchester, Vermont, United States. He earned a BA in foreign affairs at the University of Virginia and an MA and PhD in political science at the University of Wisconsin–Madison. He teaches courses and conducts research broadly in the areas of comparative and international political economy, regionalism and global governance, and Canadian and North American politics and has published extensively in article, chapter, and book form. He is co-editor of *Globalization and Food Sovereignty: Global and Local Change in the New Politics of Food* (University of Toronto Press, 2014), *North America in Question: Regional Integration in an Era of Political Turbulence* (University of Toronto Press, 2012), and *Contentious Politics in North America: National Protest and Transnational Collaboration Under Continental Integration* (Palgrave Macmillan,

2009) and author of *Defying Conventional Wisdom: Political Movements and Popular Contention Against North American Free Trade* (University of Toronto Press, 1998). He has held the Fulbright Research Chair in North American Studies at Carleton University, Ottawa, Canada, and has twice been a Visiting Researcher at Carleton's Institute of Political Economy.

Abigail B. Bakan is a professor in the Department of Social Justice in Education (SJE) at the Ontario Institute for Studies in Education (OISE) and cross-appointed to the Department of Political Science, University of Toronto. Her research is in the area of anti-oppression politics, with a focus on intersections of gender, race, class, political economy, and citizenship. Her publications include *Theorizing Anti-racism: Linkages in Marxism and Critical Race Theories* (co-edited with Enakshi Dua; University of Toronto Press, 2014), *Negotiating Citizenship: Migrant Women in Canada and the Global System* (with Daiva Stasiulis; University of Toronto Press, 2007), *Critical Political Studies: Debates and Dialogues from the Left* (co-edited with Eleanor MacDonald; McGill-Queen's University Press, 2002), and *Employment Equity Policy in Canada: An Interprovincial Comparison* (with Audrey Kobayashi; Status of Women Canada, 2000). Her articles have appeared in *Race and Class, Social Identities, Rethinking Marxism, Politikon, Socialist Studies, Atlantis, Signs, Canadian Journal of Law and Society*, and *Studies in Political Economy*. Her current SSHRC-funded research, with Yasmeen Abu-Laban, addresses processes of human rights regarding race, gender, and Indigeneity in the context of United Nations world conferences. Their co-authored recent volume, *Israel, Palestine and the Politics of Race: Exploring Identity and Power in a Global Context*, is published by I.B. Tauris Publishers, an imprint of Bloomsbury (2020).

Jalal Barzanji is a highly respected Canadian-Kurdish writer and journalist. He has published eight books of poetry, a memoir, and numerous critical columns. After his two-year imprisonment by Saddam Hussein's regime in the late 1980s and further political repression into the 1990s, he and his family fled to Turkey. They remained there for eleven months, eventually immigrating to Canada, where he has resided for more than twenty years. He is a City of Edmonton Hall of Fame member; he was Pen Canada's first Writer in Exile and the recipient of an honorary doctorate of letters from the University of Alberta.

Pallabi Bhattacharyya was a postdoctoral fellow in sociology and international development studies at Saint Mary's University in Halifax, Nova

Scotia, where she was a member of the Canadian Research Team for the Violence Against Women Refugees and Migrants: Analyzing Causes and Effective Policy Response project. She completed her PhD from the Department of Sociology and Criminology at the University of Manitoba. Her PhD research focuses on the rights, agency, and empowerment of refugee women and youth in Canada. In the past thirteen years, her major research experiences include projects with UNICEF; UNESCO; WHO; the British Council; the Commonwealth Youth Exchange Council program; the Child and Youth Refugee Research Coalition project by the European Union; Immigration Research West (IRW); Immigration, Refugee and Citizenship Canada (IRCC); Canadian Institutes of Health Research (CIHR); and Social Sciences and Humanities Research Council (SSHRC).

Fariborz Birjandian has served on committees, boards, and task forces related to immigration, refugees, diversity, equal rights, and the cultural arts from the local to the international levels. He became a refugee when he left his home country of Iran with his family in 1987. His involvement and work with refugees began in 1987 and has continued these past thirty-plus years. He initially began this work with the United Nations High Commissioner for Refugees (UNHCR), and once settled in Canada, he volunteered with several organizations, including the Red Cross and Calgary Catholic Immigration Society (CCIS). In his role as CEO of CCIS, he leads 300 staff members and 1,600 volunteers as they deliver approximately eighty programs and services designed to aid the settlement and integration of immigrants and refugees in Calgary, Alberta, and its surrounding communities. He has been instrumental in designing and initiating numerous methodologies related to settlement and integration, including the *UNHCR Settlement Handbook*, which is used nationally and internationally. He has received numerous awards and recognitions for his community involvement and for his commitment to ensuring that institutions, advisory groups, and all levels of government work to recognize the needs and challenges faced by newcomers, promote the creation of welcoming and engaged communities, and recognize and celebrate diversity.

Chiedza Chikawa-Araga received her bachelor's degree in accounting from the University of Oregon and became a certified public accountant after moving to Canada. She has worked as an accountant in the non-profit, private, and public sectors. Apart from accounting, she works with her father, Thomas Mapfumo, as part of his business/management team.

Michael Frishkopf (frishkopf.org, m4ghd.org) is a professor of music, the director of the Canadian Centre for Ethnomusicology, and an adjunct professor in the Faculty of Communication and Media Studies at the University for Development Studies, Ghana. His field and action research, centering on the Arab world and West Africa, includes music and Islam, music and development, global health, music as medicine, music and architecture, digital repositories, social network analysis, virtual and augmented reality, and machine learning.

Jim Gurnett works with community organizations as a consultant and as Inner City Pastoral Ministry's pastoral associate. He has been a school teacher and principal in Alberta and Afghanistan, the director of social-profit organizations such as the Edmonton Mennonite Centre for Newcomers and Bissell Centre, the founding executive director of the University of Alberta research center The Hope Foundation, an adult educator, a journalist, and a community activist. His political activity has included serving as the MLA for the Spirit River-Fairview constituency and the executive director for the government caucus at the Legislative Assembly of Alberta. He is a board member at the Edmonton Intercultural Centre. His focus is often on social justice issues and the importance of building community. His life is enriched by ten grandchildren.

Encarnación Gutiérrez Rodríguez is a professor of sociology with a focus on culture and migration at the Goethe-University, Frankfurt am Main. Previously to this position, she was a professor of general sociology at the Justus-Liebig-University Giessen. Moreover, she is an adjunct professor in sociology at the University of Alberta, Canada, and a visiting professor in CRISHET (Chair for Critical Studies in Higher Education Transformation), Nelson Mandela University, South Africa. In 2020/21, she was a Digital Senior Fellow in the Maria Sibylla Merian Centre: Conviviality-Inequality in Latin America (Mecila), São Paulo. Among her many publications is the important book *Migration, Domestic Work and Affect* (Routledge, 2010) and her recently published book *Decolonial Mourning and the Caring Commons: Migration-Coloniality Necropolitics and Conviviality Infrastructure* (Anthem, 2023). More recently, she has published with Shirley Anne Tate *The Palgrave*

Handbook in Critical Race and Gender (Palgrave, 2022), with Rhoda Reddock *Decolonial Perspectives on Entangled Inequalities: Europe and the Caribbean* (Anthem, 2021), and with Pinar Tuzcu *Migrantischer Feminismus in der deutschen Frauenbewegung, 1985–2000* (Assemblage, 2021). Her work engages with affective labour, materialities, institutional racism, racial capitalism, and the coloniality of migration.

Louise Harrington is an assistant professor in post-colonial and contemporary literatures in the Department of English and Film Studies at the University of Alberta. She works primarily on cultural representations of war and ethno-religious-national conflict in the twentieth and twenty-first centuries, specializing in the comparative study of Ireland, Israel/Palestine, and South Asia. She has further research interests in critical border studies, geocriticism, spatial literary studies, and migration. Among her publications are articles in *South Asian Diaspora*, *Postcolonial Text*, and *South Asian Review* and essays in the edited collections *The Routledge Companion to Postcolonial and Decolonial Literature* (2024), *Partitions and Their Afterlives* (Rowman and Littlefield 2019), *The Cosmic and the Corporeal: Interdisciplinary Explorations of Time, Space and Body* (Institute of Interdisciplinary Inquiry 2016), and *Tracing the New Indian Diaspora* (Rodopi 2014).

Reza Hasmath (PhD, Cambridge) is a professor of political science at the University of Alberta. He has previously held faculty positions in management, sociology, and political science at the Universities of Toronto, Melbourne, and Oxford and has worked for think tanks, consultancies, development agencies, and NGOs in the United States, Canada, Australia, the United Kingdom, and China. His award-winning research looks at the global life course experiences of ethnic minorities. He is the editor-in-chief of the *Journal of Civil Society*.

Benjamin Ho is a professor of economics at Vassar College and author of the book *Why Trust Matters: An Economist's Guide to the Ties That Bind Us* (Columbia University Press, 2021). Professor Ho applies behavioral economics tools like game theory and experimental methods to tackle topics like apologies, identity, inequality, and climate change. Before Vassar, he taught MBA students at Cornell, where he was selected as one of Poets and Quants 40 under 40, served as lead energy economist at the White House Council of Economic Advisers, and worked/consulted for Morgan Stanley and several tech startups. Professor Ho is also a faculty affiliate for the Center for Global Energy Policy at Columbia University. His research has appeared in outlets like *Management Science* and *Nature: Human Behavior*. Professor Ho holds seven degrees from Stanford and MIT in economics, education, political science, math, computer science, and electrical engineering.

Jwamer Jalal arrived in Canada as a child in a family of United Nations–sponsored Kurdish refugees fleeing war in Iraq. A University of Alberta alum, he is currently the managing coordinator of the Alberta Ministry of Health's Immigrant Youth Mental Health Initiative at the Multicultural Health Brokers Cooperative—a not-for-profit organization that started twenty-five years ago to support Edmonton's newcomers.

Solomon Kay-Reid is completing a JD at the Peter A. Allard School of Law at the University of British Columbia.

Nariya Khasanova is a PhD candidate in the Department of Political Science at the University of Alberta and master's degree holder in Sustainable Urban Governance and Peace from the United Nations–mandated University for Peace (2013). Her doctoral research examines reproductive justice in immigrant and refugee families in Canada. Passionate about migration studies, sustainable development, and human rights, she has served as a research assistant in two SSHRC-funded projects, including "The UN as a Knowledge Producer: World Conferences on Women, Racialized, and Indigenous Peoples" and "Migration and Precarity: From the Temporary Foreign Worker Program to Permanent Resident, Student and Undocumented Migrant Status." Prior to joining the University of Alberta, she was also a visiting scholar at George Washington University, a project officer at the United Nations Association in Canada, an intern at national and regional UNDP offices in Uzbekistan and Bratislava, and a policy analyst at the Government of Alberta.

Anna Kirova is a professor in the Faculty of Education, University of Alberta. She has served as Education Domain Leader and Children, Family and Youth Research Domain Leader with the Prairie Metropolis Centre of Excellence in Research on Immigration, Integration, and Diversity and on the Board of Governors of Immigration Research West (IRW). Her research focuses on the need for understanding culturally and linguistically diverse families with young children's experiences in school and the possibility such an understanding offers for culturally responsive pedagogy. Her work has been published in national and international academic journals.

Thomas Mapfumo is a world-renowned musician from Zimbabwe, known for creating and popularizing Chimurenga music, in which he incorporated Western instruments with traditional Zimbabwean instruments, singing in Shona and addressing political themes during and post the colonisation war. Chimurenga music was built on the struggle of Black Rhodesians and the country's traditional music. It was a sound that gave the natives an identity and a voice during a time when they didn't seem to have a voice. Due to his contribution to music and activism, Mapfumo received an honorary master's degree in recognition of advocacy for freedom from the University of Zimbabwe in 1999 and an honorary doctorate degree in music from Ohio University at Athens in 2001. However, as the political climate shifted in Zimbabwe, Mapfumo's music became increasingly critical of the government. He faced censorship and threats, leading him to move his family to the United States in 2000 for safety. Despite his exile, he remained committed to creating and performing music that challenged the status quo. In 2018, after fourteen years, Mapfumo returned to Zimbabwe for a concert, citing positive political changes. However, he hasn't returned since 2019 due to concerns about the ruling regime. Throughout his career, Mapfumo has been a resilient voice, using his music to express social and political dissent.

Labe Songose is an Integration Program Officer at IRCC (Settlement Network). She graduated from the University of Manitoba with a master's degree in sociology. Her areas of research interest are in immigrants' and refugees' settlement and integration, immigrant and refugee women's well-being, and immigration policies.

Dana Waissi holds a double major psychology and English degree from the University of Alberta. He is Kurdish but was born in an Iraqi refugee camp and came to Canada when he was four years old with his family and was raised in Edmonton. His goal is to continue his studies and become a neuroscientist. In tandem with his studies, Dana has also mastered the keyboard and a Kurdish instrument (Saz) and has steadily worked with various musical softwares to mix and master multilayered music tracks while curating a YouTube channel in which he showcases his musical compositions. He is also the recipient of a URI Undergraduate Research Stipend for work on Kurdish cultural production and takes every opportunity to discuss and engage in work on Kurdish identity and its place in Canadian society.

Lori Wilkinson is a professor in the Department of Sociology and Criminology at the University of Manitoba in Winnipeg, Canada. She is the Canada Research Chair-Tier 1 in Migration Futures and, in 2023, was awarded the title Distinguished University Professor at the University of Manitoba. Her current program of research centers on the resettlement and integration experiences of immigrants and refugees. She is the director of Immigration Research West, a multidisciplinary group of over one hundred members who work together to educate Canadians about the contributions of newcomers. Her research has been published in several international and national academic journals and reports to national and international governments.

Index

Page numbers in *italics* refer to tables.

Abdallah-Pretceille, Martine, 213
Abdalnour, Roy, 379, 385, 386
Abdi, Ali A., 28
Abella, Irving, 229; *None Is Too Many: Canada and the Jews of Europe, 1933–1948*, 230, 231
Abitur program, 176
ableism, 201
Adirondack Friends of Refugees and Immigrants, 79
affective communication, 331, 332
Afghan refugees, 146, 281
African music, 349–57
African National Congress, 254
Ahmed, Saifuddin, 106
Ahmed, Zakaria: "Ana Fintizarak" (I'm waiting for you), 386
Ajram, Nancy, 385
Akbarzadeh, Shahram, 108
Akthar, Zahra, 140
Albanese, Anthony, 56
Alberta: hate crimes in, 156; health services, 161; immigrant population of, 4, 162; supremacist groups, 4
Ali, Ayub, 317–18
alterity, 13–14, 199, 212, 213
American Civil Liberties Union of Vermont (ACLU-VT), 76
American Jewish Joint Distribution Committee (JDC), 230
Amin, Idi, 278
Amjad, Afshan, 210
Amnesty International, 53, 83
Anderson, Willow J., 257
Anglo-American democracies, 45

Ankara, Turkey, 287, 297
anti-austerity protests, 67, 71
anti-immigration protests, 77
anti-racism education, 212
antisemitism: definition of, 226, 227; as global trend, 235, 238; as state policy, 230
apartheid, 254–55
apologies: elements of, 249; function of, 15, 256; humanization and, 15; inter-group, 261; loss of status due to, 251; paradox of, 256, 264; with promise to improve conduct, 250–51; signals incorporated in, 251; types of, 250, 251, 263. *See also* state apologies
Arab and Middle Eastern Journalists Association, 6
Arab music, 384, 385–86
Arar, Khalid, 169
Armstrong, Felicity, 206
arts: as basis for socialization, 330; boundaries of, 32
Ashkenazi Jews, 236–37
asylum-migration nexus, 168, 170, 174–75, 189
asylum seekers: connection with terrorism and Islam, 104; illegal border crossing of, 51, 74; precarity of, 65; rights of, 170, 272; state programs for, 279–80; treatment of, 47–48, 104–5; women, 188
Auqaily, Ahmed al-, 379, 385
Australia: asylum seekers, 47–48; COVID-19 pandemic in, 49; human rights revolution, 45; immigration

Australia (*continued*)
policy, 44, 45, 46, 49; Indigenous population, 44, 46; multiculturalism, 45; party system, 47, 48; racism, 46; refugee policies, 43, 57

Baha'I faith, 93
Ballantyne, Julie, 203
Ban Vinai refugee camp, 330
Barakat, Salim, 303
Barnett, Brooks, 367
Barton, Angela, 200, 202, 205
Barzanji, Jalal: "Arrival," 294; birthday of, 287; Canadian audience of, 298, 299; "Corner," 292–93; *Dancing in the Evening Snow*, 291, 294–95; education of, 287–88; "Home in a Suitcase," 300–301; imprisonment of, 16, 29, 295–96, 297; life in Erbil, 289–90; life in Turkey, 297–98; *The Man in Blue Pajamas*, 299; native village of, 287; non-fiction writing, 299; office in Edmonton Public Library, 298–99; PEN Canada's first "Writer in Exile," 298; poetry of, 290, 291; rejection of works of, 295; self-censorship of, 291, 292, 294–95; "Tell Ewar," 296–97; trip to Canada, 298; "War," 291–92, 298
Barzinji, Mahmud, 305
being human: act of, 22
Bêkes, Şêrko, 311, 319, 320; "A Letter to God," 312, 313
Berlin Center on Integration and Migration, 186
Berliner, Paul: *The Soul of Mbira*, 350
bicultural identity, 12
Biden, Joseph, 56
"big problems," 339–40, 341
Bildik, Riza, 308
Bispo, Fernando, 361n17
Bjørneseth, Frida, 127, 143
Black, Johannah, 70
Black Lives Matter, 67, 71
Blacks Unlimited (band), 350
Blair, Charles Frederick, 229
Blatz, Craig W., 250, 251, 260, 261
Bloch, Maurice, 336
Blum, Stephen, 311
"boat people," 282
Boko Haram's recruitment music, 32
Bolter, Jessica, 54

Boochani, Behrouz: *No Friend but the Mountains*, 49
border regulations, 8, 70. *See also* Canada-US border
Borneman, John, 252
Bosnian refugees, 282
Boston Marathon bombing, 114
Botha, P. W., 255
Bourdieu, Pierre, 206
Boycott, Divestment and Sanctions (BDS) movement: government condemnation of, 233, 238, 240, 242; Israeli-Palestinian conflict and, 226, 227–28, 238–39, 242; Jewish Canadians in, 239, 241; supporters of, 240, 241
Boyle-Baise, Marilynne, 201
Branch Out program (Germany): Initial Support for Transcultural Learning: access to university facilities, 184, 185; classroom environment, 181, 183; economic hardship of attendees, 184; English-language instructions, 180; exchange of ideas on migration, 181–82; funding of, 181, 186; goals of, 12, 168, 179–80, 182; institutional limitations, 184; interactive space, 183, 185; language barriers, 184; networking opportunities, 186; outcome of, 183, 185–86; promotion of, 170; teaching module, 179; travel arrangements for participants in, 184
Brandt, Willy, 252–53
Brankamp, Hanno, 25
Bridges Not Borders (Créons des Ponts) organization, 65, 79, 80–81
British "home children" program, 282
Brown citizens: exclusion of, 12, 158–60
Brú, Federico Laredo, 228
Brubaker, Rogers, 159
Brück, Lukas, 187
Buduburam Liberian refugee camp, 342–43, 351
Burgi, Ziad, 385
Burj al-Barajneh refugee camp, 111

Calgary Catholic Immigration Society (CCIS): community partners, 99, 100; counselling work of, 97, 98; COVID-19 pandemic and, 101–2; programs and services, 100, 102; Syrian refugee crisis and, 99

Câmara, Dom Hélder, 273
Cambodian refugees, 128
Canada: antisemitism in, 227, 229, 230; asylum program, 51, 52–53, 74, 279–80; citizenship policy, 159, 160; COVID-19 pandemic in, 53; diversity policy, 158; education system, 200, 209; far-right groups, 65; foreign-born residents, 158; hate crimes in, 104; human rights revolution, 45; immigrant population of, 4; immigration policy, 44, 46, 50, 65, 78, 96, 156; Indigenous populations, 44, 46; international obligations, 53; media portrayals of, 75; mental health services in, 276–77; multiculturalism, 28, 45, 200, 308–9; national anthem, 237; party system, 52; provision of weaponry to oppressive regimes, 15; racism, 46; refugee policies, 15–16, 43, 50, 57, 74, 95–96, 269, 274–75, 279, 282; "Smart Border Plan," 50
Canada-US border: countermovement of agency and solidarity, 85; COVID-19 pandemic and closure of, 84; duality of migrant precarity along, 8; humanitarian organizations, 79; irregular crossing of, 75, 78; pro-migrant protests at, 78, 80–81. *See also* Lacolle-Champlain border crossing; Roxham Road border crossing
Canada-US Safe Third Country Agreement (STCA), 8, 50–51, 52–53, 74, 75, 80, 83, 84, 280
Canadian Border Services Agency (CBSA), 239
Canadian Charter of Rights and Freedoms, 83, 200, 280
Canadian Council for Refugees, 53, 83
Canadian Council of Churches, 53, 83
Canadian Ethnocultural Council, 308
Canadian Museum of Immigration, 233
Canadian Pacific Railway, 261
Canadian Teachers' Federation: *Dream Big Together*, 199
Canadians for Justice and Peace in the Middle East (CJPME), 240
Cantarero, Luis, 206
CANZUS countries, 44
Caring for Social Justice, 65
Castles, Stephen, 174
Center for Youth Empowerment (CYE), 342
Centre for Refugee Resilience (CRR), 98
Chan, Michael, 109
Chapman, Audrey R., 256
Chapuis, Nicolas, 110
Chattopadhyay, Sutapa, 70
Chaudhry, Shereen J., 251
Chikawa-Araga, Chiedza, 354, 361n17, 364, 374
children: contemporary wars and, 195–96; pedagogical and medical surveillance of, 206; right to protection, 196–97. *See also* immigrant youth; racialized children
Chimurenga music, 350, 351–52, 355, 374
Chinese Canadians: discrimination of, 261; rehumanization of, 260–61; state apology to, 247, 260–61, 262, 263–64
Chinese Exclusion Act, 260, 263
Chinese Head Tax, 247, 260, 261, 263
Chipaumire, Nora, 352, 362n18
Chisholm, Riley, 70
Chrétien, Jean, 257
Christopher, Gilbert, 361
Chwe, Michael, 22, 336
Cigerxwîn (pseud. of Sheikhmous Hasan), 319
citizenship, 43, 159
Claes, Rhonda, 257
clash of civilizations, 104
classism: as form of dehumanization, 201, 203
Clifton, Deborah, 257
Coalition Against Israeli Apartheid, 241
collective effervescence, 337
collective imaginary, 68
collective recognition of humanity, 22–23
Collins, Clinton, 204
coloniality of migration, 173–74
Comenius, Johan: *Orbis Sensualium Pictus*, 203
Comité d'accueil des demandeurs d'asile au Québec, 80
Comité d'accueil des migrants du Haut-Saint-Laurent, 80
Common Experience Payment (CEP), 258
common feeling, 30, 31, 336, 338, 381
common knowledge, 22
community building, 310, 311
Conquergood, Dwight, 330
contact theory, 27
contact zones, 183

contestation process, 8
COVID-19 pandemic: anti-Asian xenophobia and, 157; economic impact of, 66; government response to, 42; hate crime and, 157; impact on migrants and refugees, 42, 83–84, 101
critical self-reflection, 15
cross-group friendships, 27
Cruz, Ted: on Syrian refugees, 116
cultural wealth, 162–63
culture: theories of, 310–11, 334, 335
Customs and Border Protection (CBP), 73, 76
Czech refugees, 282

Daesh. *See* Islamic State of Iraq and the Levant (ISIL)
Dalgaard, Nina Thorup, 127
dance, 30, 31, 32, 350
Darwish, Mahmoud: "The Kurd Has Only the Wind (for Saleem Barakat)," 303, 320
Darwish, Sayyid, 386
Davin', Nicolas Flood, 203–4
Deferred Action for Childhood Arrivals (DACA), 54, 55, 72, 79
Deferred Action for Parents of Americans and Lawful Permanent Residents, 54
dehumanization: consequences of, 43; definitions of, 23, 42, 201; educational practices and, 10–14, 201, 205–7, 208–9, 211; forced migration and, 341; forms of, 201–2, 209, 212–13; immigration policies and, 7–10; media's role in, 7–10, 42; through music, 17; by oppression, 331; philosophical perspective on, 23–25; of politics, 8, 25; refugee experience of, 5, 12, 25; research on, 21, 25–26; resistance to, 26–34; system-lifeworld balance and, 339
de Klerk, Frederik Willem: apology of, 254–55, 256, 262; criticism of, 255, 263
Department of Homeland Security (DHS), 70, 73, 75–76
Derrida, Jacques: on meaning of *hôte*, 24
dialogic inquiry, 29–30
Diers-Lawson, Audra, 249
displaced persons, 29, 91, 272, 273
docility-utility: notion of, 205, 206
Doğan, Zehra, 315–16
Dorn, Walter, 307

double movement: concept of, 66, 85, 86
Dryden-Peterson, Sarah, 169, 188
Durkheim, Émile, 337, 339, 382

Edmonton: Heritage Festival, 334; refugees in, 278
education system: dehumanization and, 10–14, 201, 205–7, 208–9, 211; humanization framework, 13, 198–99, 200, 212. *See also* multicultural education
Effendi, Sabukh, 386
"effervescence" (Durkheim), 32, 337, 382
Emdad, Reza, 128
Enforcement and Removal Operations (ERO), 73
Engels, Friedrich, 22
ERASMUS student exchange program, 181, 182, 186
Erbil, Iraq, 289
Erbil Public Library: building of, 16, 289–90; transformation into jail, 295–96
Eskander, Mohammed, 385
ethical apology framework (EAF), 249
ethical behaviour, 332
ethnomusicology, 329, 331, 334, 341, 342
Eugene, Oregon: community of, 364–65; music venues, 364, 364n24, 367, 368n31; record studios in, 361n17
European Union: asylum policies, 168; border control, 173; migration policy, 171–72, 173; New Pact of Asylum and Migration (NPAM), 12, 171, 172–73; refugees in, 167, 275
Ewart, Jacqui, 106
exile: cultural identity and, 309
exploitative cheap labour, 15
Eyre, Banning, 351

Fairouz (stage name of Nouhad Wadie Haddad), 386
Fakhri, Sabah, 385
Farajallah, Iman, 196
Flanagan, Bill, 49
food banks, 274
forced migration, 340
Foroni, Francesco, 156
Foucault, Michel: concept of docility-utility, 205, 206
Foundations of Caregiver Support (Alberta Health Services), 162

Foyer du Monde organization, 80
France: immigration and naturalization policies, 159–60
free trade agreements, 68
Freire, Paulo, 23, 29, 331, 341
Frishkopf, Michael, 31, 358–63, 368n30, 374

Galvin, Kathleen T., 212
Gaza humanitarian crisis, 195
Geertz, Clifford, 310
German Academic Exchange Service (DAAD), 178–79, 187
German higher education institutions (HEIs): admission requirements, 176, 187, 188; application process, 177; funding program, 178; inclusive work in, 188; refugees in, 169–70, 175–86
Germany: access of refugees to higher education, 175–79; apology for the Holocaust, 252–53; asylum policies, 170–71, 174, 175; Federal Ministry of Higher Education and Research (BMWF), 178; immigration and naturalization policies, 159; migration to, 170; nationalism, 170; partial hospitality, 12; post-secondary higher education, 13; racism, 185, 186; sexual assaults incidents, 186; unification of, 170. *See also* refugees in Germany
Ghosh, Ratna, 28
Gibson, Margaret, 200
Giessen reception center for refugees, 180–81
Giles, Wenona, 169, 188
Gillette, Maureen, 201
Giving Voice to Hope (PAR project and CD), 342, 343, 351
Gleeson, Shannon, 69, 81, 85
Global Compact on Refugees, 8, 56–57
globalization, 8, 68
Globe and Mail, 10, 105, 108, 109, 111, 113, 117
Goicoechea, Jessie, 204
Goodale, Ralph, 113–14, 115
Gosine, Kevin, 212
Govier, Trudy, 255
Gramsci, Antonio, 85
Great Transformation of the post–World War I era, 66
Green, Al, 364n23
Groupe de Sécurité Patriotique, 65

guests, 24
Guterres, António, 41, 157

Habermas, Jürgen, 339
Halabja massacre, 313
Half Moon (film), 314
Hall, Peter, 68
Hannaford supermarket chains, 82
Hanson, Pauline, 47
Harachi, Tracy W., 127
Harper, Stephen: apology for Chinese Head Tax, 260–61, 262, 263–64; apology to Indigenous peoples, 225, 256, 257–58, 259, 263, 264; refugee policy, 51–52
Haslam, Nick, 201
Hasmath, Reza, 199
Hassanpour, Amir, 311
hate crimes, 104, 108, 116, 117, 154, 157
hearing: as form of "remote touching," 30–31
Heidegger, Martin, 207
hermeneutic phenomenology, 198
Herrmann, Steffen, 201
Hesse reception center for asylum seekers, 181
Hessian Ministry of Higher Education and the Arts (HMWK), 179
Hestia (Greek goddess), 275–76
Hezbollah, 116
Hmong refugees, 330
Hollenbach, David, 29
Holloway, Immy, 212
Holocaust, 210, 230, 232, 237, 238, 240, 248, 252–53
home: definition of, 275; Greek deity of, 275–76
homogenization practice, 198, 204–5
Horany, Dominique, 385
Hornsey, Matthew J., 261
hosho (music instrument), 350
Hoskins, Eric, 113
hospitality, 23–24
Housefather, Anthony, 233
Howard, John, 48
humanitarian organizations, 79, 80–81
humanity, 22, 23
humanization: definition of, 21, 199, 200, 332; educational system and, 199–200; forms of, 212–13; Golden Rule of, 381; interdisciplinary approach to, 21; music and, 381–82; social context of,

humanization (*continued*)
    332–33; state apologies and, 14; symbolic manifestation of, 206
human nature, 200, 203
human rights, 57, 200
Humboldt Foundation, 178
Hungarian refugees, 282
Hungary: opposition to refugees, 172
Huntington, Samuel, 104
Hussein, Saddam, 107, 290–91, 297, 299, 305, 312
Hussen, Ahmed, 52
Hutu dehumanization of Tutsis, 23
"hyper-diversity" era, 28

IAB-BAMF-SOEP Survey of Refugees in Germany, 175
"I Am Kurdistan" (Waissi), 321–25
immigrants: othering of, 11–12
immigrant youth: citizenship concerns, 159–60; community support of, 162, 163; cultural wealth of, 162–63; English-language proficiency, 158; hostility toward, 156–57, 159, 160; identity crisis, 152–55, 161–62, 163, 164–65; immersion into host culture, 162–63; integration of, 151–52; issue of belonging, 152, 153, 161; labelling of, 156–57, 158, 164, 207; language-based discrimination, 207–8; objectification of, 207; programs for, 163, 164; resettlement of, 164; resiliency of, 160–61, 162; sacrifices of, 151, 157–58, 163; schooling experience, 160–61, 204–5
Immigration and Customs Enforcement (ICE), 70, 73, 82
Immigration Refugees and Citizenship Canada (IRCC), 130, 145
Independent Assessment Process (IAP), 258
Independent Jewish Voices (IJV), 239
Indian Act of 1876, 256
Indian industrial schools, 204
Indian Residential Schools Settlement Agreement (IRSSA), 258, 259
Indigenous action plan, 257
Indigenous peoples: dispossession of, 7; injustices toward, 259–60. *See also* residential schools
Indochinese refugees, 52
intercultural education, 212–13
interculturalism, 13, 212–13, 214

International Monetary Fund, 68
international student migration, 169
International Women* Space, 185
interregnum, 85
Iran: Kurdish population of, 152, 304, 313, 315, 323; persecution of religious minorities, 93; revolutionary guards, 94
Iranian refugees, 91, 95
Iran-Iraq War, 94, 321
Iraq: Ba'athist regime in, 153, 287, 289, 290, 291, 295; Kurdish population of, 152, 153, 287, 304, 305, 315, 323; Revolutionary Command Council, 291; social realism literature, 290; US invasion of, 153, 154
Iraqi refugees, 114
Islam: global influence of, 106; media framing of, 104, 106; in relation to ISIL, 115–16; terrorism and, 107, 110; Western perceptions of, 105–6
Islamic Peril: Media and Global Violence (Karim), 107
Islamic State of Iraq and the Levant (ISIL): attacks in Iraq, 126; Islam and, 115–16; massacre of Kurdish people, 305–6; media portrayal of, 111, 115; terrorist attacks of, 110–11, 115; victims of, 112
Islamic State of Iraq and Syria (ISIS). *See* Islamic State of Iraq and the Levant (ISIL)
"Islamic terrorism" narrative, 106, 117
Islamophobia, 9
Ismaili refugees, 282
Israel: criticism of, 226, 227, 240; establishment of, 232
Israeli-Palestinian conflict, 6, 107, 195–96

Jager, Justin, 127
Jalal, Jwamer, 11
Japanese Canadians, 225–26
Jewish refugees, 14, 50, 226, 227–29, 230–33, 235, 237
Jews: advocacy organizations, 232; Muslims and, 107; Nazi dehumanization of, 23, 229, 236, 241
Josh Brown Lives organization, 79
Justus-Liebig-University (JLU) (Giessen), 168, 170, 179–83

Kamkars music, 318, 320
Kanu, Yatta, 210

Kaplan, Ida, 140
Karam, Elias, 385
Kaya, Ahmet: "How Can You Know?," 316–17
Kazemipur, Abdolmohammad, 104
Kemalist movement, 305
Kenney, Jason, 282
Khalil, Hadi, 385
Klinenberg, Eric, 16
Komagata Maru incident, 50, 226
Kondakci, Yasar, 169
Kosovar refugees, 282
Kramsch, Claire, 213
Kristallnacht, 229, 231, 240
Kronfeldner, Maria, 200, 211, 214; *What's Left of Human Nature?* 201
Kulthum, Umm, 386
Kurdayetî, 311
Kurdi, Alan: publication of photo of, 9, 51, 103
Kurdish identity: cultural production and, 16–17, 303, 304, 311–13, 323; on first-generation immigrants, 151, 154, 155, 156, 161, 162; fragmentations of, 304, 307, 309–10, 317–18; historical context of, 304–6; language and, 303, 307; poetic representation of, 319–20; Western perspectives on, 154, 306–7
Kurdish National Liberation Movement (KNLM), 313
Kurdish people: ancestral homeland, 304; birth records, 287; in Canada, 153, 155, 306, 308, 311; concerned about citizenship, 159; cultural production of, 16, 303–24; dehumanization of, 16; discrimination against, 160–61, 305, 316; division among, 320; dream of unity in, 322; in exile, 321; folklore, 318; Iraqi regime and, 153, 289; Islamic State and, 305–6; issue of belonging, 158; language and dialects, 304; living conditions, 288; music, 308, 316–19; oppression of, 289, 313, 314; poetry of, 312–13, 315, 319–20, 321–22; religious beliefs, 304; schooling, 287–88; territory populated by, 152; traditional songs, 304, 311, 316–19
Kurdistan: absence of recognized borders, 303–4; British control of, 305; civil war in, 197, 297; independence movement, 161, 305, 321; Iraqi regime and, 305; Kemalist movement in, 305; military forces of, 307–8
Kurmanji speakers, 131, 132, 135, 136, 142

labelling practices, 156–57, 158, 164, 203, 209
Lacolle-Champlain border crossing, 65–66, 81
Lake, Diedre M., 128
Lakhani, Salma, 278
lamellophone traditions, 350
La Meute (anti-Muslim group), 77
Lamont, Michele, 68
Land of Dreams farm, 100
language: discrimination based on, 207; meaning and, 208
Lausanne, Treaty of, 152
Lawlor, Andrea, 104
Layton, Jack, 259
Lesbos refugee camp, 167–68
Levinas, Emmanuel, 22
Liberian refugees, 342, 343
lifeworld, 198, 339
Lightfoot, Sheryl, 44
Lisée, Jean-François, 78
Loewenstein, George, 251

Mackenzie King, William Lyon, 229, 234
MacNevin, Joanne, 199, 210
Mahabad Republic, 315
"Make America Great Again" campaign, 71, 72
Makiadi, François Luambo Luanzo, 355n7
Mansour, Renad, 307
Manus Island detention center, 49
Mapfumo, Thomas: as artist in exile, 18, 342, 352, 358; audience of, 359; career of, 351; children of, 371; Chimurenga music, 355; collaborators of, 360–61, 362n18; concerts of, 359, 362–63; conference address, 354–57; connections with Zimbabwe, 349, 365, 368; *Danger Zone* (album), 361n17; detention of, 356; education of, 354; Eugene community and, 361n17, 364–65, 367n28, 370, 374; honorary doctorate of, 349; influence of, 374; interviews, 353, 354, 358–63, 364–73; life story of, 17, 354–58, 372–73; MDC Alliance and, 360; move to the US, 358n12, 373; Mugabe's regime and, 356–57, 358; "Ndangariro" (lyrics), 375–76;

Mapfumo, Thomas (*continued*)
nicknames of, 351; North America tour, 352; personal charisma, 353; religious views, 366; social media posts, 360; songs of, 350, 351, 356, 358, 360, 361n17, 375; travels in Africa, 354–55; University of Alberta's International Week and, 379; US tours, 362; visit to Edmonton, 353; Zimbabwean diaspora and, 359–60, 362n18, 369
Maraire, Dumisani, 363
March of the Living, 232
Marley, Bob, 350, 361
Marrus, Michael R., 249, 252, 259
Martin, Paul, 50
Martinkus, John, 106
Marx, Karl, 22
Matthes, Jörg, 106
mbira (music instrument), 350, 363, 374
mbira dzavadzimu (music instrument), 350
Mbira Renaissance (band), 353
McDonald, Anne Marie, 83, 84
McDougall, Barbara, 51
meaningfulness, 335–36
Median Empire (728–550 BCE), 310
mediated arts, 32
Migrant Justice organization, 77, 81–82, 84
migrant precarity, 65–66, 67, 69, 70, 78–79, 84, 85
migrants: exploitation of, 70; vs. refugees, 3; settler colonialism and, 4, 173–74; statistics, 3, 67–68; after World War II, 6
Mihai, Mihaela, 249, 250, 251
Milk with Dignity program, 82
Mills, Carmen, 203
Montgomery, Edith, 127
Morrison, Scott, 49
Movement for Democratic Change Alliance, 360, 360n15
MS *St. Louis*: Canada's apology to passengers of, 14, 226, 227–28, 230–36, 241, 247; in Cuba, 228–29, 234; in popular culture, 229–30; refusal for entry into the US and Canada, 229, 234; return to Europe, 230, 235; voyage of, 50, 228, 229
Mugabe, Robert: Chimurenga war and, 355n8; election of, 17; fall of, 352–53, 359; political regime of, 18, 351, 356–57, 358; rise to power, 356n10
Mujuru, Ephat, 350

Mulroney, Brian, 50, 68
multicultural education: benefits of, 27–28, 201; criticism of, 28, 198–201, 211–12
Multicultural Health Brokers Cooperative (MCHB Cooperative), 161, 162, 164
multiculturalism, 28, 160, 197, 200, 237, 308–9
music: as act of collective participation, 329, 336, 340–41; affective power of, 31, 32; attributes of, 380–81; connectedness, 336, 338–39, 341; as cultural construction, 334; dehumanization through, 17, 32; distribution of, 337–38; as form of remote touching, 335; meaningfulness of, 30, 334, 335–36, 337; memory and, 383; nationalistic, 342; power of, 17, 379, 380, 381; refugees and, 32, 330, 343; rehumanizing effect of, 329–30, 331, 333–34, 338; resilience and, 336; solidarity and, 339; sonic organization of, 31; as transcultural performance, 31, 331, 337; universal language of, 334, 335
musical resonance, 338, 340, 342, 382, 383
"Music for Global Human Development" (M4GHD), 331, 338, 340, 342
musician refugees, 384
musicking: notion of, 30
Muslims: discrimination of, 105; diversity of, 106; hate crimes against, 104, 108, 116, 117, 154; media portrayal of, 105, 106, 107; negative perception of, 106, 159–60, 209–10; relationship between Jews and, 107; travel ban, 73
mutrib (Arabic singer), 385
Muzorewa, Abel Tendekayi, 356, 356n9

Nahawand, Longa, 387
naming ceremony, 332
National Association of Japanese Canadians, 225–26
national identity, 12, 159
National Post, 10, 105, 108, 109, 111, 114
Nauru island, 48
Nazeri, Shahram, 304
Nenshi, Naheed, 112, 116
neoliberalism, 68, 69, 71
neoliberal precarity, 71, 78–79, 85
New Pact of Asylum and Migration (NPAM), 12, 171, 172–73
Newroz (Kurdish New Year), 304, 322
Nicolino, Venus, 209

Ni Frontières, Ni Prisons organization, 81
9/11 terrorist attacks, 154
North American Free Trade Agreement (NAFTA), 68, 71, 72

Obama, Barack: immigration policy, 53, 54
Obhrai, Deepak, 233
O'Brien, Peter, 159
Occupy Wall Street, 67, 71
Oliver, Sophie, 23
One Nation Party (Australia), 47
Orbis Sensualium Pictus (Comenius), 203
"organic" solidarity, 339
Organization for the Prevention of Violence, 156
Ortiz, Fernando, 183, 331
Other/othering: alterity of, 13–14; ethical relation with, 22; notion of, 203, 213, 214; recognition of, 22, 23, 26–27

Packer, Martin, 204
Pakistani Baha'i community, 95
Palestinian refugees: Canada's actions toward, 6; dehumanization of, 226, 238, 241; generations of, 111; identity crisis, 309; UN mandate, 41
Pang, Augustine, 249
Papua New Guinea, 48
Paret, Marcel, 69, 81, 85
Paris terrorist attack (2015), 9, 104–5, 109, 110, 111, 115, 116, 117
participatory action research (PAR), 340–41, 343
People's Party of Canada, 65, 78
Perez, Michelle S., 210
performing arts, 30, 32, 341
Perwer, Şivan, 308, 311; "Kîne Em?" (Who are we?), 319
Peşêw, Abdullah: "The Dagger," 319–20
Peshmerga (military of Kurdistan Region), 306, 307–8, 322
Peterborough mosque arson, 108, 109, 116
Pettigrew, Thomas F., 27
Philpot, Catherine R., 261
Pierce, Sarah, 54
Pittsburgh synagogue shooting, 231, 240
Plattsburgh Cares organization, 79
Poland: opposition to refugees, 172
Polanyi, Karl, 66, 71, 85, 86
"post-multicultural" approaches, 28

post-truth politics, 44
Pourbaix, Eilis, 342
Prairie provinces: immigrants in, 158–59
Pratt, Mary Louise, 183
precarity: duality of, 71; as hegemonic norm, 67, 70; origins and institutionalization of, 69; of place, 69; resistance to, 85–86. *See also* migrant precarity; neoliberal precarity; refugee precarity
precarity-migrant-agency nexus, 81, 85
Prince, Paul, 368, 368n31
Putin, Vladimir, 32, 341, 342

Qadi, Muhammad Yunis al-, 386
Qazi Muhammad, 315
Qubadî, Behmen, 313, 314–15
Québec: anti-immigration protests, 77–78; COVID-19 pandemic in, 83–84
Quijano, Anibal, 173, 174

Rabadi-Raol, Ayesha, 202
racialized children: achievement gap, 210; "civilizing" approach to, 203–4; labelling of, 203–4; oppressions of, 202; stereotyping of, 202, 209–10
racism: educational system and, 210; as form of dehumanization, 201, 210; mental health and, 160
Rahbani, Assi, 386
Rahbani, Mansour, 386
Rahbani, Ziyad, 386
Rane, Halim, 106
Reagan, Ronald, 68
refugee precarity, 65–66, 67, 70
refugees: abuse of, 95; access to education, 12–13, 169, 170; addictions, 278; age of, 98, 146; claim for asylum, 51, 52–53, 74, 94–95, 279–80; community support, 96–97, 100; connections to home societies, 383; COVID-19 and, 42; culture and, 33; decision to become, 92–93, 274; definitions of, 3; dehumanization of, 4, 5; emotional and psychological state of, 100–101; faith in humanity, 9; family members, 93; fear of, 3–4, 104; generosity of strangers toward, 94; genetic testing, 279; in the Global South, 56; housing for, 277–78; *vs.* immigrants, 199; initial departure of, 93–94; integration of, 74, 97–98, 146, 278, 383; international convention

Index   405

refugees (*continued*)
on, 169; intersubjective connections of, 382–83; language skills, 97; learning of foreign rules, 206; mental health issues, 128–29, 276–77, 278; *vs.* migrants, 3; multiculturalism and, 281; music and, 33; negative attitudes toward, 26, 280–81; policies addressing experience of, 98–99; prejudice toward, 26, 42–43, 282–83; racism and, 281; resettlement of, 11, 74, 91, 92, 95–98, 101, 146, 276, 278, 281–82, 308; smugglers and, 93–94; social solidarity of, 341; sponsorship of, 276; stages of experience of, 92; statistics of, 3, 41–42, 67–68, 146; story of the village along the river and, 269–72, 273; studies of, 5, 25–26; success stories, 278–79; temporary employment, 95, 97; transportation program for, 279; trauma of, 9, 94, 96, 99; vulnerability of, 97, 102; women, 175. *See also* specific groups of refugees

refugees in Germany: access to post-secondary education, 168, 176–78, 183, 187, 188–89; advocacy groups, 180; countries of origin, 175; culture of hospitality toward, 177; education level of, 176; financial hurdles, 187; German-language proficiency, 176; health problems, 187; hostility toward, 177; legal status, 183, 184; media portrayal of, 170, 177; social assistance for, 177; statistics of, 175–76, 181

refugee students: emotional and cognitive challenges, 196, 197; importance of safe environment, 198; language barrier, 207–8; loneliness and isolation, 198; school experience, 197–99; socialization of, 206–7

Refugees Welcome International, 79

rehumanization: through arts and culture, 30–34, 333, 338–39, 340; benefits of, 26; definition of, 333; via dialogue, 29–30; via inter-group contact, 27; via multicultural education, 27–29; resocialization and, 333

Rempel, Michelle, 78

Research Network on Human Rights and Migration, 186

residential schools: compensations to survivors of, 258–59; Indigenous practices and, 225; legacy of, 256–57; misconceptions about, 258; public awareness of, 258–59; purpose of, 204, 257; state apology to victims of, 225, 247, 256, 258, 263, 264

resonance. *See* socio-sonic-visual resonance

Rezai-Rashti, Goli, 209

Rezazi, Nasir, 317

right to asylum, 272

right-wing protests, 77

ritual transition, 333

Robertson, Cheryl Lee, 127, 143

Rocca, Francesco, 42

Rojhat, Melek: "Homeland," 318

Rollins, Natalia (a.k.a. Moxie), 361n17

Roma children, 204

Ross, Michael, 250, 251, 260, 261

Rothbart, Myron, 156

Roxham Road border crossing, 65, 67, 75, 77, 79, 80, 84

Roy, Nilanjana, 69

Royal Commission on Aboriginal Peoples (RCAP), 257

rumba dance, 350

Russian pro-war rallies, 342

Russia-Ukraine war, 195

Rust Belt states, 72

Saavedra, Cinthya, 210

Said, Edward, 105, 106; "Reflections on Exile," 309

Sané, Pierre, 57

Sangalang, Cindy C., 127

Save the Children International, 195, 196

Sazkar, Gare: "I Am Kurd," 317–18

Schafer, Murray, 30, 335

Scheer, Andrew, 78

schooling for refugees: curriculum, 206, 211–12; dehumanization and, 10, 209; experience of, 204; inequalities embedded in, 203; intervention programs, 207–8; language classes, 207; lunchtime routine, 206–7; rules and regulations, 205–6, 207; as sites of cultural reconstitution, 214; social structures of, 203

Schopenhauer, Arthur, 334

Schumann, Karina, 250, 251, 260, 261

Schütz, Alfred, 31, 204

Seattle World Trade Organization (WTO) protests, 66

Second Vatican Council, 282
"Secure Our Borders" demonstration, 81
Segall, Kimberly Wedeven, 310, 311
selective endorsement process, 45
Selee, Andrew, 54
Sennay, Slabe, 342–43
Settlement Worker in Schools (SWIS) program, 145
settler colonialism, 7, 44, 47, 56
Sèvres, Treaty of, 152, 305, 315
sexism, 201
Shachar, Ayelet, 45
Shadd Araban, 385
Sheyholislami, Jaffer, 309, 311
Shona musical traditions, 350, 351, 353, 371n34
Sidorkin, Alexander, 30
signalling theory, 248–49
Sikh refugees, 50, 226
Simpson, Brenda, 205
Skuza, Jennifer A., 198
Small, Christopher, 30
Smith, Bianca, 108
Smith, Wadada Leo, 352
social drama, 333, 338, 342
social exclusion: as form of dehumanization, 201, 203, 209
social pathologies, 331, 339–40
social resonance, 381, 383, 384
social transpositions, 18, 380
Socio-Economic Panel at the German Institute for Economic Research (DIW Berlin), 175
socio-sonic-visual resonance, 31, 332, 337, 341–42, 380, 381–82
Soldiers of Odin, 65, 77
solidarity, 339
Solidarity Across Borders, 80, 81
Söndergaard, Hans Peter, 128
Soukous dance, 350
South Africa: state apology for apartheid (de Klerk), 253–55, 263; Truth and Reconciliation Commission, 253–56
Souto-Manning, Mariana, 202
state apologies: as act of atonement, 248; cost of, 259, 261, 262, 264–65; efficacy of, 248, 249–50, 262–63, 264; elements of, 251; failure of, 262; loss of national status and, 251; partial, 252–53, 254–55, 264; as poisoned gift, 235–40, 241; politics of, 225–26, 228, 241, 247, 249; rehumanizing effect of, 247, 248, 251, 253–61, 262, 264; signalling theory approach to, 248–49, 256; sincerity of, 234, 264; theoretical framework of, 248–51; timing of, 230–31; trustworthiness of, 262
state sovereignty, 57
stereotypes, 209
Stewart, Jane, 199, 210, 257
Stop the War on Children: Protecting Children in 21st Century Conflict (Save the Children), 195
Storm Alliance, 65, 77, 80
Streitwieser, Bernhard, 169, 187, 188
Sultan, Khalid, 107
Surveillance on the Northern Border (ACLU-VT), 76
Swanton Border Control Sector, 76
Syria: Kurdish population of, 152, 304, 305, 315, 323; Rojava revolution in, 305
Syrian refugees: association with terrorists, 112, 116; in Canada, 9, 51, 96; community support of, 99; compassion for, 6; debate about, 116–17; dehumanization of, 9; educators' response to arrival of, 199; employment of, 175; Islam and, 105, 108, 110; local officials and, 111; media portrayal of, 9–10, 27, 103, 104, 105, 108–10, 115; methodological approach to study of, 108; religious faith of, 104, 109; resettlement of, 6, 109, 111, 113; security checks, 109–10, 113–14, 115; statistics of, 176; in the US, 74; women, 176

Tamil refugees, 50
Tampa crisis (2001), 47–48, 49, 51
Tan, Edna, 200, 202, 205
tarab music, 384, 385
Tardif, Guillaume, 386
Tarkan (Turkish pop star), 152–53
Tatlises, Ibrahim, 304
Tavuchis, Nicholas, 256
taxonomies, 329
Tea Party movement, 71
terrorism, 110, 111–12, 116
Thatcher, Margaret, 68
Theorell, Töres, 128
Thorne, Barrie, 207
Time for Drunken Horses, A (film), 313, 314
Timshel, Isabelle, 127
Todres, Les, 212
Tolley, Erin, 104

touching, 30–31
transcultural music, 17, 331
"Transpositions: Music for Resilient Communities" concert, 379–80
trauma-informed educational practices, 142, 143
trauma of refugees, 125, 128, 129
Tribeca News (magazine), 314
Troper, Harold, 229; *None Is Too Many: Canada and the Jews of Europe, 1933–1948*, 230, 231
Trudeau, Justin: apologies of, 14, 226, 227, 231–35, 236, 242, 247; campaign promises, 52; condemnation for BDS, 240; criticism of, 239; on Holocaust, 238; humanitarianism of, 52; on Jewish refugees, 237; on Muslim travel ban, 52; on Paris terrorist attacks, 111, 114; refugee policies, 8, 51, 52, 109, 110, 114
Trump, Donald: anti-humanitarianism, 55; attempt to cancel DACA, 55; border security policy, 73; and term *China virus*, 157; exclusionary rhetoric of, 56, 73; executive orders, 73, 74, 76; first days of presidency, 54; immigration policy, 54, 55–56, 67, 72–73; position on multilateral agreements, 57; refugee policy, 51, 53–54, 55; rise to presidency, 72
Trump, Melania, 55
Truth and Reconciliation Commission of Canada (TRC), 14, 225, 258, 259
t'shuvah: concept of, 239
Tunisi, Bayram al-, 386
Turkey: Kurdish population of, 152, 304, 305, 315–16, 323; music, 386–87; War of Independence, 152
Turnbull, Malcolm, 49
Turner, Victor, 333

Ugandan refugees, 278
Ukrainian refugees, 3, 5–6
Unangst, Lisa, 187
UN Convention on the Rights of the Child (UNCRC), 169, 196–97, 200, 206
UN Convention Relating to the Status of Refugees, 45–46, 53, 280
UN Declaration on the Rights of Indigenous Peoples (UNDRIP), 44
UN Protocol Relating to the Status of Refugees, 46

undocumented migrants, 73–74, 75, 76, 77, 78
UN High Commissioner for Refugees (UNHCR), 3, 41, 91, 275
Unitarian Universalists, 65
United Kingdom: "home children" program, 282
United States: asylum seekers, 51; cultural resentment in, 72; deportations from, 73–74; human rights revolution, 45; illegal border crossing, 76; immigration, 44, 46, 53, 54–55; Indigenous peoples, 44, 46; National Quota (Johnson-Reed) Act (1965), 45; racism, 46; refugee policies, 43, 53, 55, 56, 57, 74
"United to Protect Our Borders" rally, 77
University of Applied Sciences in Magdeburg, 179
University of Osnabrück, 179
University of Saarbrücken, 179
UN Office for Disaster Risk Reduction, 273
UN Relief and Works Agency (UNRWA), 3, 41
UN Universal Declaration of Human Rights, 15, 43, 57, 196, 272, 273
US Immigration Reform and Control Act, 53
'Uwis, Jamil, 386
Uzbek refugees, 114

Verdun, Amy, 69
Vermont: campaign against Department of Motor Vehicles, 82; as "sanctuary state," 77; surveillance in, 76. *See also* Migrant Justice organization
Verwoerd, Wilhelm, 255
vicarious contact, 27
Vietnamese asylum seekers, 47
Volkswagen Foundation, 178

Wahab, Abdurrahman, 306
Wahab, Mohamed Abdel, 386
Waissi, Hama Aziz: "I Am Kurdistan," 321–25
Wallace, Rebecca, 103, 104
Warsaw Ghetto Uprising memorial, 252
Wassouf, George, 385
Watt, David L. E., 128
Weima, Yolanda, 25
West Island refugee volunteers, 65
Wilder, Charlie B., 361n17

Wittgenstein, Ludwig, 208
Wohl, Michael J. A., 249, 261
Women in Exile e.V., 185
Wood, Sara, 128
World Bank, 68
World Social Forum, 71
World Trade Organization (WTO), 68, 71

Yarsanism, 304
Yazidi refugees: caregivers in families of, 143; communication challenges, 136, 137, 138–40, 141, 145; countries of origin, 125; Daesh captivity, 137, 139, 140; education of, 130, 141, 144; eligibility for social services, 145; emergency arrival of, 144; employment of, 133–34; English-language skills, 127, 135, 136, 142, 143; health care for, 134–35; illnesses of, 143; integration of, 127, 128, 129, 133, 140, 142, 143; international assistance to, 126; interviews with, 125, 130–32; language of communication of, 131, 135; marital status of, 132; mental health problems of, 127, 129, 133, 134, 137, 138, 145; migration of, 128; persecution and expulsion of, 125–26; religion of, 126; resettlement of, 126, 127, 129, 130, 132, 137, 142, 144; shortage of settlement service workers for, 144–45; study of, 130–32; translation and interpretation services for, 135–38, 143–44; traumatic experience of, 11, 125–29, 133, 135, 136, 140–44; violence against, 126, 129, 305
Yellow Vests Canada, 65
Yezidism, 304
Yosso, Tara J., 162, 163
Young, Iris Marion, 205, 209
YPG (People's Protection Unit), 305, 306
YPJ (Women's Protection Unit), 305

Zakho, Iraq, 297
Zana, Layla: *Writings from Prison*, 315
Zimbabwe: Chimurenga wars, 350, 355, 355n8; corruption, 17, 357; culture, 370–72, 374; economic hardship, 366; emigration from, 351; independence of, 17; music culture of, 350, 351, 363; political regime of, 18, 355, 356; sale of pirate CDs, 368, 369; in Western media, 357
Zimbabwe African National Liberation Army, 355n8
Zimbabwe African National Union (ZANU), 355n8, 356n10
Zimbabwe African People's Union, 356n10
Zimbabwean diaspora, 18, 352, 353, 362n18, 369–70
Zimbabwe People's Revolutionary Army, 355n8
Zimdancehall genre, 368
Zionism, 237